The Natural Goodness of Man

The Natural Goodness of Man

On the System of Rousseau's Thought

by Arthur M. Melzer

The University of Chicago Press
Chicago and London

The University of Chicago Press, Chicago 60637
The University of Chicago Press, Ltd., London
© 1990 by The University of Chicago
All rights reserved. Published 1990.
Printed in the United States of America

25 24 23 22 21 20 19 18 17 16   2 3 4 5 6

ISBN-13: 978-0-226-51978-4 (cloth)
ISBN-13: 978-0-226-51979-1 (paper)
ISBN-13: 978-0-226-22600-2 (e-book)
DOI: 10.7208/chicago/9780226226002.001.0001

Library of Congress Cataloging-in-Publication Data

Melzer, Arthur M.
   The natural goodness of man : on the system of Rousseau's thought / Arthur M. Melzer.
   p. cm.
   Includes bibliographical references.
   ISBN 0-226-51978-3 (cloth). — ISBN 0-226-51979-1 (paper)
   1. Rousseau, Jean-Jacques, 1712–1778. 2. Philosophical anthropology—History—18th
century. I. Title
B2138.M3M44 1990
194—dc20   89-20587
                                                                                CIP

⊚ This paper meets the requirements of ANSI/NISO Z39 48-1992 (Permanence of Paper).

To My Mother and Father

Contents

We are sick with evils that can be cured; and nature, having brought us forth sound, itself helps us if we wish to be improved.

SENECA

(and the epigraph to Emile)

. . . that evil is buried more deeply in humanity than the cure-all socialists think, that evil cannot be avoided in any organization of society, that a man's soul will remain the same, that it is from a man's soul alone that abnormality and sin arise, and that the laws that govern man's spirit are still so unknown, so uncertain and so mysterious that there cannot be any physicians, or even judges, to give a definitive cure or decision.

DOSTOEVSKY

Preface

I am not a Rousseauian, nor do I know anyone who is. Today one finds believing Kantians, Utilitarians, Marxists, various kinds of Nietzscheans, maybe a Thomist or two, but virtually no one calls himself a "Rousseauian." Rousseau's thought is too full of complexities and paradoxes, too extreme and dangerous (in the view of both Right and Left) and, in the end, just too strange to be embraced and inscribed as the final truth regarding human affairs. Yet if his thought does not inspire belief, it is uniquely well-suited to inspire reflection, and that would seem to be why this philosopher who has no disciples continues to have so many and such ardent readers.

Indeed, among the major writers of the Western philosophic tradition one can single out a few who, regardless of the particular content of their doctrines, claim our attention for their sheer capacity to animate and elevate our thinking—the great sirens of the mind, so to speak, as were Plato, Saint Augustine, Machiavelli, and Nietzsche. Rousseau too has this particular gift. "Of all the writers that are or ever were in Europe," remarked David Hume, "he is the man who has acquired the most enthusiastic and most passionate Admirers."[1]

What is the fascination with Rousseau? Perhaps the first thing that comes to mind is the human comprehensiveness of his concerns and vision. It is through Rousseau—inspired by the example of Greek and Roman antiquity—that the blood begins to rush back into the cramped and withered limbs of the early modern conception of man, the man of Hobbes, Descartes, and Locke. Rousseau begins to speak once again of feeling and imagination where before there had been only calculation; he revives the spirit as an object worthy of consideration in addition to the body; he assigns to statesmanship a vital part on the political stage as a supplement to the mechanical role of constitutional structures; he writes movingly of the grandeur of virtue, patriotism, and community instead of reducing all human ends to individual self-interest; he explores the erotic and romantic side of life in addition to the world of security and gain; and he bestows a new seriousness on the personal and intimate in opposition to the public world of honor and accomplishment. In a word, he boldly insists on pushing beyond the tame, manageable issue of comfortable self-preservation to confront the whole, messy, complex question of *happiness*.

To study Rousseau, then, is to confront the whole phenomenon of man, to acquaint oneself with all the issues of life, to make a grand, dizzying tour

---

[1] Letter to John Home, March 22, 1766, reprinted in Ritter (1988) p. 197.

of the human condition. Yet it is also to see what a unified, if multi-faceted, view of this whole might look like. His works induce one, as few others do, to think both broadly and synthetically about the great issues of moral and political philosophy. And if, by the end, one does not find oneself in agreement with him, one still feels moved to say, in a phrase of which he was especially fond: "I am a human being: nothing human is foreign to me."

It is not only from their content, however, but also from their remarkable style that Rousseau's writings derive their unique allure. "He wrote with an eloquence and fervour that had never been seen in prose," observed Lord Acton, who described Rousseau as "the author of the strongest political theory that had appeared amongst men."[2] As with any great writer, Rousseau's style is not an accident of his tastes or talents but the necessary manifestation of his thought. From the standpoint of formal technique, admittedly, there is nothing one could call typically Rousseauian except a brilliant and wily eclecticism: by turns lyrical and mocking, pious and paradoxical; full of epigrams, orations, historical examples, delicate vignettes, mathematical formulae, long footnotes, personal confessions, and universal proclamations. Yet amid all this variety, one still senses a forceful unity of style that emerges not from its form but its source: the genuine, personal, living voice of Rousseau. The power of his style is above all the power of sincerity.[3]

Casting off the fetters of aesthetic formalism, of dry rationalism, of partisan interest, of personal shame, he aspires to a level of honesty and sincerity never before attained. His writing, like his thought, seems to issue from the fullest, most intimate contact with life. He endeavors to speak in a fully human voice, one in touch with every corner of the human soul, and trembling with the pathos of his own personal existence.

Rousseau's voice has exercised an immense power over his readers, shaking them free of their theories and postures, showing the way back to their own profoundest cares. As depth calls to depth, his writings have the capacity to convey not only new ideas and doctrines but new energies. And that is perhaps the simplest reason why for two centuries thoughtful persons of every persuasion have returned again and again to Rousseau: not simply to learn, not necessarily to admire, but, as it were, to recharge.

Finally, Rousseau's thought fascinates us for the enormous, perhaps

---

[2] Lord Acton (1967) pp. 374-75.

[3] In his famous work on heroism, Thomas Carlyle includes Rousseau as a sort of hero of sincerity: "We name him here because, with all his drawbacks and they are many, he has the first and chief characteristic of a hero: he is heartily *in earnest*. In earnest, if ever man was; as none of these French philosophers were. Nay, one would say, of an earnestness too great for his otherwise sensitive, rather feeble nature.... There had come, at last, to be a kind of madness in him: his ideas *possessed* him like demons; hurried him so about, drove him over steep places!" (*Heroes, Hero Worship and the Heroic in History*, p. 219, emphasis in the original).

unparalleled influence that it exercised on his own and subsequent ages. As Henry Sumner Maine wrote:

> We have never seen in our own generation—indeed the world has not seen more than once or twice in all the course of history—a literature which has exercised such a prodigious influence over the minds of men, over every cast and shade of intellect, as that which emanated from Rousseau between 1749 and 1762.[4]

Although it might appear to be of only academic interest, Rousseau's immense historical influence is actually what makes him most deeply and personally interesting to us. For his works not only influenced great events of the past, as did the actions of Caesar and Napoleon, but they also shaped the thoughts and sensibilities of all succeeding generations, including our own. Rousseau is one of the progenitors of the modern mind, one of the discoverers of that world of hopes and feelings, of categories and questions in which we all now find ourselves living. And thus his writings are personally important to us—like a lost diary from our childhood—as a means to our own self-understanding and liberation.

The whole purpose of studying past philosophers, after all, beyond whatever hope we may have of simply learning from them the truth, is to try to reconstruct the genealogy of our present beliefs, the historical phenomenology of our minds. For we must begin by making conscious the forgotten sources that shape our present thinking if we are ever to become capable of thinking for ourselves.

Returning to the thought of someone like Rousseau allows us to re-enact the discovery of our present beliefs, which we now take for granted and so no longer fully understand. We can recapture these ideas in all their brash novelty and vigor, before they became accepted and venerable, before they decayed into prejudices, as they have now, when we can no longer identify their presuppositions, no longer remember anything more than a caricatured version of the alternatives to them, and thus no longer stand clear of them to judge their worth.

Specifically, to return to Rousseau is to re-enact that revolution in thought and feeling that led us from an ethic of perfection and self-transcendence to one of selfhood and non-alienation, from reason to feeling, self-mastery to spontaneity, and self-knowledge to sincerity. It is to witness the change in sensibility that leads many today to feel the superiority of the noble savage or the artistic bohemian to the dutiful member of society. It is to observe the birth of our modern preoccupation with secular compassion, our reduction of the human problem to the problem of oppression, our latent

---

[4] *Ancient Law*, p. 51. Rousseau's direct political influence was greatest during the period of the French Revolution, "during the few years," as Auguste Comte asserts, "when the *Social Contract* inspired more confidence and veneration than were ever obtained by the Bible or the Koran" (*Systeme de Politique Positive*, vol. III, pp. 596-97; quoted by Derathé [1964] p. cx). His *philosophical* influence has been much more diffuse and long lasting.

hostility to technology and commerce even in the midst of prosperity, our vague longing for nonorganic community, our temptation to replace representation with participatory democracy, and distributive justice with generality or fairness. Rousseau may not be the only source of these ideas—our ideas—but each of them bears the stamp of his powerful influence.

To describe that influence in a somewhat different way, Rousseau may be said to have inaugurated the "radical tradition" of philosophical discontent with modernity which, since his time, has formed a permanent and integral part of modernity itself—culminating today in the declaration of a new, "post-modern" era. Standing at the threshold of the "modern age" inaugurated by the American, French, and Industrial revolutions, the threshold of that long journey toward technological, welfare-capitalist/socialist, liberal, mass, democratic society that today still goes by the name of "modernization"—Rousseau was the first to cry, "stop." And in presenting his classic diagnosis of the ills of modern society—the loss of social and psychic unity—he defined the problem which succeeding generations of critical thinkers would try to solve.

Of course, Rousseau was not simply the first to cry stop to modernization, since many had done so before him in the name of the *ancien regime* and the old monarchic and Christian principles. But he was the first to do so as a more advanced adherent of the new modern ideas. The Enlightenment and the new Party of Reason had plenty of enemies; Rousseau was its first *defector*, its first "dialectical" opponent. His defection, moreover, turned out to be the founding event of a since unbroken tradition of modern self-hatred, of protest against modernity arising from within the modern camp, and the first clear indication of the theoretical instability and continuously self-devouring character of the modern revolution.

In other words, Rousseau became the prototype of the modern alienated intellectual: the thinker who agrees with the modern rejection of the principles that underlay the classical and Christian worlds, but who nevertheless loathes the new world that these modern ideas have created. Knowing the man-made character of this world, and blaming it for the unhealthy state of his own soul, he seeks the restoration of the world and his soul through a still more radical, progressive application of these modern ideas.

By exploring all the diverse ways in which societies or individuals might be transformed and restored, Rousseau's works planted the seeds of almost all later forms of radicalism: of the communist and anarchist Left as well as of the romantic and fascist Right.[5]

Thus, our intellectual world, in all its diversity, is to a remarkable extent constructed out of fragments of Rousseau. And if his distant and difficult

---

[5] As François Furet (1981, p. 31) writes, "Rousseau may well have been the most far-sighted genius ever to appear in intellectual history, for he invented, or sensed, so many of the problems that were to obsess the nineteenth and twentieth centuries."

works continue to hold a strange fascination for us, that is perhaps due not only to the human comprehensiveness of his thought and the extraordinary energy of his writing, but also to our sense that we need him in order to understand ourselves. It is a necessary step on the road to knowing and clearing our minds that we confront the sense in which we are all in fact unconscious "Rousseauians."

*   *   *

There exists today a vast critical literature on Rousseau, one deploying every kind of interpretive technique and viewing his thought from every imaginable angle. It would appear that by now no promising avenue of approach, no matter how oblique or unusual, has been neglected. And yet it seems that a case can be made—to state baldly here what is argued at length in the Introduction—that precisely the most obvious and potentially useful approach has for one reason or another been overlooked, that the most simple and straightforward book has not been written. Rousseau tells us—repeatedly and insistently—that his thought, although it appears to be both disjointed and self-contradictory, is really quite consistent. Indeed, not just consistent: it forms a rigorous, unified system. And this entire system, he adds, is built upon a single new principle: the doctrine of the natural goodness of man. Rousseau claims to be a rigorous systematist and that in order to understand him it is essential to grasp his system as a whole.

If for the moment we assume, as is seldom done, that all of these statements can be taken at face value, then Rousseau's philosophy would itself seem to solicit a very specific exposition. First, one needs to determine what Rousseau means by "the natural goodness of man" and what if anything is really original about this principle. Second, one should explain on what basis Rousseau believes it to be true, what arguments or proofs he gives for it. Finally, one should draw out the consequences of this principle and try to show how it accounts for the major features of his constructive or programmatic writings. Or, to speak only of the aspect of his thought to which I primarily confine myself in this work, one must explain how "the natural goodness of man" systematically produces the *Social Contract*. Through such an exposition, were it possible, one might reasonably claim to have understood Rousseau—the parts and the whole of his thought—in the specific manner in which he himself declares he must be understood. The present work attempts such an exposition.

Acknowledgments

A first book is precious for the opportunity it affords of acknowledging one's long accumulated debts. The first and greatest one is to my parents for benefits I could never hope to repay or begin to describe. To them this book is dedicated.

To Allan Bloom, who writes so beautifully of philosophic education, I owe the beginning of my own, including my interest in Rousseau. He together with Werner Dannhauser first taught me how to seek myself in distant times and places, to be captivated by the awe-inspiring power and delicacy of great minds, and to be thrown back on my own mind by their disagreements. Harvey C. Mansfield, Jr., a brilliant lecturer and a sober friend, opened new doors to the *Social Contract*, as to so many other works, through his new interpretations of modern politics. Judith Shklar was a wonderful source of insight, skepticism, and encouragement, especially, of course, on the subject of Rousseau.

It is a fond pleasure to thank Harold Ames, Robert Kraynak, and Clifford Orwin, my oldest intellectual companions, and Jerry Weinberger and Richard Zinman, my close friends and colleagues, for their friendship and conversation. So many of the ideas that appear here in print were formed in the crucible of discussion with them. Among others who saw the manuscript in various parts or drafts, I would particularly like to thank Christopher Bruell, Alan Grimes, and Jack Paynter. Joel Schwartz and the reviewers for the University of Chicago Press read the manuscript with great care and perception, helping me to make many significant revisions. With a generosity I have long admired and profited by, my sister, Sara Melzer, gave of her time and her keen appreciation of the French and English languages. Almost every page bears the mark of her improvements. I am deeply indebted to Arlene Agus for her editing, her moral support, and the brightness of her eyes.

I should like to thank the Mellon Foundation, the Earhart Foundation, and the Institute for Educational Affairs for their generous financial support. Earlier versions of some of the ideas in chapters 4, 5, and 8 can be found in "Rousseau and the Problem of Bourgeois Society," *American Political Science Review*, December, 1980, and in "Rousseau's Moral Realism: Replacing Natural Law with the General Will," *American Political Science Review*, September 1983. An earlier version of some sections of chapter 13 originally appeared as "Rousseau's 'Mission' and the Intention of His Writings," *American Journal of Political Science*, May 1983.

Abbreviations

The following abbreviations and editions have been used in referring to Rousseau's works. Where accurate and readily available English translations exist I have quoted and cited these. Otherwise, the translations are my own and citations are to *Oeuvres complètes* (4 vols.; published under the direction of Bernard Gagnebin and Marcel Raymond; Paris: Gallimard, Bibliothèque de la Pléiade, 1959-69). Where possible, I have included references to book, part, letter, or chapter (as the case may be) as well as page number. Citations of the *Social Contract*, for example, are in the form "book-chapter: page" (e.g. III-2: 82).

d'Alembert	*Letter to M. d'Alembert on the Theatre*. Translated by Allan Bloom. In *Politics and the Arts*. Ithaca, N.Y.: Cornell University Press, Agora Editions, 1968.
Beaumont	*Jean-Jacques Rousseau citoyen de Genève à Christophe de Beaumont, archevêque de Paris*. In *Oeuvres complètes*, vol. IV.
Bordes	*Preface of a Second Letter to Bordes*. In *The First and Second Discourses Together with the Replies to Critics and Essay on the Origin of Languages*. Translated by Victor Gourevitch. New York: Harper & Row, 1986.
Confs.	*Les Confessions de Jean-Jacques Rousseau*. In *Oeuvres complètes*, vol. I.
Corsica	*Projet de Constitution pour la Corse*. In *Oeuvres complètes*, vol. III.
Dialogues	*Rousseau juge de Jean-Jacques. Dialogues*. *Oeuvres complètes*, vol. I.
Emile	*Emile; or, On Education*. Translated by Allan Bloom. New York: Basic Books, 1979.
FD	*First Discourse*. In *The First and Second Discourses*. Translated by Roger D. Masters and Judith R. Masters. New York: St. Martin's Press, 1964.
Frags.	*Fragments politiques*. In *Oeuvres complètes*, vol. III.
GM	*Geneva Manuscript*. In *On the Social Contract with*

	Geneva Manuscript and Political Economy. Translated by Judith R. Masters. Edited by Roger D. Masters. New York: St. Martin's Press, 1978.
Guerre	*Que l'état de guerre naît de l'état social*. In *Oeuvres complètes*, vol. III.
Hero	*Discours sur cette question: Quelle est la vertu la plus nécessaire au héros*. In *Oeuvres complètes*, vol. II.
Imitation	*De l'imitation théâtrale*. In *Oeuvres complètes de J. J. Rousseau*, vol. 1. Paris: Hachette, 1884.
Languages	*Essay on the Origin of Languages*. In *The First and Second Discourses Together with the Replies to Critics and Essay on the Origin of Languages*. Translated by Victor Gourevitch. New York: Harper & Row, 1986.
Last Reply	*Last Reply [to Bordes]*. In *The First and Second Discourses Together with the Replies to Critics and Essay on the Origin of Languages*. Translated by Victor Gourevitch. New York: Harper & Row, 1986.
LM	*Lettres morales*. In *Oeuvres complètes*, vol. IV.
Mals.	*Quatre lettres à M. le Prèsident de Malesherbes*. In *Oeuvres complètes*, vol. I.
Montagne	*Lettres écrites de la montagne*. In *Oeuvres complètes*, vol. III.
Narcissus	Preface to *Narcissus*. In *The First and Second Discourses Together with the Replies to Critics and Essay on the Origin of Languages*. Translated by Victor Gourevitch. New York: Harper & Row, 1986.
NH	*Julie, ou la nouvelle Héloïse*. In *Oeuvres complètes*, vol. II.
Observations	*Observations [to Stanislas, King of Poland]*. In *The First and Second Discourses Together with the Replies to Critics and Essay on the Origin of Languages*. Translated by Victor Gourevitch. New York: Harper & Row, 1986.
OC	*Oeuvres complètes*.
PE	*Discourse on Political Economy*. In *On the Social Contract with Geneva Manuscript and Political Economy*. Translated by Judith R. Masters. Edited by Roger D. Masters. New York: St. Martin's Press, 1978.
Philopolis	*Letter to Philopolis*. In *The First and Second Discourses Together with the Replies to Critics and Essay on the*

Origin of Languages. Translated by Victor Gourevitch. New York: Harper & Row, 1986.

Poland   *Considérations sur le Gouvernment de Pologne*. In *Oeuvres complètes*, vol. III.

Polysynodie   *Polysynodie de l'abbé de Saint-Pierre*. In *Oeuvres complètes*, vol. III.

Reveries   The *Reveries of the Solitary Walker*. Translated by Charles E. Butterworth. New York: New York University Press, 1979.

SC   *On the Social Contract*. In *On the Social Contract with Geneva Manuscript and Political Economy*. Translated by Judith R. Masters. Edited by Roger D. Masters. New York: St. Martin's Press, 1978.

SD   *Second Discourse*. In *The First and Second Discourses*. Translated by Roger D. Masters and Judith R. Masters. New York: St. Martin's Press, 1964.

Introduction

Anyone gripped by an earnest desire to understand Rousseau's thought cannot help being daunted by the existence of an enormous secondary literature notorious for its disagreements and bitter disputes. No other philosopher, it is probably fair to say, has been as variously interpreted and misinterpreted as Rousseau. Given this fact, it is perhaps best to begin the study of his works not with the direct question—what do they mean?—but with a second-order question that may show how to answer the first: what is it that has made them so uniquely difficult to understand?

Beyond the difficulties that must naturally attend the effort to understand a mind greater than one's own, a mind distant also in time and place, I think one can point to four unique factors that have made Rousseau particularly hard to interpret. In ascending order of importance: Rousseau's "biography," his great philosophical and historical influence, the apparent contradictions in his thought, and, finally—what Rousseau himself emphasizes—the necessity but great difficulty of grasping his thought as a single, systematic whole.

Rousseau's Biography

The first great source of Rousseau misinterpretation has been the extraordinary strangeness of his personality and life, which has made it very difficult for scholars to treat his arguments seriously as arguments rather than as symptoms. His personality was riddled with psychological eccentricities: his desire to be spanked and to expose himself, his strange illnesses, his love affair with a woman he called "mama," his paranoia. To this strange personality add a very unusual and turbulent life: his childhood spent in strict Calvinist Geneva, his youth as an engraver's apprentice, a vagabond, a lackey, a music teacher, a secretary to the French ambassador to Venice, an aide to a French tax-collector, his marriage to a linen worker, Thérèse, his transformation at middle-age into the most celebrated philosopher in all of Europe, and his eventual decline into a restless fugitive fleeing persecution, both real and imagined. To top it off, Rousseau rubs our noses in all these facts by writing his *Confessions*, with its revelation of the most intimate details of his life. More than any other thinker before or since, Rousseau allows, invites, indeed almost demands biographical and psychological reductionism. And, in equal measure, he has received it.

But it is Rousseau's explicit contention that the strangeness of his life and personality is precisely what made it possible for him to uncover the strange, hidden truth about human nature. Certainly, until we have understood and judged his ideas on their own merits, we are not entitled to psychologize them away.[1]

Rousseau's Influence

The second factor rendering accurate interpretation difficult—even while making it more important—is Rousseau's unprecedented influence. Thinkers who have been *philosophically* influential tend to get buried under the beliefs of their disciples, necessitating a delicate process of excavation to separate out their original thought from the similar yet different views that they inspired in others. Rousseau, in particular, was a far more complex and less "settled" thinker than virtually any of his disciples. The common tendency to read their thought back into his—making him, say, a Romantic or a Kantian—has tended to distort his meaning, especially by oversimplification.

The situation is even worse if a thinker should be *historically* influential, playing an important role in momentous cultural and political upheavals; for then partisan interests forcibly rework him into an ideological ally or enemy. Because of Rousseau's enduring historical influence, the secondary literature has hardly known a moment's rest from this sort of distortion. First, he was exalted by some and vilified by others for the role played by his writings during the French Revolution, after that, for his influence on the Romantic movement, and, later still, for his contributions to socialism and for the part he played in the rise of totalitarianism.[2] His works have been dragged into virtually every major ideological battle of the last two centuries—and have been deeply scarred as a result. Of course, no serious student of ideas can or should ignore the dangers of Rousseau's thought, which are very real. Only they are dangers best defused by understanding.

Rousseau's Unsystematic and Contradictory Writings

A still greater obstacle to understanding has been the internal character of Rousseau's writings: they appear to be both unsystematic and self-contradictory. It is difficult to deny that Rousseau's style of writing is unsystematic. Believing that if one speaks to men's hearts, their minds will follow, he tends to paint rather than to argue. His works are as much novels as treatises. He refrains from analyzing and dissecting his ideas precisely because his purpose is to bring them to life. But this style, while certainly

---

[1] Kelly's (1987) commentary on the *Confessions* provides an excellent account of Rousseau's own view of the development of his personality and its relation to his philosophical discoveries. The best biography of Rousseau is Cranston (1985), an invaluable source of information. See also Guehenno (1966).

[2] See Gay (1954) pp. 4-8.

part of his appeal, often leaves the reader with the difficult task of figuring out Rousseau's argument for himself.

Worse still, this style often conceals the very presence of an argument. Due to the very skillfulness of his literary art, Rousseau's writing appears artless, as if it were merely an unreflective and feverish effusion of strongly felt sentiments. He seems to be something of a poet or a visionary but certainly not, as Bertrand Russell assures us, "what would now be called a philosopher."[3] It appears that he calls upon us not to think but only to feel, and that all it really means to "understand" Rousseau is to enter sympathetically into his unique "vision."

Related to this point is the common assumption—and it is difficult to overstate how completely it conditions all our responses to Rousseau—that whatever he may be saying, and however interesting it may be, it is not *hard*. He is not intellectually difficult as are, say, Aristotle or Kant, and we will not be called upon to think hard, develop long, subtle chains of reasoning, rack our brains. In this way, Rousseau's poetic and unsystematic style, attractive as it is, has thrown his readers off the scent of his argument and dissuaded them from applying the necessary kind and degree of exertion.

This problem is of course made worse by the second charge in this accusation: Rousseau's writings are not only unsystematic but actually self-contradictory. And indeed, we seem to find no fewer than four major contradictions in his works.

The first, the most obvious, and the most famous of these is a conflict between the radical individualism found in the *Second Discourse* and the radical collectivism found in the *Social Contract*. One may also include in this first contradiction certain other antitheses that follow from it: a conflict between Rousseau's praise of solitude and of community, of idleness and of activity, of spontaneity and of self-conquest, of gentleness and of martial valor, of cosmopolitan humanitarianism and of exclusive patriotism.

Second, a conflict exists between, on the one hand, Rousseau's extreme egalitarianism, his extravagant praise of the people, his demand for unlimited popular sovereignty, his insistence on pure, direct democracy, and, on the other hand, his elitism, his disparagement of the people, his insistence on the necessity of a civil religion, his advice to the legislator and even the executive power to mold and manipulate the people, and other seemingly antidemocratic or authoritarian political measures.

Third, Rousseau follows Montesquieu (and precedes Burke) in emphasizing the importance for politics of established custom, historical context, and regional variation, in embracing the fundamentally conservative principle that "freedom is not the fruit of every climate" (*SC* III-8: 92). But this prudent, statesmanlike flexibility and conservatism is contradicted by his doctrinaire, unhistorical, and universally subversive declaration that every

[3] *History of Western Philosophy* p. 684.

state not strictly in accord with the almost impossibly demanding principles of the *Social Contract* is illegitimate.

Finally, the fourth contradiction—which can be viewed as the source, or at least a compendium, of the other three—concerns the question of where Rousseau belongs in the history of political thought. On the one hand, he seems clearly to be a modern, Enlightenment figure, influenced primarily by such theorists as Hobbes and Locke with their individualism and social contract theory, their egalitarianism, and their proclamation of universal principles of legitimacy based on the elemental goal of self-preservation. On the other hand, Rousseau seems to turn his back on modernity in disgust and return to the nobility of the classical world, to Plato and Plutarch, Cato and Lycurgus, Rome and Sparta, with their collectivism, their inegalitarianism, and their appreciation of the rare and complex conditions required to establish a regime that will raise its citizens to the highest peaks of virtue.

In looking over this list, one is struck by the fact that it contains not the sorts of ambiguities and tensions found in all writers, but stark polarities. Although Rousseau emphatically denies that his writings are really contradictory, even he does not deny, he rather openly laments, that they often appear to be so.[4] And this undeniable appearance of contradiction is perhaps the single greatest cause of the extraordinary difficulty that scholars have had in understanding him.

Our results to this point might be summarized by saying that for two centuries, Rousseau's thought has appeared as a contradiction wrapped in a willful distortion inside an aberrant personality.

Rousseau's System and His Contradictions

We turn finally to Rousseau's own explanation for the misinterpretation of his writings (a problem that greatly concerned him ever since the publication of the *First Discourse*). His thought, he maintains, will always be misunderstood and even appear contradictory unless it is grasped comprehensively, as a single, systematic whole, and, for a variety of reasons, his readers have been disinclined or unable to do so.[5]

Virtually everyone familiar with Rousseau is aware of his famous claim

---

[4] See *Dialogues* III: 932; SC II-4: 62n, II-5: 65; *Emile* II: 93; *OC* III: 71n, 105-6.

[5] *Dialogues* III: 932; *Mals.*, 1136; *SC* II-4: 62n, II-5: 65. Although there have been a number of commentators who, taking Rousseau at his word, have sought the underlying unity of his thought, there has been little consensus as to what that unity is. For a brief survey of such views, see Peter Gay (1954) pp. 17-24. I will attempt to respond to some of the more important of these views in the course of presenting my own. In general, it seems to me that to be judged successful, a statement of Rousseau's system must be able to resolve the four contradictions mentioned above, and it must be able to explain the content of his major writings, not just the easy cases like the *Second Discourse*, which is obviously about the natural goodness of man, but also the tough cases like the *Social Contract*, in which this principle is never once mentioned.

to be systematic, and many of his interpreters accept it in the abstract; but when it comes down to analyzing his writings, they have tended to dismiss it, discouraged by his unsystematic style and, above all, by his contradictions. Rousseau's readers, then, seem to have been caught in a circle: they have failed to seek the system because of the contradictions and have seen contradictions because they have failed to find the system.

To break out of this problem, it might be useful to attack it from both ends: to ask those who believe the contradictions to be real how they explain Rousseau's commission of such obvious and elementary mistakes; and to ask Rousseau in greater detail how his thought could appear to be so contradictory if in fact it is perfectly consistent.

Two explanations have most commonly been given for Rousseau's inconsistencies. Reduced to bare essentials, the first asserts that he changed his opinions over time and the second that they are real contradictions, but he didn't notice them.

According to the first view, one must interpret Rousseau "genetically": his thought developed over time, and thus what appear to be contradictions can be explained as merely changes of mind. After all, many thinkers have, on their own testimony, changed their opinions in fundamental ways.

But this view runs directly counter to Rousseau's own testimony that his opinions did not change in any important respect over the course of his writings. "I wrote on diverse subjects," he asserts, "but always with the same principles: always the same morality, the same belief, the same maxims, and, if you like, the same opinions" (*Beaumont*, 928; see 933, 935; *Mals.*, 1136; *Dialogues* I: 687, II: 829, III: 932-34). This claim, which he repeated throughout his life, is made all the more plausible by the fact that he began writing at the relatively mature age of thirty-eight, that all of his major philosophical works were written in a period of only twelve years, and that all sides of his contradictions appear in all of his works, albeit in different degrees.

The second view is one that is more often assumed than stated explicitly. It holds that Rousseau was drawn in opposite directions by the competing desires or external influences acting upon him, and, because of the extremely unsystematic character of his mind, he was incapable of resolving—because incapable of perceiving—the resulting inconsistencies in his thought. This view carries the advantage that it accounts for both Rousseau's contradictions and his repeated denials of them. Furthermore, Rousseau himself seems to endorse it when he complains of the deficiencies of his mind: "I take pleasure in meditating, searching, inventing; my disgust is in putting things in order, and the proof that I have less reason than *esprit* is that the transitions are always what cost me the most" (*OC* I: 1128-29). Again:

> My ideas take shape in my head with the most incredible difficulty.... From this comes the extreme difficulty that I find in

writing. My erased, smudged, tangled, undecipherable manuscripts
attest to the pains they have cost me . . . . it is at night in my bed
and during my insomnias that I compose in my head . . . . Some of
my sections I have turned over and over in my head for five or six
nights before they were fit to be put onto paper. (Confs. III:
113-114)[6]

Rousseau was simply incapable of thinking systematically, the argument
runs, and so was unaware of the contradictions in his thought.

It strains credulity, however, to think that he could have been simply
unaware of the obvious contradictions that every college freshman sees in
his works, especially when he expressly acknowledges that they contain the
appearance of contradiction. When a genius complains about his mental
defects, moreover, we must not be over hasty in concurring. Rousseau may
indeed have lacked the sort of analytical brilliance that one finds in a thinker
like Hume or Kant, but that did not prevent Hume from pronouncing him
"a very fine Genius" and Kant from proclaiming him the veritable Newton
of the moral world.[7] If Rousseau repeatedly asserts that putting his ideas in
order always required a conscious and painful effort, that surely does not
entitle us to conclude that he could not or did not make that effort, especially
when he informs us that, on the contrary, his keen awareness of his
weakness moved him to make special efforts in just this area. A more
accurate conclusion is that of Hippolyte Taine, who, after quoting this very
same passage, continues:

But on the other hand, in this burning furnace, under the pressure
of this prolonged and intense meditation, his style, incessantly
forged and reforged, acquires a density and a hardness that one
does not find elsewhere . . . . Moreover, the pieces of his writing
are linked together; he writes not just pages but books; there is no
logician more strict. His demonstration is woven stitch by stitch
over one, two, three volumes, like an enormous web without exit
where, willingly or unwillingly, one remains held. He is a systematist who, turned in on himself, with his eyes obstinately fixed on
his dream or on his principle, penetrates into it a little more each
day, unravels its consequences one by one, and always keeps the
webbing as a whole in his grasp.[8]

This passage, written by a determined opponent of Rousseau's thought and
influence, describes quite beautifully, I think, the character of his writing
and also reflects very closely Rousseau's own understanding of himself.

[6] See Letter to Deschamps Sept. 12, 1761, reprinted *OC* I: 1844. This passage also shows
just how much art is involved in the appearance of spontaneity in Rousseau's style.

[7] Letter to John Home, March 22, 1766, reprinted in Ritter (1988) p. 197. Regarding Kant,
see the excerpts from his notes reproduced in this same volume, pp. 207-8.

[8] *L'Ancien Régime*, pp. 352-53.

Taine's tribute forms a nice introduction as we turn to hear Rousseau explain how his thought could appear so contradictory if in fact it is rigorously consistent. At a certain point in the *Social Contract* Rousseau states with some exasperation: "All of my ideas fit together, but I can hardly present them simultaneously" (II-5: 65).[9] Rousseau has a new and complex view to put forward which can only be understood as a whole; but it cannot be *presented* as a whole, not "simultaneously," but only successively within and also among his several works. His readers, he claims, have always seen "contradictions" in his works because they have impatiently seized upon partial, half-explained, and one-sided presentations as if they were complete and definitive.

But why, we are entitled to ask, have his readers repeatedly made this same mistake? And why does this problem plague him so much more than other writers? Rousseau gives two answers. The first, to which he gives primary emphasis (and which will be considered at greater length momentarily), places the blame on his readers. Turning around the accusation just directed at him, he claims that they are unaccustomed to truly systematic thinking such as he alone practices, for "nothing is so contrary to the philosophic spirit of this century" (*Dialogues* III: 934; see 932).

The second reason for his readers' repeated failure to grasp his thought as a whole has to do, Rousseau acknowledges, with the way he wrote his books. For various reasons, he never made a comprehensive statement of the whole (although *Emile* comes closest), nor do his separate books form an ordered development, in which one work picks up where the other leaves off. Rather he allowed his system to dribble out in disconnected parts (*Bordes*, 114-15; *Confs.* VIII: 388; *Dialogues* III: 933). It seems to me that this second reason is actually the more important one and that Rousseau is thus somewhat more to blame than he himself acknowledges. The general point may be stated as follows: Rousseau's *thought* is indeed exceptionally systematic—but his *writings* are exceptionally unsystematic. This radical incongruity between thought and presentation has been the primary source of all our misunderstandings.

The incongruity is no accident, for Rousseau's thought culminates precisely in a praise of idleness, solitude, and disdain for the life of the writer. True, Rousseau also strongly desired to serve humanity, but the systematic presentation of his ideas was not necessarily the best means of doing so. His head was always filled, he explains, with a hundred different literary projects—as well as a desire to throw away his pen—and thus which of these projects ever came to fruition owed a great deal to chance (*Confs.* IX: 407-10). Just consider Rousseau's writings. No other philosopher ever wrote so many of his major works on questions or topics that arose

---

[9] See p. 62n: "Attentive readers, please do not be in a hurry to accuse me of inconsistency here. I have been unable to avoid it in my terminology, given the poverty of the language. But wait."

accidentally and were not of his own devise: the *First* and *Second Discourses* (and the unfinished *Discourse on This Question: "What Is the Virtue Most Necessary to a Hero"*) were all written as entries in academic prize competitions, the preface to *Narcisse*, which is "one of my good writings," as an introduction and apology for his play by that name (*Confs.* VIII: 388), the *Discourse on Political Economy* as an article for the *Encyclopedia*, the works on the Abbé de Saint Pierre at the behest of the abbé's family, the *Letter to d'Alembert* as a reply to the *Encyclopedia* article on Geneva, the works on *Corsica* and *Poland* at the request of representatives of those countries, the *Letters from the Mountain* and *Rousseau Juge de Jean-Jacques* in response to attacks on him and his writings, the *Confessions* at least partly at the behest of his publisher (*Confs.* X: 516), and finally *Emile*, "the best of my writings," was "begun to gratify a good mother" and "the authority of friendship caused this project, although *less to my taste in itself*, to be closer to my heart than all the others" (*Confs.* XI: 573; *Emile* Preface: 33; *Confs.* IX: 409, emphasis added). Remarkably, the *Social Contract* appears to be the only one of Rousseau's philosophical works that he wrote more or less under his own steam, and even that was only an extract from a larger work, his *Political Institutions*, on which he worked on and off for about twenty years before abandoning. It is not only Rousseau's style, then, that is unsystematic and prone to hide his argument, but also the very sequence and topics of his major works.[10]

In Rousseau, then, one confronts a very anomalous situation. A systematic thinker but an accidental author, he spoke out only in fortuitous, externally motivated pieces. And in composing them his method was to "cannibalize" his philosophical system: to take his ideas out of their place in the whole and reassemble them in order to address the particular topic at hand. That is why, for example, one finds that terms which have a special meaning in Rousseau's system, like the "general will," the "sentiment of existence," "virtue," or "law," are often used in one book and defined in another. Similarly, conclusions stated in one of his works may be ultimately based on premises defended only in some other, often later, work. For example, the central thesis of the *First Discourse*—that the arts and sciences are morally and politically corrupting—has seemed so strange to

---

[10] The externally motivated character of most of Rousseau's writings has also had the effect of making those writings far more complex, by forcing Rousseau to try to do two things at once. In *Emile* and the *Second Discourse*, for example, Rousseau's primary purpose is to prove the natural goodness of man and draw out some of its consequences, but this purpose must be interwoven with the different (although not unrelated) official purpose of the writings—to present a plan of education, and to show the origin of inequality. In a letter to a friend, Rousseau writes: "You say quite correctly that it is impossible to produce an Emile. But I cannot believe that you take the book that carries this name for a true treatise on education. It is rather a philosophical work on this principle advanced by the author in other writings *that man is naturally good*" (Letter to Cramer, October 13, 1764, italics in the original).

many of its readers because it is based on a premise that is stated and supported only in later works: that moral and political health is possible only in a small, spartan community of public-spirited citizens. (Given this unstated premise, his conclusion is fairly obvious and indeed a commonplace of classical political theory.) To exaggerate somewhat, Rousseau took the various pieces of his unified system of *thought*—its concepts, ideas, and arguments—and scattered them unsystematically throughout his *writings*.

This incongruity between thought and writing has not only hidden Rousseau's system from view, but also made his works appear positively confused and self-contradictory. For, on the one hand, it has rendered his writings exceedingly *interdependent*. Since they are made up of disconnected fragments of a single system, they are intimately linked together—all the more so for being linked unsystematically, not book to book, so to speak, but rather sentence to sentence or idea to idea, a premise here to a conclusion there. Thus, as Rousseau states, his works are "inseparable and form together a single whole," they "explain themselves each by the others."[11] Of course, on a certain level, they are meant and able to stand alone, but ultimately they are incoherent unless cross-referenced at every point.

Yet, on the other hand, since they are linked so unsystematically, they *appear* precisely to *stand alone*. They appear to be the very opposite of what they are. In this way, Rousseau's readers have been encouraged to treat completely interdependent works as if they were completely independent. Mistaking fragments for completed wholes, they necessarily find conclusions without premises, terms without definitions, and doctrines without the arguments that explain the limits of their applicability—they find, in short, that Rousseau is contradictory or incoherent.

The Nature of Rousseau's System

We must find the system, then, that Rousseau has dismantled and scattered among his desultory writings. But what does Rousseau mean by his "system"? The issue is somewhat slippery, for in one sense Rousseau is clearly disdainful of systems. He makes a distinction between what he calls the "systematic spirit" and the "spirit of observation," the former being the tendency to generalize boldly, constructing a system of abstract and universal principles, the latter being a cautious adherence to empirical observation and concrete facts (*LM*, 1090, 1093; *Emile* Preface: 34, V: 386-87). Like most of his contemporaries, like most of ours, he has a visceral distrust of the systematic spirit, believing that the greatest danger in philosophy lies in vainly overestimating the power of reason. All wisdom begins in skepti-

---

[11]*Mals.*, 1136 (Rousseau is referring to the two *Discourses* and *Emile* here), *Beaumont*, 950-51; see *Dialogues* III: 932-33.

cism or in a certain intellectual modesty and retrenchment. Regarding his own thought he insists: "instead of yielding to the systematic spirit, I grant as little as possible to reasoning and I trust only observation. I found myself not on what I have imagined but on what I have seen" (*Emile* IV: 254).[12]

Rousseau attacks here what we may call the "systematizer": one who, vainly reasoning with too little appeal to experience, ends up forcing things to fit together. Yet what he claims to *be* is a "systematic thinker": one who hates "systematizers" but nevertheless believes that a genuine philosopher can never stop *asking* how the whole fits together, never abandon this quest and question. Unlike the mere collector of ideas and insights, Rousseau continually seeks—albeit cautiously, skeptically, empirically—a unified vision.

He claims, moreover, that in this important respect he is unique among his contemporaries, as he would seem to be among ours.[13] The other thinkers of his time have all allowed their understandable horror at the "systematizers" of the seventeenth century (or in our case, of the nineteenth) to turn them away from the reasonable and necessary concern with "systematic thinking," with comprehensiveness and unity. They have allowed themselves to be stampeded into the grasp of a narrow precision or a shallow eclecticism.

This problem is compounded by a related one: since the Enlightenment, the philosophers have all lost their necessary distance from society. Beneath the surface, they are all "men of letters," trained in and for society; and their whole attitude toward thinking is shaped by the restlessness and love of novelty found there, by the need to keep up, to have something to say, to be in print, and above all by the impatient and luxurious eclecticism that picks and chooses among ideas, that extracts from everything the interesting or pleasing part and throws away the rest (*Beaumont*, 967; *FD*, 52-53). The taste and habit have been lost for that quiet, sustained, and comprehensive meditation Rousseau calls "systematic."

But Rousseau himself, with his sincere longing for the truth and his taste for solitude and meditation, is different. Describing his works, he states:

> These books are not, like those of today, collections of detached thoughts upon each of which the mind of the reader can repose. They are the meditations of a solitary; they demand a sustained attention which is not too much to the taste of our nation. When one insists on seeking to follow their thread one must return to them with effort and more than once. (*Dialogues* III: 932; see 829)

Alone with his thoughts, cautiously, relentlessly, in long unbroken chains of reasoning, he endeavors to think things through to the end, to hold fast

---

[12] See *Emile* II: 110, IV: 214n2, 268. For the views of Rousseau's contemporaries see, for example, the article "Philosopher" in the *Encyclopedia*.

[13] Regarding our own time, consider MacIntyre (1981) p. 10.

to the questions through all their mutations, to draw out and test all of the consequences of his beliefs, to unify his understanding, to see life whole.[14]

But Rousseau's claims for himself extend further—to the assertion that, through such holistic thinking he eventually attained an actual vision of the whole, a philosophical system. On the basis of a long period of reading, thinking, and especially of uniquely wide-ranging observation, he came to a crucial new insight, which first crystallized in his mind during a sudden vision, the so-called illumination of Vincennes. It was early autumn 1749; Rousseau was walking from Paris to Vincennes, where his friend Diderot had been imprisoned.

> I had in my pocket a *Mercure de France* that I began to leaf through along the way. I came upon the question of the Academy of Dijon, which gave rise to my first writing [the *Discourse on the Arts and Sciences*]. If ever anything was like a sudden inspiration, it is the movement that occurred in me at that reading; suddenly I felt my mind dazzled by a thousand lights.... Oh Monsieur, if I had ever been able to write a quarter of what I saw and felt under that tree, with what clarity I would have shown all the contradictions of the social system; with what force I would have exposed all the abuses of our institutions, with what simplicity I would have demonstrated that man is naturally good, and that it is solely by these institutions that men become wicked. (*Mals.*, 1136; see *Confs.* VIII: 351; *Dialogues* II: 828)

Rousseau saw, moreover, that this new insight constituted "the fundamental principle of all morals," and by drawing out all of its consequences, he constructed a comprehensive system of moral and political philosophy (Beaumont, 935).[15]

The system Rousseau claims to possess, then, must not be confused with the sort of rationalistic, Cartesian, deductive system that he so distrusts and disdains. Rousseau does not begin from a rationally self-evident first principle and build from there, but rather ascends to his first principle—the natural goodness of man—through a variety of different arguments each involving both reasoning and observation. And even then, the conclusions he deduces from this principle are not left to stand solely on the ground of that deduction but are themselves tested empirically. Rousseau's thought should also be distinguished from the sort of grand metaphysical system that includes all of nature and heaven in its sweep. His thought is certainly not indifferent or unrelated to questions beyond the human sphere, but, to

---

[14] Remember that this difference between Rousseau and others in the capacity for systematic thinking is his first and preferred explanation for why his readers have always failed to see the whole of his thought. To the extent that he is right, then the most neglected aspect of his philosophizing happens to be precisely the one from which we have the most to learn.

[15] See 951; *Dialogues* III: 932-36, 828-29, 687; *Mals.*, 1135-36; *Confs.* VIII: 351.

the extent possible, it endeavors to be metaphysically neutral. His "system" proper is a theory of humanity, a philosophy of morals and politics.

This account of the sources of Rousseau misinterpretation, if accurate, shows what must be done in order to understand him correctly. One must approach each one of his different writings on its own terms, paying scrupulous attention to its specific and often idiosyncratic "occasion": the unique intention, angle of approach, and audience that gives each work a somewhat different color and perspective. But in view of their utter interdependence, one must also study all of them together—and not just successively but, as it were, simultaneously, joining them not just book to book but, again, idea to idea in an effort to put back together again what Rousseau has dismantled, the complex, systematic whole of his thought. And one must also strive to recover, in the process, his art of comprehensive thinking.

In studying Rousseau, I have tried to proceed in this manner and, in the present work, I attempt to lay out the reassembled system of his thought. To keep the book within manageable proportions, when I turn to the constructive part of Rousseau's system, I limit myself primarily to his political thought and attempt to demonstrate how the *Social Contract* and the *Political Economy* can be understood, and only understood, as strict consequences of the principle of natural goodness.

It is hoped that through an elaboration of this kind, we may learn the most about Rousseau's philosophical thought, and also the most from it.

Part One

The Meaning of Rousseau's Fundamental Principle

1

The Natural Goodness of Man

"The fundamental principle of all morals," Rousseau proclaims, "on which I have reasoned in all my writings . . . is that man is a being that is naturally good." The reader who carefully studies his various works will see "everywhere the development of [my] great principle that nature made man happy and good but society depraves him and makes him miserable" (*Beaumont*, 935-36; *Dialogues* III: 934). It is curiously difficult, however, to grasp or feel the significance of this "great principle" owing to its deceptive simplicity as well as its numbing familiarity. Worn down through two centuries of use, it has lost all sharpness and specificity, becoming a tiresome platitude more likely to discourage than stimulate reflection. We must begin, then, by extricating Rousseau's thought from that of his imitators and popularizers and restoring his revolutionary new principle to something of its original meaning and vitality.

Who Is Good and What Is Goodness?

To whom does "the natural goodness of man" attribute goodness? If the very mention of Rousseau's name often raises an indulgent smile, that is because it is usually assumed that his famous principle is a tender-minded, pollyannish affirmation, indeed the classic statement, of the basic goodness of human beings as we know them. Yet nothing could be further from the truth. "Man is wicked," Rousseau affirms of those around him, "sad and continual experience spares the need for proof" (*SD*, 193). Rousseau speaks of civilized humanity with a disgust and contempt that yield nothing to Saint Augustine, and which earned him, during his lifetime, the reputation not of a pollyanna but a misanthrope. Voltaire, for example, attacked the *Second Discourse* as a "book against the human race."[1] In truth, Rousseau's indictment of the human race—his now classic diagnosis of the ills of modern society in terms of the loss of social and psychic unity—is one of the most important elements of his thought, virtually defining the problem that later generations of thinkers would try to solve, and forming the inaugural event for what has since been a continuous tradition of post-Enlightenment lamentation over the waywardness of modern man. Far from being an affirmation of civilized man's goodness, then, Rousseau's principle is a penetrating new account of his extraordinary badness.

---

[1] Quoted in *OC* III: 1379.

Rousseau *does*, of course, attribute goodness to men, but only to "natural" men who are free of the corrupting effects of artificial society. In the unqualified sense, this means the presocial, arational, subhuman, brutelike "natural man" portrayed in the *Second Discourse*. However, certain other, less extreme human types also qualify as relatively natural and "good." The primitive savage, denizen of a later epoch where men have developed most of their faculties and live together in loose tribes, is said to be "essentially good" (*SD*, 151). In civilized times, there is Emile, eponymous hero of Rousseau's educational treatise, who is raised on the fringes of contemporary society. Through extraordinary artifice, the development of his faculties and desires is reordered to harmonize with and preserve much of his primitive goodness. In a loose sense, the citizen, the zealous patriot living in the legitimate state described in the *Social Contract*, reconquers his original goodness, if in an entirely new and unnatural form. Finally, as explained in the autobiographical writings, Rousseau himself, the philosopher or artist, preserves his natural goodness through genius, solitude, and extraordinary strength of soul. These rather disparate human types, the central characters in the large *dramatis personae* of Rousseau's writings, are those he calls good

What, then, is meant by "goodness"? Here, Rousseau's thought tends to be obscured by the contemporary attitude toward this word or concept, which we somehow feel compelled to define in a narrowly moralistic sense, even as we find that sense insipid. Rousseau, who understands the concept in a more capacious, full-bodied way, employs it here in a double, relative sense: man is by nature good *for himself* and also good *for others*. Rousseau's strongest claims concern the first: man is naturally good for himself, meaning well-ordered and self-sufficient, hence happy. None of his natural inclinations are bad, that is, harmful, illusory, impossible, or contradictory. His desires are all proportioned to his needs and his faculties to his desires. And on a still deeper level, prior to all desire, he has within himself a fundamental source of contentment, a joy in mere existence.

Man's natural goodness for others is more ambiguous. It does not mean rationally "moral," since natural man is subrational and amoral; nor does it primarily mean that man is moved by a positive inclination to love and help others, nor even that he is always gentle. Natural man is occasionally violent, and tribal man even cruel or vindictive. The primary meaning of this goodness is negative. By nature, man lacks a specific desire to harm others, and, even more important, he lacks all the needs, passions, and prejudices that now put his interests in essential and systematic conflict with others. He is naturally self-sufficient and content, and therefore strife with others is never intrinsically pleasant, it is rarely useful, and it troubles his inner repose.

There is also, however, a positive content to this goodness. By "identifying" with others, natural man experiences rudimentary feelings of compassion which discourage him from engaging in unnecessary violence. In civilized man, these feelings develop into a natural conscience, an inner "voice of nature." Yet Rousseau argues that this inner voice is weaker than the artificial passions and vices that inevitably develop along with it in society. Thus, most civilized men do hear the inner voice, but only in moments of detachment and recollection; they forget it as soon as they act. If a civilized man were raised like Emile, however, then natural pity or conscience, unopposed by artificial passions yet stimulated by an artificially developed imagination, would lead to a genuine benevolence of feeling and action. Such is the limited (and only partly natural) positive content of man's goodness for others.[2]

Taken as a whole, then, the principle of natural goodness may be said to involve three basic elements: an assertion that by nature man is good for himself and others, a "misanthropic" characterization of the evil of civilized man, and, bridging the gap between the two claims, a demonstration that man's present evil derives wholly from the corrupting effects of society. Through this third element, Rousseau initiates the philosophic tendency, which has dominated almost all subsequent thought, to understand the human problem in terms of historical, social, or environmental causes rather than natural or divine ones.

Rousseau's Opponents

The meaning of the principle of natural goodness can be sharpened, and some of its momentous consequences brought to light, by identifying the thinkers Rousseau is attacking and the doctrines he is trying to refute. Since he regards this principle as altogether new, there is a sense in which he is attacking simply everyone who preceded him. This sweeping category, however, can be resolved into three primary opponents: Christian thought and especially the doctrine of original sin; early modern political theory, particularly the thought of Thomas Hobbes; and classical political philosophy, especially in its Platonic strain, with its starkly dualistic theory of human nature. That *is* pretty nearly everyone in the Western tradition.

The Church doctrine of original sin is the most obvious, and no doubt most eagerly targeted, of Rousseau's opponents. All of his writings, he claims, aim to demonstrate that "there is no *original perversity* in the human heart, and that the first movements of nature are always right" (*Beaumont*, 937-38, emphasis added). The history of the species sketched in the *Second Discourse*, and that of the child in *Emile*, are obviously meant to confront the biblical account of the Fall, supplying an alternative explanation of the origin of evil that exculpates man by shifting the blame onto society. Similarly, the *Confessions*, as the very title implies, is intended as an alternative to the work of Saint Augustine, the classic exponent of the original sin doctrine. Through a detailed personal confession, Rousseau tries to demonstrate that his own numerous sins "came to me much more from my situation than from myself" (*Mals.*, 1136).[3]

---

[2] *Beaumont*, 935-37; *LM*, 1088, 1105; *Dialogues* I: 687; *Emile* IV: 223-36, 287-93; *SD*, 95-96, 130-33. Regarding the ambiguities in Rousseau's discussion of pity, see Plattner (1979) pp. 82-87.

[3] For discussion of this theme in the *Confessions*, see Kelly (1987), Hartle (1983), and Burgelin (1952) pp. 311-17.

Rousseau also attacks the doctrine of original sin on internal and scriptural grounds. To the traditional argument, for example, that only this doctrine can explain the mystery of the origin of human evil, he responds: "We are, you say, sinners because of the sin of our first father, but why did our first father himself sin? Why cannot the same reason which you use to explain his sin be applied to his descendants without original sin?" (*Beaumont* fragment, 1013). Moreover, the view that contemporary men are guilty for a sin of their most distant ancestor, and that their natures, corrupted by that sin, now force them to sin again, cannot, he argues, be reconciled with God's justice (ibid.). Finally, Rousseau points out that the "doctrine of original sin, subject to terrible difficulties, is not contained in scripture as clearly or harshly as it has pleased the Rhetor Augustine and our theologians to claim" (*Beaumont*, 937-38).

In opposing this doctrine, of course, Rousseau may be viewed as following a nearly universal tendency of philosophic thought in the eighteenth century. Nevertheless, as Karl Barth wrote of Rousseau: "the Church doctrine of original sin has seldom . . . been denied with such disconcerting candor and force and in so directly personal a way."[4]

By replacing the doctrine of original sin with the principle of natural goodness, Rousseau is, of course, not merely correcting what he takes to be a false opinion, but also combating a harmful and dangerous one: "How I hate the discouraging doctrine of our hard Theologians!" (*Beaumont*, 940n). His hatred of it appears to rest on two grounds.

First, it leads to a cruelly repressive morality, one that condemns our spontaneous inclinations as sinful, that curses nature and poisons life. Since human beings can never fully comply with this antinatural morality, it also burdens them with constant feelings of failure, self-hatred, and guilt. By declaring that "the first movements of nature are good and right," Rousseau clearly seeks to lift this burden of guilt and to restore life to men's souls by putting them back in touch with their natural impulses and energies (*Dialogues* I: 668).

Rousseau's second and greater objection to the doctrine of original sin, however, is that it actually weakens morality. Indeed, as compared with later thinkers such as Nietzsche and Freud, Rousseau places surprisingly little emphasis on guilt and the "life-destroying" character of overzealous Christian morality. He believes that men are more often corrupted than repressed by such a morality.

Human beings are fairly skeptical, intractable, and resistant to morality, in Rousseau's view, and therefore this extreme, antinatural morality most often simply fails to take hold. And in failing, it casts all moral restraint into disrepute.

> A young and beautiful girl will *never despise her body*, she will never in good faith grieve for the great sins her beauty causes to be

---

[4] Barth (1959) p. 108.

committed, she will never sincerely shed tears before God for being a coveted object, and she will never be able to believe within herself that the sweetest sentiment of the heart is an invention of Satan. Give her other reasons that she can believe within and for herself, for these will never get through to her. (*Emile* V: 392; emphasis added)

"By exaggerating all duties," Rousseau claims, "Christianity makes them impracticable and vain" (*Emile* V: 374). In aiming too high, asking too much, and opposing the natural sentiments, the morality based on original sin produces not sincerely moral individuals, but only a few guilt-ridden believers and a great many cynics, hypocrites, and libertines.

Rousseau seeks to promote a more realistic and effectual morality by building on certain salutary passions such as patriotism, romantic love, and pity. But once again, such a morality is crippled by the doctrine of original sin because, by cursing the passions, it stunts the full development of these useful moral sentiments.

Furthermore, the doctrine of original sin tends to destroy men's sense of freedom and moral responsibility, for it teaches that they are all born sinners, that it is not within their power to avoid evil, that they have no free will. It makes them passive, slavish, and resigned to their own sinfulness while they wait for God in His mercy to save them. Consequently, Rousseau believes he accomplishes something "that is both most consoling and most useful" in showing that "all these vices belong not so much to man as to man badly governed" (*Narcissus*, 106). He seeks to embolden humanity to take control of its own destiny. When people see that evil derives from society rather than from their sinful natures and that it may be cured or ameliorated through human as distinguished from divine action, they will recover a sense of freedom and dignity, a feeling of responsibility for their lives, and a moral determination to improve them.

In one last, obvious way, the doctrine of original sin undermines morality: it encourages men to despise mankind. The Christian priest shows us:

all men as monsters to be stifled, as victims of the Devil whose company can only corrupt the heart and cast us into Hell. And what is most peculiar is that after all of these beautiful declamations, the same man gravely exhorts us to love our neighbors, that is, this whole troop of rascals for whom he has inspired us with such horror. (*OC* IV: 19)

Christianity may command us to love others but it inspires us to hate them. The doctrine of natural goodness, on the other hand, promotes a genuine love of humanity based on compassion. By replacing the image of man as a born sinner with that of a born victim, it brings secular compassion to the fore as the only reasonable and proper attitude toward mankind.

In sum, Rousseau not only refutes but, as it were, turns the Church doctrine of original sin on its head, charging that, through its overly demanding and misanthropic morality, it itself creates many of the evils it is supposed to combat: guilt, corruption, slavishness, and hatred. By contrast, Rousseau's own doctrine will genuinely combat these evils by revealing their true cause in this mistaken view of human nature and by fostering a new, more effectual morality based on compassion for a victimized mankind.

The second main target of Rousseau's principle is Thomas Hobbes. Although I would argue that in some sense all of early modern political thought is an intended opponent, this more complex view is best discussed later. The doctrine of natural goodness is obviously meant to confront and refute Hobbes's famous doctrine that man's natural condition is a war of all against all. At times, it can seem that Rousseau wrote the *Second Discourse* for no other purpose than to refute, point by point, the *Leviathan*'s argument regarding the state of nature.[5]

Hobbes is, of course, very much in agreement with Rousseau's objections to Christianity and is no more inclined than he to view man as sinful; but he does see man as naturally selfish in a way that makes him extremely bad for others. We are not born sinners but born enemies. And he concludes, as many had before him, that because of this natural badness, man is not capable of free or democratic government, for freedom is only as good as those who exercise it. Given their nature, men need to be governed by an absolute monarch who rules with an iron hand. In short, based on his harsh view of human nature, Hobbes gives the classic defense of repressive, absolute government.

There is also a classic counterposition: man is good and therefore capable of free government—but this is not the position taken by Rousseau, who agrees that men today are at least as bad as Hobbes maintains. What the principle of natural goodness asserts is that man's present badness is not a consequence of his own nature but of the structure of society and especially of the repressiveness of existing governments. In a startling reversal similar to his argument against original sin, Rousseau blames political repression for the very evils that had been cited throughout history to excuse it. He agrees that men must be good to be capable of free government, but he adds that they must be free to be capable of goodness. In this way, the principle of natural goodness leads to Rousseau's fierce republicanism.

The third target of Rousseau's doctrine is the dualistic view of human nature found in Plato and most other classical as well as Christian authors—the view that man's nature is "bad," not necessarily because it is sinful in the eyes of God or because it is bad for others but because it is bad for himself: self-contradictory. Such a view asserts that the human soul or personality is not naturally one, unified, or self-consistent, but composed of two disparate and possibly antipathetic elements: reason and passion. We are hybrid creatures, half god and half beast; rational animals, pulled in one direction by the disinterested, idealistic, rational part of our nature and in another by the selfish, irrational, physical part.

---

[5] See Plattner (1979) pp. 65-70 for a good presentation of this refutation.

We are naturally at war with ourselves—born schizophrenics.[6]

In classical times, the dualistic view was challenged by the Stoic school, which maintained a doctrine akin in certain respects to that of the natural goodness of man. The soul, they argued, contains only one element or power: reason. All vice or self-conflict arises not from a separate, irrational force within us but from the errors or prejudices of reason itself, errors caused by the influence of society. Seneca states these points most clearly: "you are mistaken if you suppose that our vices are inborn in us; they have come from without, have been heaped upon us . . . Nature does not ally us with any vice; she produced us in health and freedom."[7] It is generally acknowledged that the Stoics and especially Seneca had a considerable influence on Rousseau, as he himself would seem to acknowledge by using a passage from Seneca—asserting man's natural goodness—as the epigraph for his most comprehensive work, *Emile*. Rousseau can in a sense be viewed as carrying on their argument against Plato and others in support of the natural unity of the soul.

Against this third opponent, then, Rousseau asserts his principle that "nature made man happy and good"—meaning now that man is naturally good for, or not in conflict with, himself. Rousseau identifies a single activating principle within us: not indeed reason but "self-love" or the desire for preservation, which is the "source of our passions, the origin and principle of *all* the others" (*Emile* IV: 213, emphasis added). If man as we know him experiences division and conflict within his soul, that is because self-love undergoes certain modifications in society which have "*alien causes* without which they would never have come to pass; and these same modifications . . . change the first object [of self-love] and go against their principle. It is *then* that man finds himself *outside of nature* and sets himself in *contradiction with himself*" (ibid., emphasis added). "Alien causes" arising in society are responsible for dividedness and self-conflict. By nature, man is one.

Understood as a rejection of classical dualism, Rousseau's doctrine has its most far-reaching implications, extending and radicalizing the consequences of the attack on Christianity and Hobbes. The dualistic theory of the soul has always carried the implication that living well requires "virtue" in some sense. The central task of life is not to "let go," but rather to get a grip on oneself: to create some kind of rational order out of the natural chaos of one's soul. And this requires two things: wisdom and strength—wisdom to know the proper order or hierarchy among the various competing elements within us, and

---

[6] See for example, Plato *Republic* 436a-442a, 588b-589b; Aristotle *Ethics* 1177b27-1178a5; St. Thomas Aquinas *Summa Theologica*, I qu. 8a2, II-I qu. 23a1. It should be mentioned that although Plato is traditionally regarded as the archetypal psychological dualist (and metaphysical dualist), actually he asserts that his discussion of the parts of soul in the *Republic* is provisional and that the soul, in its pure, undistorted form, may in fact be one. See *Republic* 435d, 504b, 611b-612b, *Phaedrus* 230a. (Rousseau himself inclines to this interpretation of Plato; see *Imitation*, 365n.) Still, such unity would not be "natural" in the Rousseauian sense of original and spontaneous.

[7] *Letters to Lucilius*, XCIV 55-56. See Diogenes Laertius on Zeno VII 89. Bevin (1913) pp. 100-104, Gould (1970) pp. 132-33.

strength or will power to enforce that order within our souls and our lives. It
thus follows directly from the dualism of our nature that to live well we need
wise self-mastery, rational self-rule, in a word: "virtue."

Rousseau's principle of the natural unity of man overturns this tenet of
virtually all prior moral philosophy. He argues that outside society (but only
there) such contradictory impulses in the soul would not arise in the first
place, rendering unnecessary "virtue" of any kind (and not just overly
repressive Christian virtue), and making possible the new moral posture
Rousseau calls "goodness": the effortless indulgence of one's naturally
good and unified inclinations, the total surrender to "being oneself." For
the "good" man, spontaneity replaces strength or self-control, for his only
goal is to let go as much as possible. And sincerity replaces wisdom, for his
task is not to choose rationally among the competing natural elements
within him, but only to embrace what genuinely comes from himself and is
therefore good, and to reject what comes from society, which is alien and
divisive. In this way, Rousseau's principle inaugurated the great moral
revolution that dethroned "virtue" in favor of "goodness," that replaced
wisdom and self-control with the new ethic of sincerity and spontaneity.

Furthermore, Rousseau's rejection of psychological dualism and the
necessity of virtue leads him to a new emphasis on human equality and the
dignity of all men. The dualistic theory has always carried inegalitarian
implications because it means that living well is an uncommonly difficult
task. Nature itself discriminates against the mass of humanity, reserving
psychic health and happiness for the natural elite who are strong and wise
enough to know how to rule their naturally wayward souls. On these points,
the Western philosophic tradition prior to Rousseau was essentially of one
opinion: the mass of human beings are, if not born sinners, then born
failures, natural losers, because they are unable to pass the difficult test that
life itself imposes, that of unifying their naturally divided souls.

But Rousseau's principle means that a unified and healthy soul is the
natural heritage of man as such, and thus that human life poses no problem
(or rather no *natural* problem) that all men are not equipped to solve.
Rousseau is the first and greatest philosophic defender of what may be
called the "sufficiency of mediocrity." In principle, all human beings are
equal to the task of life. In this way, the doctrine of natural goodness
redeems the dignity of the people from the traditional contempt of the
philosophers (just as it redeemed them from the misanthropy of Augustinian
Christianity) and promotes a new spirit of humanitarianism.

It must be emphasized, however, that these points about the ethic of
goodness and the naturalness of unity apply in an unqualified sense only to
those who have completely escaped society; and, in civilized times, such
withdrawal is possible only for superior individuals of philosophic or
artistic genius. But in a qualified sense they also apply to all those who live
in relative isolation, like early savages and free peasants or farmers. They
lead to Rousseau's subversive new preference for the common people—

simple, backward, and provincial—over the civilized, cultured, urban elite.

The classical doctrine of psychic dualism, and Rousseau's rejection of it, also have certain specifically political consequences. Although perhaps no classical thinker defined the world of viable political alternatives quite so narrowly as did Hobbes, still most of them saw that world as strictly limited by the fixity of nature, and especially by the problematic dualism of human nature. Accordingly, Rousseau's principle, which rejects that fixity and dualism, has the effect not only of overturning Hobbes's narrow argument for absolute monarchy but also of liberating politics from the whole spirit of classical moderation. If the fundamental source of vice or self-conflict is not in nature but in society, then perhaps it could be overcome by reordering society. In principle, then, Rousseau opens up radical new hopes for politics, utopian, messianic, and also potentially totalitarian, hopes that it can transform the human condition, bring secular salvation, make all men healthy and happy.

For various reasons, Rousseau himself, as distinguished from some of his followers, did not travel very far down the new road he opened up. Even if it is true that society has made men bad, it does not necessarily follow that bad men, armed with this knowledge, will be able to create a new society that will make men good. Rousseau's principle did lead him to entertain striking new hopes that a properly ordered republic could transform and cure men's souls; however, he remained extremely pessimistic about the possibility of creating such republics.

Having observed Rousseau's principle in confrontation with its main opponents—Saint Augustine, Hobbes, and Plato—we have seen particularly what it denies: men are naturally good in that they are not born sinners, enemies, or failures. To see more clearly what it affirms, and to understand Rousseau's doctrine for how society must be changed, we must turn to examine his actual argument for man's goodness and his specific account of how society corrupts men.

On the General Spirit of Rousseau's Thought

Before leaving this general, introductory plane, however, one longs to find something still more fundamental that might be said about Rousseau's principle, something that would make it possible to see its essence and distinctiveness at a single glance, to grasp it as a single vision of life.

It is a common practice in intellectual history, sometimes openly acknowledged, sometimes not, to regard abstract philosophical systems as ultimately the expressions of certain basic, underlying postures toward life. "There are certain sects, which secretly form themselves in the learned world," remarks David Hume, and

> they give a different turn to the ways of thinking of those who have taken part on either side. The most remarkable of this kind are

the sects founded on the different sentiments with regard to the
dignity of human nature; which is a point that seems to have
divided philosophers and poets, as well as divines, from the beginning of the world to this day.[8]

The seemingly perennial and unchanging dispute regarding human nature
has especially encouraged the view that, beneath all their reasoning, philosophers are really guided by an elemental attitude of either "realism" or
"idealism"; or that there is essentially the pessimistic and the optimistic
posture toward life. Even Plato acknowledges the importance of "courage"
and "moderation" as two fundamentally opposite philosophic temperaments.[9] William James, however, is the thinker most famous for encouraging this kind of analysis. As deflating and simplistic as it may seem, he
asserts, "the history of philosophy is to a great extent that of a certain clash
of human temperaments."[10] And the temperaments he distinguishes are
essentially the same as those just mentioned: the "tough-minded" (pessimistic, realistic, empiricist, irreligious, and so forth) and the "tender-
minded" (optimistic, idealistic, rationalistic, religious).[11] Although he does
not name names, it is pretty clear he would regard, say, Hobbes as a classic
example of the tough-minded and Plato of the tender-minded.

Accepting these categories, at least for the moment, where would one place
Rousseau? Can we identify a fundamental temperament underlying his system? We have seen enough of his thought to avoid categorizing him as a simple
optimist. The matter grows more complex when we consider that he attacks *both*
Hobbes and Plato. But the full complexity of this issue does not emerge until
one considers, as we have not yet done, that, although he ultimately attacks them,
Rousseau also draws upon the thought of both Hobbes and Plato, that they are
probably the two thinkers who had the greatest influence upon him.[12]

[8] "On the Dignity or Meanness of Human Nature," in *Essays Literary, Moral and Political*,
p. 45.

[9] See Republic 503c-504a, 535a-536b. See also Pascal's distinction between the "esprit de
geometrie" and the "esprit de finesse" at the beginning of the *Pensées*.

[10] *Pragmatism and Four Essays from the Meaning of Truth*, p. 19.

[11] Ibid., p. 22.

[12] Most scholars have noted the important influence of one of these two thinkers on
Rousseau, although few have noted both. Regarding Plato, Hendel (1934) stands out as the most
sustained Platonist reading of Rousseau. Vaughn (1915, p. 2) remarks: "In the crucial years of
his growth [Rousseau] was the whole-hearted disciple of Plato." Ernest Barker (1964, p. 452)
states: "It is with Rousseau that Plato's political theory begins to exercise that steady influence
on thought which it has exercised ever since." See also Plamanetz (1963) pp. 385, 386, 388-90,
Burgelin (1952) pp. 568-69, Grimsley (1972) pp. 53-55, and Millet (1967) "Le Platonisme de
Rousseau." Silverthorne (1973, p. 235) points out that there are fifty-eight references to Plato
in Rousseau's works, more than to any other source except Plutarch and the Bible (although, in
general, counting references is a very poor means of judging influence in Rousseau). It is also
worth mentioning that in the *Nouvelle Héloïse* (V-3: 565) Plato is said to be St. Preux's "master"
and in the *Confessions* St. Preux is said to be modeled on Rousseau himself (IX: 430).

This is only to restate the fourth contradiction mentioned in the Introduction: Rousseau as both an Enlightenment and classical figure. Somehow he
combines the two opposite tendencies.

On the one hand, Rousseau is extremely hard-headed and skeptical (although this fact has been generally neglected).[13] He is full of cynicism
regarding contemporary civilization, mercilessly unmasking and debunking
everything revered or exalted: the *philosophes* no less than the Church, the
bourgeoisie as well as the monarchy. Moreover, his approach to the study of
man is scientific and anthropological, his epistemology is empiricist, his
psychology is egoistic and reductionist, his political theory is based on self-
preservation, and his view of natural law is skeptical in the extreme. And more
radically than anyone before him, he argues that man, in his true nature, is not
fashioned in the image of God nor is he Aristotle's rational animal; he is a
solitary, amoral, arational, subhuman brute. As Voltaire not unfairly observed,
"No one has ever employed so much intelligence in the effort to make us
beasts."[14]

And yet, despite all of this undeniable hard-headedness, it seems that
Rousseau somehow ends up on the high-minded, idealistic side. He overflows
with enthusiasm and sentimentality. He burns with zeal for the goodness and
dignity of man, the nobility of virtue, the splendor of romantic love, and the
sweetness of intimacy. He is filled with contempt for the baseness of modern
philosophy and consumed with admiration for everything ancient, for
Roman heroism and Spartan virtue, Christian purity and Platonic sublimity.

No less a figure than Adam Smith, reporting on the *Second Discourse* for
the *Edinburgh Review*, remarked on this puzzling combination in Rousseau
of realism and idealism, of the Enlightenment and classicism, of Hobbes and
Plato: "It is by the help of [Rousseau's] style, together with a little philosophical chemistry that the principles and ideas of the profligate Mandeville [a
"Hobbesian"] seem in [Rousseau] to have all the purity and sublimity of the
morals of Plato."[15] Throughout the present work, as we try to understand
Rousseau's philosophy, we will come across this puzzling mixture again and

---

Regarding Hobbes, Bertrand de Jouvenel (1947, p. 101) writes: "Rousseau was profoundly
influenced by Hobbes, so much so that one can speak of a '*hobbisme retourné*'." Derathé (1950)
demonstrates at length and with great precision how much Rousseau's psychology and also his
political concepts of contract, sovereignty, and "civil persons" owe to Hobbes (pp. 100-113,
134-41, 217-22, 308-20, 400-402, 432-36). Althusser is really making the same point when he
states: "Rousseau's theoretical greatness is to have taken up the most frightening aspects of
Hobbes" (1972, p. 136). See also Barzun (1947, p. 40), Georges Davy (1953) and (1964) "Le Corps
Politique selon le *Contrat Social* de Jean-Jacques Rousseau et ses antecedants chez Hobbes," and
Taylor (1965) "Rousseau's Debt to Hobbes."

[13] Masters (1968) has been extremely important and influential in restoring due attention to this
side of Rousseau's thought.

[14] Voltaire to Rousseau, 30 August 1755, quoted in *OC* III: 1379.

[15] *Edinburgh Review*, 1755. Quoted by Plattner (1979) p. 64.

again, this unique synthesis of Plato and Hobbes.

If one is looking, then, for a certain primal something in Rousseau that lies deeper than his system, that is more revealing than his principle, one will not find it in either of the supposedly elemental and perennial "temperaments" identified above, but, on the contrary, in the new spirit or movement of thought that somehow allows him to be both at once, the novel "philosophical chemistry," in Smith's phrase, through which he manages to sublimate Hobbes into Plato, the curious, complex *idealistic realism* that I will argue structures his thinking on the deepest level.

We may conclude by trying to give a provisional indication of its meaning. If we reconsider, for example, Rousseau's attack on the Church doctrine of original sin, we see that he is initially moved by a spirit of skepticism and realism, doubting the truth of this established doctrine and questioning the efficacy of the demanding morality based upon it. Rousseau then takes his skepticism a crucial step further by arguing that this "sacred" doctrine and this too exalted morality have actually corrupted man and indeed have themselves caused many of the evils that they blame on man's fallen nature. But this striking conclusion, the result of extreme realism, issues in the new and idealistic consequence that man's elemental nature may be much better than had formerly been supposed and may itself supply the basis of a more effectual morality. In this way, Rousseau's very realism prepares and issues in a new idealism.

To state it still more formulaically: Rousseau's skepticism debunks all of the purportedly "higher" things in human nature and affairs and, more, actually blames them for causing all of the evils they are supposedly needed to cure. But in doing so it *exculpates* man's *lower*, bodily nature, which had always been falsely condemned, showing it to have an unsuspected goodness upon which one might base the unity and happiness formerly sought in the "higher." This is the unique "philosophical chemistry" through which Hobbesian realism is made to issue in Platonic sublimity. Extreme skepticism directed at the "high" for the sake of idealism regarding the newly exculpated "low." Such is the general philosophical spirit—idealistic realism—that lies behind Rousseau's system and his revolutionary new principle of the natural goodness of man.

The generalizations offered here will be fleshed out and, it is hoped, substantiated in what follows. As we descend into the complex and entangling details of Rousseau's argument, they may also help us to hold in mind a more synoptic view of what is happening, where we are going, and what is at stake.

Part Two

Rousseau's Proof of the Principle
of Natural Goodness

2
The Inner Goodness of Existence: The Introspective and Psychological Arguments

For Rousseau, the natural goodness of man was no mere hypothesis but a great and noble truth of which he was firmly persuaded and which inspired in him all the eloquence and passion that distinguish his writings. Neither was it a mere "vision," although it first crystallized in his mind in the visionary "illumination of Vincennes," but rather a thesis which he claimed to have rationally "demonstrated" in his works (*SD*, 193, *Beaumont*, 945), to have established as an "incontestable maxim" (*Emile* II: 92), to have proved "with a clarity so luminous, with a charm so touching, with a truth so persuasive that no nondepraved soul could resist the allure of [my] images and the force of [my] reasons" (*Dialogues* I: 687; see *Mals.*, 1136). What, then, is Rousseau's proof?

Not being what we have called a "systematizer," Rousseau presents not a single, geometric deduction for his principle but rather a series of distinct arguments employing different kinds of evidence, each drawing upon both observation and abstract reasoning. There is, however, an overall, two-part strategy to his proof, discernible in the following passage from *Emile*:

> Let us set down as an incontestible maxim that the first movements of nature are always right. There is no original perversity in the human heart. [1] There is not a single vice to be found in it of which it cannot be said how and whence it entered. [2] The sole passion natural to man is *amour de soi* [self-love] . . . [which] in itself or relative to us is good and useful. (*Emile* II: 92; see *Beaumont*, 936)

Rousseau alludes here to two distinct forms of demonstration: a negative proof, which demonstrates man's natural goodness indirectly by showing the external, social origin of all his present vices, and a positive proof, which attempts to show directly that the fundamental principle of our nature, "self-love," is good.

In presenting the positive proof, Rousseau will employ two separate arguments, the first drawing on introspective evidence and the second based on psychological theory. His presentation of the negative proof also has two parts: a third argument that appeals to historical or anthropological evidence, and a fourth argument—which will prove to be the most important—concerning the nature and structure of society. Closely related to the negative argument is also Rousseau's new characterization of civilized man's evil, for through this characterization he

identifies the specific vices that must be shown to derive from society in order
to exonerate man's nature. These four arguments—interrelated but separable
for purposes of analysis—plus the new description of human evil constitute
Rousseau's "demonstration" of the natural goodness of man.[1]

---

[1] Missing from this list of arguments, it will be noticed, is any reference to the theological
and metaphysical views that Rousseau presents in *Emile*, albeit not in his own name but as the
"Profession of Faith of the Savoyard Vicar." Some scholars, Pierre-Maurice Masson (1916) still
being the classic example, regard the Savoyard Vicar's views as the ultimate first principles of
Rousseau's system; others have taken a more guarded or skeptical position. Judith Shklar (1969,
p. 108), for example, asserts that Rousseau himself was "a complete agnostic." Part of the
ambiguity surrounding the "Profession of Faith" arises from the fact that when a thinker states
as insistently as Rousseau that the belief in God, free will, and immortality is absolutely
indispensable for the moral virtue and happiness of ordinary men, one is driven to suspect that
even if he himself did not believe, he might say that he did. One's suspicion can only increase
when Rousseau explicitly asserts the necessity of just such myths in his discussions of the
legislator and the civil religion in the *Social Contract*. (*Emile* IV: 312n, 314-15; *GM* 195; *SC*
II-7: 67-70, IV-8: 124-32; *NH* V-5: 588; *OC* III: 700-706, IV: 1142-43; *Confs*. IX: 435-36.)

Furthermore, certain elements of the "Profession of Faith" flatly contradict Rousseau's views
as presented elsewhere. Unlike Rousseau, for example, the vicar is a stark psychological dualist,
seeing man as a compound being composed not only of a bodily element but also of a spiritual
element which "raise[s] him to the study of eternal truths, to the love of justice and moral beauty"
(*Emile* IV: 278; cf. 213). Thus, while Rousseau recognizes a natural "conscience" in man, it is
said to derive from *bodily* self-love through identification or compassion; but for the vicar
conscience is not mere compassion but a "love of order" and a "Divine instinct, immortal and
celestial voice" (cf. *Emile* IV: 235, 235n and *SD*, 95 with *Emile* IV: 290-92). Similarly, the vicar
claims that man is "by his nature sociable, or at least made to become so" and that God placed
man on earth in order to practice morality, whereas the *Second Discourse* clearly argues that the
evolution of both society and morality were wholly accidental and unnecessary (*Emile* IV: 290,
281; *SD*, 95, 140). Accordingly, the vicar also posits the existence of a binding natural law, which
the *Second Discourse* denies; and the whole message of the *Social Contract* is that men must
follow not natural law but the general will. In the latter work, Rousseau also asserts that "I am
mistaken when I speak of a Christian republic; these two words are mutually exclusive.
Christianity preaches nothing but servitude and dependence. . . . True Christians are made to
be slaves. They know it and are scarcely moved thereby; this brief life is of too little worth in
their view" (*SC* IV-8: 130). But clearly Rousseau himself, a fierce republican, preaches anything
but "servitude and dependence."

Finally, the "Profession of Faith," unlike Rousseau's other works, is based not on reason
alone, and not on revelation, but on the "inner sentiment" (which is not to be confused with
introspection). The vicar will "accept as evident all knowledge to which in the sincerity of my
heart I cannot refuse my consent" (IV: 269-70). At the very least, then, one must distinguish
between Rousseau's philosophical thought based on reason alone and his religious thought
based on the inner sentiment. And whatever he may believe regarding the validity of the latter,
it cannot be regarded as the basis of the former. Indeed, one sees throughout Rousseau's
philosophical works that, although he often makes supplementary arguments that refer to God
or to man's free will, he expressly avoids basing his major claims on these arguments (see *SD*,
113-14, 167; *SC* I-8: 56). We are justified, therefore, in excluding these theological arguments
when looking for the rational "demonstration" Rousseau claims to have given for his principle.

It should be mentioned, however, that if viewed in a theological context, Rousseau's
principle takes on one further layer of meaning: it forms a new ground for theodicy. See especially
Lanson (1912), who views this as the key to Rousseau's thought.

The Introspective Argument

How do we learn the truth about human nature? In Rousseau's rather skeptical view, it is not by observing men's external behavior, and still less by reasoning about their speeches or common opinions, because all social men are actors, who constantly lie and dissemble. From the standpoint of knowledge as well as politics, Rousseau believes that one can only trust oneself. Only introspection can reveal the truth about man. This conclusion had already been reached by Hobbes who exhorts his readers, in a famous passage in the introduction to the *Leviathan*, to "read thyself. . . . For this kind of doctrine admitteth no other demonstration" (p. 20). As Rousseau puts it in *Rousseau Juge de Jean-Jacques*: "From where could the painter and apologist of nature, which is today so disfigured and calumniated, have taken his model if not from his own heart. He described it as he sensed himself" (III: 936).[2]

Despite this apparent methodological agreement, however, Rousseau and Hobbes come to opposite conclusions about human nature, due to a crucial difference in their understanding of the introspective method. Rousseau claims that human nature not only is hidden by men's dissimulation but also is both "disfigured and calumniated," as he states in the above passage. Society's artificial environment has utterly "disfigured" man's true nature; and the passions arising in society motivate all men to "calumniate" human nature—the oppressed impelled by envy and hatred, the oppressors by contempt and self-justification (*SD*, 91-92; *Emile* IV: 225, 243-45, 262-63; *OC* IV: 18-19; *NH* II-17: 249). Accordingly, the proper philosophical method requires not only introspection but solitude, withdrawal, detachment. "A retired and solitary life, a lively taste for reverie and contemplation, the habit of returning to himself and seeking there in the calm of the passions these first traits that have disappeared among the multitude—only this enabled him to recover them" (*Dialogues* III: 936). Not any man, but only one such as Rousseau, who is utterly detached from society, will be relatively free of both disfigurement and calumnious passions, and thus both able and willing to see the truth through introspection.

Yet Rousseau does not altogether exclude other men from access to the truth and thus from the intersubjective confirmation of his discoveries. The traits of man's real nature, "so new for us and so true *once traced out* [by Rousseau], find once again at the bottom of men's hearts the attestation of their justice; but they would never have reappeared there by themselves if the historian of nature had not begun by removing the rust that hid them" (ibid.). Rousseau expects the validity of his introspective discoveries to be confirmed in the hearts of his readers.

Using this new method—detached introspection—to uncover man's original nature, what does one find?

---

[2] In this work Rousseau speaks of himself in the third person. See also *SD*, 95, 183; *Confs.* VIII: 388. From the very first mention Rousseau makes of his principle, in a footnote to one of his several defenses of the *First Discourse*, the introspective basis is evident: "man is naturally good, as I believe, and as I have the good fortune to feel" (*Last Reply*, 73n). Rousseau claims that ever since his youth he felt himself to be naturally good (*Dialogues* II: 828).

> Let us return to ourselves. . . . Let us examine, all personal interest
> aside, where our inclinations lead us. Which spectacle gratifies us
> more—that of others' torments or that of their happiness?. . . Is it in
> heinous crimes that you take pleasure?. . . Iniquity pleases only to
> the extent one profits from it; in all the rest one wants the innocent
> to be protected. (*Emile* IV: 287)[3]

Stripped of all external rewards and taken purely in itself, harming others
naturally repels us. Conversely, goodness or benevolence, consequences
aside, seems to please us, to gratify and fulfill our nature, for it comes
naturally and leaves us with a feeling of warmth, peace, and contentment.
Think of the moments of real happiness in your life. Aren't they all associated
with sentiments of love and goodness? "I know and feel," Rousseau reports,
"that to do good is the truest happiness the human heart can savor" (*Reveries*
VI: 75). These simple and obvious experiences prove that man's true nature
inclines to goodness (for others).

Most thinkers, Hobbes included, have agreed that by nature man takes no
pleasure in cruelty purely for its own sake.[4] Furthermore, most would agree
that *if* true inner peace or contentment is possible on earth, it will not be found
in fighting or harming others but in some condition of harmony and goodness.
The question is: is such inner tranquility to be found as easily as Rousseau's
argument assumes—in simple warmheartedness—or even found at all?

Plato would argue, for example, that although we may take some limited
pleasure in helping others, the deeper feelings of peace and contentment to
which Rousseau appeals here are sentimental and false, stemming from the
momentary illusion we all occasionally cultivate that we are fundamentally
safe or at one with others. But being the mortal and selfish creatures that we
are, we are not safe and at one, and therefore these warm but illusory feelings
cannot show us the truth about our nature and good.

Plato would agree, however, that these feelings are not wholly illusory but
rather pale reflections or divinations of the true peace and contentment to be
attained not through simple goodness and warmheartedness but through a
difficult, philosophic transcendence of our exposed and mortal bodies. And
the attainment of this true inner peace by the philosophic few does result in
a kind of gentleness or goodness for others. Thus Plato agrees that the
summum bonum or ultimate perfection of human nature does involve goodness (and in this teleological sense, goodness is natural to man); but of course
men are not "naturally" in a state of perfection—that is, not primitively or
spontaneously so—hence not "naturally good" in Rousseau's sense.

On the contrary, the inability to attain this longed for state of absolute

---

[3] The Savoyard Vicar is speaking. Similarly, "envy, covetousness, hate . . . torment the man
who experiences them" (*Emile* IV: 223). See also *SD*, 130-33; *Dialogues* I: 687; *LM*, 1106-15.

[4] "That any man should take pleasure in other men's great harms, without other end of his
own, I do not conceive it possible" (*Leviathan* p. 53).

safety and peace on the part of the great mass of ordinary human beings inclines them rather to anger and violent irrationality (if also to occasional moments of sentimental goodness). Thus Plato maintains: "surely some terrible, savage, and lawless form of desires is in every man . . . this becomes plain in dreams."[5]

Hobbes would go even further in attacking Rousseau's argument, denying that goodness is natural even in the limited sense acknowledged by Plato. A state of true peace and contentment is not merely difficult for men but impossible; it is not a true object of human nature. Those warm feelings of goodness and repose that we occasionally experience are not only false or sentimental, he points out, but cloying and tedious as well. The real moments of felicity in life are moments of victory. "Read thyself" with honesty, Hobbes insists, and you will agree:

> The felicity of this life, consisteth not in the repose of a mind satisfied. For there is no such *Finis ultimus*, utmost aim, nor *summum bonum*, greatest good, as is spoken of in the books of the old moral philosophers. Nor can a man any more live, whose desires are at an end, than he, whose senses and imagination are at a stand. Felicity is a continual progress of the desire from one object to another.[6]

Life *is* desire: the ceaseless need to move forward, progress, acquire. Contrary to Plato as well as Rousseau, then, man has no love of goodness rooted in a longing for harmony, inner repose, or contentment. Goodness is in no sense natural; and iniquity, although not intrinsically pleasant, is intrinsically useful owing to the naturally limitless character of human desire. Thus, all men are naturally enemies.[7]

Rousseau responds that men who make such arguments "always forget the sweet sentiment of existence, independent of all other sensation" (*OC* IV: 1063). The experience of this sentiment reveals not only that man does indeed long for repose (contrary to Hobbes), but also that by nature he *possesses* it (contrary to Plato). In an argument characteristic of the whole movement of his thought, Rousseau embraces Hobbes's skepticism regarding the perfection that Plato locates above men, but then rediscovers that perfection at the base of man's being. Relying here on his method of detached introspection and the privileged access to the truth that it gives him, Rousseau asserts:

> The sentiment of existence, stripped of any other emotion, is in itself a precious sentiment of contentment and of peace which alone would suffice to make this existence dear and sweet to anyone able to spurn

---

[5] *Republic* 572b.

[6] *Leviathan* XI: 80. See *De Homine* XI-15: 54.

[7] In one sense Hobbes's man is less "good" than Plato's because he hasn't even the longing for rest and goodness. But since he also lacks the wildness and irrationality that, in Plato's view, results from the frustration of this longing, he is in another sense more "good." He is selfish and naturally in competition with others, but sane, rational, and willing to compromise for peace.

all the sensual and earthly impressions which incessantly come to
distract us from it and to trouble its sweetness here-below. But
most men, agitated by continual passions, are little acquainted
with this state and, having tasted it only imperfectly for a few
moments, preserve only an obscure and confused idea of it which
does not let them feel its charm. (*Reveries* V: 69)

Anyone who, removing himself from the illusions and insincerity of society, succeeds in reestablishing contact with this vital center of his being
knows with inner certainty that he has found a stratum of human nature
deeper than the one that Hobbes or Plato describes.

Rousseau does not simply deny what these thinkers assert, that men as
we now see them are inclined to iniquity—either by a restless desire for
progress or a frustrated desire for rest. But these desires, he claims, are only
distortions created by society, distortions of something more fundamental
that he has rediscovered. Man's deepest self is absolute and self-sufficient,
and thus his deepest experience, the "first movement of nature," is neither
restless desire nor frustrated longing but contentment, peace, and a grateful
love of existence. Man is naturally good for himself, in this sense—and
therefore good for others. He is a fundamentally satisfied being and, as
such, nothing drives him into conflict with others; he rather flees conflict
as destructive of his repose and contentment. Due to the sentiment of
existence, then, man is by nature good: at peace with himself and others.

His goodness for others acquires a more positive content, moreover,
through the "expansiveness" of his contentment and love of existence. As
Rousseau proclaims, "I love myself too much to be able to hate anyone
whatever. That would be to constrict or repress my existence, and I would
rather extend it over the whole universe" (*Reveries* VI: 81). Under the right
circumstances this natural expansiveness inclines men to a positive goodness or benevolence. Thus, those simple feelings of warmth and contentment arising from an act of common goodness are not sentimental or false
after all, and, in putting us back in touch with them, Rousseau reveals to us
the truth about ourselves: goodness fulfills and iniquity violates our nature.

Introspection first suggested to Rousseau the idea of man's natural
goodness, and it supplied him with much of the inner content of that idea.
But by itself this argument is inconclusive and even circular. The very
legitimacy of the method of detached introspection, for example, is based
on a premise that it cannot really supply by itself; namely, that man is not
naturally a political being, that the true human self is the private self found
through solitary introspection and not the social self, known through men's
public deeds and speeches.

Rousseau assumes, moreover, that the results of his own introspections,
unique and strange as they are, reveal the elusive truth about human nature
as such; and he assumes this on the ground that he, unlike all other men,
has remained relatively natural and free of disfigurement. Yet how can he

know that he has remained natural unless he already knows the truth about human nature? Perhaps his attainment of a peace and plenitude that other men do not seem to have experienced so fully can render his naturalness likely, but how can he be certain that his experience is not in fact the result of certain secret and illusory hopes, or of a forgetting of reality rather than the fullest contact with it, or of some idiosyncratic proclivity or artificial technique that reveals nothing about the core of man's nature?

Indeed, one is struck by how trusting Rousseau is of introspection. He is so impressed with the social origins of lying and deceit that he considers it safe to assume that, isolated from society, men will be honest with themselves. That assumption is what allows him to substitute the method of detached introspection or, more generally, of "sincerity" for Socratic dialectics or whatever other method one might find, like Freudian analysis, to free us from the lies that we tell ourselves. Rousseau's evident belief that men have no natural need to lie to themselves would seem to be a consequence of his principle of man's natural goodness and self-sufficiency, but for that reason it ought not to be the crucial presupposition of the method used to prove that principle.[8]

Whatever Rousseau might have thought of these specific objections, it is clear that he too believed that the introspective argument was not sufficient. He claims to have possessed this introspective awareness since his youth, whereas he did not fully formulate and embrace his principle of natural goodness until much later, in the "illumination of Vincennes." Presumably the latter event was not possible until Rousseau attained the insights contained in the three further lines of argument presented in his works.

The Psychological Argument

Rousseau's second argument, like the first, is part of his "positive" proof, which attempts to give a direct, positive demonstration of the goodness of human nature. It is based on psychological theory, on a new doctrine of "self-love" as the fundamental principle of human desire and motivation.

"The source of our passions," Rousseau argues, "the origin and the principle of all the others, the only one born with man and which never leaves him so long as he lives is *self-love*," the goal of which is self-preservation (*Emile* IV: 212-13, emphasis added; see II: 97; *SD*, 95, 221-22). And this self-love is "always good and always in conformity with order," that is, "in itself or relative to us [it] is good and useful; and since it has no necessary relation to others, it is in this respect naturally neutral. It becomes good or bad only by the application made of it" (*Emile* IV: 213, II: 92; see *Dialogues* I: 668-70; *Beaumont*, 936). Consequently, motivated by self-love, man is naturally good for himself and naturally neutral or innocent toward others.

[8] At the end of his life Rousseau wrote in the *Reveries*: "the 'know thyself' of the temple of Delphi [is] not as easy a maxim to follow as I had believed in my *Confessions*" and "the true and primary motives of most of my actions are not as clear even to me as I had long imagined" (IV: 43; VI: 75). On this theme see Starobinski (1971) pp. 216-17.

On what is this argument, or these assertions, based? Where does Rousseau get his particular notion of "self-love" or "self-preservation"? And how does he know that human self-love does not in fact include contradictory inclinations that would put us in conflict with ourselves or aggressive inclinations that would put us in conflict with others?

A. Rousseau's Theory of Self-love

To some extent, Rousseau's psychological doctrine is merely a formalization of what he has discovered through introspection, but clearly he also relies upon other, more theoretical considerations and arguments. Unfortunately, he does not elaborate these thematically or in any one place, and therefore our effort to reconstruct his thinking will be somewhat conjectural in places.

To get a general feel for the issue, as well as to become acquainted with theories with which Rousseau himself was no doubt familiar, we might briefly consider some earlier views of this subject beginning with the classic discussion presented in Cicero's *De Finibus*. In this dialogue, Cicero suggests that there are essentially two possible views regarding the fundamental source or principle of human desire: the hedonist view that we desire pleasure or the absence of pain (this being understood as the greatest pleasure) and the view that we desire self-preservation. The first view, espoused by the Epicureans among others, holds that pleasure is the good, pain is evil, and men desire life for the sake of pleasure. The second view, adopted most notably by the Stoics but also, it is claimed here, by Plato and Aristotle, maintains that not pleasure, but life itself is the primary object of human desire; we do not desire life for the sake of pleasure but rather pleasant things for the sake of life. Otherwise stated, men love not pleasure but themselves, consequently they desire to preserve themselves.[9]

Defending the theory of self-love or self-preservation, Marcus Cato, an interlocutor in *De Finibus*, observes: "Immediately upon birth...a living creature feels an attachment for itself, and an impulse to preserve itself and to feel affection for its own constitution and for those things that tend to preserve that constitution."[10] Observation seems to show that we seek, for example, the health and good condition of our bodies and, more generally, the preservation of our lives not merely as a blind reflex, not simply from fear of death, not out of love of pleasure, but from an attachment and affection for ourselves.

If men are to be capable of loving themselves, however, they must first of all be objects to themselves, they must sense themselves. Thus, Cato continues: "It would be impossible that they should feel desire at all unless they sensed themselves and to this extent loved themselves."[11] Self-awareness is

[9] *De Finibus*, V 7.

[10] Ibid., III 4-5.

[11] Ibid.

a necessary precondition of self-love (and conversely, because men love themselves, they naturally take delight in their awareness of themselves).

But what exactly is this self that is sensed, loved, and preserved? In the classical view, as presented by Cicero, it is understood teleologically. "All nature is self-preserving, and has before it the end and aim of maintaining itself in the *best* possible condition *after its kind*."[12] It is acknowledged that: "At the outset this tendency is vague and uncertain, so that it merely aims at protecting itself whatever its character may be; it does not understand itself nor its own capacities and nature."[13] But later, men clearly manifest an inclination for growth and self-development; and when the simple self-awareness which is necessary for self-love of any kind evolves into self-knowledge, then this inclination leads them to seek "life in accordance with human nature developed to its full perfection and supplied with all its needs."[14] Thus, in the fundamental inclination of "self-love," the self one truly senses and loves is not one's actual, individual self with all its peculiarities and defects, but one's perfected nature, one's essence as a human being, which calls to and attracts one. In other words, the classical conception of "self-preservation" involves "self-actualization": one seeks not merely to avoid dying, but to live, to *be*, and—more—to *be fully*, which means to be entirely the *kind* of thing that one is, to actualize all of one's potentials, to fulfill one's nature, to realize completely the Idea, the formal and final cause that is the ground of one's being.

Turning to modern thinkers, one finds a doctrine of self-preservation at the heart of the thought of Thomas Hobbes, among others, where it is drastically reinterpreted on a nonteleological, "naturalistic," and negative basis. Nature does not work through the attractive power of forms but by the ceaseless motion and mutual resistance of extended bodies. Accordingly, human self-preservation is not the attraction to one's ideal nature or the positive love of one's being, but the endless fleeing or overcoming of death. Indeed, "life" *has* no positive, inner content. Man feels himself only in pressing against what is other. He exists only in moving ever forward, opposing or appropriating what is not him. That is why it is so fundamental and so obvious to Hobbes that rest or contentment is impossible, that "life is perpetual motion," that "idleness is torture," and that "felicity is a continual progress of the desire, from one object to another."[15] Self-preservation drives man to pursue not indeed power, but power after power, for only thus does he experience (as well as strengthen) his faculty of resistance to death which is his life itself. Hobbes acknowledges, then, the restless inclination in men toward growth and development on which the

[12] Ibid., V 9-10, emphasis added.

[13] Ibid., V 8-9.

[14] Ibid., V 9-10.

[15] *De Homine* XI-15: 54, XI-11: 51; *Leviathan* XI: 80. See *De Homine* XI-6, 7: 48-49; *De Corpore* XXV-12, 13: 159-62; *Elements of Law* VII: 207-9.

classics had based their teleological understanding of self-preservation; but he understands this inclination not as growth toward a natural perfection and repose but as ceaseless motion, measured not by an end approached but by dangers and challenges left behind. In Hobbes's famous analogy, life is a race without a finish line, in which "continually to out-go the next before, is *felicity*. And to forsake the course, is to *die*."[16] In short, Hobbes has a doctrine of self-preservation, but, naturalistic and negative, it is disjoined from a doctrine of self-love: man's deepest experience is opposition and not attraction. His "life" and "self" have no positive, internal content that he might love, but exist only as a motion against what is other.

Returning to Rousseau, we find that he agrees with Hobbes in rejecting the teleological understanding of "life" and "self" that underlies the positive, classical interpretation of self-preservation, but he considers the resulting negative interpretation implausible, as well as repellent. If one simply observes not anxiety-ridden urban man, whom Hobbes describes very well, but peasants or savages or lower animals—a cat slowly stretching, curling up in a corner, and purring to itself—is it not obvious that idleness is not torture but a pleasure for living creatures, that a "delicious laziness" and not restless motion is what is most natural? "To do nothing," Rousseau suspects, "is man's primary and strongest passion after that of self-preservation" (*Languages* IX: 266n; see *SD*, 118, 208; *Dialogues* II: 846). Observation suggests that the root of life, "the first movement of nature," is not a negative relation to the other, but a positive affection for oneself and for simply *being*.

It seemed to Rousseau that the philosophers of his century were so caught up in understanding and controlling external nature that they had not adequately turned their reflection back on themselves. They had neglected to ask what it really meant to be alive as a human being (*SD*, 91, 183). The naturalistic understanding of man prevailing in his time, which certainly he himself did not wholly abandon, needed to be supplemented by the self-knowledge that the knowing subject had of itself. A new Socrates, Rousseau saw the necessity for an independent, human understanding of the human. And on this basis he seemed to perceive that life had an inner content beyond the mere avoidance of death, that man is something more than the sum of his exertions against the other.[17]

In order to develop his own, nonteleological and yet positive interpretation

---

[16] *Elements of Law* IX-21: 225.

[17] Karl Barth argues that through this return to man and to himself Rousseau brought the Enlightenment to a close and inaugurated the "age of Goethe." "For the eighteenth century, rejoicing in its command of all things, had *not* asked after...man himself, for all the importance man had assumed for it." But a "whole world revealed itself to [Rousseau] when he gazed into himself. He did not do this in the manner of the individualism of his time, which looked within in order to go out again at once into the outside world, desiring to apprehend, form and conquer." For Rousseau "[e]xistence was not just a predicate, not entirely a matter of how I conduct myself towards the outerworld. It was definitely not just acting and suffering. Existence was a beautiful, rich and lively inner life of its own" (1959, pp. 109, 110).

of self-preservation, which would do justice to these observations and reflections, Rousseau appears to have reasoned as follows. The confrontation with external objects, which Hobbes regards as constitutive of our life and self, presupposes that we first perceive these objects. Perception necessarily precedes desire or resistance. But as Locke, following Descartes, points out: "It [is] impossible for anyone to perceive without *perceiving* that he does perceive...and by this everyone is to himself that which he calls *self*." All perception or awareness is inseparable from self-awareness (the copresence of the two constituting "consciousness," as the word began now to be used). We have "an intuitive knowledge of our own existence, and an internal infallible perception that we are. In every act of sensation, reasoning, or thinking, we are conscious to ourselves of our own being."[18] Thus, prior to all desire and all relation to the other, there exists an absolute self accompanying sensibility or awareness as such.

It seems that Rousseau seized upon this new concept of the self—"consciousness," the perceiving subject, the thing that thinks and senses, in a word, the Cartesian "ego"—finding in it the positive self he had hypothesized and experienced. For it is stable and at rest, despite the ceaseless motion of the desires or of matter. It is positive or absolute, rising above the negative, other-relatedness of the Hobbesian conception. And yet it is nonteleological, existing not through a relation to some eternal essence, nature, or formal cause, but merely through its indubitable presence to itself. Thus, Rousseau took the momentous step of reconstituting a theory of self-preservation and self-love based on the new conception of the self as "consciousness."[19]

The first thing assumed by any positive theory of self-preservation, we have seen, is that men must *sense* themselves; therefore Rousseau asserts: "Man's first sentiment was that of his existence, his first care that of his preservation" (*SD*, 142). And by this famous "sentiment of existence" Rousseau means precisely the "intuitive knowledge" that we exist as a perceiving thing, mentioned above by Locke. This sentiment is not the perception of any particular object, like our own body, nor is it the introspective knowledge of any internal object, like the soul; rather it is the awareness of "the 'I' to which he. . . relate[s] all his sensations," the

[18] *Essay Concerning Human Understanding* II-27 (11): v.I, 449, emphasis in original; IV-9 (3): v.II, 305.

[19] There might seem to be an unbridgeable gulf between Descartes, who defines the self as a *res cogitans*, a "thing that thinks," and Rousseau, who was the first to deny that man is the rational animal. But the passages from Locke quoted above show that the Cartesian ego exists, and knows itself, in every form of perception—not just in thinking. And Descartes himself maintains that "[b]y the word thought I understand all that of which we are conscious as operating in us. And that is why not alone understanding, willing, imagining, but also feeling, are here the same thing as thought" (*Principles of Philosophy* I-9: v.1, 222; see *Meditations* II: v.1, 153). Rousseau does not really stray so far from Descartes, then, in defining the self as, essentially, a "thing that feels."

self-awareness of the conscious subject, of the Cartesian ego (*Emile* I: 61).
That is the self that we sense in the "sentiment of existence."[20]

This same self, Rousseau goes on to assert, forms the true object of human
self-love or the desire for preservation. It is as conscious subjects that we love
and seek to preserve ourselves. That is why the sentiment of existence, which
for Descartes and Locke is a mere item of knowledge, is, for Rousseau, the
source of man's greatest delight. And that is why self-preservation is now
understood to aim not at the protection of the body's "vital motions," as Hobbes
maintained, and not at the realization of one's objective "nature," as in the
classical view, but at the preservation and heightening of one's "existence,"
one's elemental awareness that one is, one's consciousness. "To live is not to
breathe," Rousseau asserts, "it is to act; it is to make use of our organs, our
senses, our faculties, of all the parts of ourselves which give us the *sentiment
of our existence*." Self-preservation is not merely a fear or resistance to death
but a positive love of life. And this love is newly interpreted as "the desire *to
exist*. All that seems to extend or strengthen our existence flatters us, all that
seems to destroy or compress it distresses us. That is the primitive source of
all our passions" (*Emile* I: 42, emphasis added; *OC* II: 1324-25, emphasis
added).[21]

B. The Psychological Argument for Natural Goodness

Because man is motivated by "self-love," Rousseau had argued, he is
naturally neutral toward others and good for himself. But how could he know,
we asked, that self-love did not include either aggressive inclinations that
would put us in conflict with others or contradictory ones that would put us in
conflict with ourselves? These questions can now be answered by drawing out
the implications of Rousseau's new psychological theory.

The life or existence that is the object of man's love is not only positive and
absolute, as distinguished from the negative and other-related Hobbesian
conception, but also, contrary to the teleological classical view, it is always

---

[20] In taking this first step, Rousseau is by no means alone. Due to the immense influence of
Descartes and Locke, as well as to the metaphysical and moral neutrality of the concept of
"consciousness," some form of this concept was adopted by almost all eighteenth-century thinkers,
especially in France, and, along with it, some version of the expression "sentiment of existence."
The phrase is to be found in such disparate writers as Malebranche, Montesquieu, Buffon, Mme
d'épinay, Delisle de Sales, Claude Buffier, Charles-Georges Le Roy in his *Encyclopedia* article
"Homme," the abbé Prévost, Marie Huber, the abbé de Lignac, and Maupertuis. For some, the
sentiment of existence was only of epistemological interest, while others integrated it into a
religious understanding of the soul. Most secular thinkers attached it to an essentially hedonistic
understanding of morals and psychology. A few seem to have employed it in a doctrine of
self-preservation akin to the one we find in Rousseau, most notably the latter's friend and rival in
love, Saint-Lambert. (See Poulet [1978] and [1980], Spink [1978], and Mauzi [1960] pp. 109-40,
293-300.) Still, it is no accident that the "sentiment of existence" is primarily associated with the
name of Rousseau, who attributes to it a unique importance and power, as will be seen.

[21] On these general themes, see also Burgelin (1952) pp. 115-48.

there within one, whole and complete. Rousseau is certainly not the first to have claimed that there is a natural sweetness to mere life but he seems to be the first to have made that sweetness the final end of life and the root of all happiness. Most of the thinkers who spoke of the "sentiment of existence," for example, also described it as pleasant, but they did not attribute to it such completeness and self-sufficiency. They did not go on to conclude, as Rousseau does, that man possesses the ground of his happiness and being within himself.[22] Perhaps that is simply because they failed to integrate it into a comprehensive new doctrine of self-love. Or perhaps Rousseau's account of it is attainable only if one also goes on to assume that we social, rational, civilized men are disfigured and alienated, so that special efforts are necessary to rediscover this experience in its true fullness. It seems likely, however, that Rousseau's innovation also consists in his having ventured further down the road pointed to if not travelled by Descartes, that of taking the *ordo cognoscendi* for the *ordo essendi*, of identifying one's being with what one infallibly knows about oneself. That is, Rousseau seems more inclined (albeit confusedly) to understand the "sentiment of existence" metaphysically rather than psychologically, to see in it not a mere feeling or particular experience but something that actually reveals and constitutes our true being. Somehow, a man exists not through his relation to God or to the essence of man but through a relation to himself. Our being *is* our presence to ourselves, our sentiment of existence.[23]

However one might explain its basis, Rousseau's new doctrine of self-love has the clear effect of locating man's completed existence

---

[22] A striking example is John Norris, an English disciple of Malebranche, who asserts: "Besides those particular Sensations of Pleasure which are occasionally and upon some certain impressions excited in us, we cannot but find a certain general sentiment of pleasure that accompanies our *Being*, and which does not come and go, off and on, as our other sensations do, but remains fixed and permanent, and maintains one constant and uninterrupted steadiness. Though we have no particular occasion of joy, or incitement of Pleasure from anything without, from any of those sensible objects which surround us, though all things about us are silent, and our thoughts too are no way engaged upon any object extraordinary, yet we feel a certain pleasure in our very *existence*, not in our being thus and thus, in this or that state of mind and body, but absolutely and simply in our *being*, in our being conscious to ourselves that we are. This general pleasure of *mere being* (for so I think it may be fitly called), everyman may much better experiment than I can describe" (*Practical Discourses*, v.3, p. 187; quoted by Poulet [1980] p. 45).

Yet, notwithstanding this remarkable account of the sentiment of existence, Norris is not the least inclined to attribute to man any inner resources or self-sufficiency. "[A]s Man receives his being from God, so he depends upon God's continual influence for the continuation of it, insomuch, that should God never so little withdraw it, he must necessarily fall back into his First Nothing." "To thee then, *O Father of Spirits*, I give up and devote my whole self, for I am entirely from thee, entirely by thee, and therefore entirely thine" (*Treatises upon Several Subjects*, pp. 101, 107).

On the pleasure of mere life, see also Aristotle's *Ethics* 1166a-b. And see Brochard (1926) for the suggestion that the ancient Epicureans placed this pleasure at the center of happiness.

[23] This is to view Rousseau as taking the crucial first step toward the concept of the self-defining, self-grounding subject, to be developed later by the German Romantics and Hegel. See Charles Taylor (1975, pp. 13-29) for an excellent brief account of this concept.

at his source rather than in his end. The ultimate object of self-love, in Rousseau's view, is not some perfected form high above one, but the deepest thing within one. The Good is whatever is most one's own. Whence the magic for Rousseau of sincerity, withdrawal, intimacy, introspection, and self-absorption, for, on his new principles, this is how one draws closer to being.

One might even say that his doctrine rests on a new, individualistic or Romantic or antiteleological teleology: each thing exists most fully precisely by ignoring the call of "order"—of "ends" and "essences"—by remaining free and wild, by cleaving to its inner uniqueness and particularity, by "being itself." In other words, Rousseau's theory of self-love leads to a radical new kind of individualism, not merely political but, as it were, ontological. Each man, containing the source of his happiness and of his being within himself, has no essential connection to anything outside him, whether social or metaphysical. This would seem to be one ground of Rousseau's generally undefended assumption that men are by nature asocial and solitary. And from this individualism follows the first half of Rousseau's psychological argument: motivated by self-love, wholly absorbed in and sufficient to themselves, men are naturally neutral or innocent toward others.

The second implication of Rousseau's theory of self-preservation concerns the natural unity or self-consistency of the soul. Consciousness, the self we love and seek to preserve, is not an "object" with a certain nature or essence, a "thing" with qualities. It is not an object but a subject, revealed or constituted by an awareness not of *what* but of *that* we are, a sentiment of pure existence, of sheer "thereness." But whereas a thing or object is divisible and may be composed of several parts, the conscious subject (as distinguished from its presentations) can have no internal articulation; it is a unit, a point, an indivisible atom of existence. "The sensitive being is indivisible and one. It cannot be divided; it is whole, or it is nothing" (*Emile* IV: 279n).[24] Therefore, self-love, based on this conscious subject, must itself be unitary or self-consistent. This would appear to be the basis of the second half of Rousseau's psychological argument: motivated by self-love, man is naturally good for himself, not only because he possesses his end within himself, but also because he is fundamentally one.

An obvious objection might be raised to both parts of this argument. Precisely if self-preservation is the principle of human motivation, then man's most fundamental desire is in direct contradiction with the most fundamental fact of his nature, his mortality. Consequently, regardless of whether preservation is initially understood in positive or negative terms, mustn't the fear of death become the dominant fact and experience of human life? And isn't

---

[24] Compare Descartes (*Passions of the Soul* I-47: v.1, 353): "For there is within us but one soul, and this soul has not in itself any diversity of parts."

that why, as many thinkers have pointed out, the consciousness of our existence, while pleasant on one level, is also a terrible burden and source of anxiety?[25] Driven by this gnawing fear, moreover, men become locked in a vicious struggle, as they compete for money, status, power, and honor in a frantic effort to fortify themselves. Human self-love, then, by no means leaves men neutral or innocent with respect to others.

Just as surely, the fear of death also puts each man in conflict with himself. The lower animals, ignorant of death, can be whole in their bodies and in their love of themselves, but human beings know that self-love is a lost cause. The awareness of death twists men's desire for preservation against themselves, causing them to hate their bodies as the source of their exposedness and mortality. They are driven to fight against their natural, selfish inclinations, hoping either to force themselves into harmony with some larger social or cosmic order that promises protection, or even to detach themselves entirely from their mortal selves. Thus, human self-love is certainly not a source of rest and unity.

Rousseau's response to this classic objection is as simple as it is radical: he denies that the fear of death is natural.[26]

> It is believed that man has an intense love for his own preservation, and that is true. But it is not seen that this love, in the way in which we feel it, is in large part the work of men. By nature man worries about his preservation only insofar as the means to it are in his power. As soon as these means escape him, he becomes calm and dies without tormenting himself uselessly. The first law of resignation comes to us from nature. Savages as well as beasts struggle very little against death and endure it almost without complaint. (*Emile* II:82; see I:55)

The very awareness of death is not natural, Rousseau argues, because savage man has no foresight and even civilized man begins as a blank slate. Of course, the latter may quickly learn the abstract fact of mortality, but the palpable idea of one's own annihilation actually arises rather late and only with difficulty (*Emile* IV: 222, 224). What unnaturally speeds up the process, and what inclines us, once we have formed the idea of death, to become unnecessarily obsessed with it, is our rebellion against it, our effort constantly to think about the future in order to master fate and postpone death indefinitely. But we rebel thus against necessity only due to spoiledness, foolish prejudices, and ulti- mately *amour-propre* (vanity), none of which are natural. On the contrary, "the first law of resignation comes to us from nature." Rousseau has an extraordi- nary faith in the power of resignation which would seem to trace back, in turn,

---

[25] As Pascal remarks, "the natural poverty of our feeble and mortal condition [is] so miserable that nothing can comfort us when we think of it closely." Thus "the pleasure of solitude is a thing incomprehensible. . . . The king is surrounded by persons whose only thought is to divert the king, and to prevent his thinking of self. For he is unhappy, king though he be, if he think of himself" (*Pensées*, no. 139).

[26] See the beautiful discussion of this issue in Bloom (1979) pp. 9-10.

to the character of self-love which, being not only positive but complete, has an inner sweetness and inertia that is able to keep men from reorienting their lives in a negative, reactive, or rebellious direction. On Rousseau's understanding, then, death need not cast its shadow on life, deforming it in the ways described above. Although life is indeed always fragile and precarious, the natural desire for preservation in no way turns us against our fellows or ourselves. Indolently absorbed in the positive pleasure of being alive, completely resigned to the necessity of death, we are naturally inclined to live in benign indifference to others and in oneness with our natural, bodily selves.

C. Additional Consequences of Rousseau's Theory of Self-love

We have seen the psychological argument for the natural goodness of man. Before leaving this essential topic—Rousseau's new theory of human desire and motivation—it is worth examining a few further implications that will prove crucial at later stages of the argument.

If self-love is the "desire to exist," the question naturally arises whether, once one exists and has secured one's preservation, there is any further goal to life? Self-love, Rousseau replies, means that "all that seems to extend or strengthen our existence flatters us, all that seems to destroy or compress it distresses us. That is the primitive source of all our passions" (*OC* II: 1324-25; see *Dialogues* II: 805-6). As this passage implies, we naturally incline not only to delight in our existence, and not only to preserve it, but also to *increase* it. Although qualitatively complete in itself, our existence is nevertheless still capable of degrees, of a more and a less: "This degree of existence or, better, of life, is not always the same, it has for us a certain latitude, it is susceptible of growth or diminution" (ibid.). For example, in raising a child, Rousseau urges: "it is less a question of keeping him from dying than of *making him live*." Not all who live, then, are equally alive. "The man who has lived the most is not he who has counted the most years but he who has most *felt life*" (*Emile* I: 42, emphasis added). Thus self-love, the "desire to exist," includes a desire for *more life*: to be more awake, more vital, more intensely *there*.

According to Rousseau, two things primarily determine the degree of our existence: extent and unity.[27] Regarding extent, we have already heard Rousseau encourage the development of all of the faculties so that one may experience all the possible modes of awareness and activity. But men also possess an impulse for self-extension and a capacity for "identification" that leads them to expand their existence over other beings, in order to feel more broadly or to be more vividly present to themselves.[28] In this expansive impulse Rousseau recognizes, as Hobbes had too in his own way, something resembling the classics' teleological inclination to growth and development. But in

[27] Regarding "unity" and "extent" as the two determinants of existence or reality, see F. H. Bradley (1968) pp. 214-17, 364.

[28] See *Emile* I: 67, II: 80, 98, 159, III: 168, 192, IV: 213; *Reveries* VII: 92, 95; *Dialogues* II: 805-6; *Confs.* II: 58.

Rousseau's view, beyond the development of our most primitive faculties and the satisfaction of our elementary sexual urge, this impulse has no natural end or object. It is a pure, goalless expansiveness, a formless energy, *elan*, or libido. This fact is largely responsible for the remarkable malleability that characterizes the human species, in Rousseau's view, as well as for the possibility of the "psychic-engineering" in which he engages. By raising men with the proper experiences, images, and opinions, one can direct their expansiveness into any number of forms: romantic love, religion, compassion, patriotism, humanity, the love of nature, and so forth.[29] But having no truly natural and suitable object, man's impulse to extend his existence always tends to bring disappointment or danger, leading Rousseau frequently to exhort men to "draw your existence up within yourself" (*Emile* II: 83).[30] Man's expansiveness risks alienating him from himself and weakening the more fundamental condition of full existence: unity of soul.

Unity is natural to man, but almost everything that happens to him in society works to destroy it. The protection or restoration of unity is therefore crucial to maintaining or increasing our existence. In order to feel our whole existence, our existence must be whole. Every moment and aspect of our existence must be gathered, harmonized, united, so that, one with ourselves, we exist fully, undiminished by division or conflict, with nothing held back and nothing left out. The issue of unity will turn out to be at the core of Rousseau's critique of civilized society.

A second important consequence of this new theory of self-love is that it leads to or at least encourages Rousseau's extreme denigration of reason and his corresponding elevation of feeling or sentiment. Rousseau agrees with the familiar point found in Hobbes that, in their behavior, men follow their passions and not their reason, but he also goes beyond the issue of behavior to the question of what man is. Man has a positive self and existence, for Rousseau, but it is not as a rational animal. On the contrary, reason, which understands only "objects," projects us out into the external world—the world of things, comparisons, means, interests—and thus positively alienates us from our true self.[31] "To exist, for us, is to sense"; to exist more is to feel more; and he "has lived the most…who has most *felt* life" (*LM*, 1109 [see *Emile* IV: 290]; *Emile* I: 42, emphasis added). Rousseau begins, or at least greatly extends, the cult of feeling: the view that through feeling as such, regardless of content—and not through knowledge—one exists more and moves closer to being.

[29] See *Reveries* VI: 81, VII: 95; *Mals.*, 1140-41; *Dialogues* II: 827; *Emile* IV: 235n; *LM*, 1112, 1116.

[30] See *LM*, 1112-13; *Reveries* VIII: 110-11; *Dialogues* II: 810, 827. For a nice discussion of this issue, see Grimsley (1972).

[31] Rousseau makes a strong distinction between "ideas" (the stuff of reason) and sensations or sentiments, the former involving comparison or relation, the latter being immediate and absolute. Our existence, he emphasizes, is grasped through a sentiment (*Emile* I: 61). It cannot be known through an idea or by reason. Indeed, the natural operation of self-love is "a pure affair of feeling in which reflection plays no part" (*Dialogues* II: 806).

A related point that emerges from Rousseau's psychology is a new emphasis on "perspectivity." Men's lives grow from within, and the core of their existence is not reason, which is inherently common and public, but feeling, which is private and idiosyncratic. Thus Rousseau has a keen sense of how trapped we all are in our own unique perspectives, how differently we see the same world, how little we understand—as we live our lives alongside each other—what it is really like for others. It is particularly difficult, on his view, to comprehend the lives of people in a different time and place. To give this last point a name, Rousseau was the first to develop what later came to be known as the "historical sense."[32]

One final consequence of Rousseau's psychology is what might be called "the power of the inner" or alternatively "the natural intractability of man." In Rousseau's view, men are naturally closed in on themselves, individual monads whose happiness and being come from within. And for this reason it is extremely difficult for anything that comes from without to gain a real hold on them, whether it be knowledge one would like to impart to them, or a religion one would like to impose, or political authority one wants to assert. Men must always learn everything by and for themselves, find belief by searching their own hearts, see in authority the expression of their own wills. Only the inner and immanent, only what sincerely grows and emerges from within, can be real for men. Do what you will, they go their own way, they slip every snare, they are naturally free in this sense. Of course, by developing false needs, they eventually become caught in the web of society, but even then they remain remarkably uncontrollable, so that it is never very clear who has caught whom. Moved by self-love, men are "individuals," who truly respond only to the inner and are utterly intractable from without.

Conclusion

We have seen Rousseau's "positive" proof for his principle as embodied in the introspective and psychological arguments. Although the main shortcomings of the former have been indicated, I am reluctant to engage in much evaluation of the latter, not only because the theory of self-love on which it is based raises extremely difficult questions which could not be adequately treated here, but also because one cannot be altogether confident that this reconstructed theory is in fact Rousseau's. I will limit myself to a few obvious difficulties.

The most clearly questionable aspect of Rousseau's theory is his denial of the naturalness of the fear of death, which allows him to portray self-love as positive, as "all loving and sweet in [its] essence," despite the fact that the self we love faces immanent annihilation (*Dialogues* I: 669). Man is unmoved or

---

[32] "I have often noticed that, even among those who most pride themselves in knowing men, each hardly knows anyone but himself" (*Confs.*, 1148). In fact, Rousseau claims, men can scarcely even know themselves because, unable to see into the souls of others, they lack a crucial "term of comparison." It is in order to provide the latter—the first bridge over the chasm of human subjectivity and isolation—that Rousseau writes his *Confessions* (see 3, 1148-55).

undistorted by death because by nature he knows how to resign himself to necessity, according to Rousseau. But to accept "necessity" one must first recognize it, and is this crucial concept natural or even accessible to most men? As Rousseau himself writes:

> Man began by animating all the beings whose action he felt. . . . During the first ages men were frightened of everything and saw nothing dead in nature. The idea of matter was formed no less slowly in them than that of spirit, since the former is an abstraction itself. . . . Stars, winds, mountains, rivers, trees, cities, even houses, each had its soul, its god, its life. (*Emile* IV: 256)

To be sure, civilized men no longer view the world quite so animistically, but they are scarcely more capable of viewing the major events of their lives, and especially their own death, in terms of abstract, impersonal necessity. Mustn't one agree with virtually the whole philosophic tradition as against Rousseau that "learning how to die" is the rarest and most difficult of human achievements?

One reaches a similar conclusion by reflecting on the implausibility of the description of childhood given in *Emile*. "Indifferent to everything outside of himself like all other children, [Emile] takes an interest in no one." "The child raised according to his age is alone. He knows no attachments other than those of habit. He loves his sister as he loves his watch" (*Emile* IV: 222, 219). Rousseau assumes that the child, as also savage man, is naturally solitary, self-sufficient, and individualistic. But don't children—and savages—clearly manifest, albeit along with contrary inclinations, a longing for oneness with the parent—and the group—a longing that stems from fear of separation, freedom, and individuality? And doesn't this famous "separation anxiety" and "escape from freedom" demonstrate the presence of just the sort of natural, primordial fearfulness that Rousseau attempts to deny? In other words, the two most striking presuppositions of his system—that asociality is natural to man and that the fear of death is not—are closely related and seem equally implausible.

Another, more general problem with Rousseau's theory is that when he speaks of man's "existence" and even of degrees of existence, he leaves it unclear whether he is speaking on the metaphysical or the psychological level. The classical doctrine of self-love is based on a teleological metaphysics that gives meaning to the notion of degrees of being, but Rousseau, while rejecting teleology, makes no systematic attempt to elaborate an alternative metaphysics that might account for such phenomena.[33] If nevertheless he does mean to be making metaphysical claims, as I have suggested, then these claims would seem to be highly questionable. Taking the *ordo cognoscendi* for the *ordo essendi*, they identify what one is with what one knows first or with certainty

---

[33] Burgelin (1952, p. 32) suggests that Rousseau found traditional metaphysics inadequate to the phenomenon of human existence but without being able to replace it with a "philosophy of existence."

about oneself; but man's true being is not necessarily the same as that by which he knows that he exists. The sentiment of existence certainly shows me *that* I am but not necessarily *what* I am. It does not reveal or constitute the whole of my nature.

If, on the other hand, Rousseau's theory is purely psychological, then there is no real necessity and little phenomenological plausibility to the identification of the "existence" or "self" that we love and seek to preserve with the conscious subject. We love our bodies, for example, and not merely because they are necessary for the preservation or heightening of our consciousness.

At any rate, on the basis of Rousseau's explicit statements, as well as his curious neglect to elaborate thematically his theory of self-love, it would appear that he relied primarily on the introspective argument. What is very clear is that the centerpiece of both arguments, and the core of the positive meaning of man's natural goodness, is Rousseau's specific understanding of the sentiment of existence.

Yet no positive argument for man's natural goodness, whatever its basis, can hold out against the fact of man's present evil—an indisputable fact, in Rousseau's view—unless it is supported by a demonstration of the nonnatural, external origin of human evil. That is the task of Rousseau's "negative proof," embodied in his historical and social arguments.

3

A Species Transformed:
The Historical Argument

What is the origin of evil? Although virtually all prior philosophers had assumed that the misery and wickedness of men as we know them reveals and grows out of certain permanent features of human nature, Rousseau suspects, along with most religious accounts of humanity, that some momentous event must have transformed the human race. Originally it was made for something better. "Nothing is so sad as the fate of men in general," Rousseau observes, "nevertheless, they find in themselves a devouring desire to become happy which makes them feel at every moment that they were born to be so" (*OC* IV: 13). Is this universal feeling, commonly dismissed as an unfounded hope, actually a divination of the truth?

It is hardly plausible, after all, that nature, which established such order everywhere else, should have made man for such disorder. Whether it was God, natural teleology, or some evolutionary process that produced the various natural species, clearly all of them are well ordered, possessing natural desires for the things their bodies need and natural faculties for obtaining the things they desire. Only in our species do the needs, desires, and faculties not fit together; and only among us are there wars, slavery, murder, and suicide. Precisely because present men are so extraordinarily bad, Rousseau reasons, it is unlikely that their badness is natural. Some historical event, then, must have changed them (*Frags.*, 477, 509).

What caused Rousseau to take this strange hypothesis seriously, however, is that he was among the first to recognize the strikingly "historical" character of man's being, the extreme malleability of his nature over time. The classical thinkers all tended to regard man's fundamental nature as given and immutable (although its form and degree of development might vary with circumstances). This view was dealt its most famous blow by John Locke, who argued that nothing but the elemental desire for pleasure and aversion to pain is innate and that all the rest of man's "nature" has been acquired through association or habit.[1] But Locke's theoretical individualism—which leads him to conceive of

---

[1] *An Essay Concerning Human Understanding* I-2 (3): v. I, 66-68; II-21 (29): v. I, 330-31. See, however, *Some Thoughts Concerning Education* paras. 103-5, where Locke suggests men have an innate love of dominion.

the mind as a bundle of discrete ideas, the personality as an assortment of separate inclinations, and society as a collection of independent individuals—leads him to understand man's malleability as simply his capacity to acquire different particular ideas or inclinations as a result of the different particular experiences he may chance to have. Rousseau, on the other hand, conceives of men's minds and characters as constituted by certain overarching forms—by conceptual and personality structures—which tend, in turn, to be shaped by the overarching form of the social environment. Rousseau therefore interprets human malleability in a far more radical way, believing that different economic, social, and political structures produce human beings with fundamentally different modes of awareness and ways of life. Consequently, he draws the revolutionary conclusion, as Locke did not, that "the human race of one age [is not] the human race of another" (*SD*, 178).[2] In a word, Rousseau was the first to discover "History." And as such, he became the first to render at least possible the startling hypothesis that the human species as we now know it—with its obvious and universal badness—is completely changed from its original form.

To show that such a hypothesis is not merely possible but plausible, however, Rousseau must substantiate his vague suspicion that mankind was originally good and, above all, he must show what real event occurring in our history could have so transformed and corrupted this original nature. Rousseau establishes both of these points merely by working through more consistently the view of human nature adopted by Hobbes and, in one degree or another, most thinkers who followed him. Man is not the political and civilized animal that Aristotle teleologically assumed him to be. By nature men live not in complex, political societies but rather in some sort of primitive, prepolitical "state of nature."

Man's original goodness becomes obvious, Rousseau argues, if one simply subtracts from his present nature all the traits that he could only have acquired in organized society (something that previous thinkers had done insufficiently due to their lack of the "historical sense"). According to the familiar argument of the *Second Discourse*, natural men, living dispersed in the woods or later gathered in loose tribes, could not have developed their reason, foresight, and imagination to any great degree and consequently could not have formed many desires beyond the natural ones for sleep, food, and sex—and certainly none of the desires that now make men so bad. And given the natural abundance of food supplied by nature, and of sex supplied by females (who have no estrous cycle or period of exclusion), given also the nonexistence of vanity or *amour-propre* (which requires more social contact and intelligence than natural man had), and given the presence of rudimentary feelings of pity which prevented men from inflicting needless harm, men must have been essentially at peace with themselves and others. Rousseau does not deny that a natural man (and

---

[2] Rousseau sees himself as waging a constant battle against "this fine adage of ethics, so often repeated by the philosophical rabble: That men are everywhere the same"—an adage so often repeated despite, or perhaps because of, the great influence of Locke's epistemology and psychology in the period of the Enlightenment (*SD*, 211; see *Narcissus*, 106n).

especially a tribal savage) may have occasionally harmed another, "but it is not possible that he acquire[d] the habit of evil doing, for that could in no way be useful to him" (*Narcissus*, 106n; see *SD*, 102-41; *Last Reply*, 73). Due to the limited development of their faculties, then, men were naturally self-sufficient and therefore naturally good.

If the human species was originally good for this reason (a reason somewhat different from that given by the introspective and psychological arguments), what historical event could have changed it so much? The answer is obvious. At a certain point late in their history—about ten thousand years ago, as we now know—men abandoned their natural environment by forming large, organized societies with agriculture, a division of labor, private property, and coercive government. This event, which so radically and unnaturally changed man's environment, surely must have altered his malleable nature in various ways. Consequently, this monumental historical event, whose reality can hardly be doubted, might reasonably be used to explain all the evil that this originally good creature now displays.[3]

[3]This account of the state of nature, the most famous of Rousseau's arguments, is also the one most open to obvious criticism. Rousseau's extreme individualism (undefended except in the arguments considered previously, which are not made here in the *Second Discourse*) led him to the doubtful assumption that man was naturally solitary and that not even the family is natural. True, he does regard the tribal stage as the best for man and even suggests that perhaps it is actually his natural state (*SD*, 151; see Masters [1968] pp. 135-36; Plattner [1979] p. 75), but even his understanding of the tribe seems questionably individualistic, neglecting the considerable power of custom, kinship ties, and natural deference.

Another difficulty is that Rousseau debates whether men are naturally carnivorous (inclining, incorrectly, to the negative), but only to help decide if the family is natural, if food was easily obtainable, or if men had natural conflicts of interest (see notes E, H, and L). He never discusses the possibility that man may have the general, instinctive aggressiveness of a carnivore (see Clark [1979]). And of course he is not aware of more recent discoveries regarding the presence in virtually all social vertebrates of both territoriality and "pecking orders"—*amour-propre* of sorts (see Maclay [1972]).

Finally, there is a rationalism to the account, a faith that the behavior of (natural) men and animals can be deduced directly from their basic survival interests, which does not accord with the facts. As Jane Goodall amply documents, chimpanzees will occasionally engage in infanticide, cannibalism, murder, and something like gang warfare, and often without any clear precipitating event or change in the environment. In one particularly gruesome incident, she recounts how three female chimps forcibly seized the baby of a member of their own troop and, as the mother looked on, devoured it, while occasionally caressing or embracing the mother. Such behavior might ultimately be explicable, but it could hardly have been deduced *a priori*. (See Goodall [1986] pp. 351, 268, 283-85, 318-56, 503-22.)

Yet all these difficulties notwithstanding, contemporary anthropology tends to confirm that the stage of primitive "segmental" societies (as distinguished from the later "chiefdom" stage)—in which the human species spent 99 percent of its history—was characterized by a fair amount of equality, voluntariness, leisure, and "goodness" (see Service [1975] chap. 3). See Lévi-Strauss (1984, p. 391) for a cautious endorsement of the view that "the way of life now known as neolithic" was probably the best that man has experienced up to this point.

Empirical Evidence

Of course, this argument remains highly conjectural, but it is also supported, Rousseau emphasizes, by empirical observation—provided only that such observation is made properly, as it has not been in the past. One of Rousseau's minor "projects" is in fact to reform the empirical study of man (in virtue of which many today consider him the founder of anthropology).[4] Most classical and Christian thinkers, misled by teleological assumptions, have made the mistake of looking for the "natural" in the civilized and developed rather than in the primitive and the infantile. Even thinkers who have explicitly rejected teleology have somehow remained caught in this error, for philosophers live in cities and they are, of all men, those with the greatest stake in the supposed nobility of reason; therefore, they have always tended, consciously or unconsciously, to the proud identification of rational urban man with man as such. Thus philosophy must make a conscious effort to free itself from this professional prejudice; it must learn to get into the country (as Rousseau did), to mingle with humble farmers and peasants, to "study. . . diverse peoples in their remote provinces," to travel to those distant lands where men have remained in the savage state, and to prefer the company of children to adults (*Emile* V: 469; see *Guerre*, 612; *SD*, 210-13).[5]

And even when philosophers have their primitive subjects before them, they must constantly fight against the ever renascent tendency to view them teleologically, as merely deficient modes of civilized adults. It is owing to this tendency, for example, that "childhood is unknown," although children are all around us. "The wisest men," Rousseau asserts, "are always seeking the man in the child without thinking of what he is before being a man." And he adds: "This is the study to which I have most applied myself" (*Emile* Preface, 33-34). In short, Rousseau is attempting to revolutionize the empirical study of human nature by showing that it requires certain heretofore unsuspected exertions and abilities: a willingness of the thinker to abandon assumptions that may ground his dignity as a thinker, a scrupulous resistance to every kind of teleological thinking, and a keen anthropological imagination or historical sense.

Practicing this new empiricism, Rousseau finds that "all nations appear much better when they are observed in this way [in their provinces]. The closer they are to nature the more they are dominated by goodness." Conversely, he observes that "the more [men] come together, the more they are corrupted. The infirmities of the body as well as the vices of the soul are the unfailing effect

---

[4] See "Jean-Jacques Rousseau, Fondateur des Sciences de l'Homme" by the eminent French anthropologist Claude Lévi-Strauss (1962), who calls Rousseau "our master and brother" (1984, p. 390).

[5] Rousseau also proposes certain other means for furthering "the study of men, which certainly is yet to begin" (*Confs.*, 3). In the *Second Discourse*, he suggests there is a need for scientific experimentation, and very delicately proposes the mating of a human with an orangutan to see whether the latter is actually man in his natural state (pp. 93, 209). In a very different way, he sees his *Confessions* as contributing a vital new resource to the empirical study of man by providing the first totally honest human self-portrait (*Confs.*, 3, 1148-55). Rousseau calls on us to dig deeper on two fronts: into the past and into the self.

of this over crowding. Man is, of all the animals, the one who can least live in herds. . . . Cities are the abyss of the human species" (*Emile* V: 469, I: 59; see *Last Reply*, 73; *Frags.*, 509; *NH* Second Preface, 14, 19, II-16: 242). In the cities and upper classes one sees men ceaselessly complain of their lives and blame their unhappiness on nature. And yet:

> I dare to pose as a fact that there is not perhaps in the higher Valais a single montagnard discontented with his almost mechanical life, and who would not willingly accept, even in place of paradise, to be ceaselessly reborn in order to vegetate thus perpetually. These differences make me believe that it is often the abuse that we make of life that makes it a burden to us. (*OC* IV: 1063)

Thus observation as well as reasoning suggests that artificial society has deformed men, who, in their natural, precivilized environment, were good and happy.[6]

If Rousseau's argument went no further than this it would still remain rather uncertain and conjectural. It claims only that some vague "something" in the momentous transition to civilized social life must have deformed men and caused their present evil. And in this form, the argument is exposed to an obvious and common objection: the "something" that perverts man is not really society, which after all is nothing more than the individuals who compose it, but man's own latent evil. By developing men, society only awakens the vicious tendencies dormant within them. Thus it is not society itself that corrupts, but foresight, which teaches man the fear of death, and imagination, which suggests a hundred new desires, and reason, which arouses man's *amour-propre*. Consequently, the undeveloped, subhuman brute Rousseau describes may well be good and may even be the true natural man, but that is all more or less irrelevant. The crucial fact remains that a certain degree of evil is inseparable from the development of the higher faculties that truly constitute man's humanity.[7]

But this important objection, and indeed most discussions of the principle of natural goodness, miss the point for want of looking beyond the historical argument to the last but most important stage of Rousseau's proof: the fourth, "social" argument. Guided by the foregoing historical conjectures, Rousseau switches to the present and to an altogether different form of analysis: to political science, in the broad sense, to an examination of the fundamental basis and structure of society as such. And through this separate, sociopolitical

---

[6] Rousseau's empirical observations were based on his travels through Europe and through all social classes. As Jacques Barzun (1947, p. 30) remarks, "Rousseau was the only man of genius who traversed eighteenth-century society from the bottom to the top. He was the only one who did not take root and stay fixed. . . . He got an anthropologist's view of his culture."

[7] As a contemporaneous critic of the *Second Discourse* wrote: "No one has ever doubted these truths, which signify nothing else than that in a state where man would be reduced to the condition of the beasts, he would not have the vices of a man," Anonymous, *L'Année Littéraire* vol. 7; Lettre 7 (n.p., 1755), p. 157, quoted by Plattner (1979) p. 78.

analysis, Rousseau discovers something that he claims had never been seen before, what he calls "*a secret opposition* between the constitution of man and that of our societies" (*Dialogues* II: 828). This discovery was really the crucial event for Rousseau, for it showed that the corrupting effect of society does not derive from the mere development of our higher faculties and latent evil, as the above objection would have it, but indeed from society itself, from a heretofore unseen "contradiction of the social system" (*Mals.*, 1135).[8]

Contrary to the usual presentations of Rousseau's principle, it is not his new historical or anthropological conjectures about the primitive state of nature but rather his new theory of society that constitutes the true core of his argument for the natural goodness of man.[9] Rousseau himself makes this point explicitly in the "history of my ideas" sketched out in a few pages of the *Letter to Beaumont*. He had noticed man's remarkable evil and had searched for its cause:

> I found it in our social order, which, at every point contrary to nature which nothing can destroy, continually tyrannized it and made it continually reclaim its rights. I followed *this contradiction* in its consequences, and I saw that it alone explained all the vices of men and all the evils of society. From which I concluded that it was not necessary to suppose man wicked by his nature when one could point to the origin and progress of his wickedness. (*Beaumont*, 966-67)[10]

While Rousseau's introspections, his psychological theories, and his historical conjectures strongly inclined him to the belief in man's natural goodness, what really caused him to embrace his principle in the "illumination of Vincennes" was his discovery of the structural contradiction of society. For this insight enabled him for the first time concretely to display and trace out the social origin of all man's present badness.[11]

Before turning to this argument, we might pause briefly to consider the question of what if anything is historically unique about the doctrine of natural goodness. This question, which will help to clarify further the meaning of Rousseau's doctrine, will also confirm from a different point of view the central importance of his theory of the contradiction of society.

---

[8] The whole point of *Emile*, for example, is to show that a man could develop his foresight, imagination, and reason without destroying his natural goodness, so long as he were sheltered from the effects of society.

[9] Rousseau in fact claims that he gave the clearest demonstration of his principle in *Emile*, where the state of nature is not discussed at all (*Beaumont*, 935; *Dialogues* I: 687, III: 933, 934).

[10] See 936; *Dialogues* I: 687, III: 934; *Emile* II: 92; *Guerre*, 612.

[11] In Rousseau's famous description of the "illumination of Vincennes" in the *Letters to Malesherbes* he makes no mention of introspection, psychological theory, the sentiment of existence, or the state of nature, but only of "the contradictions of the social system" and the "abuses of our institutions" (pp. 1135-36; see also *Dialogues* II: 828; *Beaumont*, 936). Furthermore, the whole constructive part of Rousseau's thought, his proposed cure for the ills of society, is based almost exclusively on this analysis of the contradiction of society.

Rousseau's Precursors

Many writers have dismissed the doctrine of man's natural and primitive goodness as a strange and implausible conceit unique to Rousseau, while others have charged that it is entirely derivative, or even stolen, from the work of others. In fact, doctrines akin to Rousseau's have been quite common in the intellectual history of the West, but the most important features of his doctrine are unique to him.

Rousseau's view obviously has something in common with the long Western tradition of pastoral poetry. Especially in oppressive, aristocratic, over-civilized ages like Rousseau's own, men have often turned their imaginations to the simplicity, contentment, and innocence of rustic life. However, while Rousseau shares and approves of this taste, his thought cannot be identified with or reduced to it. These common idyllic longings, in his view, are seldom more than an aristocratic recreation, "a resource for a rainy day," as he puts it (*Emile* IV: 223).[12] Indeed, the pastoral art form—stylized, measured, and complacent—seems to betray a greater appreciation of poetic refinement (hence of urban sophistication) than of genuine rustic simplicity. It is not a sincere or thoroughgoing questioning of civilized life, but rather a particular means of adorning it.

A somewhat more radical literary movement, and one more important for Rousseau, emerged in the sixteenth century sparked by the discovery and exploration of the new world. All Europe was overcome with fascination and curiosity regarding the savage inhabitants of the Americas, a curiosity that called forth a constant stream of books by voyagers, as well as the new literary genre of "imaginary voyages"—both describing the life and customs of the Indians. And for the most part, this literature, which reached its peak in the eighteenth century, portrayed the savages as good.

Yet only to a limited extent could this widespread movement be called a precursor of or influence upon Rousseau, for it was and remained primarily a *literary* movement. In particular, the imaginary voyages (and to a considerable extent the real ones as well) were written to satisfy a taste for the exotic or to moralize, using the savage's goodness as a means to reveal and accuse the moral failings of civilized men. Thus the "goodness" of these literary savages often consisted in the perfection of all the civilized virtues. It was understood that these sentimental and moralized accounts were not a scientific hypothesis. Although Rousseau's own depiction of savage life is certainly not without a literary dimension, his overriding interest is philosophical, and his radical conception of natural man as good but brutish, amoral, and subhuman clearly owes very little to the literary "noble savage."[13]

---

[12] See *Emile* V: 474: "It is not even true that people regret the golden age, since those regrets are always hollow."

[13] See Atkinson (1924 and 1971), Chinard (1913), and Fairchild (1961). The last suggests that the term "noble savage" was first used by John Dryden in *The Conquest of Granada* (1670-71). "Le bon sauvage," the French counterpart, was in use even in the sixteenth century, according to Atkinson (1924). Rousseau never uses either term.

Rousseau does make some use of the real voyages, quoting several times in the *Second Discourse* from Prévost's compendium—but only to support points he has already made on other grounds. Other grounds are necessary because "I have spent my life reading accounts of travels, and I have never found two which have given me the same idea of the same people" (*Emile* V: 451). In his time, "there are scarcely more than four sorts of men who make voyages of long duration: sailors, merchants, soldiers, and missionaries," and such men "have known how to perceive, at the other end of the world, only what it was up to them to notice without leaving their street;...those true features that distinguish nations and strike eyes made to see have almost always escaped theirs" (*SD*, 211; see 189, 204-10, 213). The writers of real voyages have all lacked that eye for cultural differences and human malleability, that "historical sense" which forms such a crucial part of Rousseau's own science and doctrine of man.[14]

The true precursor of Rousseau's views is the philosophic tradition of "primitivism" (as A. O. Lovejoy has labelled it), which long ago made all of the serious points contained in the above literary movements. It is no exaggeration to say that, with varying degrees of sincerity and enthusiasm, almost every major classical thinker praised the life of early or primitive man, with the strongest views being expressed by the Cynics and late Stoics, especially Seneca. Rousseau was aware of these writings and seems to have been particularly influenced by the views of Lucretius, Plutarch, Seneca, Tacitus, and, among modern thinkers, Montaigne.[15]

The currency of primitivist doctrines in antiquity is hardly surprising considering that classical thought as a whole saw little value in technology, popular enlightenment, luxury, or empire—all the benefits (or all the vulgar benefits) of civilization. And on the other hand, the classics greatly admired austerity, courage, self-sufficiency, and the simple life, which are commonly found among savages. Moreover, most classical thinkers agreed that, whatever perfections civilized society ultimately makes possible for the few, it also made available to all a great many new sources of moral corruption. One reads everywhere how luxury, public opinion, bad examples, partisan strife, inflamed ambition, envy, greed, jealousy, vanity, loose morals, evil companions, constant change, and immoral doctrines corrupt men in society.

Nevertheless, in contrast to Rousseau, this philosophic primitivism, as well as the various forms of literary primitivism described above, never actually went so far as to claim that man is "naturally good" and that society itself is the source of all evil. For one thing, they understand the goodness of happy shepherds and primitives as mainly a negative thing: carefree and innocent, they are free of all the vices of civilized decadence. But there is little inclination to claim, as Rousseau does, that they have a positive goodness and plenitude

---

[14] A notebook of Rousseau's preserved in the library at Neuchâtel contains many pages of references to and extracts from Prévost's *Histoire générale des voyages*. See Pire (1956) for an interesting account.

[15] See Lovejoy (1935). *SD*, 130, 152; *Emile* epigraph; *FD*, 45, 42, 42n. See Morel (1909).

stemming from something like the sentiment of existence, that they have not only avoided corruption and *un*naturalness but live closer to *completed* nature, which lies at the origin and not in the end.

Second and even more important, the pre-Rousseauian primitivists all take the view stated in the objection mentioned above, that shepherds or primitives, like children, are innocent only because undeveloped; that civilized society corrupts men only because, by developing them, it brings out their latent but natural tendency to vice. Some of the Stoics, it is true, had a doctrine of natural goodness that blamed society for all corruption. Yet their doctrine, based on certain abstract arguments about the unity of the will, never really attempted to explain how, if men had no evil within them, society could cause it to emerge. Moreover, for the Stoics man is social by nature, so that in the end they do not deny that man's corruption is necessary if not in every sense natural. As Seneca writes, "there is no man to whom a good mind comes before an evil one. . . . Learning virtue means unlearning vice."[16] Even this Stoic doctrine, then, does not approach the radical blame of society and total exculpation of man that forms the heart of Rousseau's doctrine. Perhaps the single clearest indication of the difference is his praise of absolute solitude. Others had advocated withdrawal from public life, but no one prior to Rousseau recommended the avoidance of society as such.

Despite the undeniable similarities and influences, then, Rousseau went a crucial step further than all the various primitivist traditions that preceded him. He is the first philosopher to go beyond the familiar regrets for the loss of innocence, beyond the commonplace moralisms about corruption in society, and beyond the view that society merely develops man's latent vices, to the claim that *society itself* is structurally inclined to deprave men who, by nature and free of such deformation, are positively good and happy.

This brief comparison with earlier views thus leads to the very same conclusion we drew from an analysis of Rousseau's own writings, from his self-description, and from the logic of his argument: what is unique and decisive in his doctrine is his concept of the sentiment of existence, and, above all, his new theory of the contradiction of society, which allows him to exculpate human nature. This theory is the true centerpiece of his thought, although it has never quite been recognized as such or received a fully adequate elaboration.

To sum up, impelled by a sense of the sheer implausibility of men's extraordinary evil, heartened by his new, more sensitive observations of peasants and children, guided by his assumption of human malleability and the unnaturalness of civil society, and above all, inspired by his introspective feeling and psychological theory that man is naturally good, Rousseau strongly suspected that there must be some problem with society itself, some hitherto unseen corrupting factor, that was the true cause of all man's present evil. Guided by this theoretical hypothesis, as astronomers were guided by

[16] Seneca *Epistles* 50.7.

their calculations in discovering the outermost planets, Rousseau became the first to uncover the hidden and fundamental "contradictions of the social system." That epoch-making discovery is what enabled him to shift the blame for all of man's evil onto society itself, to free human nature from the accumulated calumnies of all previous ages, and to perceive for the first time in history the natural goodness of man.

"A violent palpitation oppressed me, swelling my chest," Rousseau writes of his moment of illumination on the road to Vincennes.

> No longer being able to breathe while walking, I dropped under one of the trees along the avenue, and passed there a half-hour in such an agitation that in getting up again I noticed the whole front of my jacket soaked with my tears, which I had not even noticed having shed. (*Mals.*, 1135)

4

Rousseau's Characterization of Civilized Man's Evil

We have arrived at Rousseau's central argument: man's extraordinary evil, which has always appeared to be rooted in nature, is actually attributable to a heretofore unseen contradiction in the structure of society. To follow this argument, however, it is first necessary to understand what it attempts to explain. Precisely what does Rousseau mean by "man's extraordinary evil"?

Rousseau tells us that an intense awareness of man's evil was the starting point of his philosophic reflection, and we can see for ourselves the indignation and bitter contempt he harbors for the degraded condition of civilized humanity. Also, historically, Rousseau's restoration, in modern, secular terms, of the concern with health of soul and his passionate condemnation of modern man from this new moral perspective was one of the most influential aspects of his thought. Yet, for all the importance, vehemence, and fame of Rousseau's denunciation of men's evil, its specific content is remarkably unclear, at least to judge by the confusion and dispute that has always surrounded it.

In his writings, we do not in fact find the sort of accusations to which we are accustomed from the Christian and classical moralists but rather a seemingly diffuse collection of new complaints and discontents. Civilized men, we hear, are all actors, hypocrites, and role-players. They are plagued by ceaseless desires and labors. They are effeminate, enervated, and lacking in "force and vigor of the soul." They are overly concerned with what others think of them. And they are unjust and exploitative. That is the basic list. Certainly there is some truth to each of its items, but it is difficult to see what ties them all together or even what is so terrible about these accusations as to justify Rousseau's obsessive concern with "man's evil." In the end, most of his readers, I suspect, come away from the *First* and *Second Discourses*, with their thunderous declamations, wondering just what is bothering Rousseau.

Underlying Rousseau's diffuse litany of accusations, I will argue, are the twin evils of *injustice toward others* and especially *disunity of soul*. And beneath these, in turn, stands the most fundamental evil: the loss of "existence."

Injustice

The most immediately intelligible and powerful of Rousseau's accusations against civilized humanity is that of injustice. So powerful, in fact, that many scholars have been tempted to say that all the other accusations are merely "aesthetic," that his passionate protest against injustice and oppression is the vital center of his thought, and indeed that Rousseau's world-historical significance consists in his being the first philosopher to recognize oppression as the central human problem. This view of Rousseau will prove to be correct, but not in the sense in which it is usually presented.

Man's evil is obvious, Rousseau declares, when "a handful of men [are] glutted with superfluities while the starving multitude lacks necessities" (*SD*, 181). Indeed, all civilized men, he argues, operate on the evil assumption that "wrong done to one's neighbor is always more lucrative than services. Therefore it is no longer a question of anything except finding ways to be assured of impunity; and it is for this that the powerful use all their strength and the weak all their ruses" (*SD*, 195). The weak, it should be noted, are no less unjust than the strong, in Rousseau's view, but since they are less effective, he speaks more of oppression than of crime, although he has both in view. Thus, the grand spectacle of history, he proclaims, shows everywhere the "violence of powerful men and the oppression of the weak" (*SD*, 97). And this hideous spectacle of universal injustice, Rousseau writes, fills him with an "inextinguishable hatred...against the mistreatment suffered by the unfortunate people and against their oppressors" (*Confs.* IV: 164; see *Mals.*, 1145).

Is this the true core of Rousseau's indictment of civilized man? Injustice and oppression, are they the whole of human evil in Rousseau's conception? From his writings, it would seem that they are not; and from the standpoint of unaided human reason, it would seem that they cannot be, for one is simply not entitled to conclude from the sole fact that men harm one another that they are evil, wicked, or blameworthy for doing so. Today, when moral and political thought tends to assume as an absolute and unargued first principle that oppression is evil—indeed the only evil—it is very important to be reminded that this principle is not self-evident and that earlier thinkers like Rousseau did not assume that it was.

Rousseau is in fact well versed in the morally skeptical arguments presented, for example, in the first two books of Plato's *Republic*, arguments said there to represent the views secretly held by most people. Thrasymachus, one of the interlocutors, presents a view of the world that entirely agrees with Rousseau's. He too looks behind the facade of order and justice and sees everywhere nothing but crime, exploitation, and oppression. But in contrast to Rousseau, he stresses this fact not in order to demand justice but to attack it. For what does it prove, after all, if not that men are wolves whose natural good, whose fulfillment and happiness, require injustice and preying upon others? A just man is not good, virtuous, or admirable but rather repressed, cowardly, foolish—alienated in some manner from the full development and expression of his true nature.

In fact, one is not even entitled to speak of "justice." What is good for the wolves is necessarily bad for their prey, and conversely; consequently, there is no imaginable state of affairs that would be for the good of *all*, hence just. What men commonly call "justice"—refraining from the active harm of others—is in fact harmful and oppressive for the wolves and so is no more just than its opposite. One may of course pity the fate of the oppressed. One may also regret that the world is so constituted that the good of one always requires the harm of another. But if one is strong and honest one will also admire the excellence of the masters, of those who have fulfilled human nature and succeeded in doing what, in truth, all men desire to do. To call them names, to label them "unjust," "evil," or "immoral" might be a useful tactic for the weak in their battle against the strong, or it might just be an irrational outburst of fear or resentment. But it is not a truthful or honest position. In short, if the exploitation of other men is part of the perfection and fulfillment of human nature—as men's universal tendency to it would strongly suggest—on what grounds can one condemn it as evil?[1]

Thus, although men harm and oppress one another, that fact alone does not mean that they are evil or unjust. And if Rousseau's indictment condemns men for being unjust (which it does), it must go beyond the mere fact of exploitation to include a refutation of this argument, a critique of the life of mastery. It must demonstrate, in short, that there is a kind of harm, different from the harm of being oppressed, that one suffers by being an oppressor. This second kind of evil, then, whatever it may be, must form an integral part of Rousseau's condemnation of injustice. Consequently, exploitation—the harm done to the oppressed—*cannot* stand alone as the whole of civilized man's evil.

There is, however, a widespread tendency among readers of Rousseau to ignore or reject this conclusion, a tendency brought to full clarity in Ernst Cassirer's classic interpretation. Rousseau differs from all prior moral thinkers, he argues, precisely in being a proto-Kantian demanding the realization of justice—of the Categorical Imperative or the General Will—regardless of eudemonistic or utilitarian "consequences." Rousseau's concern was not to "inquire into happiness or utility; he was concerned with the dignity of man." That dignity requires men to refrain from exploiting and oppressing others regardless of what they naturally desire or what makes them happy. Rousseau went beyond eudemonism, Cassirer claims, to the moralistic view that "there is no value to human existence on this earth if justice is not brought to triumph."[2] Thus Rousseau's indictment of civilized men is, as first suggested, a purely moralistic attack on their injustice as something inherently wrong and bad in itself. Injustice, and it alone, is human evil.

---

[1] See Plato *Republic* 336b-354c, *Gorgias* 481c-486e. See also Nietzsche, *Genealogy of Morals* I-13. One might, of course, condemn exploitation on the basis of a Utilitarian notion of collective happiness, constructed by summing the private happiness of all individuals. Rousseau did not take this view. Where there is no common good, such a construct corresponds to nothing real; therefore, there is no reason for the individual to prefer it to his private good.

[2] Cassirer (1954) pp. 70-71. See also Cassirer (1963) p. 56. Others who interpret Rousseau in a similar way include Gurvitch (1932) pp. 260-79 and Levine (1979).

This famous "Kantian" interpretation, however, misrepresents the character of Rousseau's concern for justice. Unlike Kant, Rousseau still adheres to the traditional view that the good is prior to the right, or that the value (and content) of justice must ultimately be judged before the bar of happiness. Rousseau states with remarkable force and clarity that one can require human beings to live justly only if it is fundamentally good for them to do so:

> If moral goodness [or justice] is in conformity with our nature, man could be *healthy of spirit* or *well constituted* only to the extent that he is good. If it is not and man is naturally wicked, he cannot cease to be so without being corrupted, and goodness in him is only a vice contrary to nature. If he were made to do harm to his kind as a wolf is made to slaughter his prey, a humane man would be an animal as depraved as a pitying wolf, and only virtue would leave us with remorse. (*Emile* IV: 287, emphasis added)[3]

Rousseau agrees with Thrasymachus that if man is "naturally wicked" like a wolf, then justice would be "a vice contrary to nature," a form of corruption and depravity. Thus the mere fact of human injustice is not by itself sufficient grounds for blame or regret. One needs a further doctrine, a critique of mastery showing that in fact wickedness is not our natural good, that the life of exploitation is harmful for the oppressor no less than the oppressed, that unjust men are somehow not "healthy of spirit or well constituted."

Rousseau formulates his critique of mastery, or rather summarizes its conclusion, in the most famous sentences of the *Social Contract*: "Man was born free, and everywhere he is in chains. One who believes himself the *master* of others is nonetheless a *greater slave* than they" (I-1: 46, emphasis added).[4] Again, in *Emile*: "Dependence on men, since it is without order, engenders *all the vices*, and by it, master and slave are *mutually corrupted*" (*Emile* II: 85, emphasis added; see *SD*, 156, 173-77, 193-203). Some sort of enslaving "corruption of soul" which afflicts the oppressors as well as the oppressed is the more fundamental evil that establishes and constitutes the evilness of injustice.

This conclusion is confirmed by a simple and striking fact, yet one always ignored by those who would see in Rousseau a Kantian moralist (as well as those who see a morbidly sensitive and wounded man consumed by pity or

---

[3] The Savoyard Vicar is speaking. For the same view in Rousseau's own name see *GM* I-2: 157-63; *Emile* IV: 235, 235n, 314-15, 314n. Cassirer does not deny that there are eudemonistic *elements* in Rousseau, but claims that his radical demand for law and freedom can only be understood in terms of an underlying Kantianism ([1954] pp. 55-58, 62, 69-71, 126-27; [1963] p. 57). I will try to show in the course of this work how Rousseau's unique emphasis on law and freedom can be understood, and only understood, in terms of his eudemonistic principles.

[4] These two famous and crucial assertions are assumed and never proved in the *Social Contract*. This work presupposes the critique of mastery given in the *Second Discourse* and *Emile*, and if one reads it without reference to these other works, as Rousseau urges one not to do, one will be misled in the direction of a Kantian interpretation.

ressentiment). In the very rare cases where injustice, violence, or oppression does not cause corruption but rather prevents it, he *does not condemn it*. For example, while praising the great strength and vigor that children had in the state of nature, Rousseau notes approvingly: "Nature treats them precisely as the law of Sparta treated the children of citizens: it renders strong and robust those who are well constituted and makes all the others perish" (*SD*, 106). Similarly, he points out that later, when men progressed to the tribal stage, "it was up to the terror of revenge to take the place of the restraint of laws," and thus "vengeances became terrible, and men bloodthirsty and cruel" (*SD*, 150, 149). This fact does not hinder Rousseau in the least from declaring the tribal stage to be "the best for man," "the happiest and most durable epoch," and "the veritable prime of the world" (*SD*, 151). The point becomes even clearer when we get to civilized times. What, after all, are Rousseau's two great political models but Rome and Sparta! In a manner far more reminiscent of Nietzsche than Kant, he praises the one as the "model of all free peoples," despite its ceaseless imperialism, and the other as a "republic of demi-gods rather than men," despite its extensive slavery (*SD*, 80; *FD*, 43). In the *Social Contract*, Rousseau's supposedly most Kantian work, he does not shrink from defending Sparta's policy and even from attacking those who would moralistically condemn it:

> There are some unfortunate situations when . . . the citizen can only be perfectly free if the slave is completely enslaved. Such was Sparta's situation. As for you, modern peoples, you *have* no slaves, but you *are* slaves. You pay for their freedom with your own. You boast of that preference in vain; I find it more cowardly than humane. (III-15: 103, emphasis added)

Rousseau sees the undeniable injustice and oppression of Rome and Sparta but he refuses to condemn them, for in the end what clearly counts more for him is the health of soul, the magnificent strength and freedom, of the men they produced.

In sum, Rousseau's understanding of evil does place a great, indeed unique, emphasis on oppression and injustice, but ultimately the badness or blameworthiness of injustice is grounded on the still more fundamental evil of corruption of soul. We need to ask, then, what Rousseau means by such corruption (and, eventually, why it is produced by injustice).

Disunity of Soul

The human corruption that forms the core of man's evil and misery, according to Rousseau, is psychological conflict and division, the loss of a unified, integrated personality, what I will call "disunity of soul." "The cause of human misery is the *contradiction* that exists between our state and our desires, between our duties and our penchants . . . ; *render man one* and you will make him as happy as he is capable of being" (*Frags.*, 510, emphasis added).

At the beginning of *Emile*, Rousseau gives his classic portrait of the disunified man.

> Always in contradiction with himself, always floating between his inclinations and his duties, he will never be either man or citizen. He will be good neither for himself nor for others. He will be one of these men of our days: A Frenchman, an Englishman, a bourgeois. He will be nothing.
>
> To be something, to be oneself and always one, a man must act as he speaks; he must always be decisive in making his choice, make it in a lofty style and always stick to it. (*Emile* I: 40)

A little later he speaks again of the "contradictions . . . we constantly experience within ourselves."

> Swept along in contrary routes . . . forced to divide ourselves between these different impulses, we follow a composite impulse which leads us to neither one goal nor the other. Thus, in conflict and floating during the whole course of our life, we end it without having been able to put ourselves in harmony with ourselves and without having been good either for ourselves or for others. (*Emile* I: 41)

That is Rousseau's description of disunity of soul, the core of civilized man's evil.[5]

What is so bad about it? The most obvious answer is that this constant inner conflict is painful or tormenting, but Rousseau's indictment of civilized men does not portray them as particularly tormented. In both of these passages, he describes them as "floating" rather than violently torn; more generally, he accuses them of having extensive, restless, and frivolous desires but not deep, powerful, or tormenting ones. Indeed, Rousseau, like Nietzsche, denounces men with such zeal and boldness precisely because he regards them as "happy slaves" who need to be roused from a shocking complacency and a strange blindness to their own degradation. Rousseau praises, on the other hand, the virtuous patriot as a man who escapes the evils of disunity, even while emphasizing that such virtue involves great struggle.

If the evil of disunity does not consist in inner struggle or pain, then it must consist in the absence of unity, where unity is somehow conceived as a positive good. But what can this good be beyond the freedom from pain and strife? "Existence" is Rousseau's answer. The basic principle of human nature, we have seen, is self-love, which inclines man to delight in, preserve, and increase

---

[5] On the epoch-making influence of this diagnosis Karl Löwith writes: "Rousseau's writings contain the first and clearest statement of the human problem of bourgeois society. It consists in the fact that man, in bourgeois society, is not a unified whole. On the one hand, he is a private individual, and on the other, a citizen of the state, for bourgeois society has a problematic relationship to the state. Ever since Rousseau, the incongruity between them has been a fundamental problem of all modern theories of the state and society" (1964, p. 232).

his existence. And the primary means for maintaining or heightening one's existence, according to Rousseau, is unity.

The case would be otherwise if civilized man had a natural or divine end—a specific activity, form, and unity intended for him—for then he would achieve full existence through the actualization of that end. But, for Rousseau, civilized man, an accidental being with acquired faculties and inclinations, has no such end, and therefore the issue of his full existence becomes liberated from any specific content or natural activity. It no longer matters *what* a man is so long as he is it wholly and consistently. "Unity of soul," as a purely formal condition, becomes (along with "extent") the sole determinant of existence and thus the primary good. Accordingly, disunity of soul, being the direct negation of existence, becomes human evil itself.

Unity over Time

To form a more concrete understanding of disunity we need a richer appreciation of the meaning of unity and of its relation to existence. Unity of soul, as Rousseau understands it, seems to have two components. Since man's existence gets divided by the flow of time as well as by the conflict among his inclinations, the oneness he seeks requires both "unity over time" and "unity of will or inclination."

The importance of unity for existence is perhaps clearest in the first respect: unity over time. To live in the extensionless point of the present, immersed in the flux of time and sensations, is to perish every instant. In order truly to exist, to have a self and a life, one must have duration: unity or self-sameness over time. Accordingly, Rousseau asserts that "the life of the individual begins," and he becomes "capable of happiness or unhappiness," only when "memory extends the sentiment of identity to all the moments of his existence, and he becomes truly one" (*Emile* II: 78).

Yet memory alone cannot forge a complete temporal unity, and part of us remains caught in the flux. Our natural inclination to expand our existence attaches us to various things in the world. But all worldly things—and our love for them—are in flux. "Everything around us changes. We ourselves change, and no one can be assured he will like tomorrow what he likes today" (*Reveries* IX: 122). The self thus has an inconstancy and discontinuity that leads Rousseau himself to complain of his "weekly souls" (*OC* I: 1110).

Furthermore, although memory unifies our existence by revealing and attaching us to our past and future selves, it also makes possible, by this same act, the alienation from our present self. Living in the past through nostalgic longing or in the future through desire and hope, we are always ahead of or behind ourselves—never wholly united with ourselves.

Thus, the fullness of existence for which we long requires a perfect unity over time in which the two difficulties just discussed are overcome. In this condition, which Rousseau calls having a "state," the awareness of one's self remains constant despite the flux of time and events; and the self, no longer alienated to the past or future, is complete and wholly present in every moment. In the *Reveries*, Rousseau describes the condition as:

> A simple and permanent state . . . where the soul finds a base sufficiently solid on which to rest entirely and to *gather there all its being*, without the need to recall the past or encroach on the future; where time is nothing for it, where the present lasts forever without even marking its duration and without any trace of succession, without any other sentiment of privation or of enjoyment, of pleasure or of pain, of desire or fear, but this alone of our existence, which sentiment is able to fill the soul entirely. (*Reveries* V: 68)[6]

The rare state of perfect temporal unity described here—that of Rousseau the solitary dreamer—is not compatible with life in civil society. But at least approximations to it are possible in more ordinary circumstances.

Consider, for example, the life of domestic simplicity led by Julie and Wolmar on their rustic estate in the *Nouvelle Héloïse* (V-2: 527-57). A quiet, simple, and uniform life of daily routines and seasonal festivities, it contains nothing exciting, impressive, or intensely pleasant. Yet there is a great charm in the picture of this life as a whole; and the charm is precisely that: the life is a *whole*. It is not a mere sequence of disconnected activities and experiences, but a "life," a unified manner of being, a kind of "state." All of one's actions have an order and necessity through which they contribute, each in a different way, to the preservation and expression of the same way of life. Each of the day's activities is like a different note in a single melody. A life such as this approximates the unity of a "state," because the self is neither altered over time nor divided by it. In all the changing times and aspects of one's life one is always living the same life, always being the same person; and thus each moment of life is lived in the presence of one's life as a whole.

Through such temporal unity, one exists or "feels life" more—not because one has filled it with extraneous pleasures and excitement, but because life's own native power has been gathered up and unified. The full reality of one's existence is allowed to shine through undiminished. One feels life whole.[7]

With this in mind, one begins to understand all that is lost through disunity. One of the items on Rousseau's "list of accusations" is that civilized men fill their lives with ceaseless desires and labors. Unlike the idle natural man who "breathes only repose and freedom," social man is "always active, sweats, agitates himself" (*SD*, 179). Part of the evil of this condition is the resulting fatigue and frustration. But the primary evil is the loss of unity over time, the loss of "repose" and of the plenitude of existence found in it. Man's constant needs and desires, projecting him into the future and away from his present

---

[6] Emphasis added. I have altered the translation.

[7] *NH* V-2: 553; *Emile* III: 187n; *Emile et Sophie, OC* IV: 899. For somewhat different treatments of the theme of time in Rousseau, see Poulet (1956) pp. 158-84, Van Laere (1968), and Temmer (1958).

self, make him say: tomorrow I will *live*, today I will *prepare* to live. Spending his life thus "on the way," he is never "there" and at rest. He never knows a moment when he possesses all that he wants and thus possesses himself; never a moment when he embraces his present existence and says: let this moment last forever. Continually postponing his existence, he dies without ever having lived.[8]

Unity of Inclination

To exist fully, we need not only unity over time but also unity of inclination. We must be wholly where we are, but also wholly *what* we are. Our basic desires must be harmonious and noncontradictory, so that we have the same goal and are the same person in every part of our self.

If the soul is not unified in this sense, because of either natural causes (as Plato, for instance, maintains) or historical ones (as Rousseau will argue); if instead, it is some monstrous combination of heterogeneous parts, each with its own nature and inclination, each warring with the others to rule the soul and direct our lives; and if, moreover, we fail to impose any order on this inner chaos, then we can have *no existence* at all. It is the total disintegration of the self—madness.

To exist at all, one must have an integrated personality, some measure of oneness with oneself. To exist fully, we must be fully "coherent," with all parts of ourselves pulling in the same direction. All of our inclinations and cares must fit together in a coherent whole, giving us a focus and center of being. Then, gathered together, one with ourselves, we exist wholeheartedly—with nothing in conflict and nothing left out. We attain the heightened feeling of reality that comes from being *all there*. With the full weight of our existence pressing down on a single point, we exist with all our being.

With these benefits of unity in mind, one begins to understand Rousseau's condemnation of civilized man as "always in contradiction with himself, always floating between his inclinations and his duties." The evil of his disunity is not that he may feel some inner strife and pain but that "he will be nothing." He has not wholly fallen to pieces, but the division or fragmentation of his self severely attenuates his existence and diminishes his feeling of life.

Indeed, this diminution of life is readily observable, Rousseau claims, in the enervation, "spiritual pettiness," and lack of "force and vigor of the soul" characteristic of civilized men—another item on the list of accusations (*FD*, 36-37; see 54-56; *SD*, 111, 164; *Emile* IV: 335; *Frags.*, 546). Unified souls harness the total energy of their "desire to exist" in a single direction. They are

> healthy souls, whose force, without perhaps exceeding that of common souls, produces much more effect, because it acts *wholly along the same line*, it loses none of its effect in oblique directions, and it always strikes *all at the same point*. (*Dialogues* I: 669, variant C, emphasis added; see *Hero*, 1273)

[8]*SD*, 179, 193, 195; *Emile* II: 79, 82-83, V: 411; *OC* II: 1326; *Dialogues* II: 818, 823.

Lacking "alignment," the social man's force of soul is both scattered and turned against itself. "Vile and cowardly even in their vices. . . there hardly remains enough life in them to move" (*Emile* IV: 335). Disunity of inclination saps the vigor and vitality of their souls.

Conclusion

A major element of Rousseau's originality was his restoration, on modern principles, of the philosophical concern with the state of men's souls. Because of this concern, his thought begins, as would that of most thinkers who followed him, from a posture of moral revulsion and protest at civilized man's evil. But Rousseau restores this concern only by developing a fundamentally new conception of evil. Unlike earlier, Christian and classical moralists, it is no longer understood in terms of the transgression of divine commands or the lack of conformity to natural ends, but in the terms provided by Rousseau's new theory of self-love. The positive goal of human desire is existence, which is maintained or enhanced through *formal* unity. Hence psychic disunity is the core of human evil, and it underlies all the disparate and somewhat untraditional accusations that constitute Rousseau's new indictment of civilized humanity, including the crucial accusation of injustice (although how injustice produces disunity remains to be seen).[9]

Furthermore, only in light of this reinterpretation of the meaning of human evil can one make sense of Rousseau's "social argument," his fourth and most important proof for the principle of natural goodness. For Rousseau certainly does not believe that society is the cause of, say, men's failure to transcend all egoism and selflessly love their neighbors as themselves. If this specific failure were the true essence of evil, then men would indeed be evil by nature. Only because human evil is nothing but disunity of soul and mutual exploitation can it be entirely attributed, as Rousseau will now attempt to show, to a heretofore unseen "contradiction of society."

---

[9]One may form a good idea of the influence of Rousseau's new conception of evil, or at least of the importance of the phenomena he describes, by considering the terms of analysis made current by later thinkers, terms such as: "Divided self," "hollow men," "alienation," "identity crisis," "inauthenticity," "other-directedness," and so forth.

5

The Contradiction of Society:
The Social Argument

How can society alone be the cause of all men's injustice and disunity of soul? Perhaps, by putting men's interests in artificial opposition, society might produce injustice, but it could not create a division inside men's very souls unless the human soul were already a composite of distinct parts capable of opposing each other. For this reason, the phenomenon of human self-conflict has almost always been explained by means of some theory of the multipartite character of human nature, whether the parts be reason and passion, eros and thanatos, soul and body, nature and free will, head and heart, spirit and matter, devil and angel, or whatever.[1]

Rousseau, however, proclaims the natural unity of man and the social origin of all dividedness. He does so, despite the above argument, by claiming that psychic disunity consists not in a conflict of distinct ends or parts of soul, created by nature, but in a conflict of end and *means*, created by society.

The real heart of Rousseau's "social argument," then, is his account of the process by which unified natural man has been transformed into the divided civilized man because of a contradiction between his single natural end and

---

[1] Virtually all psychological theories that divide the personality into parts employ, implicitly or explicitly, the argument first used in Plato's *Republic* (436a-442a): men desire opposite things simultaneously, and by the principle of non-contradiction, the same thing cannot do contrary things at the same time; therefore, the soul must have more than one part. See also Thomas Aquinas, *Summa Theologica* qu. 8a2, II-I qu. 23a1.

The religious doctrine of the Savoyard Vicar, for example, contains a dualistic view of the soul based on just such reasoning: "In meditating on the nature of man I believed I discovered in it *two distinct principles*; one of which raised him to the study of eternal truths, to the love of justice and moral beauty, to the regions of the intellectual world whose contemplation is the wise man's delight; while the other took him basely into himself, subjected him to the empire of the senses and to the passions which are their ministers, and by means of these hindered all that the sentiment of the former inspired in him. In sensing myself carried away and caught up in the combat of these *two contrary motions*, I said to myself, 'No, *man is not one*'. . . . let him who regards man as a *simple being* overcome these contradictions, and I shall no longer acknowledge more than one substance" (*Emile* IV: 278-79, emphasis added; see *Beaumont*, 936). Rousseau's own belief in man's natural unity involves a rejection of the higher element postulated here and in most earlier views. Man is naturally asocial, amoral, and unmetaphysical: he simply loves himself (*Emile* IV: 213).

the means required to secure it in society. This process of "soul division" is best examined first on the individual or psychological level, and only later on the political level, where the "contradiction of society" can be viewed more comprehensively as the cause not only of psychic disunity but of social injustice.

The Origin of Disunity from Personal Dependence

As described in the *Second Discourse*, the development of disunity of soul essentially involves two steps: the loss of self-sufficiency due to the rise of unnatural desires; then the loss of unity through the growth of dependence on other human beings. In the first stage of the state of nature, man's desires, limited to those for food, sleep, and sex, were well within the reach of his natural powers, making him self-sufficient and one. But the invention of permanent huts, what Rousseau calls the "first revolution," eventually gave rise to new comforts and needs, to the family, love, and loose tribal society, and to the first developments of language, reason, and *amour-propre*. The emergence of these new desires made it increasingly difficult for men to maintain their primitive self-sufficiency.

Nevertheless, this "tribal" stage, during which men still managed to remain self-sufficient, constituted a "golden mean between the indolence of the primitive state and the petulant activity of our vanity [*amour-propre*]" (*SD*, 150-51). Men had now become somewhat vengeful and cruel toward enemies and had slightly compromised their perfect, animal-like unity of inclination, but these evils were more than compensated for by the greater development of their faculties, the elevation of their sentiments, and their rudimentary social contacts based on pure affection or identification (as distinguished from mutual need). These changes clearly increased their capacity to "feel life," and therefore Rousseau praises the tribal stage (and by no means the primitive state of nature, as is sometimes thought) as "the best for man," "the happiest and most durable epoch," and "the veritable prime of the world" (*SD*, 151).[2]

This happy condition continued, Rousseau maintains, for as long as men applied themselves "only to tasks that a *single person* could do and to arts that

---

[2] See *Emile* II: 80; *Beaumont*, 936-37; *Frags.*, 476-78; *GM* I-2: 158-59. It is often thought that Rousseau considers *amour-propre* by itself to be the direct cause of disunity, as he seems to assert in a number of passages (see *SD*, 179, 222; *Emile* IV: 213-14; *Dialogues* I: 669). But it should be clear from his paean to the tribal savage, as well from his praise of Emile and of the patriotic citizen, that *amour-propre*, uncorrupted or rightly directed, is compatible with a high degree of unity (although incompatible with the perfect animal unity that natural man possessed and to which the solitary dreamer aspires in a way to return). *Amour-propre* is in fact "the first and most natural of all the [acquired] passions" (*Emile* III: 208), and although it certainly plays a very great role in man's corruption, if it were identical to man's evil, there would be very little left to Rousseau's assertion of man's natural goodness, and no hope at all for his return to goodness. The excessive emphasis on *amour-propre* has tended to obscure the true villain of Rousseau's analysis, "personal dependence." (The interesting study by Charvet [1974], for example, suffers from this defect.)

did not require the *cooperation* of several hands." Eventually, however, there occurred the most fateful event of human history, the beginning of all evil, the true Fall: "the moment one man *needed the help* of another." This fatal moment, which "ruined the human race," came with the second "revolution": the development of the division of labor as a result of the invention of agriculture and metallurgy (*SD*, 151-52, emphasis added). This great change brought others in its wake: the establishment of private property, labor, inequality, the perfection of the faculties, the heightening of *amour-propre*, constant conflict, the creation of the state—the third "revolution"—and its decline into despotism (*SD*, 152-78). But all of these evils have at their heart the initial condition that first led to their development: the dependence of one human being upon another human being, what Rousseau calls "personal dependence." For reasons to be considered later, Rousseau sees a great difference, indeed a diametrical opposition, between needing others and loving them. And he regards the advent of this new human relation, mutual need, as the true source of all man's injustice and disunity of soul.[3]

One is struck by the radical simplicity of Rousseau's claim. How could needing and helping others, the most elemental social phenomenon, be the root of all human evil? Rousseau's general thesis is that personal dependence is self-contradictory, and that the disunity of man's soul arises from the internalization of this contradiction. But to understand this thesis let us begin further back with the general phenomenon of man's use of means, of which the dependence on other human beings is just a special case.

The lower animals have their needs and they pursue them directly. And like a lion lunging after its prey, if they fail to attain their object, then they soon stop and give up completely, resigned to necessity and restored themselves. Indeed, animals can scarcely conceive of any other course of action. But men, as soon as their minds develop, begin to turn their attention to the pursuit of "means," of things not good in themselves but useful for the acquisition of future goods. This indirect approach to the satisfaction of our desires is capable of taking on a life of its own, alienating us from our true needs and from ourselves.[4]

---

[3] That the agricultural revolution was the decisive event in the development of civilization and the state is generally accepted today, as is the view that this progress beyond primitive society brought a tremendous increase in inequality, war, and oppression. All the early civilizations seem to have been horribly despotic. There is no widely accepted explanation of these changes, however, but a Marxist variation on Rousseau's argument has enjoyed considerable popularity. See Fried (1967) and, for a critique, Service (1975) and Haas (1982). See Sagan (1985) for a Freudian interpretation.

[4] Hobbes sees this capacity to be concerned with means as such, to consider an object from the point of view of all the things that might be done with it, as the distinctive faculty of the human mind. See *Leviathan* III: 29. See Strauss (1959, p. 176n) on the central importance of this point for Hobbes's thought.

Dependence on external means of any kind—a knife, a bow, a pair of shoes—alienates us in some degree from ourselves. Rousseau emphasizes that only natural man, naked and free, has the experience of "constantly having all of one's strength at one's disposal . . . of always carrying oneself, so to speak, entirely with one" (*SD*, 107; see *Emile* III: 176). The problem with external means is not just that they are separable from us but *intractable*: using them always involves at least a momentary abandonment of our natural inclination and end while we obey the laws that govern the functioning of the means. To control, we must obey. As technology becomes more complex and demanding, especially after the fatal invention of agriculture, this "obedience to the means" begins seriously to compromise our freedom and unity. In a word, it becomes "work." Rousseau emphasizes that man has a "mortal hatred . . . of continuous labor"—a *mortal* hatred because work begins man's Fall from the fullness of existence in depriving him of repose, in postponing his existence and dividing him from himself (*SD*, 118; see 179, 208; *Dialogues* II: 823). Men had to be broken in over a long period of time before they would submit to the yoke of continuous labor.

Why, then, do men continue their obedience to the means if it so clearly contradicts their end? The answer lies in the vast new needs they acquire at the same time, partly from imagination, which suggests new pleasures and delights, and partly from *amour-propre,* which pushes them to surpass the accomplishments and power of others. But there is also a self-contradiction in the very pursuit of means that makes it self-sustaining. The power needed to acquire, protect, and use a means is often greater than, or at least different from, the power one acquires *from* the means, so that the acquisition of means or power actually increases one's need for power. For instance, in seeking power we acquire things; in acquiring things we extend ourselves; in extending ourselves we increase our insecurity, hence our need for power. Consequently, once a man begins to acquire means, he cannot stop; he is drawn into a self-perpetuating quest for ever more power. Rousseau's point, in other words, is similar to Hobbes's most famous psychological tenet:

> I put for a general inclination of all mankind, a perpetual and restless desire of power after power, that ceaseth only in death. And the cause of this, is not always that a man hopes for a more intensive delight, than he has already attained to; or that he cannot be content with a moderate power: but because he cannot assure the power and means to live well, which he hath present, without the acquisition of more.[5]

The pursuit of means is self-contradictory, hence self-sustaining and endless. Rousseau simply adds to Hobbes's observation that because it is

[5]*Leviathan* XI: 80.

self-sustaining, requiring constant obedience to the means, it alienates us from and contradicts our original end.[6]

The contradiction of power does not fully come into play, however, unless the means we seek to use are human beings, the most uncontrollable of all objects. As we have seen, Rousseau's theory of self-love, with its emphasis on the "power of the inner," on man's radical asociality and self-enclosedness, leads him to a strong belief in man's intractability. It is almost impossible to control or use human beings, to externally compel their genuine cooperation or obedience. "Nothing is less stable among men," Rousseau insists, "than those external relationships which . . . are called weakness or power, wealth or poverty" (*SD*, 97; see 107; *GM* I-2: 158; *PE*, 216). Always unstable, power over men endlessly begets a need for more power. It is above all *social* means, personal dependence, then, that is self-contradictory. Only by an all-consuming and endless attention to others can one succeed in getting them to serve oneself.

This is Rousseau's crucial new insight, and he sees its application everywhere. Even if it is only a small child one is trying to control, he warns prospective tutors: "The master commands and believes he governs. It is actually the child who govern . . . she always knows how to make you pay a week of obligingness for an hour of assiduity" (*Emile* II: 119-20). More generally, he shows how men's selfish need for the services of others makes them "anxious to oblige one another from dawn to dark" (*FD*, 39). Their very selfishness forces them into an insincere "sociability" and "selflessness." Of course, some men acquire a direct power over men below them, but usually only by submitting to the power of those above them: "A little parvenu gives himself a hundred masters to acquire ten valets" (*Montagne* VIII: 842n). And even at the top of the hierarchy, one finds that rulers and tyrants too are slaves of their power, spending all their days trying to protect it. "Whoever is master cannot be free, and to reign is to obey. Your Magistrates know that better than anyone, they who like Othon omit no servility in order to command" (*Montagne* VIII: 841-42; see *SD*, 173; *Dialogues* II: 891; *Reveries* VI: 83-84). The tyrant may appear to be free and powerful since he frequently makes others do what they do not want to do; but in fact he is enslaved, for, to keep and use this "power," he must constantly do what *he* does not want. The famous declaration that Rousseau places at the beginning of the *Social Contract*, often dismissed as idle rhetoric or construed as proto-Kantian moralism, is in fact a precise formulation of this crucial social-psychological contradiction: "One who believes himself the master of others is nonetheless a greater slave than they."

---

[6] Rousseau's familiar formula "all wickedness comes from weakness" is merely another way of stating that evil derives from man's fall into the world of means (*Emile* I: 67; see IV: 282, 282n; *Reveries* VI: 81-82; *SD*, 129). The whole of Marx's thought is nothing but an elaboration of this central idea that the human soul, in its historical fragmentation and alienation, has been produced by the contradictions inherent in the use of means.

Rousseau's clearest statement of the contradiction and of its central importance for his thought occurs in *Emile*:

> Your freedom and your power extend only as far as your natural
> strength, and not beyond. All the rest is only slavery, illusion and
> deception. Even *domination is servile* when it is connected with
> opinion. . . . To lead [others] *as you please* you must conduct
> yourself *as they please*. . . . Never will your real authority go
> farther than your real faculties. . . . Take everything, usurp every-
> thing; and then pour out handfuls of money, set up batteries of
> cannon, erect gallows and wheels, give laws and edicts, multiply
> spies, soldiers, hangmen, prisons, chains. Poor little men, what does
> all that do for you? You will be neither better served, nor less robbed,
> nor less deceived, nor more absolute. You will always say, "*We want*,"
> and you will always do *what the others want*.
>
> The only one who does his own will is he who, in order to do it,
> has no need to put *another's arms* at the end of his own; from which
> it follows that the first of all goods is not authority but freedom. The
> truly free man wants only what *he* can do and does what he pleases.
> That is my *fundamental maxim*. (*Emile* II: 83-84, emphasis added)[7]

Mastery is slavery, for to command one must obey. Based on his premise of
man's utter intractability, Rousseau argues that all personal dependence, all
social power, all efforts to rely on or use other men is self-contradictory and
enslaving.[8]

And that is truly Rousseau's "fundamental maxim" because it shows that
man's Fall did indeed occur at "the moment one man needed the help of
another." It demonstrates how personal dependence has enslaved all civilized
men and eventually destroyed the unity of their souls.

Yet this famous accusation that all men in society are "slaves" brings to a
head what would seem to be the questionableness of Rousseau's whole
argument. One is inclined to say that whatever discomfort Rousseau himself
may have felt in the drawing rooms of eighteenth-century Paris, the average
person does not feel enslaved by his "personal dependence." And why should
he? If he depends on the good will of others, is their good will so hard to obtain?
Or if he endeavors to manipulate and use others, is that task really so onerous
and difficult as to be enslaving? Isn't it in fact quite enjoyable, at least for those
skilled at it, those combining the courage and cleverness extolled by the likes

---

[7] Regarding the futility of wealth, and the enslavement of the rich man to his riches, see
Emile I: 56, IV: 345-54.

[8] Rousseau's fundamental maxim can be seen as a radicalization of the classical critique
of the tyrant: he is a slave of his power, which is dangerously unstable, and must spend all his
time protecting his position and his life against his ubiquitous enemies (see Plato *Republic*
578c-580a and Xenophon *Hiero*). The "radicalization" results from Rousseau's belief that
every form of social power, and not just tyranny, is unstable owing to man's natural asociality
and intractability.

of Thrasymachus? Finally, if the pursuit of social power were as self-defeating and enslaving as Rousseau claims, men would long ago have seen this and given it up.

Rousseau expects this very objection, however, for it is just what men would say if they were such as he believes them to be. Yes, you men in society do not feel your enslavement, Rousseau's argument continues, but only because you have internalized it. From infancy you have felt the necessity of serving and manipulating others to satisfy your own selfish desires so that long before you could understand what was happening to you, you became broken in and "socialized." And even now, you sense on the deepest level of your being that you could not last two days without the help of others, without the food, shelter, and clothing that you yourself do not produce. You know that your life is not in your own hands. Consequently, while you remain fundamentally selfish, your life and death dependence on other human beings has molded your habits so that you instinctively act as society requires. Unlike the patriotic citizen, you do not genuinely love and live for society, which remains for you a mere means. But it is a means so necessary and general as to be more important to you than any momentary and particular selfish end. Thus your very selfishness has trained you to serve society eagerly and habitually if ultimately insincerely.

Desiring to serve, you social men no longer feel how enslaved you are by your self-defeating dependence on society. "It is the same for freedom as for innocence and virtue—their value is felt only as long as one enjoys them oneself, and the taste for them is lost as soon as one has lost them" (*SD*, 164). Only men of unbroken unity of soul, like the savage and like Rousseau, recognize, suffer under, and flee the enslavement of society and power. "What a sight the difficult and envied labors of a European minister are for a Carib? How many cruel deaths would that indolent savage not prefer to the horror of such a life" (*SD*, 179). But you civilized men, broken and tamed, cannot see the horror. Having long since fallen from the plenitude of uncompromised unity and selfhood, you no longer remember or regret what you have lost in submitting to the yoke of your social position and power.[9]

The contradiction of personal dependence, then, has enslaved social men although they do not feel it; and the internalization of their enslavement—which prevents them from feeling it—splits their souls. Here, then, is the true source of disunity. Man does not have within him two naturally distinct and conflicting elements. Rather he has internalized the contradiction of personal dependence, through which the force of his unitary self-love is made to push against itself, end against means. He is divided between his selfish desires and

---

[9] "There are few men with hearts healthy enough to know how to love liberty" (*Montagne* VIII: 842n). Consider also the epigraph that Rousseau chose for the *First Discourse* and again for *Rousseau Juge de Jean-Jacques*: "Here I am the barbarian because no one understands me." A sense of futility is a constant undertone in Rousseau's rhetoric and is responsible for much of its shrillness, for he knows that precisely if what he is saying is correct then no one will understand or believe him.

the internalized need "selflessly" to serve others which that very selfishness produces. His soul is divided by a *selfish selflessness*.

This derivation of disunity of soul from personal dependence—the veritable centerpiece of Rousseau's thought—can be made somewhat more concrete if we consider more closely the selfishly motivated service to others that social man is required to perform. As compared to later thinkers, Rousseau makes remarkably little mention of the "problem of work," that is, the one-dimensional and deforming jobs men must perform in order to fit themselves into the economy. He is concerned rather with the destruction of men's unity of inclination resulting from the deforming moral and social postures men must assume to fit into society. As Rousseau points out in the most famous item on his "list of accusations," social men are forced to become actors and hypocrites, constantly hiding their true feelings. "Incessantly politeness requires, propriety demands; incessantly usage is followed, never one's own inclinations" (*FD*, 38). One must find out what qualities bring honor and influence. "It is necessary to have them or affect them; for one's own advantage it was necessary to appear to be other than what one in fact was, to be and to seem became two altogether different things" (*SD*, 155).

This split between being and seeming, inner and outer, is the most profound form of the disunity of inclination afflicting civilized men. The dissimulation required is not an occasional lie, nor the sort of deceit that can be undertaken in a calculated, detached, and self-possessed manner. Rather it is the full-time "role" men unconsciously adopt through socialization, the ingrained pretense to concern for others and to "respectability" that makes one an accepted member of society (see *OC* IV: 56, variant b). Social man—needing sustenance and security, desiring honor, and caught up in the self-augmenting pursuit of power—is in a position of utter dependence on society, a dependence he is scarcely aware of because he feels it so constantly and deeply. His dissimulation is correspondingly deep, requiring him to falsify his inner life to the point where he hardly has desires and beliefs of his own. He passes his life claiming to others and to himself that he cares about what he does not care about, feels what he does not feel, and believes what he does not believe. He somehow realizes all the while the falseness of his inner life because he feels within himself the readiness to change in the face of changed social circumstances. But he no longer knows how to find his true cares, feelings, and beliefs. Due to his role-playing he has lost his natural self, but he *is* not his role. He is neither himself nor what he pretends to be; therefore, he is nothing. He does not live, he only pretends to live.

> Everything being reduced to appearances, everything becomes factitious and deceptive: honor, friendship, virtue, and often even vices, about which men finally discover the secret of boasting; in a word, always asking others what we are and never daring to question ourselves on this subject, in the midst of so much philosophy, humanity, politeness, and sublime maxims, we have only a deceitful and frivolous exterior. (*SD*, 180; see *Dialogues* II: 818)

All that remains inside of men is the general or formal selfishness of the pursuit of power, while the positive, concrete notion of who they are and what they want has been yielded up for use as a means for the manipulation of others.[10]

It is important to notice in this portrait of the divided civilized man that it is not his social conformism as such but its root in personal dependence that is the cause of his disunity; for the patriotic citizen, who is no less "conformist," is not divided. The difference between them is that the citizen *loves* his fellow-citizens and does not *need* them; therefore, he is sincere and internally unified because his desire to serve others in order to win their honor and affection coincides with his genuine love and concern for them. But the "selfless devotion" to others of the ordinary social man—his politeness, conformism, and respectability—is merely the contradictory, hence insincere and divisive, product of his selfishness. It is a *selfish* selflessness. He is divided between his selfish ends of security, honor, and power and the endless, all-consuming, and insincere "services" to others made necessary by his very selfishness, by his devouring need to use these intractable human beings as means.

Loving Others versus Needing Them

This summary, with its contrast between the citizen and the social man, brings to the fore the fundamental (and questionable) presupposition of Rousseau's argument: the radical opposition between loving others and needing them that forms the ground of his peculiar concept of "personal dependence." By "loving" others is meant caring for them in some sense for their own sake; whereas "needing" men is caring for them as a means to one's own narrow self-interest, to one's honor or profit. (Of course, in a larger sense, to love someone is to need them, but this need of the heart is essentially different from the exclusive, selfish need at issue here.)

The traditional view of this question is that human beings are by nature social, so that their material need of one another is also a source of genuine gratitude, respect, and love. Needing others and loving them naturally go together, and this combined relationship forms the basis not only of private friendships but also, when elaborated through the division of labor, of the larger political order. Personal dependence, on this view, can be a source of genuine social harmony.

Rousseau does not deny that within the family and among lovers and friends, needing and loving can go together, but he cautions against the traditional error of taking these lesser societies as models for the greater. Outside this charmed circle, men are fundamentally selfish, lacking the natural sociality that leads to gratitude or to love of the larger, mutually beneficial order. The only other principle of human nature recognized by Rousseau is a capacity for "identification," which, under the right circumstances, allows men to expand their self-love over others. The combination of these two premises results in Rousseau's unique concep-

---

[10] The resulting human type is nicely described by Allan Bloom (1979, p. 5): "He is the man who, when dealing with others, thinks only of himself, and on the other hand, in his understanding of himself, thinks only of others."

tion of loving and needing as opposite, mutually exclusive tendencies (*Emile* IV: 213, 234; *PE*, 209-11; *Reveries* VI: 74-78).

Where men do not need they can love, Rousseau maintains, because the strength and wholeness of independence is what spurs them to expand their beings, and the equality of independence inclines them to identify with one another.[11] Moreover, mutual love tends to exclude mutual need, for it inhibits men from taking the fatal first step in the self-augmenting pursuit of social means.

But as soon as one man needs the help of another and looks upon him as a useful object, the bond of identification is broken, the positive energy of self-reliance is lost, and love disappears. Then all that remains to determine their relations is pure selfishness. One man needs the other, but has no loving desire to give help in return, nor does the other have a desire to help him. Their selfish interests may coincide in a few respects, but they will conflict in many more. Therefore, their relation of dependence necessarily tends toward enmity and exploitation. The more desperately each man depends on the services of others, the more he must be driven to wish—if only secretly and, as it were, against his will—that the others serve him without reciprocity, that they be his slaves. Of course, the need for others may begin moderately enough, but it necessarily feeds on and augments itself owing to its self-contradictoriness. Consequently, "the moral picture, if not of human life, at least of the secret pretensions of the heart of every civilized man," Rousseau claims, is to be "the sole master of the universe" (*SD*, 195). Needing others—personal dependence—necessarily destroys every vestige of love and becomes a purely exploitative relation.[12]

Thus, once again it is the premise of man's radical selfishness and asociality, as well as of man's natural intractability, that leads Rousseau to his central argument, which is somewhat shocking to common sense as well as to most earlier thought: his claim that loving and needing others are opposites and that all human evil began at "the moment one man needed the help of another."

[11] *Emile* IV: 229, 235n; *Poland* IV: 966; *Corsica*, 914-15. Rousseau's view culminates in the claim that "one is truly sociable only to the extent that one loves to live alone" (*Art de Jouir*, *OC* I: 1175).

[12] It is this reasoning that also leads to what Rousseau calls his "great precept of morality, but destructive of all social order, to never place oneself in a situation of being able to find one's advantage in the harm of others" (*Dialogues* II: 824; see *Mals.*, 1137; *SD*, 133, 194). For example, "Two years ago Lord Marshal [Keith] wished to place me in his will. I opposed this with all my strength. I told him that I would not for anything in the world know that I was named in anyone's will, and even less in his." This precept, he continues, "is true philosophy, the only one really suited to the human heart. Every day I penetrate further into its profound solidity and I have examined it in different ways in all my recent writings" (*Confs.* II: 56).

The Contradiction of Society

Having seen on the psychological level the process through which the individual is corrupted through personal dependence, we can turn to a more political and synoptic view of Rousseau's theory of the "contradiction of society" as the source not only of psychic disunity but of social injustice. Based on his strong distinction between loving others and needing them, Rousseau identifies two fundamentally different kinds of society: one based on the social bond of mutual love, identification, or patriotism; the other based on mutual need, personal dependence, or enlightened self-interest. For reasons we have just seen, these two social bonds, and the two kinds of society based on them, tend to be mutually exclusive: "For it is indeed impossible to tighten one of these bonds," Rousseau asserts, "without having the other relax by as much" (*Narcissus*, 105n).

The first kind of society is found, according to Rousseau, in two very different historical conditions: in the primitive, tribal stage of history, prior to the fatal invention of the division of labor, and also later, in those rare places like Rome and Sparta where the perfection of the art of legislation has led to the creation of a genuine city united by militant patriotism. The second, self-interested kind of society exists wherever tribal societies have decayed and imperfect states been established—which is to say, more or less everywhere in civilized times. Accordingly, when Rousseau makes his various claims about "society," he means the latter kind of society.

Rousseau also speaks of "modern" or "bourgeois" society, which is defined by the most extreme predominance of the bond of personal dependence and self-interest. In Rousseau's view this exaggerated reliance on self-interest has been produced by the conscious efforts of modern philosophers, motivated by their individualistic and materialistic theories and their anticlerical intentions. Hence, Rousseau's general thesis that "society" is contradictory and corrupting is also intended as a particular attack on modern bourgeois society and on the Enlightenment philosophers who helped to create it.

Rousseau states his insight into the contradiction of society (and especially of modern society) perhaps most forcefully in the preface to *Narcissus*.

> Of all the truths I submitted to the judgement of the wise, this is the most arresting and the most cruel. All our writers regard the crowning achievement of our century's politics to be the sciences, the arts, luxury, commerce, laws, and all the other bonds which, by tightening the knots of society among men through *self-interest*, place them all in a position of *mutual dependence*, impose on them *mutual needs* and common *interests*, and oblige everyone to contribute to everyone else's happiness in order to secure his own. These are certainly fine ideas, and they are presented in a favorable light. But when they are examined carefully and impartially, the advantages which they seem at first to hold out prove to be open to considerable criticism.
>
> It is quite a wonderful thing, then, to have placed men in a position where they cannot possibly live together without obstructing,

supplanting, deceiving, betraying, destroying one another! From now on we must take care never to let ourselves be seen such as we are: because for every two men whose interests coincide, perhaps a hundred thousand oppose them, and the only way to succeed is either to deceive or to ruin all those people. That is the fatal source of the violence, the betrayals, the deceits and all the horrors necessarily required by a state of affairs in which everyone pretends to be working for the others' profit or reputation, while only seeking to raise his own above them and at their expense. (*Narcissus*, 105)[13]

Beneath the apparent order of society and the high-culture that adorns it, men falsify and divide themselves in order to manipulate and exploit others.

The simple cause of all this evil is the fundamental contradiction on which society is based. The *essence* of society is to unite men through the contradiction of personal dependence, to derive men's selflessness and sociability from their very selfishness. This social bond does indeed hold men together, but because it is a contradiction, it puts men in conflict with others and with themselves, it generates both injustice and disunity. Let us consider each in turn.

"Our needs bring us together in proportion as our passions divide us, and the more we become enemies of our fellow men, the less we can do without them" (*GM* I-2: 158). Society rests upon our selfish needs, and, by stimulating *amour-propre* and the self-augmenting pursuit of power, it infinitely increases them. Needing to use others, wishing secretly to enslave them if we could, and also being in competition with them, we become their enemies. Yet, though we are enemies, we cannot separate, for our *need* of each other is precisely what makes us enemies. The more we are enemies the closer we are bound together. As a result, society is nothing but a system for secret exploitation. It drives us simultaneously toward and away from others, binding us together by making us opposed; it thus organizes us for mutual crime and injustice.

Looked at from the other side of the contradiction, society drives us simultaneously toward and away from *ourselves.* By increasing our selfishness it makes us love others less, but need them more. And given the natural intractability of man, to control others we must abandon ourselves. Lacking the force truly to enslave others or to be unjust all the time, we must become "sociable" and polite, we must slavishly court, deceive, and manipulate others. These activities are all forms of selfish selflessness, and that is the contradiction of inclination generated by society. Social man spends his life serving others precisely because he cares only about himself.

In sum, due to the contradiction of society—of sociability produced from selfishness—man is "good neither for himself nor for others." Because he is sociable as well as selfish, he lacks unity; because selfish as well as sociable,

---

[13] See *FD*, 51; *SD*, 156, 172-75, 193-95; *Beaumont*, 936; *PE*, 216-17. For a discussion of this passage and related ideas, see Keohane (1978) and Lovejoy (1961) pp. 153-215.

he lacks justice. Injustice and disunity are two sides of the same coin, and society—based on the contradiction of personal dependence—is the cause of both.

The Natural Goodness of Man

This simple but ingenious theory of society, this discovery of the "hidden contradiction" of personal dependence, is, by Rousseau's testimony, the great realization that caused him to embrace his principle in the "illumination of Vincennes" (*Mals.*, 1135-36; *Beaumont*, 966-67). It enabled him to go beyond the general historical hypothesis that some vague "something" in the rise of artificial society might have corrupted man, to point to a specific process still going on before our eyes that explains the genesis of both injustice and disunity, the precise evils afflicting civilized men in Rousseau's new analysis. This discovery is also what sets Rousseau apart from the pastoral poets and philosophic primitivists of the past by demonstrating that primitives are good and civilized men bad not because society merely occasions the development of man's latent evil, but because the contradiction of society imposes on man an alien deformity. Finally, this theory forms the basis of the whole "constructive" part of Rousseau's thought, which seeks ways to cure men's deformity. Rousseau's social argument, in short, is the core of his proof for the natural goodness of man and the true centerpiece of his thought.

This conclusion is supported by the fact that the social argument embraces the curious double movement of thought—"idealistic realism"—that, as suggested at the beginning, characterizes Rousseau's philosophy on the broadest level. The first tendency of his mind is one of realism and bitter skepticism, questioning the value of society and civilization with all their lofty pretensions to tame, moralize, and elevate man. Rousseau pushes this skepticism beyond the commonplace doubts as to whether society fully lives up to its claims, pushes it to the realization that this noble institution is positively harmful, and that by virtue of its inner contradiction it is in fact the hidden cause of all the evils it claims to cure. Through this initial movement of skepticism and cynicism, Rousseau shifts all the blame for man's present evil onto society itself, and by doing so he "idealistically" exculpates human nature, showing it to be good and indeed a possible basis for the happiness and benevolence that had formerly been hoped for from society. Thus the central argument of Rousseau's thought has the precise structure of "idealistic realism": its extreme skepticism directed at the noble and "high"—its revelation of the corrupting "contradiction of society"—leads to a radical new idealism regarding the "low"—the instinctive, primitive, inner, natural goodness of man.

We have now seen the four arguments plus the characterization of human evil that together constitute Rousseau's proof for the natural goodness of man. One cannot but be struck, as Rousseau no doubt was, by the neatness with which all the parts fit together and reinforce each other, by the elegant coherence of the whole. The fundamental assumption running throughout is that man is by nature a highly asocial, self-sufficient, inwardly contented animal. This assumption, revealed by Rousseau's introspection and elaborated by his psychological theory, supplies the positive content of man's goodness. It also encourages Rousseau to define human evil in terms of the lack of formal unity rather than the lack of conformity to some substantive end established by nature or God. It leads him to regard the formation of civilized society as an epoch-making transformation of man's natural environment. Finally, it underlies his theory of the self-contradictoriness of "personal dependence" and his argument that society, based on this contradiction, is the true source of injustice and disunity—of all human evil as he has just redefined it.

Despite this internal coherence, however, the basic assumption of man's extreme asociality is never really established and it strikes one today, as it did most premodern thinkers, as difficult to sustain. Nevertheless, we will be in a better position to evaluate the validity of the principle of natural goodness after we have seen it in action: seen what it is able to explain, what insights it opens up, what reforms it calls for, what events it predicts—in short, seen its consequences.

The Human Problem

By presenting a new characterization of man's evil as well as a new explanation of its origin or cause, Rousseau's principle of natural goodness amounts to a fundamental redefinition of the human problem. Before turning to the solution Rousseau proposes and the other consequences of his principle, it would be useful to conclude by characterizing somewhat further the epoch-making changes Rousseau has wrought in our conception of the human problem.

In general, by arguing that all evil arises from the corrupting effects of artificial society, Rousseau transforms the human problem into a merely social or historical issue where before it had been thought to be a natural or divine one. The ambiguous effects that this great change has had on politics have already been mentioned—the raising of energetic but dangerous new hopes that through political action one might transform the human condition itself.

But now that we have seen precisely where Rousseau's principle locates the social source of evil, we can see its more specific consequences. Evil derives from "personal dependence," and therefore from those political conditions that especially embody or produce dependence; namely, inequality, oppression, and servitude, to use these terms in their broadest sense. Hence Rousseau declares: "I hate servitude as the source of *all the evils* of the human race" (*Beaumont*, Fragment, 1019, emphasis added). This is an extraordinary and fateful declaration.

No one would deny that servitude and oppression are among the evils men face. But are they the only ones, as Rousseau boldly declares here? Most thinkers have answered emphatically: No. For corruption of character, the sickness of the soul, is certainly an evil different from oppression of the body, and indeed greater than it. Furthermore, the evils of the soul tend not only to eclipse those of the body but even to counteract their importance, because, in the complexity of the human condition, the task of eliminating the soul's evil is often in direct conflict with the elimination of bodily evil or oppression. The Old Testament would seem to suggest, and the New Testament to insist, that the experience of servitude is an important condition for moral development. Indeed, Rousseau goes so far as to assert: "Christianity preaches nothing but servitude and dependence. . . . True Christians are made to be slaves" (*SC* IV-8: 130). In one degree or another, the monotheistic religions have taught that the mortification of the flesh plays an important part in the purification of the soul.

Among classical thinkers, too, the perfection of the soul was thought to require some kind of servitude, although not one's own. Almost all ancient philosophers expressed a preference for aristocracy, despite its obvious oppressive tendencies, because, in order for at least some men to be able to acquire and exercise virtue, they must have the education, the leisure, and thus the wealth that (in preindustrial times) can be secured only through the relative servitude of a large lower class. And even those ancient philosophers who praised, or cities that established, democracies, never seriously questioned the necessity of slavery.

To make the point more broadly, the biblical and classical traditions, despite their great differences, agreed that the human condition is tragically complex, that the various real goods of life do not fit together. It is often thought today that these earlier traditions were "tender-minded" (to return to William James's vocabulary), with their belief in divine or natural order, in contrast to the disillusioned tough-mindedness of contemporary thought. But that is to miss the quiet, stern, unsentimental hardness of their view of life (as well as the tender idealism that lies beneath modern realism). Both earlier traditions, but especially the classical, emphasized that human life is characterized by certain permanent or at least humanly irresolvable tensions—whether between the good of the soul and of the body, or between the welfare of the few and the many, or between social justice and individual perfection.

This complex, qualified, conflicted attitude toward human affairs, and toward oppression or bodily suffering in particular, was first challenged in an open and unambiguous way by Thomas Hobbes, who indignantly dismissed all such exalted claims about man's need for moral or spiritual perfection as so many clever lies invented by ambitious elites in order to dominate and oppress the people. Without apology, he discarded all concern with the soul and reduced the complexity of human affairs to the simple, unitary goal of preserving men or preventing widespread violence and bodily harm.

Hobbes's preference for absolute monarchy as the best means to this goal made him many enemies, but the infamy attaching to his name also attests to the fact that this goal itself represents a forced and ugly simplification. It is unconvincing as well as degrading to regard the elimination of war or oppression as the sole end of life and to dismiss all concern with the dignity or perfection of the human soul as an irrational obstacle to the efficient protection of the body. For as loudly as violence and oppression may proclaim their evil, in the end one cannot escape the quiet fact that safety is not happiness and that a nation free of oppression can still be miserable or debased.

Here is where Rousseau enters with his fateful principle of natural goodness, which maintains precisely that nonoppression by itself *does* lead to happiness and health of soul, and which thus elevates Hobbes's simplification to include the exalted concerns of classical and Christian thought. When Rousseau declares that oppression or servitude is "the source of all the evils of the human race," he is not denying, as Hobbes is, the importance of that other and greater evil, corruption of soul, but rather tracing the cause of corruption back to oppression. "Dependence on men . . . engenders all the vices" (*Emile* II: 85). In this way, Rousseau unites into one the evils of soul and body. He thus renders Hobbes's ugly reductionism noble and comprehensive: he takes the *whole* human problem, in all its classical and biblical complexity, and reduces it to the problem of oppression.

In other words, the surface impression from which we began—that what is philosophically unique and historically momentous in Rousseau is a new level of concern with injustice and oppression, an urgent new demand for strict right—was not mistaken. Only this critical change must be properly understood. It does not result from some increased awareness or personal experience of the injustice of the world, as if this were not sufficiently known before. And it is not the product of an incipient Kantianism, a new, moralistic faith in justice as something necessary for its own sake regardless of consequences. Rather it is due precisely to a new analysis of the *psychic consequences* of injustice and oppression. Prior to Rousseau virtually all thinkers had, in a sense, granted something to the moral skepticism of Thrasymachus in their refusal simply to condemn oppression as the worst thing, in their quiet admission that strict justice is not the only or highest good. But Rousseau's theory of society constitutes the most thoroughgoing refutation of Thrasymachus, the greatest "critique of mastery," the most radical statement of the harmfulness of oppression and the goodness of justice, ever made. All corruption of soul, indeed "all the evils of the human race" result from oppression.

This revolutionary simplification of the human problem has had momentous consequences. It is moral and political dynamite. By breaking down the moderating complexity of classical thought while at the same time rising above the narrow and enervating simplicity of early modern thought, by replacing the seemingly permanent tension in human affairs between the goals of excellence and nonoppression with the unification and mutual reinforcement of these goals, by collecting and unifying all of life's disparate evils into one, single "enemy," Rousseau's simplification did much to produce the striking increase in moralistic passion and political urgency characteristic of later philosophy. More specifically, it marks the philosophical beginning of what may very generally be called the modern "left," the party of nonoppression, strict fairness, and equality. For it has enabled the left for the first time, not merely to combat, but to *take over* the issue of its traditional opponent, the Christian or aristocratic right, to add all of the grandeur and nobility of "human perfection" or "health of soul" to the urgency of nonoppression and, under this unified banner, to march forward unopposed (or, rather, opposed only by its less radical cousin, the liberal center, with its qualified defense of inequality based on economic efficiency and a less utopian, middle-class notion of virtue).[14] The ultimate expression of the process started by Rousseau is Marxism with its promise that merely by eliminating the exploitation of man by man the human problem will be permanently solved and all men will live in wholeness and completion.

Rousseau himself, however, cannot be said to have agreed with any of the movements to which his thought gave rise. He does not favor communism, socialism, or even liberal democracy. A very different solution is required, he thinks, for the problem he has elaborated.

---

[14] To the Catholic thinker Jacques Maritain, for example, the most striking and dangerous thing about Rousseau is his secular appropriation of Christian themes, his "mimicry of sanctity, changing of the heroic life into a religious enjoyment of self." "He turns our hunger for God towards the sacred mysteries of sensation, towards the infinite of matter." Rousseau "hallows the denial of grace" (1929, pp. 112, 115).

Part Three

The Consequences of
Rousseau's Principle

6

Curing Humanity:
Rousseau's Solutions

Rousseau seeks to heal the wound of civilization. Having discovered at last the true nature of the human sickness, he hopes to devise for the first time a genuine cure. It is a notorious fact, however, that Rousseau's constructive writings present not a single, clear solution but a complex array of puzzling and seemingly contradictory proposals. Yet, behind this appearance, there is a logic to Rousseau's solutions which can be discerned if one keeps in view his unique understanding of the problem.[1]

The General Character of Rousseau's Solutions

The first thing to notice about Rousseau's constructive thought is that it is not limited to securing men's minimum rights to life, liberty, and property, but includes the ultimate goals of justice and happiness. Believing that he has discovered the social origin of all evil, it is all evil that he seeks to cure. In this respect his thought breaks with the dominant tendency of early modern and liberal thought and returns to the loftier or more utopian ends of Christian and classical philosophy. Yet Rousseau undertakes this "return" precisely through a more advanced development of modern principles. This gives his quest for solutions a wholly unique character.

The evils of human life began with man's accidental departure from his natural state of animality and solitude. He is not Fallen but Risen. Thus, for Rousseau, the quest for happiness and the good life can no longer be understood as it had been by almost all previous philosophers: as a pursuit of the *natural* life for which man was made and "intended," the specific life to which his natural needs, instincts, and faculties all point. Having gone irrevocably beyond his natural life as an animal, man is now on his own, homeless and free, without nature or instinct to guide him, an accidental being who must try to invent an altogether new life and happiness for himself.

Similarly, Rousseau himself, "the philosopher," can no longer play the part

---

[1] We are concerned here with Rousseau's solutions in theory, that is, with his theoretical understanding of what would be required to cure men of the problem he has discovered. Only in chap. 13 will we address the practical questions of what specific reforms Rousseau believed possible in his own time and how he hoped to promote these reforms by means of his various writings.

of the reverent and contemplative wise man, pointing out to men their natural form, the path of life prepared for them by God or nature. He himself must break new paths. From now on, the philosopher must be an active and self-conscious creator, an artist of humanity and technician of the soul. In his search for solutions, he must invent new ways of arranging men's artificial needs, inclinations, and faculties to create new human beings with some new form of happiness.

But if man's natural life and constitution no longer serve as a standard, what is to guide this human engineering? If human beings are such malleable creatures who can be brought to desire almost anything, on what basis would one choose one way of life as preferable to another?

We know Rousseau's answer: lives are to be evaluated by their degree of existence, which is to say, by their measure of "extent" and especially of unity of soul. But this standard is a nonsubstantive or formal one. There is no particular right content to civilized man's life, no necessary objects of desire, no proper activity, no specific fulfillment. Any way of life of reasonable extent is good, regardless of content, provided only that it is internally consistent. Rousseau is the first thinker thus to complete man's liberation from God and nature: to abandon all substantive standards, natural or divine, and to replace them with the formal standard of psychic unity or noncontradiction.

With this in mind, we turn to Rousseau's particular proposals. If the contradiction of society, selfish selflessness, is what divides man against himself and others, then he can be restored to unity and justice by inducing him to embrace totally either side of the contradiction: complete selfishness or complete sociability. To eliminate divisive personal dependence men must be either wholly separated or wholly united. In more political terms: "Give [man] over entirely to the state or leave him entirely to himself, but if you divide his heart you will tear it" (*Frags.*, 510; see *Emile* I: 39-41).

Within the framework of all earlier forms of thought, recommending two antithetical ways of life as equally good would be a glaring contradiction. It makes sense only on Rousseau's new "coherence theory of happiness": any content will do so long as it is self-consistent. Thus, having reduced the human problem to the contradiction of personal dependence, Rousseau's constructive thought necessarily bifurcates into two conflicting ideals: extreme individualism and extreme collectivism—the only two paths, though opposite ones, to the single goal of unity.

This fundamental bifurcation can be found even in the character and self-presentation of Rousseau, who tried in some sense to live each of the opposite solutions. In some contexts we meet "*pauvre* Jean-Jacques," the solitary, self-absorbed, unique individual, whereas in others we meet "J. J. Rousseau, Citizen of Geneva," selfless patriot and courageous publicist.

Forming part of the two antithetical solutions, moreover, are also certain other, derivative antitheses that are found in Rousseau's writings: the praise of solitude and also the praise of community; of idleness and laziness and also of activity and vigor; of sincerity, naturalness, and spontaneity and also of self-conquest and social control; of sensitivity, gentleness, sentimentality, and compassion and also of manliness, courage, hardness, and patriotism; of the importance and essential equality of women and also of their complete disenfranchisement; of artistic creativity and also of moralistic opposition to the arts. The copresence of all these antitheses, which so many scholars have taken to represent a confusion, a contradiction, or a peculiar change of mind in Rousseau, are in fact just the opposite: the logical consequence of his analysis of society's contradiction and indeed a testament to the rigorous and unflinching consistency of his thought.

What Rousseau's two opposite ideals have in common may also be described as "freedom." The individualistic solution aims at what Rousseau will call "natural freedom," the collectivist, political solution, at a very different "civil and moral freedom." This unique emphasis has led many to identify Rousseau as the originator of the "philosophy of freedom" developed later by German Idealism.[2] He certainly was the first to regard freedom not merely as a by-product of the good life or as one precondition among many, but as its essential condition. There are two related reasons for this. First, for Rousseau the good life no longer consists in conformity to man's given, objective nature—with the ultimate renunciation of freedom implicit in such conformity—but in the attainment of a formal unity that man himself must freely invent. Second, he finds that unity is lost through personal dependence, especially as embodied in the social condition of inequality, oppression, or servitude; therefore, all restorations of unity must involve freedom. Having declared: "I hate servitude as the source of all the evils of the human race," it clearly follows, as he states elsewhere, that "the first of all goods is . . . freedom" (*Beaumont* Fragment, 1019; *Emile* II: 84).[3]

The Individualistic Solution

The most obvious and natural way to avoid the contradiction of society is through complete solitude. Rousseau elaborates this generally impractical solution primarily for the sake of a few rare individuals, although he also hopes that it will have the general effect of encouraging the provincial populations and others who already live in relative isolation to remain there and to resist the corrupting allure of city life.

With arguments reminiscent of the Stoics and other ancient moralists, Rousseau tries to instill in men a wise and disillusioned moderation that

---

[2] "The principle of freedom emerged in Rousseau" (Hegel, *Lectures on the Philosophy of History*, vol. III p. 402). See also Strauss (1953) pp. 278-79; Bosanquet (1965) pp. 218, 221; and Manent (1977) pp. 177-95.

[3] The Kantian interpretation of Rousseau, of course, explains his emphasis on freedom in terms of a new concern for moral autonomy. But such a concern cannot easily explain his praise of natural freedom and the idle, solitary life, or, more generally, the whole systematic bifurcation of his thought.

restrains their pursuit of means and detaches them from the false goods of society. But going beyond these earlier thinkers, Rousseau seeks to detach men from society itself, and to this end he draws upon the radical theoretical individualism at the root of his principle. Thus arises the "Romantic" Rousseau, who tries to turn men back on themselves, to make them more introspective and even narcissistic, to reorient them toward the world of the private, the intimate, and the emotional, to convince them of the sacredness of their individuality, the inviolability of the "self," and the importance of "freedom" understood as escape from society and convention. Similarly, through his descriptions and praise of wild nature, he tries to give men's hearts a new interest that frees them from their bonds to society and other men.

The highest and purest form of this individualistic solution is that lived (or aspired to) by Rousseau himself, the solitary artist and romantic dreamer. Having philosophized his way free of the false needs and hopes engendered by civilized life, the artist withdraws from society and lives in perfect independence or "natural freedom," as did primitive man. Restored in this way to his original goodness, he nourishes his unified soul on the sentiment of his own existence, while also occasionally expanding his existence over all of nature—as revealed to him by his developed mental faculties—and over the communities of kindred spirits painted for him in sweet reveries by his highly developed artistic imagination.

One major purpose of Rousseau's voluminous autobiographical writings—the *Confessions*, *Rousseau Judge of Jean-Jacques*, and especially the *Reveries of a Solitary Walker*—is to describe the character of this most unified and natural of civilized ways of life. They also describe the bizarre and unnatural conditions that were needed to create it: Rousseau's precocious sensuality, his illnesses and belief he would die young, his awkwardness in society, his long romantic involvement with his patroness (whom he called "mama"), the hostility toward him of all established parties, and so forth. If one begins within civilization, the road back to natural goodness, as these works present it, is almost insanely unconventional.

In *Emile*, Rousseau tries to formulate a less extreme if also less perfect form of the individualistic solution by showing how an ordinary child without philosophic genius, if raised from birth with the proper method, might attain a high degree of unity even within society. The education described in *Emile* is a true masterpiece of psychological engineering, an ingenious collection of strategies, schemes, and manipulative techniques designed to rearrange the elements of civilized man into a moral and harmonious whole. The crucial scheme at the heart of the education is to raise Emile in absolute and total "freedom"—while also controlling virtually everything he does. The tutor (Rousseau) never issues a single order or command but leaves Emile free to do as he likes, subject only to the constraints of his physical environment. Yet, by manipulating that environment behind the scenes, he secretly determines Emile's every experience and action. In this way, the wise tutor regulates the development of Emile's faculties and inclinations, while also keeping him free of all dependence. Growing up in a world strictly bounded by *things* but not by *wills*, Emile never learns to use and serve other men but only to recognize necessity and resign himself to it. Evil is thus eliminated at its source: from the start, Emile is prevented from getting caught up in the contradictory and self-augmenting pursuit of social means.

Rousseau's project, however, is to create a man who can live healthily even in society, so Emile cannot remain forever sheltered from personal contact and dependence, nor wholly free of *amour-propre* and the other dangerous desires that necessarily arise in society. Therefore Rousseau employs two further devices. While Emile is still detached from others and able to view them dispassionately, Rousseau teaches him to read hearts and to live in the world of private feelings rather than the false world of public claims. He shows Emile all the weakness that men hide behind their displays of pomp and cheer, and keeps constantly before Emile's eyes the image of human suffering. When Emile eventually enters society, then, his *amour-propre* is not inflamed by envy but rather soothed by—and even channeled into—*pity* for the misfortunes of others. Through this proud and generous compassion, Emile is inspired with a love for other men and with a distaste for the attempt to use them; and *amour-propre*, which is generally the greatest source of personal dependence, is in this way made to fight against it.[4]

The tutor also makes important use of another dangerous social passion: sexual desire. He delays, purifies, and elevates Emile's desires, directing them to an imaginary "Sophie," a perfect woman. The intense longings thus produced create in Emile an elevation of sentiment and a noble romanticism that keep him moderate, chaste, and detached from the imperfect objects of this world during this most turbulent, dependent, and potentially corrupting period of life. They also inspire within him a moral idealism, a love of goodness, virtue, and ultimately of God that remains with him for the rest of his life. Eventually Emile meets his virtuous Sophie, and thereafter his love of goodness is mingled with and supported by his desire to please her. They marry and raise their family in rustic retreat, protected by relative isolation, pity, love, and God from the need or inclination to depend on others.[5]

Although Rousseau's individualistic solutions have the distinct advantage of being more natural—more in accord with man's instinctive selfishness and individuality—they are possible (in their purity) only for a few isolated and rare human beings. One must either be a philosopher or be raised by one. To restore a whole society to goodness and unity, one must move in the opposite direction, to the collectivist ideal. Before attempting to analyze the highly legalistic and abstract doctrine through which Rousseau presents his political solution in the *Social Contract*—which will occupy us for the remainder of the

---

[4] On the general theme of compassion and Rousseau's pivotal role in elevating it to the central virtue of our time, see the excellent discussion by Orwin (1980).

[5] See the brilliant summary of *Emile* in Bloom (1979).

book—let us survey the most distinctive features of that solution to see how they follow systematically from the new definition of the human problem embodied in Rousseau's principle.[6]

The Political Solution

In Rousseau's system, if men cannot be completely separated, they must be completely united. They must never live with others while caring only for themselves. Hence the mission of the political solution is quite simply this: to find a form of association that completely eliminates man's natural selfishness and individuality, or, failing that, eliminates all of its effects.

The extreme unnaturalness of this collectivist enterprise is obvious from the start. For all their artificiality, the individualistic solutions still build on our spontaneous inclinations and, in promoting them, Rousseau can even make use of the rhetoric of "return to nature." But the political solution is not merely artificial or nonnatural but *anti*natural, requiring the wholesale remaking of human beings through social engineering. Rousseau's new formal standard of unity or noncontradiction gives him a standpoint outside of nature from which to call for its complete conquest.

One can understand on this basis the immoderate and radical, not to say totalitarian, tendency of Rousseau's thought. On his principles, successful political life is not the smooth and regular functioning of an organic community, but a state of permanent war against the strongest inclinations of an asocial and solitary animal. Radical expedients are required—a total denaturing environment—in order to keep such beings in a condition of communal mobilization.

The "antinatural" character of politics also helps to explain the general complexity and strangeness of Rousseau's proposals. There can be no simple, ready-made, "natural" means of combatting nature; one must fight a messy battle using every available means. In fact, Rousseau's political scheme can be seen as a combination of three more or less distinct lines of attack, which I will call the "psychological," the "political," and the "moral and religious." Treating each in turn, we can unfold Rousseau's political theory as a systematic, multilayered attack on human selfishness and individuality.

A. The Psychological Level

If we need to collectivize men completely, the most direct approach would be to alter their very psychology, to reprogram their minds and transform their inclinations. That is what Rousseau attempts on the first, psychological level. "Good social institutions," he declares, "are those that best know how to denature man, to take his absolute existence from him in order to give him a relative one and transport the *I* into the common unity, with the result that each

[6] As Iring Fetscher points out: "The essence of Rousseau's republic can be better understood if one starts from its *function*, its *purpose*, rather than from its formal structure as depicted in the *Contrat Social*" (quoted by Crocker [1968] p. 102).

individual believes himself no longer one but a part of the unity and no longer feels except within the whole" (*Emile* I: 40). Rousseau would uproot men's innate selfishness and merge them together like bees in a hive, so that, without the need for *political force* (the second level) and without the need for *moral self-conquest* (the third), they will spontaneously act as one.

What institutions are capable of producing such a psychological transformation? Clearly, the most important would be a rigorous public education that teaches and breeds patriotism. Education, Rousseau therefore declares, is "certainly the State's most important business" (*PE*, 223). His model here, as in most things, is Sparta "where the law attended principally to the education of children and where Lycurgus established morals which almost allowed him to dispense with adding laws" (*SD*, 173).

But if this education is really to take hold, if men are to live for the community not occasionally and halfheartedly but every day and without reserve, then certain "material" conditions are also necessary. For example, the community cannot be a sprawling mass-society, anonymous and abstract, like the modern nation-state, but must be, like the ancient city-state, "of a size limited by the extent of human faculties" so that the "sweet habit of seeing and knowing one another turn[s] love of the fatherland into love of the citizens" (*SD*, 79; see *SC* II-10: 74, III-13: 100). Similarly, the city must be fairly homogeneous so that there is a single community to love, and not a pluralistic collection of diverse ethnic groups or competing economic interest groups. Therefore, a developed, complex economy with a highly ramified division of labor should be avoided. Under most circumstances, a simple, agricultural economy is best. Above all, a relative equality of fortunes must be maintained to minimize class conflict, and sumptuary laws should be used to prevent the acute selfishness, rivalry, and personal dependence generated by luxury, "the worst of all evils in any state whatever" (*SD*, 199). Indeed, one should discourage the commercial spirit altogether, and, without promoting imperialism, one should foster "that warlike ardor and that spirited courage which suit freedom so well and whet the appetite for it" (*SD*, 81).

The spontaneous, all-encompassing communal feeling produced by these institutions will find its greatest expression in public festivals where "each sees and loves himself in the others." But even at other times, the citizens' days must be filled as much as possible with the public business, leaving no time for a dangerous idleness when people might begin to return to themselves (*d'Alembert*, 126; *Poland* II: 957-58). Finally, this public devotion, inherently fragile because contrary to nature, must be carefully protected through public censorship of the arts and sciences, or even their total elimination as private pursuits (*SC* IV-7: 123-24; *FD*, 36-37, 62-64).

If by these various social and economic arrangements one could actually remake men psychologically, then the contradiction of society would be altogether dissolved. No trace of selfish selflessness could exist where all were selflessly united, sharing a single, communal identity. No two men would ever confront each other as separate individuals. In the very midst of society, without the use of force of any kind, men would attain perfect unity of soul and perfect justice: they would be one with themselves in their complete, spontaneous oneness with others.

Such total psychological transformation is not possible, however, because nature cannot be wholly overcome. According to Rousseau, "art, which can disguise, bend, and even stifle nature, cannot change it altogether. It extends the germ of our passions rather than giving it a contrary direction as would be necessary to make us truly civil, that is to give us that civility of heart which would make us prefer others to ourselves" (*Emile* 1st version, *OC* IV: 56; see *GM* I-2: 158-60). No institutions can ever overcome the fact that men are distinct individuals, each with his own separate body, his own pleasure and pain, life and death. The problem of society, therefore, cannot be solved on the psychological level. Of course, it remains vitally important to pursue it as far as possible, but, do what one will, society will always fundamentally remain a union of separate, self-interested individuals.

B. The Political Level

Since eliminating all selfish inclinations is impossible, only one means remains of saving men from personal dependence: the external expression of these inclinations must be suppressed through *force*. That is the aim of the specifically political level of Rousseau's solution (and, in a different way, of the moral and religious level as well). Indeed, for this reason, the essence of politics (and morality), in Rousseau's view, is force.

How can it be good for men, however, to be *forced* against their natural inclinations? In the context of society, it must constantly be recalled, my own natural inclinations become harmful to me. To be free to follow my selfish interests in society—genuine though they may be—is bad for me, not only because others are then free to do the same at my expense, but also because then I begin to use others and get trapped in the contradiction of personal dependence. And no gains made by using others can possibly compensate me for the resulting loss of my freedom and unity of soul. Political rule, legitimate force, must thus be used to save me from myself, to free me from the dangers of my own inexpungeable selfishness.

In other words, within society, a general policy of selfishness (as distinguished from an isolated selfish act) is self-contradictory and enslaving; therefore, the *true* selfish interest of each man is that he—and all others—be made unselfish, by psychological transformation to the extent possible and, for the rest, by force. This is the meaning of Rousseau's infamous and paradoxical statement that the citizen "will be *forced* to be free. For this is the condition that . . . guarantees him against all personal dependence" (*SC* I-7: 55, emphasis added). If men were selfless by nature, then, within society, they might also be free by nature. But since they are naturally and unalterably selfish, they can be unified and free only through force.

Rousseau is thus a wholehearted "statist." By forcibly repressing (as well as partially transforming) man's natural selfishness, the legitimate state is the true and indispensable agent of man's salvation. "Only the force of the state," Rousseau flatly declares, "creates the freedom of its members" (*SC* II-12: 77).[7]

The state's saving mission is rendered extremely difficult, however, by the natural intractability of man, the tenacity and deviousness of human selfishness. Every society contains ambitious men of superior wealth, position, or intelligence who employ all their means to evade or undermine the state's force. It is necessary, therefore, to expand and protect the force of the state, to close every loophole through which it might be evaded, and remove every vantage point from which it might be attacked. That is why, in the *Social Contract*, Rousseau systematically removes literally every external limit on the force of the state, whether in the "private sphere" below it or the moral absolutes above. He argues that the sovereign power cannot be bound by a constitution or limited by natural law, that it is inalienable, indivisible, and infallible, that it possesses the right of life and death, and in short, that the sovereign power is "entirely absolute, entirely sacred, and entirely inviolable" (*SC* II-4: 63). Not only a statist, Rousseau is an extreme absolutist.[8]

At the same time, Rousseau of all men is aware that absolute power can lead to oppression. But it is precisely his heightened concern with oppression, *private* as well as political, that leads him to argue that absolute state power is indispensable. Therefore, the political task cannot be to limit the state's force, as liberal thought maintains, but only to ensure somehow the salutary use of its unlimited force. To this end, Rousseau requires that sovereign power be placed in the hands of the most pure and direct democracy. Even representative democracy he rejects as illegitimate.

Accordingly, Rousseau's political writings contain the most extreme defense of absolutism and, in the same pages, the most extreme demand for democracy to be found in any major philosopher before or since. Many readers, viewing only part of his thought, have accused him sometimes of being an

[7] On force as the central virtue of the state see also *SC* II-6: 67, II-7: 68, II-11: 75, IV-2: 110n. Of course, Rousseau has in mind not only actual force but also the threat of it, as well as the pressure of public opinion. The very presence of force, moreover, eliminates much of the need to use it because it suppresses not only the external expression but also the spiraling *growth* of men's selfish desires by preventing them from ever getting started in the self-augmenting pursuit of social means.

[8] Again: "The social compact gives the body politic absolute power over all its members" (*SC* II-4: 62). Two passages are sometimes raised in objection to this claim. "Each person alienates through the social compact only that part of his power, goods, and freedom whose use matters to the community" (ibid.). And: "The right that the social compact gives the sovereign over the subjects does not exceed, as I have said, the limits of public utility" (*SC* IV-8: 130). However, the immediate sequel to the former passage states: "but it must also be agreed that the sovereign alone is the judge of what matters." That the sovereign possesses "absolute power" does not mean that it will choose to exercise total or arbitrary control over everything, but only that nothing outside of itself has the legitimate right to set a limit to what it does. Rousseau believes that so long as this power is exercised by the general will, it will be incapable, by its own internal nature, of exceeding "the limits of public utility."

authoritarian or totalitarian, sometimes of being a radical democrat or anarchist. In fact, Rousseau takes the unique position that good politics is possible only in the meeting of these mutually offsetting extremes: the power of the state over the individual and of the citizens over the state must both be brought to a maximum. In a phrase, Rousseau's political solution takes the form of "democratic absolutism." Only where each citizen is utterly subject to the state, and where the state is entirely subject to the combined citizenry can naturally selfish human beings be made to live together in health and freedom.

But a democratic government, it will be objected, is still eminently capable of abusing its power through a tyranny of the majority. Rousseau's primary response to this obvious problem (as will be argued later) is to balance the authority of the democratic sovereign by giving a large role to the executive power, which, structured as an elective aristocracy, will also provide a means for injecting superior talent and intelligence into the officially egalitarian state mechanism.

There is, however, a still more fundamental difficulty: even if the state's absolute power should remain well-intentioned and be used only to force men to be free of dependence on each other, won't it necessarily create in the process an even greater dependence on itself? Isn't the citizen's utter subjection to the rulers just as corrupting and psychologically divisive as obedience to other men in society? Or, to phrase it in the terms of an oft-repeated objection, isn't this whole political enterprise of "forcing men to be free" simply self-contradictory?

Far from ignoring this difficulty, Rousseau considers it the central problem, and regards his solution to it as the veritable secret of politics, the ground of the very possibility of salvation through the state. "By what conceivable art," he writes, "could the means have been found to subjugate men in order to make them free...? How can it be that they obey and no one commands, that they serve and have no master...? These marvels are the work of the *law*. It is to law alone that men owe justice and freedom" (*PE*, 214, emphasis added). By "law" Rousseau means a general rule on which all have voted and to which all are equally subject, a *general will* as distinguished from the personal will of an individual. Where law, in this specific sense, rules, it does two things: it necessarily "forces men to be free" of dependence on others, because it prevents men from doing to others anything they have willed to prevent others from doing to them; and yet, in the act of "forcing," it creates no new personal dependence, since it is itself an impersonal, general will.

The latter point is made with particular clarity in a passage which, according to Rousseau, does nothing less than "resolve all the contradictions of the social system."

> There are two sorts of dependence: dependence on things, which is from nature; dependence on men, which is from society. Dependence on things, since it has no morality, is in no way detrimental to freedom and engenders no vices. Dependence on men, since it is without order, engenders all the vices, and by it, master and slave are mutually corrupted. If there is any means of remedying this ill in society, it is to *substitute law for man* and to arm the general wills with a real

strength superior to the action of every particular will. If the laws of
nations could, like those of nature, have an inflexibility that no human
force could ever conquer, dependence on men would then become
dependence on things again (*Emile* II: 85, emphasis added).[9]

Law is "the most sublime of all human institutions" (*PE*, 214). It is what makes
possible the whole political enterprise—"to subjugate men in order to make
them free." So long as the awesome force of the democratic absolutist state is
only exercised through general laws, it can be safely relied upon to enforce the
freedom of each citizen, without, in the process, ever subjecting anyone to a
private will. Thus, to promote the absolute and invincible rule of law, to
"substitute law for man," to establish the sovereignty of the "general will,"
becomes the central goal of Rousseau's political schemes.

The originality and significance of this conclusion is somewhat obscured
by the fact that almost all philosophers have emphasized the advantages of a
government of laws rather than of men. Given the extraordinary benefits
Rousseau expects from the rule of law, the provision of happiness and health
of soul, he seems to be returning in particular to the classical conception of
law. The latter is nicely epitomized in the reply of the Pythagorean to a man
who asked him the best means of educating his son to virtue: "Let him be born
in a city with good laws."[10]

It is important to see, however, that, in contrast to Rousseau, the classical
view bestows its praise not on lawfulness as such or "generality," but rather
on the substance of good laws. The value and essence of law is not its formal
generality but its wise and morally edifying content which guides the citizens
to virtue and happiness. Indeed, on the classical view, it is precisely the formal
characteristics of law, its blind fixity and impersonal generality, that ultimately
limit its usefulness by making it a rather clumsy vehicle for wisdom. That is
why Plato argues that philosopher-kings, who could supply direct and individ-
ualized guidance, would dispense altogether with the rule of law.

Rousseau's view on these points is just the opposite: the value and essence
of law inheres not in its particular content but in its formal characteristics. He
bestows his extravagant praise on *law as such*, regardless of content. And as
to the superiority of the rule of philosophers to the rule of law, he asserts that
"the worst of laws is still better than the best master" (*Montagne* VIII: 842-43).

His new position follows directly from his principle. The source of all evil
is the condition of obedience or personal dependence. Therefore even the best
master, the philosopher-king, constitutes a great evil because the helpful
content of the commands he issues can never compensate for the harm he does
simply by issuing commands. Conversely, law as such, regardless of content
(and thus even the worst of laws), is a great good because by its very form—its

[9] Note again how much importance Rousseau places on giving the state and law "a real
strength" and "an inflexibility that no human force could ever conquer."

[10] Diogenes Laertius VIII-1.5.

generality and impersonality—it produces freedom from personal dependence, hence health and unity of soul.

In other words, having reduced the totality of the human problem to dependence, and thus human salvation to freedom, Rousseau reduces the whole enterprise of politics to the following: "This is. . . the great problem of state-craft: to find a form of government that puts *law above man*"—law understood formally as general will (Letter to Mirabeau, July 26, 1767, emphasis added). Again:

> That noble question of the best possible government seemed to me to reduce itself to this one. What is the nature of the government suited to form a people that is the most virtuous, the most enlightened, the wisest, and in sum the best, to take this word in its largest sense. I thought I saw that this question was very close to this other one, if indeed it was different from it. What is the government which by its nature always holds closest to the law? (*Confs*. IX: 404-5).

The most exalted political end, health of soul, which the classical thinkers sought to promote through the rule of rare, substantively wise, morally uplifting laws, is in fact attainable through the rule of *law as such*, that is, the absolute and invincible dominion of general rules on which all have democratically voted and to which all are equally subject.

C. The Moral and Religious Level

Here, another well-known objection arises. As cleverly designed as these institutions are—the legalistic democratic absolutist state—they are not nearly as safe or foolproof as Rousseau has allowed himself to believe. And although he surely intends to oppose tyranny, in practice he encourages it by putting all his faith in institutional mechanisms that are so easily corrupted.

Rousseau himself, however, wholly endorses the insights that lie behind this objection—and they are what lead him to the third level of his solution. Contrary to the usual assumption, he is not offering the foregoing political prescriptions as an "institutional solution" whose success is guaranteed automatically, structurally, and regardless of the moral character of the citizenry. Indeed, Rousseau considers the faith in "institutional solutions" a delusion typical of modern political thought. He endeavors to restore the ancient awareness of "how impossible it is for any establishment whatever to function in the spirit of its institution if it is not directed in accordance with the *law of duty*. They [should] realize that . . . for the maintenance of the government, *nothing* can replace *good mores*" (*PE*, 217, emphasis added).

Without internal moral restraints the citizens will always find ways of evading the laws, regardless of statutes, policemen, and punishments; similarly, the magistrates will always find ways of turning the government into a tool of exploitation, no matter how institutions are arranged, divided, and balanced. In short, Rousseau seeks to resurrect the view of the "ancient politicians [who] incessantly talked about morals and virtue"—the view that governments and institutions are ultimately only as good as the people who compose them (*FD*, 51; see *SC* III-15: 102, IV-7: 124, II-12: 77; *PE*, 217; *Poland* VII: 977). Politics cannot be successfully separated from morality: only where the force of duty motivates the citizens to obey the law voluntarily, say, 80 percent of the time, can political institutions be successfully used to enforce the law for the remaining 20. To instill "morals and virtue," then, is the aim of the third level of Rousseau's political solution.[11]

Rousseau returns to this well-known classical theme, however, only on the basis of a fundamentally transformed conception of "morals and virtue" (one which would be extremely influential for all later thought). Unfortunately, the meaning or ground of this transformation is very difficult to understand because it is nowhere thematically explained but rather takes shape gradually through three interrelated assertions or themes scattered among his works. First, there is the famous, enigmatic definition of "moral freedom" presented without preparation or explanation in the *Social Contract*: "the impulse of appetite alone is slavery, and obedience to the law one has prescribed for oneself is freedom" (*SC* I-8: 56). Second, Rousseau declares that a man attains virtue simply when "his private will conforms on all matters with the general will" (*PE*, 218). "Morality" becomes purely formal, consisting in generalizing one's will.

Third, Rousseau puts new emphasis on the element of inner force in morality. "The word *virtue*," he likes to point out, "comes from the word *force*" (*Emile* V: 444, I have altered the translation). He even goes so far as to formulate a new moral distinction between "virtue" and "goodness" that hinges precisely on the issue of force. The term "virtue" (and also "moral freedom" and "morality") he reserves for moral action performed contrary to inclination, through self-conquest. "Goodness," on the other hand, is unforced, spontaneous behavior that happens to conform to the standards of morality.[12] In fact, Rousseau attaches such importance to the phenomenon of self-forcing that he asserts that man's essence or specific difference consists not in reason, as had always been thought, but rather in man's unique inner power to conquer his natural impulses at the behest of law or duty (*SD*, 113-14; *SC* II-4: 63-4).

These new assertions regarding the nature of human virtue can be made intelligible if we simply continue our consideration of the political role of "morals and virtue." If morality is introduced as something necessary for the proper functioning of the state, then its essential characteristics will be shaped by those of the state. For reasons we have seen, Rousseau's polity is necessarily a *self-legislating* body that cures men by *forcing* them, contrary to their natural selfishness, to follow *law as such*, the general will. "Virtue," which motivates men to support and obey this state, will have the same distinctive form.

But having derived this definition from the needs of the state, we need to

[11] The third level differs from the first in that here it is not a question of psychologically redirecting the natural inclinations but of morally combatting or transcending them.

[12] *Emile* V: 444-45, 473; Lettre à M. de Franquières *OC* IV: 1142-433; *GM* II-4: 191.

clarify whether, by "morality" or "virtue," Rousseau simply means "political virtue," the qualities individuals must have for the state to function properly, or also "genuine virtue," the qualities that constitute the health of soul or intrinsic excellence of the individual himself. Rousseau replies, more emphatically than any previous thinker, that "political virtue" is the same as "genuine virtue," that good citizenship is identical with health of soul (within society). Forcing oneself to obey the law or to generalize one's will—as painful as this must be for naturally selfish beings—is intrinsically good for one. Rousseau takes this position for two, or perhaps three, distinct reasons.

First and most obvious, virtue not only supports the state in its effort to force men to behave lawfully and remain free of dependence, it also constitutes a separate moral route to this same end. Through virtue, defined as forcing oneself to will generally, the citizen forces himself to be free. And since such freedom from personal dependence is the sufficient condition for psychic unity, in Rousseau's view, it follows that virtue in this new formal sense is indeed the true excellence or health of the human soul.

The same point emerges from Rousseau's famous statement regarding moral freedom: "the impulse of appetite alone is slavery, and obedience to the law one has prescribed for oneself is freedom." This sentence both restates Rousseau's new definition of virtue—self-forced obedience to the general will—and gives a highly elliptical explanation of why it is good, of why *this* is human virtue.

"The impulse of appetite alone is slavery." How is it so? Certainly not inherently and absolutely, for then the whole individualist solution, which promotes natural spontaneity, could not be recommended by Rousseau as a form of freedom and happiness (see *Dialogues* II: 823-24). The doctrine of natural goodness utterly rejects the view that our natural appetites are inherently sinful or slavish. "All the first movements of nature are good and right" (*Dialogues* I: 668). If the impulse of appetite is slavery, it must be due merely to the effects of society. This is only to restate Rousseau's central discovery: man's selfish instincts, which are good by nature, necessarily lead to contradictory personal dependence within society, and so in that unnatural environment produce "slavery."[13]

Within society, then, only "obedience to the law . . . is freedom." Rousseau is no pain-loving Puritan, and yields to no one in the longing for ease, spontaneity, and "letting go." But within society, the only noncontradictory will is a general will, and the only man who can be self-consistent and free is the self-combatter, the moralist, the "man of principle" who, renouncing forever all naturalness and spontaneity, lives his life in self-forced obedience to the general will. Thus, in society, "moral freedom" as Rousseau defined it becomes human excellence, for only through it can social man be free, unified, and healthy.

This first argument for Rousseau's definition of virtue enables us to assess

---

[13] Since Rousseau's main proof of the goodness of man's original nature is his demonstration of how perverted it necessarily becomes in society, we should not be surprised to find the discoverer of "the natural goodness of man" telling the citizen that nature is the enemy.

more clearly the character of the change it initiates in the history of morality. Rousseau's view contrasts sharply with the more capacious conception of human virtue which Aristotle, for example, expressed in eleven distinct virtues. For Rousseau, this quality is now reduced to one thing: self-forced obedience to law as such. Moreover, as compared to earlier conceptions, Rousseau's virtue is also strikingly formal in character. It tests each desire not by its content—by whether it promotes the specific fulfillment of our nature—but by whether it can be "generalized," whether we would will that everyone act on such a desire. The reason for these differences is that the task of virtue is no longer to elevate us to the perfection of our various natural faculties and activities, but only to prevent us from ruining our original goodness through using each other. In other words, Rousseau produces this moral revolution: virtue is no longer defined "vertically," in terms of the fulfillment of some higher human end (which does not exist), but simply "horizontally" as the proper relation to other human beings, as good citizenship, as justice in both a narrow and formal sense. When all evil is understood as using other men as means, moral excellence is reduced to formal fairness or generality.

This account contains an obvious problem, however, which will lead to the second reason for Rousseau's redefinition of virtue. If the paramount goal of his solutions is to restore unity of soul, and if virtue, as he himself insists, is nothing but inner struggle and self-combat, how can it produce psychic unity? The argument has been that by forcing men to act unselfishly or lawfully, virtue eliminates the great social source of disunity, personal dependence. That is true. But obviously, in the process, virtue creates a disunity of its own: a permanent inner conflict between men's natural, selfish desires and the demands of the general will. In what sense, then, can the function of virtue and its value to the individual be the production of unity?

Rousseau concedes the point: through force or virtue one can never return men to anything like their original, natural unity of soul, based as it was on unity of inclination. He argues, however, that virtue or moral freedom has the power to create an altogether new kind of psychic unity—a moral unity—which is wholly independent of the inclinations and which can therefore be maintained despite their permanent conflict.

What occurs in an act of virtuous self-conquest is not the overpowering of one natural impulse by another but the triumph of that unique human faculty to resist or rise above all natural impulses: "the voice of duty replaces physical impulse and right replaces appetite" (*SC* I-8: 56; see *Emile* V: 444-45). Through virtue, social man finally completes his needed conquest of nature—not, as on the first level, by altering his natural inclinations, but by rising above them, by freeing his activity and his identity from them. The virtuous man will continue to *feel* his natural appetites and impulses, but he will cease to follow them, cease to live for them, cease to *be* them. In becoming a "moral being," he shifts the ground of his existence. He sheds his former, natural self, based on what he feels and desires, and relocates his existence in a new, moral self, based on what he respects and wills. And on this new moral plane, he is able to create and enforce a coherent self, a unified existence, despite the permanent conflict of his desires.

The production of psychic unity in this new, moral form is the second basis of virtue's intrinsic usefulness to the individual. The virtuous citizen will attain "unity of will" in place of the "unity of inclination" he has permanently lost by forcibly adhering to a single, unified set of moral principles or laws. In the same way he will attain "temporal unity," for, over time, the "man of principle" will always be doing and being the same thing, since all of his various actions would represent so many instantiations of the same, unchanging general principles.

Of course, the utility of this new unity would be unclear if unity of soul were understood merely "negatively" as the absence of the pain of inner conflict. In such terms the very possibility of a unity produced by altering not man's inclinations but his "identity" would be unintelligible. The value and possibility of moral unity is intelligible only on the specific interpretation we have seen: unity as a means to the positive good of "existence."

In these terms, the virtuous citizen attains a genuine and choiceworthy unity, despite the conflict of his inclinations, for he *exists more*. Rousseau describes the unified man as follows: "to be something, to be oneself and always one, a man must act as he speaks; he must always be decisive in making his choice, make it in a lofty style and always stick to it" (*Emile* I: 40). Virtue is a painful self-conquest, but it gives the citizen an energetic and unshakable sense of who he is and what he stands for. He is fully mobilized, forcefully united, and intensely alive.

In sum, Rousseau identifies human virtue with "self-forced obedience to the general will" as the specific quality needed for the proper functioning of both the state and the soul. It produces psychic unity both negatively, by forcing men to be free of dependence, and positively, by creating an altogether new, moral self. In other words, moral freedom is a means, first, to civil freedom, second, to moral unity—and both for the sake of unity of soul.[14]

Rousseau's whole political solution culminates, then, in the third, moral level. To cure social man it is not enough to modify his spontaneous inclinations or to limit him through political institutions; one must wholly transform his identity, his self, his locus of existence. That is why Rousseau emphasizes that the legitimate state necessarily produces: "a remarkable change in man, by substituting justice for instinct in his behavior and giving his actions the morality they previously lacked" (*SC* I-8: 55; see *Emile* V: 473). Natural men

---

[14] Here, finally, we learn Rousseau's answer to the crucial question raised but not resolved in chap. 4: how is morality or justice, which seems to be merely society's good, also the good of the individual and therefore binding upon him? Rousseau's answer—that it unifies his soul—is the same as that given in Plato's *Republic* (see 350d-352b, 441d-444a), except that the unity Plato has in mind is the harmonious ordering of man's naturally multipartite and hierarchical soul, whereas Rousseau's unity is a forced and artificial self-conquest made necessary in society by the artificial rending of man's naturally unified soul. Consider also Bergson (1935, p. 15): "Obligation, which we look upon as a bond between men, first binds us to ourselves."

must not merely come to *behave* morally but to *be* "moral beings." Within society, unity can exist only for a moral being, only as moral unity.

The central issue of Rousseau's politics thus becomes: what must be done to make human beings virtuous or moral? How are naturally selfish, lazy, and solitary animals to be turned into energetic self-combatters who live only for their duty to the community and the law?

The first thing Rousseau emphasizes is the need for certain *beliefs*. Moral enthusiasm requires a belief in the doctrine of free will, for example (*Emile* IV: 280-81; Lettre à M. de Franquières, *OC* IV: 1145). Even more important, to be inspired to make this strenuous self-conquest men must be, as it were, in love with virtue, and believe with all their hearts in its divine beauty or absolute worth. Such lofty and romantic claims, however, go well beyond the two merely utilitarian arguments described above concerning the usefulness of virtue for psychic unity. Therefore, to make men capable of virtue and of receiving its utilitarian benefits, Rousseau needs to make a third and very different argument that idealizes virtue as something absolute and necessary for its own sake, independent of any mere eudemonistic or utilitarian benefit.

Consequently, Rousseau proclaims the sacred beauty or absolute worth of virtue, albeit in somewhat different terms in his different writings.[15] In the *Social Contract*, he does so through his statement on moral freedom: "the impulse of appetite alone is slavery, and obedience to the law one has pre-scribed for oneself is freedom." Above, we interpreted this passage to mean that natural appetite is "slavery" not in itself or absolutely, but merely under the deforming conditions of society. But it must be acknowledged here that, as the passage actually reads, appetite is condemned and freedom praised absolutely. In the same context, virtue or moral freedom is praised as that which "alone makes man truly the master of himself" (*SC* I-8: 56). In short, Rousseau attempts here to bestow on virtue the splendor of self-creation, absolute freedom, or what later came to be called "autonomy."[16]

The single most important belief for the virtuous man, however, is in God's existence—a God who rewards virtue and punishes vice in the afterlife and

---

[15]*SC* I-8: 56; *Emile* V: 473. See also *OC* III: 86n, where Rousseau quotes Montaigne to the effect that it is our duty to praise virtue as beautifully as possible.

[16] Of course there are other ways to depict the intrinsic worth of virtue. Rousseau is the first to glorify virtue in this particular way—in terms of the dignity of an absolute and formal freedom instead of the admirableness of conformity to the specific perfection of human nature. He is the first, in other words, to praise freedom or self-mastery not as a means to the fulfillment of man's higher end but as an end in itself. There seem to be three reasons for this change. First, virtue *cannot* (truthfully) be praised in substantive terms because, in Rousseau's understanding, man has no higher nature or end. Second, virtue *need* not be praised in such terms because the virtue that Rousseau desires to promote—from his desire to foster unity of soul—is formal, requiring nothing more than obedience to law as such. Third, virtue *must* not be praised in substantive terms because that would tend to destroy it. It would create a moral standard above the city's laws and thus undermine the absolute and unquestioning law-abidingness that is the core of virtue (as will be seen in chap. 8).

who vouches for the "sanctity of the social contract and the laws" (*SC* IV-8: 131). For the nonbeliever, it is simply "impossible to be a good citizen" because he is incapable of "sincerely loving the laws, justice, and of giving his life, if need be, for his duty." Virtue, in Rousseau's view, is absolutely inseparable from religious belief (*SC* IV-8: 130-31).[17]

To transform men into moral beings these three beliefs—God, free will, and the beauty of virtue—are absolutely necessary, but not sufficient: certain political conditions are also needed. Rousseau is not a "moralist" who sees virtue as a natural force in the soul to be activated by preaching the right beliefs. On the contrary, he is a radically political thinker who views the moral consciousness as an artificial creation of the state. Morality can no more be separated from politics, he believes, than politics from morality; and a purely "moral solution" to the human problem is no more possible than a purely "institutional solution." If virtue was first introduced as a means to make the state function properly, ultimately the well-ordered state is a means to transform men into virtuous citizens.

By scrupulously enforcing the laws, for example, the state constrains and habituates men to behave virtuously, while also making it safe for them to do so without fear of being taken advantage of. Also, public honor and esteem, when rightly directed, play a crucial role in promoting virtue. "What was the motive of the virtue of the Lacedaemonians," Rousseau goes so far as to assert, "if not to be *esteemed* virtuous?" (*Frags.*, 501, emphasis added; see *Corsica*, 937-38; *SD*, 175; *PE*, 219).

But the primary political means for promoting morality is patriotism, for "it seems that the sentiment of humanity evaporates and weakens as it is extended over the whole world. . . . Interest and commiseration must in some way be

---

[17] See *GM* III-2: 195-96; *Emile* IV: 291-92, 312n; Lettre à M. de Franquières *OC* IV: 1142. The question naturally arises whether Rousseau himself adheres to these "moral beliefs," and, if he does, whether they in fact do not constitute the true basis of his moral thought, which we have heretofore mistakenly neglected. Specifically, does Rousseau's political solution culminate in the goal of creating "moral beings" not, as I have argued, for the sake of unity and happiness, but rather for the sake of moral freedom, that is, not because the moral self is the only noncontradictory and unified self possible within society, but because, as Kant might argue, it is simply of infinite intrinsic worth? In chap. 4, I presented some reasons why I believe the Kantian interpretation of Rousseau cannot be sustained, and still other reasons will emerge later. Perhaps it suffices to answer here that Rousseau was notoriously tentative in his discussions of these three beliefs, and he strongly implied that, whatever they might add to the main body of his thought, the latter also certainly stood on its own (*SD*, 114, 167; *SC* I-8: 56). In general, Rousseau spends much more time speaking of the utilitarian benefits and good feelings one gets from believing in virtue than he does demonstrating the validity of such a belief (*GM* I-2: 159; *Emile* IV: 287, 291; *LM*, 1101). In the early "Fragment on Liberty" (*OC* III: 1894), he claims that "whether the acts of my will are in my own power or whether they follow a foreign impulse I do not know and I care very little to know." And in several places he admits that virtue is itself only a passion (*Emile* V: 397, 445; *NH* IV-12: 493; *Frags.*, 501). Finally, if Rousseau truly believed that "the impulse of appetite alone is slavery" not just in the context of society but absolutely, it would be very hard to make sense of the doctrine of natural goodness or the whole individualistic half of his thought.

confined and compressed to be activated" (*PE*, 219). The phenomenon of morality, Rousseau is saying here, does not really arise in and between human beings as such, but rather in patriots or citizens, in their exclusive respect for their fellow citizens. By grounding morality in patriotic citizenship, Rousseau is consciously attacking the cosmopolitanism—the ethical universalism and apolitical moralism—characteristic of his time (and, even more, of ours). He is returning to the more political and particularistic approach to morality found, for example, in Plato and Aristotle. Rousseau acknowledges that "every patriot is harsh to foreigners. They are only men. They are nothing in his eyes." But he continues: "This is a drawback, inevitable but not compelling. The essential thing is to be good to the people with whom one lives. . . . Distrust those cosmopolitans who go to great lengths in their books to discover duties they do not deign to fulfill around them" (*Emile* I: 39).[18] If one seriously seeks to promote virtue, he argues, and not merely to moralize, one must see that this difficult and unnatural state of soul rarely exists except in conjunction with particular patriotism.

In order to promote this virtuous enthusiasm, public education as well as certain specific social and economic conditions are required, as we have already seen, but certain political conditions are also especially important. And these turn out to be identical to the institutions devised, on the second level, for the purpose of safely forcing men to be free of personal dependence. Thus, on the third level, all of these political institutions receive an additional and higher justification, a new moral, or rather moralizing, significance.

Patriotism, for example, is inseparable from direct democracy, in Rousseau's view. Only where the citizens are actively involved, knowing that they control the state, will they be inspired with genuine loyalty and devotion. Thus, consent, popular sovereignty, direct democracy, the general will—all these institutions devised on the second level to make the state safe—are also embraced by Rousseau as the great and indispensable fountains of patriotism and moral enthusiasm (*PE*, 218-22; *SC* I-8: 56, III-15: 101-4; *Montagne* VI: 806-7; *SD*, 81).

And once again, the absolute rule of *law*, "the most sublime of all human institutions," proves to be the single most important condition, for through it the state actually promulgates the true morality, which consists in nothing but willing lawfully or generally. Morality *is* lawfulness for Rousseau. Furthermore, the rigorously legalistic state, which scrupulously respects the equal dignity and rights of each, inspires every citizen by its own supreme example to respect himself, to honor his compatriots, and, for these two reasons, to take his duties seriously.

This respect for the inviolability of the individual that flows from the rule of law is, for example, the primary reason for Rousseau's ardent admiration of

---

[18] See *GM* II-4: 190-92, I-2: 161-62; *PE*, 220-21. But *SD*, 160 mentions the rare true cosmopolitan.

the Roman republic: "the Romans stood out over all the peoples of the earth for the deference of the government toward private individuals and for its scrupulous attention to the inviolable rights of all members of the state. Nothing was as sacred as the life of the simple citizens." Rousseau praises this legal sanctity of the individual not for its intrinsic justice, or for the security it provides, but for its transformational effect on character. It elevated the Romans' self-understanding and produced "that love of the citizens for one another and that respect for the name Roman which aroused the courage and animated the virtue of anyone who had the honor to bear it" (*PE*, 221; see *Poland* XV: 1038-39). In short, for Rousseau the properly structured state—the legalistic, democratic, absolutist city—is, above all, a great engine of mobilization, designed to inspire men's hearts with patriotism and thereby raise their souls to virtue.

This brief summary has been an attempt to unfold Rousseau's political theory as a precise, systematic response to the human problem of personal dependence. Beginning from his new principle, one can deduce all of the unique and most characteristic features of his political thought: the elaborate and semitotalitarian institutions designed to denature and collectivize men; the democratic absolutist state that endeavors to "force men to be free" through the "most sublime" institution of the "law" understood formally as "general will"; and the return to a concern with "virtue" or "moral freedom"—redefined as self-forced obedience to law—not only as a support for the state but also as its highest purpose.

Rousseau: Liberal or Ancient?

We may complete this overview of Rousseau's political theory by trying to situate his thought within the broader movement of Western political philosophy. One prominent view on this much-debated issue holds that, whatever his deviations and oddities, his thought is ultimately "liberal," particularly given his extreme individualism, his use of social contract doctrine, his ardent support of democracy, his concern for toleration, his evident debts to Locke—and, we might add, his psychological realism.[19]

All these traits are indeed to be found in Rousseau, but to assess their true significance one should begin at the heart of the matter. Rousseau's fundamental principle—that society based on personal dependence and mutual self-interest is the source of all human evil—is the most direct possible attack on the fundamental principle of classical liberal thought (and, less directly, a rejection of all later forms of liberalism as well). Based on his principle, Rousseau argues that "negative" liberal freedom—the cherished "private sphere" secured from the "limited state"—is nothing but a freedom for oppression and disunity; that nothing good or healthy can ever come from men's private relations; that society can be rectified only

[19] See especially Cobban (1934) and Chapman (1956).

by making all human relations public and lawful; and thus that men can be truly free only *through* the state and in no way *against* it. Consequently, the "social contract," upon which Rousseau does indeed base the state, is used (as we will see) in antiliberal fashion, not to establish but to eliminate men's rights against the state. All private, natural rights are to be totally alienated in exchange for political rights, for a share in control over the absolute and unlimited state.[20]

Similarly, Rousseau is indeed a democrat, but not a liberal one. Precisely in a democracy, where there is the greatest need for public virtue, one can least afford to be liberal, he argues. There, it is necessary and (Kantian liberals notwithstanding) it is possible to legislate morality. Rousseau rejects the separation of law and morality, politics and ethics, as well as of church and state (although he tries very hard to protect toleration). He has no faith in the spontaneity of society in either moral or economic matters— no belief in the cunning of reason or the invisible hand, the march of progress or the free market. He is suspicious of liberal cosmopolitanism, wary of the arts and sciences, opposed to pluralism,[21]against technology and industrialism, appalled by commercialism, disgusted by urbanization,

---

[20] It is Rousseau's virtue as a thinker to destroy our habitual categories. We are accustomed to think in terms of the distinction made famous by Benjamin Constant (and later elaborated by Isaiah Berlin) between two kinds of liberty: "The liberty of ancient times was whatever assured citizens the largest share in exercising social power. The liberty of modern times is whatever guarantees the independence of the citizens from their government" (quoted and translated by Holmes [1984], p. 31). But the liberty of Rousseau's citizen is both and neither of these. Not being by nature a political or social animal, the freedom he desires is not ancient liberty, not that of political status or "social power" for his group. He seeks a personal, private, civil liberty—the inviolability of his rights and the freedom from all dependence. But this modern-sounding personal freedom cannot be secured through modern "independence... from their government," in Rousseau's view, but only by sharing control over a powerful and intrusive government, like that of ancient Rome or Sparta, which actively instills in everyone a respect for the laws and for the sacred rights of each. Rousseau's distinctive conception of freedom is conveyed well by this account of Sparta. "If liberty means freedom from arbitrary interference," writes Kurt Von Fritz, then "in this sense the Spartans were actually the freest of the free, and they always considered themselves as such. No Spartan could be arbitrarily punished or ordered around either by a king or an ephor, or the gerousia, or even the apella. Any command that was given had to be strictly within the fundamental law, and there was always the possibility of appeal. Yet we do not think of Sparta as a liberal country. It is doubtful whether there ever was a country in which the life of the individual, almost from the cradle to the grave, was more tightly controlled by the state than in ancient Sparta" (1954, p. 349-50).

[21] Regarding interest groups Rousseau states that the best arrangement would be to eliminate all of them, but where this is not possible then "their number must be multiplied and their inequality prevented, as was done by Solon, Numa, and Servius" (*SC* II-3: 61-62). The striking resemblance to *Federalist Paper* 10 has led many commentators, especially those defending Rousseau against the charge of totalitarianism, to argue that he is in fact a pluralist.

Yet the sentence in question shows that Rousseau is neither of these things. If a totalitarian believes that it is both necessary and possible to eliminate all organized disagreement within society, then the passage shows that Rousseau is not a totalitarian. But that does not mean he is a "pluralist" either, at least in the interesting sense of the term, according to which Madison is a

revolted by the bourgeoisie,[22] and dead set against "extending the sphere." In short, we must constantly remind ourselves that when Rousseau speaks of democracy he is thinking of Calvinist Geneva and not of Montesquieu's England, of Sparta and not of Athens.

As for the theoretical individualism at the root of Rousseau's thought, it demonstrates not that he is a member of the liberal camp but that he is a *defector* from it. He contends that individualist principles, when fully thought through, lead back to collectivist prescriptions. Let us begin, he agrees, with the liberal goal of securing the rights and welfare of the individual—whether understood as comfortable self-preservation or (as in later theories) as moral autonomy, or as rugged, self-reliant individualism, or as being true to one's unique inner self. Yet precisely because men are naturally asocial individuals, he continues, a liberal, individualistic society must necessarily produce a condition of universal exploitation and disunity where in fact no one is safe, no one is moral, no one is self-reliant, and no one is sincere. Within society, the good of the individual requires the rejection of individualism; it requires that all individuals be denatured and transformed into patriotic citizens who love the city more than themselves and their virtue more than their lives. Rousseau "defects" from the liberal camp by refuting its conclusions on the basis of its own, individualist premises.

Finally, the same point can be made about Rousseau's psychological realism. He shares with the early liberal thinkers a posture of hostile skepticism toward all of the purported higher faculties and inclinations of the human soul. But again, he soon defects from the liberals, finding them, not too harsh and hardheaded, but insufficiently so. Their much-vaunted realism is actually a prelude to an unwarranted optimism that a good society can be constructed out

---

pluralist and, say, Aristotle is not. Aristotle is quite aware that in all states the facade of public unity always conceals an underlying competition of rival interest groups. Still, he is not a pluralist because he does not advocate the lifting of that facade, does not favor the public legitimation of self-interest, does not believe that a healthy and just society can result from the *open* competition (whether free or regulated) of rival selfish forces.

Rousseau's view is the same. When he speaks of multiplying the number of groups in the state, he does not mean that this should be done through the free growth and free play of interest groups. He is against such pluralistic spontaneity. As his reference to Solon, Numa, and Servius makes clear, what he has in mind is the methodical creation by the legislator of certain official groups whose size, composition, and role is strictly regulated by law (*SC* IV-4: 116).

[22] Cobban (1934, pp. 203, 209-10) and others have pointed out that Rousseau wants to base his state on the "middle class," which is true in the sense that he seeks to avoid the extremes of both wealth and poverty: "tolerate neither opulent people nor beggars. These two conditions, naturally inseparable, are equally fatal to the common good" (*SC* II-11: 75n). But it is false if "middle class" is taken to mean the urban and commercial class. Neither Sparta nor Rome was, and if Rousseau has his way, neither Corsica nor Poland will be based on such a class (*SC* IV-4: 114; *Poland* XI: 1004; *Corsica*, 904-5, 911, 919-20). Rousseau is for the yeoman farmer. The Genevans, it is true, were largely a commercial people, but Rousseau sees this as the source of their greatest problems (*Montagne* IX: 881).

of the selfish, asocial individuals that they acknowledge men to be. Rousseau, more suspicious of men, cannot share this faith. If a truly stable and non-oppressive society is to be constructed, then men cannot be employed as they are but must be transformed into virtuous patriots—a course of action admittedly difficult but possible. Rousseau embraces it not from utopianism but precisely from a more consistent realism: if men are really what the liberal "skeptics" claim they are, then nothing less will do. Liberal realism, pushed to an extreme, returns one to a concern for virtue. In sum, Rousseau's thought, if correct, represents not just the rejection but, as it were, the dialectical self-overcoming of liberal political theory.[23]

Rousseau is thus led back to the theory and especially to the practice of the ancient Greeks and Romans. They form his true models and his great inspiration.

> When one reads ancient history, one feels oneself transported into another universe and among other beings. What do the French, the English, the Russians have in common with the Romans and the Greeks? . . . The strong souls of the latter seem to the others as an exaggeration of the historians. How can they who feel themselves so puny believe that there once were such great men? But they did exist. (*Poland* II: 956; see *Frags.*, 538-39, *Montagne* IX: 881)

So many of the features of Rousseau's solution that strike the contemporary reader as unique, bizarre, or proto-totalitarian are in fact just the standard views and utter commonplaces of classical political theory.

Yet, because Rousseau returns to ancient thought on the grounds of—as a paradoxical, dialectical result of—extreme realism and individualism, we should not be surprised to find that his thought also departs in crucial respects from that of all classical thinkers. It constitutes, ultimately, not a return at all but a new synthesis and a radical step forward to a new "postliberal" form of modernity.

Rousseau's most obvious disagreement with the mainstream of classical thought is his bitter opposition to all hierarchy and inequality, his intransigent demand for democracy, equality, and freedom. It is Rousseau, after all, who, in the words of one scholar, "effected, virtually single-handed, an epochal transvaluation in the meaning and appeal of democracy."[24] Not that democracy and equality did not have their defenders in the ancient world, but Rousseau's

[23] The proponents of the "liberal Rousseau" are correct, then, in seeing all the kinships and similarities they point out, but these are precisely what make Rousseau so dangerous to the liberal camp. He is a defector and traitor in their midst who turns all their principles and weapons against them. That is what gives his thought its Orwellian character: men must be forced to be free, individualism requires collectivism, the social contract abolishes all rights against the state, freedom and democracy require semitotalitarian control. This is how to make liberals disarmed and disoriented.

[24] Miller (1984) p. 121. See pp. 1-4, 41-43, 108-11, 158-59.

defense is unique by virtue of the radical new hopes that lie behind his egalitarian demands. For his realism too is ultimately only a prelude to an extravagant new idealism.

Perhaps the best formula for Rousseau's thought is this: a radicalized humanism that seeks to translate all of the purported benefits of the divine and transcendent, the "vertical" dimension, onto the level of the merely human and "horizontal." His understanding of the human problem, we have seen, reduces everything to the horizontal issue, other men. All the evils of human life derive from personal dependence and oppression and not from man's supposed baseness and insufficiency, his fallenness from a higher natural or divine perfection. But for a purely horizontal problem one needs only horizontal solutions. Rousseau will cure men simply by arranging them properly among themselves.

His political solution is to create nonoppression and freedom through the reign of "law" and "virtue," where these familiar classical concepts have both been redefined in a formal, democratic, and horizontal way. They have been emptied of all substantive and inegalitarian reference to a higher end or perfection of human nature, and identified with formal "generality" or reciprocity in relation to other men. Through a unique synthesis of liberal and classical thought, Rousseau develops this radical humanistic claim: he will bring true unity and happiness to men not by uplifting them to some divine or transcendent standard, but simply by preventing them from using and ruining each other.[25]

There is still one final twist. In the end, Rousseau's extreme skepticism triumphs, leading him to the view that the truly good society, even in this simplified horizontal conception, is scarcely possible. A tone of ultimate pessimism may be detected sounding from the deepest level of his political writings.

Men can never be wholly denatured or made unselfish, nor can one completely eliminate the division of labor and mutual dependence. Thus, Rousseau is forced to conclude that "in the social state the good of one necessarily constitutes the harm of another. This relation is in the essence of the thing, and nothing can change it" (*Emile* II: 105n; see *Mals.*, 1137). Of course one must try to force men to be free through law, but in the end, Rousseau concedes, "putting law above man is a problem in politics that I compare to that of squaring the circle in geometry" (*Poland* I: 955; see Letter to Mirabeau, July 26, 1767). One may devise all sorts of institutional tricks to protect the rule of law, but in the end it is always men who will rule; and only if these men were of perfect virtue would they not evade and pervert the laws, but precisely then they wouldn't need the laws. So it comes down to this: "the vices that make

---

[25] Consider the remark of Bertrand de Jouvenel (1947, p. 57): "Here is without doubt the secret of the immortal seduction exercised by Rousseau: beautiful things intoxicate him, their difficulty repels him, he seeks an easy road. He excites enthusiasm while at the same time he flatters laziness."

social institutions necessary are the same ones that make their abuse inevitable" (*SD*, 172-73).

Rousseau concedes, for example, that "the universal spirit of the laws of every country is always to favor the strong against the weak and those who have against those who have not. This difficulty is inevitable, and it is without exception" (*Emile* IV: 236n; see *SC* I-9: 58n; *Emile* V: 473). The difficulty might be rendered irrelevant if a perfect equality of wealth could be established and maintained, but Rousseau holds that this is absolutely impossible (*Frags.*, 522).

These pessimistic views, which Rousseau expressed consistently during every stage of his career, certainly do not imply that there is no better and worse among states. But they do limit what one can hope for from politics. Strangely, despite all his modern radicalism and rebellion, there is ultimately a lesson of classical moderation in Rousseau. "One of the greatest chimeras of philosophy is to have wanted to discover some form of government in which, by the sole force of the laws, the citizens might be free and virtuous. It is only in the solitary life that one can find liberty and innocence" (*Fragment sur la liberté, OC* III: 1894).[26] In the end, Rousseau's skepticism and individualism lead him to praise the tribal stage as really the best for the mass of humanity and the life of the solitary dreamer as best for men such as himself—the lives of natural unity beneath and above the moral-political realm.[27]

[26] See *Mals.*, 1137; *Dialogues* II: 823-24; *Emile* II: 105n.

[27] *SD*, 151; *SC* II-11: 76; *Dialogues* I: 668-72, II: 810-25; *Reveries* V: 64-71, VI: 76-77.

7

Rousseau's Doctrine:
The Principles of Political Right
and the Maxims of Politics

Beginning from the premise of the natural goodness of man, with its new account of the human problem, we attempted in the previous chapter to "deduce" Rousseau's political solution, to regenerate it for ourselves, as it were, and present it in our own terms.

We turn now to Rousseau's own presentation. Having seen in general how his state will function and what it will do to cure the sickness of society, we turn to his official political doctrine—for Rousseau is emphatically a thinker with a "doctrine"—as presented in the *Social Contract* (complemented by the *Discourse on Political Economy*). The main portion of Rousseau's doctrine is the "principles of political right" (so named in the subtitle to the *Social Contract*) which presents a formal, juridical definition of "legitimate" government, deduced in a precise and legalistic manner from the individual's natural right to self-preservation. To supplement these principles, Rousseau also presents the "maxims of politics" or the "science of the legislator," which treat all matters not involving strict right or legitimacy but only mere expediency or prudence.[1] The latter primarily concerns the form of the executive power and the actions of the legislator in founding the state.

The examination of Rousseau's doctrine and the argument supporting it will occupy us for the remainder of the book. But to begin we must ask why he chooses to encapsulate his political thought in this sort of formal doctrine in the first place. Such a "literary" question might seem needlessly academic—until one actually looks at the *Social Contract* and discovers that virtually none of the arguments elaborated above is to be found in that work! There is not a single mention of the natural goodness of man, there is no reference to the corrupting effects of personal dependence, there is not one allusion to the problem of disunity of soul. The crucial project of educating and mobilizing men to virtue is barely discussed and, although

---

[1] *SC* III-18: 106, III-3: 83, II-11: 76, IV-8: 130; *GM* I-4: 168, II-3: 183. See Masters (1978, pp. 20-24, 202n2; 1968, pp. 290-93, 369-409), who is principally responsible for drawing attention to this important distinction.

great stress is placed on the importance of freedom and rule of law, the explanations given for their importance are very narrow and quite different from those we considered above.

If Rousseau's ultimate ends are unity and happiness, why, we must ask, do his official political principles argue from self-preservation? If the crucial task of politics is to eliminate divisive personal dependence and to promote moral unity through the absolute rule of law and the creation of virtuous patriotism, why does Rousseau fail to say so in his major political work? And what is the reason for what he does say: what is the origin and the purpose of this abstract, narrow, legalistic juridical doctrine? We are driven, then, to raise the question concerning the form of Rousseau's doctrine—the neglect of which has led inevitably to much confusion regarding its content and meaning.[2]

Natural Constitutional Law

To begin with, what makes it even possible for Rousseau to use such a doctrine? Since he, as distinguished from Hobbes or Locke, returns to the comprehensive classical ends of virtue and happiness, how is it possible for him to generate the requirements of these elaborate goals through a narrow juridical doctrine that looks only to the conditions of preservation?

The answer is that, on Rousseau's unique principles, these two sets of requirements are the same. On the one hand, like almost all theorists and partisans of republicanism, Rousseau holds that the real threat to men's security comes not from anarchy but from oppression or dependence, hence the central requirement of preservation is freedom and the rule of law. But Rousseau also makes the new claim that the single source of human vice and disunity is, again, oppression or dependence, and thus that freedom and the rule of law are also the sufficient condition of unity and happiness. The political requirements of preservation and of happiness perfectly coincide. The principle of natural goodness has the effect of collapsing the distinction between the lowest and highest ends of politics, between Hobbesian and Platonic aims, between legitimate government and the ideal society. That is what makes it possible for Rousseau to encapsulate the requirements of his comprehensive political solution to the human problem in the narrow preservation-based juridical doctrine found in the *Social Contract*.

---

[2]On a practical level, the *Social Contract* is meant to be and is coherent in itself. Nevertheless, the problem to which this treatise is the solution is not explained, not even hinted at, within it. Rousseau presents his doctrine completely severed from the purpose or presuppositions of the doctrine. Thus in a larger, theoretical sense, it is altogether impossible to understand the *Social Contract* by itself, as Rousseau himself implies in his repeated statements that his works must be read as a whole, as well as in his explicit assertion that the *Social Contract* "should be considered as a kind of appendix to [*Emile*]" (letter to Duchesne, May 23, 1762). The primary errors into which one falls if one treats the *Social Contract* as self-contained are two: either one sees Rousseau's politics as limited to the goal of preservation or, sensing the inadequacy of this, one views him as a proto-Kantian.

Yet why would he want to do so? What could induce a thinker to prefer a narrower presentation of his thought to a broader one? The answer would seem to be: in order to have a greater practical effect.

Rousseau's "principles of political right" is an example of "natural constitutional law," a form of political theorizing that first arose in the seventeenth century.[3] As is generally acknowledged, philosophers in this period came to reject as too lofty and unrealistic the traditional claims made for the detached life of pure contemplation and began seeking a more useful and active role in the practical world. And this same spirit of psychological realism also led them to take a narrower and simpler view of the ends pursued in that world—which view, in turn, strengthened their hopes of having such a practical effect on it.

This complex change produced the rise of "natural constitutional law"—a form of political philosophy that attempts, for the first time, to settle the major question of political practice on the level of theory: to deduce directly from abstract human nature (with its single end of self-preservation) certain principles of constitutional law that are universally applicable and thus also universally binding and obligatory. In proclaiming such a doctrine, philosophers became "practical" not only in that they were now presenting immediately applicable advice but also that they were, through the power of their proclamations, taking active steps toward its realization in the world.[4]

Such doctrines derive great power by beginning from the right of self-preservation, which possesses tremendous psychological force. If one preaches to men their duties and obligations, as do earlier forms of natural law, one appeals to forces in the soul that are quite feeble in most cases, whereas when one proclaims to all men what they must do in order to preserve their lives, one speaks to their most abiding, passionate, and self-righteous concern.

Furthermore, the lowly beginning point in self-preservation also gives natural constitutional law an unprecedented rigor and intellectual power. All the loftier issues of virtue and happiness are of necessity complex, uncertain, and imprecise. Consequently no political theory based on them has ever managed to attain widespread acceptance or great intellectual force, nor has political philosophy in general ever managed to distance itself adequately from gross partisanship and sophistry—as Rousseau notes with a particularly keen sense of disgust (*SD*, 94; *Perpetual Peace OC* III: 568-69; *SC* II-2: 60; *Emile* IV: 268). What is urgently needed, then, for both the honor of philosophy and the welfare of politics, is a doctrine that is clear and distinct, a theory that can, as Rousseau puts it, "give rise to the most universal and infallible rules by which to judge a good or bad government"

---

[3] See Strauss (1953) p. 190. See also Gierke (1934) vol. I, p. 137. Derathé (1950) pp. 386ff. The complex question of how "natural" Rousseau's doctrine is will be treated later.

[4] On these points and those that follow see Strauss (1953) 190-94, 135-40.

(*PE*, 212).[5] This is made possible by beginning from the right of self-preservation.

This right serves as the political equivalent of Descartes' *cogito*: a first principle that resists all skepticism, an unshakable rock upon which to build. What happiness, virtue, or holiness may be is unclear and debatable; but no man can doubt that he exists, that it is good to preserve his existence, and that he has a right to do so. Furthermore, the necessary means to this indubitable end, the political conditions required for preservation, can be known with clarity and precision. By starting from preservation, one can make a systematic, rigorous, juridical deduction of the necessary form of the state: the natural constitutional law. This form of political theory, then, not only attains an immediate applicability and a great psychological force, but also an unprecedented legalistic rigor—and in intellectual matters, rigor is power.

Rousseau adopts this kind of doctrine not only for its general effectiveness but also because of the particular effect he desired to have. The core of his political solution is to "put law above man," to establish a rigidly legalistic society; and, by employing a highly legalistic natural constitutional law doctrine, he clearly also hoped to advance this specific end. When classical thinkers formulated their theories of the best form of government—or when we presented Rousseau's political solution in the preceding chapter—the argument was political not legalistic. It described the good one wished to promote and judged forms of government by how well they promoted it. But as any reader of the *Social Contract* will observe, natural constitutional law is more a legal than a political doctrine, conceiving the creation of the state as a juridical, contractual event. In discussing forms of government it looks less to their substantive effects than to legal issues: what kinds of contracts can men legitimately conclude, which rights must they relinquish and which retain, and so forth. Political structures are defined in terms of formal procedures, rights, and powers without reference to ends or substantive behavior. Rousseau's intention in all this is to inspire a similar legalism among the citizens of his state, to encourage them to adopt the same pedantic, punctilious, even ritualistic concern with legal forms that he himself displays in the *Social Contract*.[6]

[5]This is why one finds in the *Social Contract* an almost obsessive concern with precision. It is full of pedantic new distinctions, new definitions, and new terms, of legalistic rigor, epigrammatic clarity, and mathematical equations.

[6]The *Social Contract* can be seen as a sort of legal melodrama. It tries to convey a sense of the mystery of legal events, the beauty and elegance of a precise juridical determination of political matters, and the dramatic nobility of sacrifices made in the name of legal formality. One of Rousseau's favorite words is "instantly," which he uses to emphasize the transformative power of legal events. For example, as soon as men consent to the social contract, as if by magic "instantly, in the place of the private person of each contracting party, this act of association produces a moral and collective body" (*SC* I-6: 53; see III-1: 81, III-10: 98, III-14: 101, III-15: 103). The *Social Contract* is suffused with the high tone of ceremonious legalism (see *SC* I-4: 50n).

Rousseau has one final reason for presenting this particular doctrine: he believes that it describes how men actually think and behave, that it is descriptively as well as prescriptively true. It was stated earlier that a treatise of this kind has power in the world because it builds on men's strongest passion and draws obvious and rigorous conclusions from it. But just for this reason, men *already* think and behave as it urges them to. Of course, they do so very imperfectly, partly because they are misled by false beliefs, partly because in following the doctrine on one level they are led to violate it on another. But, taking all of this into account, Rousseau believes that only his new juridical doctrine truly explains how men behave in groups, what a state is, how it really works, what holds it together, and so forth. This is the most neglected dimension of Rousseau's theory and in many respects its most original. The "principles of political right" are put forward by Rousseau, not only as a powerful prescriptive doctrine, but also as a new descriptive theory of political behavior, a comprehensive new science of politics that should help political men to act more prudently and effectively.

To summarize, Rousseau purposely excludes from the *Social Contract* a comprehensive presentation of the human problem as he understands it and of his political solution. For his intention in that work is less to explain his solution than to promote it. He tries to focus the work as narrowly as possible, to build on self-preservation (the requirements of which fortunately coincide with those of psychic health and unity), to construct a formal doctrine which—by virtue of its direct applicability, its psychological power, its rigorous intellectual force, its strict legalism, and its new explanation of political behavior—will help to actualize the political conditions that Rousseau considers, on other, fuller grounds, to be best.[7]

Rousseau's Doctrine

We turn, finally, to the content of this doctrine. The state, for Rousseau, is an artificial invention, and therefore its ideological framework is built from five "technical" concepts, alien to common sense (even if completely familiar by now): the "state of nature," the "social contract," "sovereignty," the "general will," and the "executive."

The "principles of political right" declare that in men's original, natural condition, their "state of nature," there is no state, no natural rule or natural law to speak of, and this eventually leads to a condition of war. To secure their preservation, men need to conclude a "social contract" through which they totally alienate all their rights to a "sovereign." Sovereignty must be bestowed inalienably and indivisibly on the "general will," which is ex-

---

[7] It is sometimes suggested that in Rousseau's view the end of politics is preservation, but that a rhetoric of virtue is necessary as a means to actualize that end. I am arguing that just the opposite is the case.

pressed in general laws that are voted on by all and applied equally to each—the will of the whole community about the community as a whole. The sovereign, which can act only through general laws, must create a distinct "executive power" or "Government"[8] empowered to enforce the laws by applying them to particular individuals. The Government may take any number of different forms, however, and Rousseau's "maxims of politics" offer principles for selecting the best executive form for any given state, as well as guidance regarding how best to enforce the laws.

That is the whole doctrine, and, thus stated, it is extraordinarily simple. To understand it fully, however, has proved extremely difficult. Given what we have seen about natural constitutional law doctrines, such an understanding must involve at least three different levels. On the primary, *prescriptive level*, one must, of course, clarify why this and only this is a legitimate state and also establish exactly what institutions the doctrine requires in the legitimate state (for example, what it means on the concrete, institutional level to make the general will sovereign). Second, on what might be called the *polemical level*, one needs to understand how the doctrine has been designed to further its own actualization and to combat the doctrines and forces that, in its own interpretation of the world, are its primary enemies. Finally, on the *descriptive level*, one must grasp the new way of thinking about political phenomena, the new science of politics, that the doctrine both proclaims and practices.

The ensuing chapters will essentially follow the brief outline of Rousseau's doctrine presented above. Chapter eight discusses the "state of nature—social contract—sovereignty" stage of the argument, which is understood best, I think, if thus treated as a single unit (and here the polemical level will be particularly important). Chapters nine and ten discuss the general will, the first emphasizing the prescriptive level, the second the descriptive. Chapters eleven and twelve deal with the executive power. Finally, after treating all these theoretical issues (albeit with an eye to polemical effects), chapter thirteen focuses on Rousseau's practical intention or "mission": for whom was he writing his books and what hopes did he entertain for reform or revolution?

It cannot be denied that the issues to which we now turn wear a somewhat dry and technical appearance, but not very far beneath the surface lurk theoretical questions of the greatest moment—questions the alienation from which often makes contemporary political theory dry and technical in more than appearance.

---

[8] To avoid confusion, whenever the word "government" is used in Rousseau's technical sense of "the executive power" it will be capitalized. I have not applied this rule, however, to passages quoted from Rousseau.

8

Replacing Natural Rule and Natural Law with the Social Contract and Sovereignty

Rousseau's doctrine begins with an account of the final stage of the "state of nature," and explains how men can escape this condition by concluding a "social contract" that establishes a "sovereign." To understand this doctrine on the prescriptive and descriptive levels, we need only follow the explicit argument of the *Social Contract*; but to grasp its polemical meaning, which is never made explicit, we will have to look elsewhere. We may assume that Rousseau's theory of politics gives him a specific conception not only of what the well-ordered state is but also of what helps and hinders the creation of such a state in practice—an analysis of how the world works, of who his primary "enemies" are, of where their power comes from, of how they may be weakened, and so forth. We may assume, in short, that Rousseau's general political theory points him to a particular doctrinal strategy. But he tends to practice this strategy without describing it, so it is very difficult to figure out what it is, especially at a distance of two hundred years.

The best means of doing so are to consider briefly the historical anteced- ents of Rousseau's doctrine. Of its several constituent elements, the first two—theories of man's primitive condition and of the social contract— have in some sense existed since classical times (if not in their full technical sense), whereas the third, the doctrine of sovereignty, was first formulated in the sixteenth century by Bodin. The first thinker to put these elements together in the specific form used by Rousseau (as well as the first to define sovereignty as a form of will) was Thomas Hobbes.

For the most part, of course, Hobbes presents the same difficulty as Rousseau: he sets forth his doctrinal attack without telling us who he is attacking or why. But occasionally, in the prefaces to his books, Hobbes pauses to explain the polemical purpose or strategy of his doctrines. These few statements provide an indispensable clue to Rousseau's doctrinal strategy as well.

The Strategy of Hobbes's Doctrine

According to the most widely accepted interpretation, the key premise of Hobbes's political thought is that all men are naturally evil, unruly, and contentious. It follows that the danger of anarchy is ever present and that an absolute and all-powerful government is needed to maintain the peace. On this reading of Hobbes, however, it has always proved impossible to explain the very issue we are concerned with, the specific content of his juridical doctrine. C. E. Vaughan, for example, finds it "a strange irony" that Hobbes, "the first writer to formulate in any detail [the theory of social contract], should have perverted it to ends the direct contrary of those for which it was manifestly devised."[1] Why did Hobbes use, indeed why did he invent, the modern doctrine of the state of nature and social contract—which are generally regarded as liberal and liberating—when his whole intention was to strengthen the authority of the state? Why did he scorn the more "authoritarian" premise of traditional natural law—that man is born for society—and enthusiastically adopt the individualist principle that man is born for himself alone, hence free?

To resolve this paradox, to discover the true function of Hobbes's juridical doctrine, it is necessary to correct the mistaken view of his premises, a mistake which obscures the whole novelty of his thought. Hobbes does not assert but rather denies that all men are actively malicious or "evil." He claims only that all are selfish or self-centered and, in addition, that a small minority are strongly ambitious or contentious from a love of glory.[2] There is indeed an ever present danger of anarchy, but it does not arise from the lawlessness and disobedience of the great mass of individuals, still less from the collective ambition of the different social classes, but from the subversive activity of a few ambitious individuals. These men, by deceiving and scaring others into following them, form clans, armies, parties, sects, and other associations, and—thus empowered by the obedience of others—they resist or subvert the established government.

This is not a minor correction of the previous interpretation but a complete reversal: Hobbes claims that anarchy is a constant danger not because the masses are too disobedient, but *too obedient*. Eager for peace but easily frightened, the mass of men are "followers," too easily led by rabble rousers of all kinds—by orators, sophists, military heroes, demagogic moralists, and, above all, by ambitious priests.

We may cite Rousseau himself in support of this interpretation of Hobbes—as well as of this novel interpretation of the political problem. "Of all Christian authors, the philosopher Hobbes is the only one who correctly saw the evil and the remedy" for modern Western politics. The evil is the "internal divisions that have never ceased to stir up Christian peoples," the "perpetual conflict of jurisdiction that has made any good polity impossible in Christian states" where "no people has ever been able to figure out whom it was obligated to obey, the [political] master or the priest"

[1] Vaughan (1925) pp. 22, 12.

[2] *De Cive* Preface: 100-101, I-4: 114; *Leviathan* XIII: 99, 101.

(*SC* IV-8: 126-27). In short, it is the people's *misplaced obedience* that, by empowering the ambitious, leads to anarchy.[3]

This conception of the political problem leads Hobbes to a completely new doctrinal strategy. He realizes that, untraditional and counterintuitive though it may be, the best means for strengthening the government and ending anarchy is to disarm the ambitious by making the people *less* obedient, less receptive to authority. That is why he developed his new individualistic juridical doctrine, as he openly acknowledges. The doctrine aims to make men "the less subject to serve the ambition of a few discontented persons, in their purposes against the state."[4] Hobbes has constructed his doctrine

> for your sakes, readers, who I persuaded myself, when you should rightly apprehend and thoroughly understand this doctrine . . . that, weighing the justice of those things you are about, not by the persuasion and advice of private men, but by the laws of the realm, you will no longer suffer ambitious men through the streams of your blood to wade to their own power.[5]

Let us consider, then, how each element of Hobbes's doctrine—the "state of nature," "social contract," and "sovereignty"—relates to this declared purpose.

Hobbes's theory of the "state of nature"[6] serves the function of liberating men from all traditional forms of authority, all natural claims to rule. By establishing that men are by nature apolitical, equal, selfish, and at war with one another, it refutes all claims to leadership and throws each man back on himself. Men owe no obedience to any of the old authorities, to the old,

---

[3] This theory of politics traces back to Machiavelli, who is the first to have made this systematic distinction between the many and the ambitious and, as he openly claims, the first to argue that the people are fundamentally conservative and that all political unrest derives from the ambitious minority. See *The Prince* IX; *Discourses*, I-4, 5, 58.

[4] *Leviathan* Conclusion: 511.

[5] *De Cive* Preface: 103.

[6] While theories of man's primitive condition have not been uncommon in the history of political philosophy, this condition has not usually been regarded as the "state of nature." On a teleological understanding of nature, man's fully developed and perfected condition is his natural state. And even those who, like the Epicureans, rejected teleology but saw human nature as susceptible of a specific state of fulfillment or satisfaction were inclined to regard that condition, and not the most primitive one, as the most natural. (Lucretius, for example, believes the first men did not have families but does not therefore consider the family unnatural. See *On the Nature of Things* V, 956ff.; Nichols [1976] pp. 127-28.) It is because he rejects both teleology and the notion of a *summum bonum* that Hobbes unambiguously identifies man's natural condition with his beginnings. (Rousseau, on the other hand, reintroduces a notion of *summum bonum*, but locates it precisely at man's source or beginnings.) The additional premise that man's beginnings were apolitical—because man is not spontaneously inclined to or fit for civil society—leads to the radical division of human history into two stages: a prepolitical "state of nature" and an artificial state of "civil society." See Strauss (1953) p. 184n.

the wise, the virtuous, the great, or the holy. Hobbes undermines the claim of family, guild, class, province, church, and tradition, of all mediating institutions and subpolitical associations. Thus he creates the liberated and naked "individual"—whom he intends to leave alone to face the modern state: the resulting homogeneous, centralized, and absolute state. As Tocqueville would warn the Americans two hundred years later, individualism and tyranny go hand in hand. Hobbes is the inventor of "anti-authoritarian absolutism": his new "liberal" doctrine liberates men the better to control them.[7]

Having used the "state of nature" to refute all natural and supernatural titles to rule, Hobbes refounds the authority of the existing rulers through the doctrine of "social contract."[8] He tells men that they have irrevocably, if tacitly, consented to the rule of the established sovereign. Yet, again, a theory of contract or tacit consent seems a bizarre choice for Hobbes since it hardly produces in men a strong inclination to obey, as Hobbes himself admits, "for nothing is more easily broken than a man's word."[9] Moreover, won't it inevitably lead the people to assert a right to withdraw their consent? The use of this doctrine becomes intelligible only in light of Hobbes's new conception of the political task: not to strengthen obedience but end its misplacement. There is no danger that the people will disobey the sovereign so long as they do not obey rival authorities. And the social contract doctrine, in Hobbes's new formulation, has this specific and inimitable virtue: it supplies a reason for authority that only the established ruler can invoke, for it bases authority not on the virtue of the ruler, indeed not on any quality of his whatsoever (which some other man might claim to possess more), but solely on the consent of the people bestowed as an arbitrary gift. Let others be wiser, holier, or morally superior; only the established sovereign can claim men's (tacit) consent.

In other words, Hobbes's social contract theory accomplishes this ideological revolution: it separates the idea of "leadership" or "authority" from the whole notion of "superiority"; it creates for the first time a political legitimacy that stands independent of any moral or religious claims (which are inherently uncertain and disputable). Hobbes inverts the whole structure of the traditional state: legitimacy no longer descends from above, from the

---

[7] *Leviathan* XXII: 169-79, XX: 152-53.

[8] The notion of a social contract has, of course, had a long history (the best survey of which is still probably Gough's *The Social Contract* [1957]). But prior to Hobbes, all or most of those thinkers who used a doctrine of contract to ground political legitimacy considered the social contract, like the marriage contract, to be only the proximate cause of an institution whose form and existence were fundamentally natural. With Hobbes, however, contractarianism becomes a far more radical doctrine, for men are naturally apolitical individuals, the state is artificial, and thus the social contract is the sole cause and ordering principle of the state. See Rommen (1969) pp. 219-47; Gough (1957) pp. 67-73.

[9] *Leviathan* XIV: 105.

substantive authority of right reason or the good; it ascends from the people, it is a contractual transfer of each individual's absolute and arbitrary authority over himself. Hobbes replaces the age-old and ever disputed "noble lie" of the leader's natural or supernatural superiority with the precise "legal fiction" that the sovereign's will is your own.

But title to rule is one thing, substantive justice another. Hobbes thought it unavailing to try to end conflict over the former without also settling the question of the latter. A man's title to rule may be perfectly clear, but if a natural or transcendent standard of justice is acknowledged by which his particular laws and actions may be judged, then ambitious ideologues will use it to subvert his rule. Through the call to "justice" or "morality" the people will be induced once again to "join with ambitious and hellish spirits, to the utter ruin of their state."[10] Thus, a crucial further doctrine is needed.

> If any man shall . . . by most firm reasons demonstrate that there are no authentical doctrines concerning right and wrong, good and evil, besides the constituted laws in each realm and government . . . surely he will not only show us the highway to peace, but will also teach us how to avoid the close, dark, and dangerous by-paths of faction and sedition; than which I know not what can be thought more profitable.[11]

Hobbes aspired to be that man by virtue of his doctrine of "sovereignty."

He argues as follows. The total war prevailing in man's natural state sweeps away not only all natural titles to rule, but also virtually all morality, all substantive natural law in the traditional sense. Where all are enemies, everything is permitted.[12] (The immoralism of *raison d'état* is, in this way, at the root of the doctrine of sovereignty.) Consequently, men themselves must create their own order and rules of morality by creating the coercive legislating power that nature and God cruelly fail to provide. Men can do so only by promising to obey this power whatever it commands, for, owing to the weakness of reason, men will never agree among themselves on what is right and wrong; they must renounce reason and submit to an arbitrary decision. But such "binding arbitration" and blind obedience is rational because any well-enforced command or law, regardless of content, will produce peace, and peace is virtually the whole of the common good. Thus, law and morality, according to Hobbes, are whatever the sovereign declares them to be, whatever he wills.

[10] *De Cive* Preface: 97.

[11] Ibid., 98.

[12] More precisely, a vestigial natural law does remain, but it's overriding commandment is to obey the civil sovereign in all his commandments. Thus "the law of nature, and the civil law, contain each other, and are of equal extent." *Leviathan* XXVI: 199-200; see XV: 113-14, XVIII: 136-37, XXI: 161-62. As we will see, Rousseau's rejection of natural law is more radical and more complete.

That is the core of the doctrine of sovereignty. The natural law tradition, by contrast, had defined law as "rational command," to indicate its dual character: a law is the command of a duly constituted authority, but to be truly a law it must also be in conformity with the immutable standard of justice apprehended by reason. And of these two characteristics, the true essence and obligation of law consists in the second, not in the command of authority as such but from the intrinsic justice of what is commanded. The doctrine of sovereignty arises from a fundamental break with the rationalism of past thought, from a rejection of this uncertain and troublesome transcendent standard. It reduces law and morality to pure authority, pure will.[13] As Hobbes states: "Before there was any government, *just* and *unjust* had no being. Legitimate kings therefore make the things they command just, by commanding them, and those they forbid, unjust, by forbidding them."[14] Sovereign command, authoritative will, is the source of all "authentical doctrines concerning right and wrong, good and evil." Thus Hobbes closes off the "dangerous by-paths of faction and sedition."

In sum, Hobbes's individualistic political philosophy produces a new analysis of the political problem—anarchy is caused by the ambitious few, empowered by the misplaced obedience of the people—which leads, in turn, to a novel doctrinal strategy—individualistic or anti-authoritarian absolutism. By making the people more skeptical and individualistic, by liberating them from all moral claims grounded in nature or God, they will be "the less subject to serve the ambition of a few discontented persons, in their purposes against the state." With the ambitious thus disarmed, the sovereign will be rendered strong and absolute.[15]

The purpose of the official doctrine Rousseau elaborates in the *Social Contract* is essentially the same, or so I will argue in the remainder of the chapter. This should not be altogether surprising. Hobbes and Rousseau in fact share an identical view of the central political task (albeit with a different understanding of the ultimate goal): both are obsessed with closing off every possible challenge to the law, both seek an airtight state with an "infallible" absolute sovereign. As we will see, Rousseau also shares Hobbes's understanding of the chief obstacle to such a condition: the ambitious ideologues and moralists who escape and subvert the law through the appeal to some supposedly higher law. Having the same task and the same enemies, Rousseau adopts the counterintuitive strategy first invented by Hobbes: to shackle the ambitious by freeing the people, to strengthen the state by subverting all traditional sources of authority, to promote absolutism through a kind of "individualism."

[13] See Thomas Aquinas, *Summa Theologica*, I-II, qu. 90, a. 1; qu. 93, a. 3; qu. 95, a. 2. Strauss (1953) p. 186; Strauss (1952) pp. 157-61.

[14] *De Cive* XII-1: 244-45, emphasis in the original.

[15] For a detailed analysis of Hobbes's doctrine see the excellent study by Kraynak (1990).

To put this strategy into effect, Rousseau requires the same ideological weapons, and that is why he takes over all the juridical doctrines invented by Hobbes—whom he declares "one of the greatest geniuses that has ever existed" (*Guerre*, 611). He uses a radically individualistic "state of nature" doctrine to sweep the ground clear of all troublesome claims regarding natural rule and natural law, and then refounds both political authority and morality on new and unchallengeable grounds through the doctrines, respectively, of "social contract" and of "sovereignty" understood as pure, authoritative "will."

No one could deny, of course, that Rousseau also strongly disagrees with what he called the "horrible system of Hobbes" (ibid., 610). But these disagreements, as violent as they are, do not remove the underlying agreement, although they have done much to obscure it.

Rousseau violently rejects Hobbes's absolute monarchy, preferring instead absolute democracy, and therefore uses the social contract doctrine for a purpose not found in Hobbes: to demand that sovereignty be kept in the hands of the people. This second function of the contract—its use as a weapon for the people in the great historical battle of "peoples vs. rulers"— is the one that we today regard as the essential and even the only imaginable purpose of this doctrine.

But that is precisely why the historical connection to Hobbes is so important and revealing. It uncovers the first and in some ways more fundamental purpose of Rousseau's doctrine, its use as a weapon in the great historical battle of "political sovereigns vs. all rival moral and religious authorities." Rousseau's juridical doctrine, in other words, has two polemical meanings: it is a republican and violently anti-Hobbesian manifesto aimed against kings and despots, as has always been seen (and as will be discussed in the chapters on the general will and the executive). But it is also an absolutist and profoundly Hobbesian tract fighting for the consolidation of the modern state by attacking the scourge of religious and philosophical moralists—as will be seen in what follows.

I have stressed that Rousseau's doctrine needs to be viewed in light of its polemical purpose and strategy, but it must not be seen as mere rhetoric, for the same considerations that make it useful also make it true in his eyes. With this in mind, let us try to follow his argument.

The Rejection of Natural Rule

The primary question Rousseau asks in the *Social Contract*, to which his juridical doctrine is the answer, is: What constitutional form must a government have in order to be "legitimate," that is, in order to place its citizens under a genuine obligation to obey?

He begins his answer by asserting that political obligation "does not come from *nature*; it is therefore based on *conventions*. The problem is to know what these conventions [i.e. the social contract] are" (*SC* I-1: 47, emphasis added). But before answering this question, he must prove what he has just asserted, that rule or authority is not natural, that man is free of all obligations not originating in his own will or contract, and that the whole question of legitimacy therefore comes down to determining the terms of this conventional agreement.

Accordingly, Rousseau must undertake a study of man's true nature and condition, which leads him, for the same reasons as it did Hobbes, to an investigation of the "state of nature." The latter, presented primarily in the *Second Discourse*, demonstrates that nature has not appointed any men as rulers nor has it legislated any moral laws. As in Hobbes, the state of nature doctrine serves to liberate "the individual," to free man both from all natural titles to rule and from all substantive natural law.

The first half of the argument—the rejection of natural rule—is nothing other than Rousseau's proof for his famous claim that "man is born free." The demonstration follows directly from the character of men in the state of nature: authority can hardly be natural if men are by nature dispersed and solitary, perfectly self-sufficient, and too stupid to form even the concept of "authority" (*SD*, 102, 139-40). The *Social Contract* supplements this argument with a refutation of the particular doctrines of Divine Right, the right of the stronger, and paternal authority—doctrines less in need of a response today than in Rousseau's time (*SC* I-2, 3: 47-49; *SD*, 161-66; *PE*, 209-11; *GM* I-5: 168-74; *Emile* V: 459-60). The argument against paternal authority remains important, however, bearing, as it does, also on the classical argument for the natural right to rule of wisdom or virtue.

The classical view is based on two eminently reasonable assumptions. First, man is by nature a social or political animal who can realize his humanity only within a political community. Consequently, the individual is not born free or for himself alone but has natural duties to the community that exist independent of his will or consent. Second, men are by nature unequal. And since the community must be ruled by *somebody*, it makes sense that it should be ruled by the better rather than the worse, by the wise and virtuous rather than the foolish and corrupt, for they will do the better job. Again, this natural worthiness to rule does not depend on human conventions or contracts.

The strongest and most obvious case for the existence of such natural authority lies in the family, in the father's right to rule the children (the case for the political community being admittedly far more complex and qualified). Thus, if paternal authority, the strongest case, is refuted, the rest of the classical case for natural rule will fall with it.

It is in his attack on paternal authority, therefore, that Rousseau explicitly defends the claim, contradicting the classical view, that man is born free.

> This common freedom is a consequence of man's nature. His first
> law is to attend to his own preservation, his first cares are those he

owes himself; and as soon as he has reached the age of reason, as he
alone is the judge of the proper means of preserving himself, he thus
becomes his own master. (*SC* I-2: 47)

In a very compressed way, Rousseau responds precisely to the two points
made above. Man's natural freedom is "a consequence of his nature." How?
First, because his fundamental desire is for his own preservation, his
own selfish good. Thus he is not naturally social or political, and, born
for himself alone, he has natural duties only to himself. Yet, given the
second classical premise—that some men are wiser than others—won't the
wise be the best judges regarding the means to each man's preservation and
thus still maintain their title to natural authority? To this implicit objection,
Rousseau responds that each man "is the judge of the proper means of
preserving himself." Not that all men are equal in wisdom—they are
not—but, as he states more clearly elsewhere, "it is even more certain that
the son loves himself than it is that the father loves the son" (*Emile* V: 459).
The point again hinges on men's natural selfishness: the wisdom of other
men is ultimately less important than their otherness. Each individual can
truly trust only himself and so must rule himself.

Rousseau overturns the classical view, then, by attacking only the first
of its two assumptions. Without questioning the existence of vast inequalities of ability among men, but rejecting the view that man is naturally
social, Rousseau dismisses all claims to natural authority and demonstrates
that man is born free.[16] From this he draws his desired conclusion: "since
no man has any natural authority over his fellow man . . . there remain only
conventions as the basis of all legitimate authority among men" (*SC* I-4:
49). Natural rule is replaced by the social contract.

The Rejection of Natural Law

The second half of Rousseau's argument—the rejection of substantive
natural law—aims to establish a similar conclusion: since there is no natural
morality, the only possible basis for binding rules of right and wrong is human
agreement or will. Rousseau would replace natural law with sovereignty.

---

[16]As Gildin (1983, p.18) points out, although Rousseau's argument is often thought to
resemble Locke's in the *Second Treatise*, it is, on the contrary, a straightforward restatement
of Hobbes's reasoning. See *De Cive* I-7, 8, 9: 115-16, III-13: 143; *Leviathan* XV: 119-20. The
only difference between the two at this juncture is that Hobbes is far more egalitarian than
Rousseau, denying as he does that there are significant differences of intelligence among men
(*Leviathan* VIII: 61-62, XIII: 98). It is worth mentioning on the latter point that whereas
Rousseau's argument culminates in an extreme defense of democracy, it never makes use of
the traditional democratic argument that there is wisdom in numbers and therefore the people
should rule because, collectively, they know best. See, for example, Aristotle's *Politics*
1281a40-1281b25, and Tocqueville's *Democracy in America*, pp. 435-36.

Again the crucial premise will be the denial that man is a social animal; but equally important will be Rousseau's denial that man is the rational animal, his extreme skepticism directed at the worth and power of reason, his break with classical rationalism. As compared with the preceding argument— which is generally accepted today—this one is far more controversial and complex. It is important that we follow it with some care because it treats crucial issues almost completely ignored by contemporary moral philosophy and because it leads to what is perhaps the most epoch-making consequence of Rousseau's thought: the total liberation of humanity from all moral standards above human will.

A. That There Is No Natural Law in the State of Nature

Rousseau treats the subject of natural law with very great brevity, which has led to much uncertainty concerning his position.[17] He first makes his case in the preface to the *Second Discourse* by means of a compressed and elliptical refutation of "our jurists," by which he means Grotius, Barbeyrac, Burlamaqui, Pufendorf—the school of natural law, as it came to be called. These writers were the main authorities on moral and political matters for the Encyclopedists; and Diderot, chief among the latter, vigorously responded to Rousseau's attack in his *Encyclopedia* article entitled "Natural Right." Rousseau then defended and enlarged upon his views in an introductory chapter of the *Geneva Manuscript* (the first draft of the *Social Contract*).

We may take Pufendorf as representative of the natural law doctrine Rousseau attacks.[18] It is an explicit compromise between Hobbes and more traditional natural law. Pufendorf accepts Hobbes's individualistic social contract doctrine regarding the right to rule but emphatically rejects his doctrine of sovereignty in favor of a secular code of natural law, which he sets forth in great detail in his books.

According to Pufendorf's argument, all men originally lived in a "state of nature" in which they were free, equal, and without rule; hence, all rule arises from a social contract, as Hobbes had taught. Although men are naturally apolitical, however, they are not naturally selfish but rather social and sociable; therefore, their natural state was a social and peaceful one in which they could and did practice the law of nature as discovered by reason. Since they did so imperfectly, however, states and rulers were eventually established precisely

[17] There has been a long scholarly debate about whether Rousseau dismisses or embraces natural law. See, for example, Vaughn (1915, vol. I, pp. 16-18), Hubert (1928), Hendel (1934, vol. I, pp. 97-99, 182), Cobban (1934, pp. 115, 147-50), Gough (1957, pp. 156-57), Haymann (1943-45), Crocker (1961-62), Hall (1973, pp. 25-28), and Goldschmidt (1974, pp. 133-55). The interpretation I develop here owes the most to Masters (1968, pp. 76-89, 158-65, 316-22) and Plattner (1979, chap. 5).

[18] Baron Samuel von Pufendorf (1632-94) was a German historian and theorist of natural law. I agree with Derathé's assessment (1950, pp. 83-84) that, of all the writers of the natural law school, Rousseau seems to have the most respect for Pufendorf.

to enforce and follow that natural law—and not freely to create law with absolute sovereignty. Thus, justice, the rules of right and wrong, derive from nature, but the state and political authority are artificial, deriving from consent.[19]

Against Pufendorf, Rousseau maintains that justice is *not* natural, thereby rejecting the compromise with traditional natural law and wholly returning to the position of "Hobbes [who] saw very clearly the defect of all modern definitions of natural right" (*SD*, 129). In outline, Rousseau makes the following two-part argument. For a binding natural law to exist, two things are minimally necessary: the law must be known to men or adequately "promulgated," and it must be enforced or sanctioned. Now, in the original state of nature, Pufendorf's rational principles of natural law cannot be known; later, when they may be known, they are not by nature enforced.

The first half of the argument follows directly from Rousseau's premise of man's asociality: since reason cannot develop without society and language, solitary natural man could not possibly have known, hence could not have been subject to, any rational laws of nature.[20] Moreover, even if one should grant to Pufendorf and the others that man was sociable and rational in the primitive state of nature, the difficulty would still remain because:

> they all establish [natural] law upon such metaphysical principles . . .
> that it is impossible to understand [it] and consequently to obey it
> without being a great reasoner and a profound metaphysician; which
> means precisely that men must have used, for the establishment of
> [civil] society, enlightenment which only develops with great diffi-
> culty and in very few people in the midst of society itself. (*SD*, 94)[21]

These objections, based on abstract reasoning, are confirmed by the facts of history: "One easily sees that the healthy ideas of natural right and the brotherhood of all men were disseminated rather late and made such slow progress in the world that it was only Christianity that generalized them sufficiently" (*GM* I-2: 162).[22] Thus the first precondition of natural law—

---

[19]*Droit de la Nature* II-2, II-3, VII-1, VIII-1.5. See Rommen (1947) pp. 77-88, Derathé (1950) pp. 36-41.

[20]Although Rousseau claims that there is no natural *law* in the state of nature—that is, an obligatory moral code to which men can and must knowingly submit—he claims that there is a natural *right*—a natural way of relating to one another that men follow blindly and instinctively. As a result of their fundamental inclinations of self-preservation and of pity, natural men followed, without knowing it, what Rousseau calls the "maxim of natural goodness": "Do what is good for you with the least possible harm to others" (*SD*, 133; see 94-96). The development of reason, however, by extending the passions and weakening pity, destroys this natural right (*SD*, 95-96, 132).

[21]The meaning of his point about the "establishment of [civil] society" will become clear in a moment.

[22]See *Droit de la Nature* II-2.10.

that it be promulgated or known by nature—is not met.

But even if these supposed laws of natural justice were known, the second half of the argument continues, they would not be morally binding or valid because they are not by nature enforced. To appreciate this argument concerning the sanctions for morality it is important that one not "Kantianize" the essentially heteronomous natural law tradition. Rousseau and his opponents all agree that, to be valid and binding, the demands of natural law must be rooted in the inclinations and fulfillment of human nature.[23] As Burlamaqui puts it, natural law is the collection of "those rules which nature alone prescribes to man, in order to conduct him safely to the end, which everyone has, and indeed ought to have, in view, namely, true and solid happiness."[24]

For a rule of justice to be valid or obligatory it must promote the natural good of all when all follow it. But in addition, it must have a force or sanction—stemming from the power of reason, from a benevolent passion, or from some external agent, natural or divine—which can guarantee to each that the others will indeed follow it (or at least compensate them for others' disobedience). "To be acknowledged among us," Rousseau states, "justice must be reciprocal" (SC II-6: 65). Therefore, if "natural law" is not by nature enforced and generally obeyed, and if it is thus harmful to those who do obey, then this law cannot be naturally binding or valid. In other words, one cannot wholly separate the question of the validity of a moral standard from that of its force in the world.[25]

Now, Rousseau argues that in the later stages of the state of nature reason does in fact develop, along with extended desires and (nonpolitical) society. Theoretically, men could then form a rational conception of "justice" or of a "common good." But we find that "the development of society stifles humanity in men's hearts by awakening personal interest, and that concepts of the natural law . . . begin to develop only when the prior development of the passions renders all its precepts impotent" (GM I-2: 159). After the full development of reason Rousseau's state of nature becomes essentially the same as Hobbes's, a "most horrible state of war," and at this point his

[23]SD, 93. *Droit de la nature* II-2.14. Grotius *Law of War and Peace* I-1.

[24]*Principes du Droit Naturel* I-1.1. See SD, 93.

[25]Our ability to interpret not only Rousseau but the whole history of political philosophy has been greatly impeded by the influence in our time of an unexamined and largely unstated Kantian moralism that makes us insist, as previous ages had not, that the eudemonistic or heteronomous consideration of "sanctions" not be relevant to the issue of moral obligation. Thus, we no longer raise or understand the question of whether morality is supported by nature, or by the state, or by God. This explains the three most striking characteristics of contemporary moral philosophy as compared with the thought of the past: it is indifferent to the issue of morality's "naturalness" (hence also to the "state of nature" as an historical issue), it is extremely unpolitical, and it sees no philosophical need to raise the religious question.

objection to natural law is also the same. Rousseau imagines a man in this state speaking as follows:

> I am aware that I bring horror and confusion to the human species but either I must be unhappy or I must cause others to be so, and no one is dearer to me than myself. . . . Everything you tell me about the advantages of the social law would be fine if while I were scrupulously observing it toward others, I were sure that all of them would observe it toward me. But what assurances of this can you give me . . . ? Either give me guarantees against all unjust undertakings or do not expect me to refrain from them in turn. (*GM* I-2: 160; see *SC* II-6: 66)

Lacking a natural sanction, the rules of "justice" were naturally harmful to follow and therefore not obligatory or valid.

In sum, Rousseau repudiates the natural law compromise of Pufendorf, Diderot, and the others, whereby justice is natural though the state artificial. He shows that the supposed natural law known and followed in the state of nature "is truly an illusion, since the conditions for it are always either unknown or impracticable and men must necessarily be in ignorance of them or violate them" (*GM* I-2: 159).

Although the argument is quite straightforward and plausible, what remains unclear is its relevance. Traditional natural law doctrines, after all, were not explicitly based on the thesis that natural law was known and followed in a prepolitical state of nature, so what significance have Pufendorf's assertion of this thesis and Rousseau's denial? We must try to reconstruct the philosophical bearing of the debate we have just witnessed, which, for some reason, we no longer engage in and no longer understand.

B. The Significance of the State of Nature

Pufendorf and Rousseau agree in adopting Hobbes's view that politics and the state are not natural. This new premise is what forces Pufendorf beyond the traditional view, for if justice is to be *natural*, it cannot owe its existence to the state, which is artificial; therefore, it must exist prior to the state, in the "state of nature."

But isn't this merely a quibble over names? One wants to say that in our present civilized world certain moral laws clearly exist that are both known and followed, and therefore they are valid and binding whether or not one chooses to call them "natural." Yet a serious philosophical issue is at stake in the use of this word, and it concerns the relation of this moral law to the state and its laws. If the moral law derives its force directly from nature—as is the case if and only if it already existed in the state of nature—then it constitutes a binding natural standard above the state to which the latter can and should be made to conform. On the other hand, if the moral law did not exist in the state of nature, then it must owe such reality as it now possesses to the state and positive law, and in that case it cannot constitute an independent, natural standard above them. On the contrary, the moral law is then an artificial human creation, wholly subordinated to the needs of the state. Thus the historical debate over the character of the state of nature is a debate over the relative causal and ontological priority of morality on the one hand and the state or positive law on the other.

Let us try to make this more precise. Rousseau does not deny altogether the existence of an objective standard of justice. His argument is not that of an ancient Sophist nor that of a contemporary positivist or relativist. He acknowledges that "whatever is good and in accordance with order is so by the nature of things, independently of human conventions . . . there is without doubt a universal justice emanating from reason alone" (*SC* II-6: 65). Men have, or rather can be made to have, a common good; and one can easily imagine rules which, *if* generally known and followed, would promote that good. But Rousseau scorns those thinkers who consider this a sufficient basis for a doctrine of natural law or, as we might say today, for a "theory of justice." For, to be genuine moral laws, these rules must be *in fact* generally known and enforced (*SD*, 95). Thus one must raise the further question of whether that crucial condition is ever met. Pufendorf and Rousseau both agree that it is (hence both believe that a valid morality does or can exist). But one must ask: Is the condition met directly, through the natural force of the rules themselves—in which case they constitute a natural law—or only indirectly, through the agency of a human invention, the (legitimate) state?

Hobbes, for example, takes the latter position. Justice lacks a natural sanction and thus does not exist in the state of nature; it has no force of its own and owes such existence as it ever attains to the state's enforcing power. But then what grounds the power and cohesion of the state? Since the state cannot be built upon men's natural obedience to and knowledge of justice, which by hypothesis does not exist, it must be built on nonmoral foundations: on the passion of fear and on "sovereignty," on the agreement to accept the sovereign's will as *definitive of* "justice." Of course, foolish moralists who have grown up within this artificially created moral order and who, failing to raise this crucial question of *origins*, assume that it is natural, will moralistically demand that citizens obey the sovereign only when his commands seem just. They will attempt to make morality, which is purely a by-product of the state, into its foundation. Such moralism will only destroy the state and, with it, all morality. Justice, Hobbes shows, cannot constitute a "natural law" independent of the state and its laws. The state alone is the creator of any and all human obligation.

Pufendorf, on the other hand, finds this view repellent and implausible. He replies: "It is not to be conceived that civil governments could ever have been established, or after their establishment, preserved, if there had not been something just and unjust antecedent to their existence."[26] Reversing Hobbes's

---

[26]*Droit de la Nature* VIII-1.5.

argument, he maintains that one cannot explain the existence and cohesion of civil society except as a result of the natural power of morality. The objective standard of justice, naturally known and obeyed, is a real force in the world, he asserts, which predated the state, gave rise to it, and now maintains it. This standard therefore constitutes a genuine natural law: a direct, obligatory code for men's behavior, a binding standard independent of the state and positive law, and superior to them.[27]

But Rousseau, we have seen, convincingly refutes this view by showing that in the state of nature justice is either not known or not enforced. In truth, Pufendorf has an extremely difficult position to defend, for once one denies the naturalness of the state it becomes very difficult to maintain the naturalness of morality. One is driven to make rather extreme, moralistic, and implausible claims for the direct, natural force of justice, unaided by the enforcing and promulgating powers of the state.

Yet, in refuting Pufendorf's moralistic view of the self-subsistence of morality, Rousseau does not merely restore but goes beyond the Hobbesian view, for he argues that morality is utterly dependent on the state not only for enforcement but also for the full development of man's reason and moral consciousness. It is the state and it alone that has "produced a remarkable change in man by substituting justice for instinct in his behavior" (*SC* I-8: 55-56).[28] In the *Confessions*, Rousseau formulates this as follows: "My perspective had been greatly extended by the historical study of morality. I had seen that everything is basically tied to *politics*, and that, however one tried, no people would ever be anything except what the nature of its government would make it be" (*Confs.* IX: 404-5, emphasis added).[29] In a sense, Rousseau's view constitutes a return to classical political philosophy with its strikingly political approach to all human phenomena, with its claim that man's whole moral and cultural life is determined by the constitution or regime, by "the nature of its government." But by combining this classical premise of the "primacy of the political" with the modern, Hobbes-

---

[27]Positive laws violating the natural law, for example, are not binding. *Droit de la Nature* VII-8.2, VIII-1.

[28] See *GM* II-2: 182, *SD*, 94, 133; *SC* II-7: 69. In one respect, of course, Rousseau moves closer to Pufendorf. He agrees that the state cannot be held together by force or fear alone, but is essentially dependent on the morality or virtue of the citizens. But Rousseau makes it very clear that this morality, so far from being natural, is positively antinatural and that it is wholly a creation of the state.

[29] Though he is most often considered a moralist and a "moral thinker," Rousseau claimed to differ from most of his contemporaries precisely in being a *political* philosopher. He could well have been describing himself when he wrote in a fragmentary biography of the Abbé de St. Pierre: he was persuaded that "morality was not the most important science for the happiness of men, but rather politics or the science of government was; and that a single wise law could make incomparably more men happy than could a hundred good treatises of morality. . . . He applied himself uniquely to the science of the government of states and was surprised to find so few men who applied themselves to the same study" (*OC* III: 665).

ian premise of the "artificiality of the political," Rousseau produces a new and radical separation between the whole moral-cultural world and nature. The state is an artificial human creation and so is the morality which it alone produces and makes possible.

In sum, the modern premise that politics and the state are not natural produces this crucial historical debate regarding the state of nature—regarding the relative priority of morality and the state—and this stark philosophical choice between the moralism of the school of natural law and the immoralism of the doctrine of sovereignty.

Rousseau takes the latter view. He does acknowledge the existence of an objective standard of order or justice, discoverable by the wise. But by proving that it is not promulgated or sanctioned in the state of nature, he shows that it does not obligate us by its own nature, it does not constitute a "natural law" in the sense of a code of morality binding on the individual and the state. The objective standard cannot be realized "morally," through direct appeal to it. It (or at least something like it) can be realized only politically and indirectly, through the actions of the (legitimate) state—or so Rousseau will argue. "Law comes before justice and not justice before law" (*GM* II-4: 191). There is no natural law to define the state and positive law; rather the legitimate state will define justice.

Rousseau's argument, and indeed the relevance of the whole debate concerning the state of nature, is open to one further objection: humanity has made progress. Even if the state was at first indispensable for the teaching and enforcement of morality among savages, that historical fact is now perfectly irrelevant, for man has gradually become tamed, enlightened, and moralized, and this inner moral progress has long since freed justice from its utter dependence on the state. Today the objective standard of order or justice—whose existence Rousseau acknowledges—is directly accessible to our minds just as its demands have taken direct root in our inclinations or characters, and therefore, although not altogether "natural," it certainly constitutes a standard above the state and an obligatory moral law.[30]

C. The Critique of Progress and Enlightenment

To evaluate this objection, Rousseau would argue, one must distinguish between two very different cases. First, in the rare places where a genuinely legitimate state has come into being, there will indeed be genuine moral progress: naturally selfish men will be transformed into virtuous citizens. But this "progress" results not from man's gradual development and progress over time, but from the accidental intercession of a wise legislator. Moreover, this citizen morality, so difficult and strenuous and so inseparable from patriotism, will still remain utterly dependent on the "father-

[30] The faith in progress is one of the primary reasons why the issue of the state of nature, as an historical question, is completely ignored in contemporary moral and political theory.

land"and on the comprehensive moralizing environment created by the state. It will not be a standard independent of the state. And to treat it as if it were, to appeal to it in preference to the positive law, would be destructive of the state.

As for the rest of the civilized world, which of course is what the above objection has primarily in view, Rousseau simply denies that it has experienced any genuine progress. Based on his fundamental insight into the contradiction of society, Rousseau believes that "civilization" as it has spontaneously developed through history is a sham, a trap, a piece of collective hypocrisy, which disguises but in no way abolishes the two original obstacles to natural law: as in the state of nature, justice is not sufficiently known and not adequately enforced.

Consider the question of moral knowledge. Obviously, reason has made immense progress since primitive times and elaborate concepts of justice and theories of natural law have developed in society. Rousseau nevertheless denies that the mass of men have become so rational as to have access to a true understanding of justice. "The art of generalizing ideas," he asserts, "is one of the most difficult and belated exercises of human understanding, will the average man ever be capable of deriving his rules of conduct from this manner of reasoning?" (*GM* I-2: 161; see II-2: 182 and *SC* II-6: 67). But the cause of men's moral ignorance is not so much a lack of intelligence or education, as the corrupt state of their characters, which in turn derives from the structure of society and the state. Thus, there is no natural law above the state, able to judge and correct it, because where the state is corrupt, so will be men's opinions of the natural law. Regardless of our intellectual progress, then, there has been no social or moral progress and men still do not have that direct access to the moral truth that would be necessary to make it directly binding upon them.

Pufendorf and other moralists would respond that Rousseau's argument makes the condition of men's moral knowledge too dependent on the state, for in enlightened times this dependence is overcome through the activity of moral philosophers who, liberated from the prejudices of their time and political environment, promulgate to the rest of mankind the timeless truths of morality. Pufendorf thought this was particularly true in his own time, thanks to recent progress in the science of natural law. As Barbeyrac explains in the introduction to his translation of Pufendorf, all natural law doctrines before Grotius failed to "contain a complete body of morality such as descends to the utmost degree of particularity and where everything is digested into the very best order and method possible."[31] But now the natural law school has constructed such a rigorous and detailed *code de nature* to serve as a direct guide for the conduct of life and affairs. Owing to

[31] Section 28. According to the *Encyclopedia* as well, natural law was "known only imperfectly to the ancients, their wise men and their philosophers have spoken of it most often in a very superficial way" ("Right of Nature" [1965] p. 194).

the progress of reason, the natural law is now adequately promulgated in the books of philosophers and so constitutes an effective and binding standard.

Rousseau rejects this position, however, as still too sanguine about the power of reason—about the possibility of enlightening the world or injecting wisdom into human affairs. As he wrote to a society of Swiss reformers:

> You wish to begin by teaching men the truth in order to make them virtuous [*sage*], whereas on the contrary it is necessary first to make men virtuous in order to make them love the truth. The truth has almost never done anything in the world. (Letter to Tscharner April 29, 1762)

If a well-ordered state has not already eliminated the corrupting effects of society and rendered the people honest and moral, philosophers will never succeed in imposing the truth on them from above.[32]

Furthermore, even if the people were willing to listen and able to understand, they would not know who to listen to since the philosophers do not agree among themselves.

> It is not without surprise and scandal that one notes the little agreement which prevails on . . . [natural law] among the various authors who have discussed it. Among the most serious writers one can hardly find two who are of the same opinion on this point. (*SD*, 94; see *Emile* IV: 268-69)

The weakness of human reason is such as to prevent the unanimity necessary for philosophy to be a salutary political guide.

This important difficulty is exacerbated due to the presence of sophists and counterfeit philosophers. Genuine philosophy will always remain the preserve of the few "sublime geniuses capable of piercing the veils in which the truth wraps itself, a few privileged souls able to withstand the folly of vanity, base jealousy, and the other passions to which a taste for letters gives rise" (*Narcissus*, 107; see *FD*, 62). But as enlightenment progresses, the taste for letters spreads to men without genius and especially to men who are incapable of resisting these dangerous passions. Thus, of the guidance offered by the "philosophers," Rousseau writes: "I sought for the truth in books; I found there only falsehood and error. I consulted authors; I found only charlatans who make a game of fooling men, who have no other law than their interest, no other God than their reputation" (*Beaumont*, 967; see *Emile* V: 458). These sophists and abusers of reason, who become more abundant as reason and enlightenment progress, have left the people further and not closer to a genuine knowledge of justice.

---

[32] Rousseau was obsessed with the fact that he too is not understood. Consider, for example, the epigraph he used for both the *First Discourse* and *Rousseau Juge de Jean-Jacques*: "Here I am the barbarian because no one understands me."

In sum, the great intellectual progress made since primitive times has
not provided men with adequate moral knowledge, because reason still
remains a weak and superficial faculty, because society corrupts men's
hearts as it develops their minds, and because reason's abuses—error,
prejudice, and deceit—have progressed at an equal pace with the truth.
Therefore, in civilized society, as in the state of nature, there is no binding
natural law, for it remains insufficiently promulgated.

Regarding the second obstacle to the existence of natural law—the lack
of sanctions—Rousseau maintains again that civilization has brought no
genuine progress. Of course immense technological advances have been
made, and one might think that this would end the economic scarcity and
conflict that made justice impossible in the state of nature. Instead, it has
aggravated that conflict. The development of man's reason and productive
capacities has been outpaced by the progress of the new desires that reason
liberates. Thus, overflowing with goods, society is still filled with competition and strife.[33]

Furthermore, the progress of the arts has made that strife more dangerous
by greatly enhancing men's power. The invention of metallurgy and then
of gunpowder led to the development of deadly new instruments of force.
And to these were added something ultimately more deadly: the art of fraud.
The progress of reason and technology, then, have only made men more
competitive and more dangerous—and so still less able to afford justice.

The "progressivists" and moralists that Rousseau is attacking might
respond as follows. It has always been admitted that the development of
reason and the arts destroys man's primitive innocence, unleashing a host
of dangerous desires and capacities. But the development of reason also
gives men the means to master these dangers. Reason and rational morality,
whatever their power in the state of nature, are now a real force in men's
souls, a force that suppresses immoderate desires, that tames and civilizes
men, that promotes justice. Can one seriously claim that civilized men are
no more moral than savages and that contemporary society provides no
more support for justice than did Rousseau's late state of nature? To be
sure, civilized man has more desires and craft than the savage; he also has
more principles.

Rousseau agrees that the worth of civilization stands or falls with
reason's power to master the evils that it itself has produced. But in his
view, it does not have this power, and rather than mastering the dangerous
passions it has unleashed, it is mastered by them. Without denying the
obvious fact that moral ideas have undergone a great development since
primitive times, he makes the same two points regarding moral progress as
he made regarding technological progress: first, the ideas of justice or

[33] Rousseau is correct in asserting that the savage spends less time working than civilized
man (*SD*, 150-2, 179). It has been observed that primitive hunter-gatherers average about thirty
hours of work per week (see Sahlins [1972] chap. 1).

morality that grow up in most societies, far from controlling our selfish passions, actually stimulate them further. And, second, they provide these stimulated passions with dangerous new weapons as well.

The advent of moral concepts and beliefs has actually stimulated the passions because it greatly strengthens that which underlies all passion: the hope of success. As Rousseau points out, "wishes without hope do not torment us. A beggar is not tormented by the desire to be king" (*Emile* V: 446). All the unnecessary desires owe their growth to man's hopes for getting and keeping, and these hopes in turn have grown through man's creation, in fact and in his mind, of a *moralized* world. The hope and passion for great wealth, for example, could not exist, could not appear in human history, until the idea and institution of "property" was created through which the precarious physical fact of possession became the moral right of ownership. Similarly, the passion for rule could not exist before physical power was supplemented by the moral idea of "authority" (*SD*, 102). These passions, once aroused, take control of the moral beliefs that created them, leading men to project onto the world an illusory moral order supporting their hopes and desires. All the great passions (even the immoral ones) are founded on such moral expectations, on a superstitious faith in oneself: my physical powers may be limited but the cosmic order is on my side. Even the man of tyrannical ambitions is a sort of "moralist" in his idealistic faith that the world can be formed into a stable and responsive order around himself (*Emile* IV: 291-92; Letter to Carondolet March 4, 1764).

In other words, if men saw the world as it truly is, they would have no passions and few desires. Wisely disillusioned and dispirited, their ambitions would be limited by the realization that "your power extend[s] only as far as your natural strength and not beyond. All the rest is only slavery, illusion and deception." Their acquisitiveness would be contained by the fact that "everything on earth is only transitory. All that we love will escape us sooner or later, and we hold on to it as if it were going to last eternally" (*Emile* II: 83-84, V: 444). But due to man's great "moral progress," that is, to the development of the moral ideas as tools of the passions, civilized man is permanently lost in a cave of illusions, where "he puts in the rank of the possible what is not possible" (*Emile* V: 445). In this way, "morality" strengthens the passions it is supposed to control.

One might reply, however, that even if this is so, morality does also teach men to combat and suppress the passions they feel. Thanks to justice and the state, we no longer experience that savage war of all against all that Rousseau describes. Just look around. Rousseau himself is witness to what we see: "the politeness of our manners, the affability of our speech [and] our perpetual demonstrations of good will" (*FD*, 39). Everywhere one sees signs of the concern for justice and right. How can one understand this except as a result of genuine moral progress?

This objection leads to the heart of Rousseau's whole critique of moral progress. He summarizes his point in the epigraph to the *First Discourse*:

"We are deceived by the appearance of right" (*FD*, 34). We are deceived in that, as compared with the late state of nature, the civilized state, with its appearance of right, is an "epoch, less horrible at first sight, but more deadly in reality" (*Frags.*, 478). And what makes it more deadly is not merely the point just considered—that our moral ideas have extended our passions—but especially this further point: the deceptive "appearance of right," like the advent of metallurgy and gunpowder, has made our extended passions infinitely more dangerous. It is a new weapon in their hands—and that is why one sees it everywhere.

> Whoever, renouncing in good faith all the prejudices of human vanity, seriously reflects on all these things, will discover at length that all these grand words of society, of justice, of law, of mutual defense, of help for the weak, of philosophy, and of the progress of reason are only lures invented by clever politicians or by cowardly flatterers to impose themselves on the simple. (*Frags.*, 475)[34]

Justice or morality, as it has spontaneously developed in human history, is the most fearsome invention of the art of fraud.

Thus Rousseau quite agrees with the moralists that an "appearance of right" is the distinguishing characteristic of civilization, yet this appearance arises not because justice has taken root in men's souls, but because it is more useful to enslave a man than kill him—and "justice" provides the means for enslaving him. Rousseau asks: "Man was born free, and everywhere he is in chains. . . . How did this change occur?" (*SC* I-1: 46). The famous question, left unanswered in the *Social Contract*, is in fact the true topic of his *Second Discourse*. As he writes near the beginning:

> Precisely what, then, is at issue in this Discourse? To indicate in the progress of things the moment when *right* taking the place of *violence*, nature was subjected to law; to explain by what sequence of marvels the strong [i.e. the great mass of men] could resolve to serve the weak, and the people to buy imaginary repose at the price of real felicity. (*SD*, 102, emphasis added)

In short, the central purpose of the *Second Discourse* is to explain how man's chains were forged through the invention of "right" and the state.

These were invented, Rousseau explains, to put an end to the state of war resulting from the growth of men's selfish desires. The inventor proclaimed:

> Let us institute regulations of justice and peace . . . let us gather [our forces] into one supreme power which governs us according to wise laws, protects and defends all the members of association, repulses common enemies, and maintains us in an eternal concord. (*SD*, 159)

---

[34] See 478, 518; *Guerre* 606, 610; *Observations*, 49-50; *Beaumont*, 937 and variant b; *Emile* IV: 236.

These are fine and true principles, Rousseau allows, but one must consider their effect and meaning in the historical circumstances in which they arose. The inventors of justice and the state could not themselves have been just or public-spirited, since these qualities arise only within the (legitimate) state. Moreover, justice and rule were needed and invented precisely because men had become so bad. Therefore, the idea of justice and the common good could only have arisen from selfish motives, hence only as a tool of exploitation. That is why the *Second Discourse* insists that the state was invented by the rich as a means of enslaving and exploiting the poor.

From the start, then, "justice" and the state were nothing but a ruse and a trap. And through history, the original deception was continually repeated: laws, magistrates, penal institutions, armies were added, but "the vices that make social institutions necessary are the same ones that make their abuse inevitable" (*SD*, 173). Unable to suppress men's unjust passions, they soon became tools of them; hence each new institution only strengthened the very evils it was meant to control. Thus did moral and political "progress"—of which the moralists are so proud—enslave the world. Born free, men are everywhere in chains—chains forged by the "appearance of right."

Men's supposed moral progress, then, which is thought to have tamed their harmful passions, has in fact not only stimulated those passions but also given them potent new weapons. Moralistic civil society is just the state of war pursued through other, more dangerous means. All civilized men are "forced to flatter and destroy one another" (*SD*, 194). Despite the appearance of progress, the second obstacle to natural law still remains: it is neither enforced nor obeyed.

To summarize, Rousseau acknowledges that there is, in heaven as it were, an objective, rational standard of order discoverable by the wise, but it does not reach down to men's reason and inclinations, it does not command and obligate men, and thus it does not constitute a binding code of morality or a "natural law." Rousseau demonstrates this through his account of the state of nature which shows that by the pure force of nature—and without the artificial aid of the legitimate state—the rational standard of order is not known and not enforced. He also proves, through his critique of progress, that the spontaneous course of history, the development of technology and morality, does nothing to remedy this situation, to give this standard its own direct access to men's minds and hearts.

Rousseau's argument against natural law has also brought one further point to light: the doctrine of natural law is not only false, it is also harmful and even malicious. In civilized times, doctrines of morality and religion always abound, but, if not "deceived by the appearance of right," one sees that these doctrines are not above the great war of selfish interests, capable of settling it, but rather the most potent weapons invented for use within that war. In Rousseau's new analysis, not only are "morality" and "natural law" not the solution, they are precisely the most insidious and dangerous expression of the problem. And whatever solution Rousseau does find to bring morality into human affairs, that solution must above all be fashioned to combat the danger of "morality." This requirement is the key to the polemical meaning of his doctrine of sovereignty.

Rousseau's Doctrine of Natural Constitutional Law

If no genuine natural law exists to show civilized men what is right and to obligate them to do it, have they any means of escaping the strife and oppression that necessarily results from the weakness of their reason and the conflict of their interests? Rousseau is clearly tempted to give the same answer as Plato: No, unless a philosopher is king or legislator. "So long as power is alone on the one side, intellect and wisdom alone on the other," Rousseau writes, "the people will continue to be vile, corrupt and unhappy" (*FD*, 64; *SC* II-6: 67). The objective, rational standard of order cannot reach the world directly, "morally," through a natural law, but only indirectly through the political activity of a wise man. He alone can bring order, justice, and virtue into the world as Lycurgus did in Sparta, not by preaching or moralizing, not by writing treatises of natural law, not even by proclaiming universal principles of right, but by *legislating*, by wisely arranging the laws and institutions, the concrete social and political relations that really determine men's characters (*Corsica* fragment, 948). No book or doctrine can replace such political activity by the legislator, nor can it even help by teaching or commanding the people to recognize a true legislator should he arise. At most, a book can help to educate future philosophers—it can give private advice to legislators as distinguished from public proclamations of universal principles.[35]

Yet it is obvious that Rousseau's *Social Contract*, while doing the former, also does the latter, that its "principles of political right" is just such a universal doctrine addressed to all men. Thus, we are compelled once again to question Rousseau's "doctrine." How does he understand what he is doing in light of the radical skepticism he has just evinced about the role of doctrines in the world? To consider for now only the most obvious question, how do his own "principles of political right" differ from the doctrines of natural law that he has just refuted?

Rousseau's doctrine, we have seen, is one of natural constitutional law. As such, it is not a moral but a political doctrine, recognizing the primacy of politics, the priority of the state to justice. It does not, like natural law, attempt to elaborate and impose on the world a transcendent code of morality; on the contrary, it seeks to establish a simple, procedural rule for defining legitimate authority or sovereignty, and then consigns to this political authority the task of both promulgating and enforcing a code of morality. But Rousseau does maintain, as we will see, that this simple rule defining legitimate authority is itself more or less adequately promulgated and obeyed,

---

[35]*Frags.*, 474; see Masters (1968) pp. 306-13.

at least in the sense that when men are not grossly misled, they have an almost instinctive awareness of when it is safe to obey an external authority.[36]

The Doctrine of Social Contract and Sovereignty

Rousseau's rejection of natural rule and natural law clears the ground for his doctrines of social contract and sovereignty. Since there are no natural rulers, men can and must create through contract any form of government that they like—so long as it is structured to guarantee their fundamental goal of preservation. But what is more, since there is no natural law, men are also free to create any rules of justice, any laws of morality, that they please, subject only to the same condition. "The social contract," Rousseau writes, "serves within the State as the basis of *all rights*" (*SC* I-9: 56, emphasis added; see I-1: 47, II-6: 66). In other words, the first characteristic of the social contract, in Rousseau's doctrine, is that it must create a *sovereign* in the Hobbesian sense: not merely a "ruler" who enforces some preexisting standard of justice, but a "sovereign" who himself creates the standard he enforces, who makes what he commands just, by commanding it, and what he forbids unjust, by forbidding it.

To make this point perfectly clear, Rousseau states in the *Discourse on Political Economy* that the sovereign's will constitutes

> the rule of what is just and unjust. This truth, let me say in passing, shows how incorrectly many writers have treated as theft the cunning prescribed to Spartan children for obtaining their frugal meal, as if everything that is required by law could fail to be legitimate. (*PE*, 212)[37]

Rousseau is referring to the Spartan practice of teaching their children resourcefulness by requiring them to steal their dinner, although one might

---

[36] It is perhaps misleading to label Rousseau's doctrine as *natural* constitutional law. Its relation to nature may be stated as follows. In the *Second Discourse*, Rousseau attempts to refute both sides of the argument over natural law: he attacks Pufendorf by showing that there is no morality in the state of nature, but also Hobbes by proving that there is no natural need for morality. Relative order and harmony prevail spontaneously because, moved by self-preservation and pity, natural men instinctively follow the "maxim of natural goodness": "Do what is good for you with the least possible harm to others" (*SD*, 133). But this instinctive "morality" (which Rousseau sometimes calls "natural law" in a loose sense) "reason is later forced to re-establish upon other foundations when, by its successive developments, it has succeeded in stifling nature" (*SD*, 96). Rousseau's principles of political right, then, are not themselves natural, but are highly artificial means for "reestablishing" something like the natural order: they are deduced from the natural goal of preservation, but they are deduced by reason, an unnatural faculty, and they require the total replacement of man's natural rights with civil rights and of his natural inclinations with the artificial ones of patriotism and virtue.

[37] Rousseau joins an on-going debate with the use of this example. Hobbes had used it to illustrate his claim that what the sovereign wills cannot be wrong. Pufendorf had replied that this law was indeed unjust and invalid since it violated natural law (*De Cive* XIV-10: 278; *Droit de la Nature* VIII-1.3). Rousseau returns to Hobbes's position.

substitute the practice of cannibalism or incest to make the point still more dramatic. Justice is whatever men collectively agree it shall be. Morality is not something externally imposed on men but merely rules that they freely invent for themselves through consent. Rousseau's thought thus marks an epoch in the liberation of man from all moral standards above his own will, from all natural or objective guidance. His doctrine of sovereignty means that men are ruled and morally guided solely by the free and arbitrary decisions of a human will.[38]

Rousseau was forced to draw this epoch-making conclusion because of his rejection of natural law, as we have just seen. But clearly Rousseau regards this radical conclusion as not only true, but also useful. Hence, before going on to the next point in Rousseau's doctrine—that the "general will" and it alone must be sovereign—let us examine why it is useful to have a "sovereign" at all. What is the purpose, the polemical meaning, of Rousseau's doctrine of sovereignty?

The single overriding mission of politics, for Rousseau, is to establish the absolute rule of law, to "put law above man." And to accomplish this, the crucial task is not so much theoretically to demonstrate the benefits of law as ideologically to disarm its "enemies." The most obvious enemies of the law are of course the rulers, the members of the executive, who always want to be above the law and masters of it. In our discussion of the executive power, we will see the unique ways in which Rousseau interprets and attempts to counteract this danger.

But rulers are by no means the only ones who seek superiority to the laws, and the failure to look beyond the familiar conflict between rulers and peoples in this context has prevented the full purpose of the *Social Contract* from being seen. The clergy, to take the most obvious example, is also an enemy of law. By asserting that the will of God is a standard above the positive laws and by making itself the sole interpreter of that will, the priesthood has carved out a lawless kingdom of its own within the state. Rousseau agrees with the rather extreme views of Hobbes on this subject: by this means Christianity has quite literally ruined the politics of the West (see *SC* IV-8: 128-30). "Communion and excommunication are the social compact of the clergy, a compact by means of which it will always be master of peoples and kings. . . . This invention is a political masterpiece" (*SC* IV-8: 127n). To oppose this lawless power, Rousseau joins with the Enlightenment *philosophes* in their historic battle against the church.

Rousseau's great novelty, however, is that he was the first to defect from the Enlightenment camp—to turn against the *philosophes*, the secular moralists, and theorists of natural law who were proliferating in his

---

[38] Consider Cobban (1934, p. 149): "Rousseau—and this was his greatest crime—submits the state to no *a priori* laws of any kind." See also Strauss (1959) p. 51.

time[39]—and for essentially the same reason: they, like other men, had their partisan interests and ambitions that endangered the rule of law. As Rousseau was among the first to see, these intellectuals constituted a new party, a "new class," a new church of secular priests seeking lawless power. While he supported their antifeudal and anticlerical mission, he saw that they acted not for the people's interest but for their own. In fact, by interest, this new intellectual class was necessarily opposed to the people and the truth, "for truth does not lead to fortune, and the people does not confer embassies, professorships or pensions" (*SC* II-2: 61). Always seeking to distinguish themselves, these men must "always think otherwise than the people," hence always "cast ridicule on the objects of their veneration" (*Frags.*, 557). In the short term they serve the rich and powerful but, like the priestly class, they help to strengthen the power of others with the intention of eventually acceding to it themselves. In the Greek enlightenment, for example, one sees that "Athens was not in fact a democracy, but a highly tyrannical aristocracy, governed by learned men and orators" (*PE*, 213).

The clearest proof of the *philosophes'* selfish ambition, in Rousseau's view, was their famous opposition to the Church, which he interpreted as merely a kind of sectarian rivalry.

> The Jesuits make themselves all powerful in exercising divine authority over consciences, and in making themselves in the name of God the arbiters of good and evil. The philosophers, unable to usurp the same authority applied themselves to destroying it; and then, in appearing to explain Nature to their docile sectarians, and in making themselves its supreme interpreters, they established in its name an authority no less absolute than that of their enemies. . . . These two groups, both imperious, both intolerant are consequently incompatible, since the fundamental system of the one and the other is to reign despotically. (*Dialogues* III: 967)[40]

Rousseau sees the intellectuals, who seek power through the appeal to nature, as fundamentally the same as the priests, who seek power through the appeal to God. That is why they are opposed. And both constitute a great threat to the rule of law—as great a threat as that posed by the rulers.

Rousseau's attack on natural law and his doctrine of sovereignty must be understood in the light of this fact. Philosophical doctrines of natural law are not only false and useless but also destructive of the one thing that can replace them, the absolute rule of positive law; they are powerful tools of ambition that endanger the one institution that can save man. Thus Rous-

---

[39] Enthusiasm for such theories was becoming so great that, as Heinrich Rommen (1947, p. 106) remarks: "eight or more new systems of natural law made their appearance at every Leipzig bookseller's fair since 1780."

[40] See II: 890, III: 964-65; *d'Alembert*, 11n; Shklar (1969) pp. 96-99.

seau views his attack on natural law not only as philosophically correct but, because correct, also as politically necessary.

In other words, Rousseau confronts essentially the same political problem as Hobbes. Both want the absolute rule of law and find the major obstacle to such rule in the abuse of "morality" and "religion" by ambitious ideologues. Consequently, both use a juridical doctrine of state of nature, social contract, and absolute sovereignty for the purpose expressly stated by Hobbes: to disarm the ambitious few by liberating the people from guidance from God or nature. Both seek to demonstrate that, in Hobbes's words, "there are no authentical doctrines concerning right and wrong, good and evil, besides the constituted laws in each realm and government."[41] For Rousseau in particular, living in a new world dominated by both Christianity and the Enlightenment, the central political task—the setting of law above men—cannot be accomplished without the help of this new juridical doctrine, a doctrine of the *sovereignty* of law.

Rousseau's Natural Law Doctrine

This interpretation can be further corroborated by briefly considering an aspect of Rousseau's writings that seems to contradict it. Probably the single greatest obstacle to the proper understanding of Rousseau's doctrine of sovereignty has been the presence in his works—in his "individualistic solution"—of an opposite doctrine, a doctrine of natural law. The citizens of the legitimate state are to receive moral guidance from the laws made by the sovereign, but what about the individuals living in the illegitimate state (who comprise the vast majority of civilized human beings)? To them, Rousseau must address an opposite doctrine. As the tutor explains to Emile:

> Laws! Where are there laws and where are they respected? Everywhere you have seen only individual interest and men's passions reigning under this name. But the eternal laws of nature and order do exist. For the wise man, they take the place of positive law. (*Emile* V: 473)[42]

In light of all we have seen, Rousseau's hopes for the popular efficacy of these "eternal laws" could not have been very great. He attempts to "remedy" the two defects of natural law—that it is not adequately sanctioned or known—by two novel doctrines presented in *Emile*: the religion of the Savoyard Vicar and the theory of conscience. (In the *Social Contract*, by contrast, there is virtually no mention of conscience; and, although there is

---

[41] *De Cive* Preface: 98.

[42] It is probably for the sake of not undermining this natural law doctrine that Rousseau stated his refutation of natural law so tersely in the *Second Discourse* and left out the second chapter of the *Geneva Manuscript* in the final copy of the *Social Contract*. The result has been the great scholarly conflict mentioned above.

a civil religion, it is said to sanction the positive laws of the city and not the conscience of the individual or the "eternal laws of nature.")

The idea that religion might provide the needed sanction for natural law (in the absence of the legitimate state) is a possibility Rousseau explicitly rejects in the *Geneva Manuscript.*

> The sublime concepts of a God of the wise, the gentle laws of brotherhood He imposes upon us, the social virtues of pure souls— which are the true cult He desires of us—will always escape the multitude. Gods as senseless as itself will always be made for the multitude, which will sacrifice worthless things in honor of these Gods in order to indulge in a thousand horrible, destructive passions. (*GM* I-2: 160)

Thus, in writing the "Profession of Faith of the Savoyard Vicar," Rousseau is trying to do what he acknowledges to be nearly impossible: in a corrupt society, to make religion a force for genuine morality.

As for the problem of knowledge of the natural law, Rousseau argues that "we have a guide within, much more infallible than all the books" (*Observations*, 37). According to the Savoyard Vicar, conscience, a moral sentiment distinct from reason, is a "Divine instinct, immortal and celestial voice . . . infallible judge of good and bad which makes man like unto God" (*Emile* IV: 290). One must agree with Bertrand de Jouvenel regarding the striking novelty as well as the inherent implausibility of this doctrine. "It is to ignore the whole immense problem of the, 'erring conscience,' . . . It is to suppose the infallibility of moral sentiment. Nothing could be more bold: it is to contradict ancient as well as Christian philosophy."[43] The doctrine is especially surprising in light of all Rousseau's arguments showing the inaccessibility of the moral truth. I would suggest that Rousseau's true understanding of the conscience was expressed by the vicar when describing his "philosophical method":

> Let us consult the inner light, it will lead me astray less than [the philosophers] lead me astray; or at least my error will be my own, and I will deprave myself less in following my own illusions than in yielding to their lies. (*Emile* IV: 269; see *Last Reply*, 86)

Rousseau's new doctrine of conscience, by promoting individual self-reliance in the realm of morality, aims to free the individual from a dangerous dependence on intellectuals and priests. This interpretation of the conscience doctrine certainly accords well with the obvious anticlerical intention of Rousseau's religious teaching. As he explains elsewhere, by "removing all human power over consciences, [it] allows no further resources to the arbiters of this power" (*Confs.* XI: 567).

---

[43] De Jouvenel (1947) p. 77.

It seems, in other words, that, in *Emile*, Rousseau proclaims a doctrine of natural law based on the infallibility of individual conscience for the very same reason as, in the *Social Contract*, he rejects natural law and proclaims a doctrine of sovereignty based on the infallibility of the general will. The two opposite doctrines have the single purpose of liberating the people from all moral or intellectual dependence on priests and philosophers—the latter doctrine by promoting total reliance on the law or the collective will, the former (and clearly inferior alternative) by urging the opposite: total moral self-reliance or moral individualism. (This is not the first time that we have seen Rousseau, in his two solutions, employ opposite means to the same goal.) Thus, the presence in Rousseau's writings of a second, contradictory doctrine seems actually to confirm the proposed interpretation, which alone makes sense of that contradiction.

To summarize, beginning from the dual premise of man's natural asociality and arationality, Rousseau liberates mankind from all transcendent guidance, dismisses all notions of natural authority and natural law, and replaces them with his doctrines of social contract and sovereignty. In proclaiming this natural constitutional law doctrine, Rousseau himself may seem to resemble the preachers of natural law whom he has just attacked, but they are in fact "doing" opposite things. To be sure, Rousseau is a thinker filled with moral passion, but his doctrine is not that of a "moralist" who teaches what justice is and exhorts men to follow it, but rather that of a specifically *political* thinker who regards such moral doctrines as not only false and pathetically ineffectual but also as the most dangerous weapons of the unjust passions they claim to control. Men cannot be made virtuous or secure by doctrines but only by living under the absolute rule of law. Yet Rousseau's doctrine of sovereignty *will* make men virtuous and secure (in a few small republics) by preventing the moral doctrines of others from destroying the rule of law. Following Hobbes's strategy of anti-authoritarian absolutism, it does not exhort men to be good but to ignore the exhortations of others.[44] It strengthens the state and law by refuting all rival sources of morality, by ending misplaced obedience, by removing all loyalties and associations that stand between the solitary individual and the sovereign.

In other words, one cannot appreciate the purpose of the narrow juridical doctrine proclaimed in the *Social Contract* without looking beyond it to another great Rousseauian theme rarely thought of in this connection: the famous attack in the *First Discourse* on the harmful political consequences of the arts and sciences, Rousseau's deep suspicion toward the Enlightenment and the intelligentsia. And ultimately, one must return once more

---

[44] In a somewhat different context, Rousseau remarks: "The best use which one can make of philosophy is to employ it to destroy the evils which it has caused. . . . Without wishing to be the guide of my contemporaries I content myself with warning them when I observe someone misleading them, and I would not need to tire them with my opinions if no one else undertook to lead them" (*Frags.*, 516-17; see *Guerre*, 609-10).

to the principle of natural goodness, to the radical analysis of the contradiction of society, in order to understand that Rousseau views virtually all the moral, intellectual, and religious phenomena that arise spontaneously within society as forms of insincerity and tools of exploitation.

Only with these points in mind, does one appreciate the urgency of eliminating all higher standards above the law, standards that have always been the exclusive property and weapon of the "intellectual class" in all its various guises. If one seeks to eliminate all personal dependence and oppression, it is at least as important to abolish such private moralities as it is to suppress private armies and to moderate private property. The doctrine of sovereignty is precisely Rousseau's attempt to establish public ownership of the means of evaluation.

9

The General Will as Sovereign

For the sake of their preservation men must conclude a "social contract" that establishes a "sovereign," not simply a ruler. The question then becomes: on whom should this sovereign power be bestowed? The "general will" is Rousseau's answer.

The general will. At last we come to Rousseau's most famous, original, and seminal concept. Unfortunately, it is also his most obscure and, one might go so far as to say, one of the most notorious and influential obscurities in the whole history of Western political philosophy.

One can form a preliminary idea of what is so original about the concept by considering that this question of who should rule, who gets the power, is, after all, the great and perennial question of politics, as old as political life itself. And through long centuries of debate, despite much disagreement about the answer, there has at least been a stable understanding of who the contenders are: a king, an aristocracy of some kind, the wealthy, the common people, a priestly class, the military, and so forth. Yet remarkably, after all of this time, Rousseau proposes a new answer, one never heard of before. The sovereign should be the "general will."

Part of the explanation for the novelty and obscurity of this answer is that Rousseau has really changed the question. In explaining who should rule the state he is actually putting forward a whole new conception of what a state, as such, is. His concept of the general will, in other words, involves nothing less than a comprehensive new science of politics, a new *descriptive* theory explaining the character of all genuine social cohesion and group dynamics.

Although it is impossible completely to separate this larger, descriptive meaning of the general will from its prescriptive meaning, the main discussion of the former will be reserved for the next chapter. Here, we will focus more narrowly on the practical and prescriptive issues: what is the general will, why must it and it alone be sovereign, where does it exist, and how, in practice, is it to be made sovereign.

Because it is both obscure and suggestive, the "general will" has a tendency to send people off in all directions, looking for precursors, influences, and offshoots. Thus here, above all, it is important to stay close to Rousseau, not only to be sure of the details but to identify the philosophical spirit at work in this doctrine, to grasp how he himself understood what he was doing.[1]

The Deduction of the General Will

In the *Social Contract*, Rousseau first mentions the general will in the climactic chapter, book I, chapter 6, where he finally proclaims the necessary terms of the social contract. At first reading, the new concept seems to be introduced fully formed, without derivation or explanation. "The general will appears abruptly," one scholar observes, "like a divinity, as Pallas Athene springing forth from the head of Zeus."[2] Its godlike appearance of being "underived" has inclined readers to the view that the general will is not in any sense a product or creation of the artificial social contract but is, in the words of the scholar just quoted, a "pre-existing reality," a transcendent moral law or a metaphysical entity that exists quite independent of men's actual wills and empirical interests.[3]

A closer reading of the chapter, however, reveals that Rousseau does in fact derive or invent the general will, deducing it, just as he does the other terms of the social contract, not from any preexisting moral imperative but from the practical requirements of human self-preservation in the artificial condition of society. The derivation is difficult to perceive, however, because Rousseau reports it in reverse order, first proclaiming his conclusion—his finished formula for the social contract—and only afterwards explaining the reasoning that produced it. To make matters worse, the whole discussion, which covers less than a page, is presented in oracular and epigrammatic fashion. Still, with some care and due attention to later discussions, the derivation can be reconstructed.

To this point, Rousseau has argued that since no political authority has been established by nature, men are driven by their desire for preservation to create such a power artificially through the conclusion of a social contract. As stated here, the first necessary feature of this contract is: "the total alienation of each associate with all his rights" to the

---

[1] For the history of the term "general will," which is by no means new with Rousseau, see Jouvenel (1947) pp. 105-12, Shklar (1973), and especially Riley (1986). As the latter has shown, the expression first emerged in debates over the character of God's will among seventeenth-century French theological writers such as Arnauld (who first used the term, in a work published in 1644), Malebranche (who gave it its greatest currency), Fénelon, and others. Later, it was employed in a more secular and political sense by Gravina, Pufendorf (or rather, Barbeyrac, his French translator), Montesquieu, Saint-Lambert, and Diderot. Rousseau was familiar with every one of these writers but used the "general will" for his own unique purposes, as the others had done in their turn.

[2] Hans Barth (1965) p. 41.

[3] Ibid.

ruling authority, which is, by virtue of this "total alienation," a "sovereign" authority.[4]

But how can men possibly risk such a "total alienation"? Where, if anywhere, can sovereign power be safely deposited?

> Since each man's force and freedom are the primary instruments of his self-preservation, how is he to engage them without harming himself and without neglecting the cares he owes to himself? In the context of my subject, this difficulty can be stated in these terms.
>
> "Find a form of association that defends and protects the person and goods of each associate with all the common force, and by means of which each one, uniting with all, nevertheless obeys only himself and remains as free as before." This is the fundamental problem which is solved by the social contract. (*SC* I-6: 53)[5]

Rousseau has devised the following solution. Sovereign authority could be safely entrusted to a political body provided that this body was such as to offer its subjects two different (but ultimately inseparable) guarantees for their security, guarantees which he summarizes in a highly compressed and elliptical manner in his famous formula for the social contract:

> the *total alienation* of each associate, with all his rights, to the *whole community*. (Ibid., emphasis added)[6]

The first and more obvious guarantee contained in this formula is that the sovereign body must be the "whole community." This means that the subjects must necessarily be members of the body that commands them and, what is more, that this body must be a *whole*, with a single, unanimous will. The subjects are not promising here to obey the mere majority but the "whole community." In the brief exegesis of the social contract formula that Rousseau

---

[4] A "sovereign" is necessary, as Rousseau explains it in this chapter, because: "if some rights were left to private individuals, there would be no common superior who could judge between them and the public. Each man being his own judge on some point would soon claim to be so on all; the state of nature would subsist and the association would necessarily become tyrannical or ineffectual" (*SC* I-6: 53).

[5] This is, of course, a strange way of posing the "fundamental problem." Other thinkers have sought to preserve security and political freedom—understood as limited government, checks and balances, majority rule, or ruling and being ruled in turn—but Rousseau is the first to demand a form of government where each citizen "obeys only himself." Similarly, in the chapters preceding this one, where Rousseau discusses rival theories of legitimate government, he poses the issue again in a very radical way, allowing no middle ground between perfect self-rule and abject slavery or even animality (*SC* I-2-4). Rousseau is driven to these extreme formulations because he is asking who should be "sovereign" and not just ruler. If one surrenders to others—to a king or aristocracy—this power of defining morality, one is indeed surrendering all freedom, all moral responsibility, all humanity. A ruling body that is in some sense "only ourselves" must be found if it is to be sovereign.

[6] Notice that this first formula for the social contract does not refer to the general will—precisely, I am arguing, because it is deriving or defining it.

presents immediately after stating it, he explains the necessity of this first provision: "as each gives himself to *all*, he gives himself to no one; and since there is no associate over whom one does not acquire the same right one grants him over oneself, one gains the equivalent of everything one loses" (ibid., emphasis added). In other words, the first provision satisfies the requirement established earlier as necessary for the subjects' safety: "each one, uniting with all, nevertheless obeys only himself and remains as free as before" (ibid.). One is safe and free because one is only agreeing to obey a body of which one is a member and whose single will is also one's own will.

The second guarantee of security built into Rousseau's formula is contained, surprisingly, in the phrase "total alienation." In his exegesis, Rousseau explains: "since each one gives his *entire* self [i.e., since there is "total alienation"], the condition is *equal* for everyone, and since the condition is equal for everyone, no one has an interest in making it burdensome for the others" (ibid., emphasis added). This crucial argument, which has tended to escape notice, is stated at greater length in a later chapter.

> The social compact *established* an *equality* between the citizens [again, through "total alienation"] such that they all engage themselves under the same conditions and should all benefit from the same rights. Thus *by the very nature of the compact*, every act of sovereignty. . . obligates or favors all citizens *equally*, so that the sovereign knows only the nation as a body and makes no distinctions between any of those who compose it. (*SC* II-4: 63, emphasis added)

In other words, Rousseau claims that owing to the "total alienation" required by his social contract formula, the sovereign body must view all the subjects as equal or indistinguishable, and it may act only through general laws that apply identically to each. And this stipulation provides the second crucial guarantee for the subjects' security: "in this institution everyone necessarily subjects himself to the conditions he imposes on others" and therefore "an individual could not be directly injured by the sovereign without everyone's being injured; but this cannot be, since it would be to want to harm oneself" (ibid.; *Emile* V: 461).[7] Clearly, such a sovereign will be "infallible" or "always right."[8]

These two guarantees, although distinguishable, are ultimately insepa-

---

[7] See *Montagne* VI: 807: the sovereign "cannot be unjust or susceptible of abuse, because it is not possible for the body to wish to hurt itself, so long as the whole wills only for the whole."

[8] For these two adjectives see *PE*, 212 and *SC* II-3: 61, II-4: 62, II-6: 67, respectively. It is important to keep in mind that this argument does not prove, and Rousseau does not maintain, that the general will can never do harm through mistaken assumptions about what is good. "One always wants what is good for oneself, but one does not always see it. The people is never corrupted, but it is often fooled" (*SC* II-3: 61). "By itself, the people always wants the good, but by itself it does not always see it. The general will is always right, but the judgement that guides it is not always enlightened" (*SC* II-6: 67). The general will can never be unjust because it can never be ill-intentioned and because one cannot be unjust to oneself; but it can be mistaken and thereby do harm.

rable, for it is only because each member of the sovereign is constrained to will only what all could will, that all end up having the same identical will. Thus, there exists a "whole community" with a single, unanimous will, as assumed by the first provision, only because the community is required to will through general laws, as stipulated in the second.

The two interrelated guarantees, elliptically stated in the social contract formula, together *define* the general will, as Rousseau indicates by now restating his formula, using for the first time the term "general will" where before he had spoken of the "whole community."[9] Rousseau makes this perfectly explicit in the formal definition he presents in a later chapter: "the general will, to be truly such, should be general in its object as well as in its essence...it should *come from* all to *apply to* all" (*SC* II-4: 62, emphasis added).[10] The general will is the will of the whole community when applied to the community as a whole.

In sum, Rousseau freely derives or invents this ingenious double generality because it provides an infallible guarantee for men's freedom and safety, and, calling it the "general will," he declares that it, and it alone, can be trusted with the sovereign power. Contrary to appearances, then, the general will is not a "preexisting reality" but an artificial construct, like the social contract itself, whose specific features are deduced from the unique requirements of human self-preservation in the unnatural, social condition into which men have accidentally evolved.

Egalitarianism and Realism

Confidence in this conclusion may begin to falter, however, as one pursues the inevitable next question: does the general will actually exist? Obviously, if such a thing as the general will, as Rousseau has cleverly defined it, actually existed, then it would indeed possess these ideal attributes (infallibility, obeying only oneself). And clearly Rousseau does think that it exists, since he demands that it be made sovereign and even asserts that it is "indestructible" (a third ideal attribute). But where, how, and why does it exist? What force is there that could constrain a whole community of naturally selfish individuals to generalize their wills, permanently and indestructibly? Essentially, two possible answers have been proposed.

Some have suggested that the force in question is the mechanism of voting

---

[9] "Each of us puts his person and all his power in common under the supreme direction of the general will; and in a body we receive each member as an indivisible part of the whole" (*SC* I-6: 53).

[10] Similarly, an act of the general will—that is, "law"—is defined as follows: "the object of the law should be general, as is the will dictating it; and it is this *double universality* which creates the true character of the law" (*GM* II-4: 189, emphasis added). Both conditions must be met. If a will is of the whole community, coming from all unanimously, but it does not *apply* to all—either because it concerns some object outside the state (e.g., an issue of foreign policy) or a specific individual or group within the state (e.g., some judicial decision)—then it is only a unanimous particular will, not a general will. See *SC* II-4: 63, II-6: 66.

and that by the general will Rousseau really means the assembly majority. But this would seem to contradict Rousseau's definition of the general will as coming from all, and also to make a mockery of the ideal claims made for it.

Troubled by the inadequacies of this answer, most interpreters have been driven back to regarding the general will, with its uniquely ideal attributes, as some sort of higher entity. Two further considerations have helped strengthen this view. Given Rousseau's great moral passion, it has seemed likely that he embraced the general will not because of the sort of practical, calculating, utilitarian considerations outlined above (however much he may like to emphasize them), but because it seemed to him objectively, inherently *right*, because it embodied his burning sense of justice, much as the very similar Categorical Imperative embodied Kant's. Furthermore, Rousseau's juridical principles are so doctrinaire and unrealistic, that is, precisely so *indifferent* to the demands of political practice, that it seems obvious that they must be the product of some moral imperative above the plane of practice and utility.[11]

It is necessary to respond to these views and objections, and to clarify the general spirit of Rousseau's political thinking. For if what we have seen of the deduction of the general will is correct, then these views, as plausible as they may seem from certain perspectives, are more than mistaken: they obscure precisely what is most important, interesting, and unique in Rousseau's theory of the general will. I believe it can be shown that the general spirit of Rousseau's doctrine is not moralistic but realistic and political, that he does not sacrifice the needs of practice to those of morality but if anything the reverse, that the general will is not a metaphysical or even a natural being but an artificial construct fashioned to meet men's practical needs, and that Rousseau's political doctrine, rather than flowing from some higher moral imperative, is made possible precisely by virtue of its conscious and radical liberation from all transcendent foundations.

The most striking evidence for these claims comes from the very aspect of the general will that is commonly thought to prove its moralistic or transcendent character: its strict egalitarianism. Since Rousseau is a passionate egalitarian it has seemed reasonable to suppose that he invented this rigidly egalitarian doctrine and moralistically clung to it despite its evident impracticality because he believed it was objectively right or just. But precisely the opposite is the case: Rousseau is an inegalitarian, and he invented this rigidly egalitarian doctrine and realistically clung to it despite its evident injustice because he believed it was necessary for practice.

Rousseau's inegalitarianism tends to be obscured by a number of factors.

---

[11] Thus, according to Hans Barth, those who have ignored "the metaphysical and theological foundation of the general will have committed an impardonable error" (1965, p. 41). A less extreme and more representative view is held by Grimsley: "Although this metaphysical basis of rational law remains for the most part merely implicit in the *Social Contract*, it is relevant to any overall interpretation of its ultimate significance for Rousseau's thought as a whole" (1972, p. 69).

His entrancing depiction of the state of nature where men are all equal because of the nondevelopment of their faculties has distracted attention from his claim that they become naturally unequal when their faculties develop. Also the brilliance and force of his attacks on *unjust* inequality have blinded readers to his acknowledgment that there is such a thing as genuine and just inequality. Finally, his new spirit of humanitarianism and well-advertised identification with the cause of the people, which obviously constitute an important step toward equality in certain respects, have mistakenly been thought to entail a repudiation of every sort of inequality.

But if one examines Rousseau's works with some tolerance for his complexity, one easily sees that he still believes in natural inequality. Indeed, far *more* than his contemporaries, Rousseau believed in "great men": in legislators and wise men, in heroes and philosophers—in innate force of soul and innate genius. It is not in Diderot or Locke or Hobbes that one finds sentences such as: "The legislator's great soul is the true miracle that should prove his mission" (*SC* II-7: 70). Or: "Cato seems like a God among mortals" (*PE*, 219). In Rousseau we find a return to something like the classical appreciation of human inequality.[12]

Of course, just because men are unequal, it does not follow that the superior may exploit the inferior. But is it not rational and just that the superior lead the inferior, rather than the reverse? As Rousseau angrily declares in the final sentence of the *Discourse on Inequality*: "It is manifestly against the law of nature, in whatever manner it is defined, that a child command an old man [or] an imbecile lead a wise man" (*SD*, 181). Conversely, there are "great men *made to guide* the others," and every one of Rousseau's writings demonstrates just how much "the others" are in need of such guidance: Emile needs the help of Rousseau his tutor, Julie and St. Preux need the godlike Wolmar, and above all, as we will see, the people need to be guided and molded by a great legislator (*Last Reply*, 66, emphasis added).[13]

One further thing follows from the existence of great natural inequalities: what is good for the superior few often is not good for the many, and vice versa. Rousseau's whole *First Discourse*, for example, with its attack on the popularization of philosophy and enlightenment, is nothing but a particular application of this principle. "I have said a hundred times over that it is good that there be Philosophers," he explains in one of his defenses of the *First Discourse*, "provided the People do not pretend to be Philosophers" (*Last Reply*, 72). Conversely, there are certain general rules concerning what is good for ordinary men, but "all rare cases are outside the rules" (*Emile* IV: 245; see II: 105). It is clear, in sum, that Rousseau strongly believes not only that men are naturally unequal but also that they are owed different treatment corresponding to their different worth (*SD*, note 'S').

Now, the general will, being a principle of strict equality, ignores this

---

[12] See Shklar (1972).

[13] See *FD*, 63; see Shklar (1964).

natural inequality among men and is therefore, in important respects, unreasonable and unjust. First, it requires the superior few to be ruled and led by laws made by the inferior multitude. And second, it makes the superior fit into the narrow mold of what is good for the inferior. Each is permitted to do only what all can do; no one is allowed to be "outside the rules." These difficulties are precisely what led all classical thinkers to regard strict equality as manifestly unjust and to have ultimate misgivings about the rule of law or the principle of "generality."

Rousseau, in fact, has even stronger grounds than the classical thinkers for considering the principle of generality to be naturally unjust for, the question of natural inequality aside, he is surely a greater believer in natural individuality. Let us not suddenly forget in the context of the general will Rousseau's radical individualism with its antinomian emphasis on diversity, individual uniqueness, and the importance of being true to one's own inner self. Thus Rousseau, the grandfather of romanticism, the great apostle of individuality, must sense very keenly how much is sacrificed and suppressed when naturally unique individuals are collectivized and everyone is forced to conform to a single general will.

If Rousseau favors the general will, then, it is most certainly *not* as the *embodiment* of justice but rather as a hardheaded and practical *replacement* for it. Doubting men's natural sociality and rationality, Rousseau claims that true natural justice—which would distribute to unique and unequal men their differing roles and goods—is not sufficiently known or sanctioned by nature. Therefore, in the extreme harshness of our condition, we are not able to do justice to natural inequality. Instead, we must build our artificial state on an artificial equality (created by the "total alienation" of the social contract), for, as we have seen, only on these terms can the double guarantee be constructed that makes possible a nonoppressive political power. Thus Rousseau invents the egalitarian principle of the general will and declares it sovereign not because it is naturally just or moral—it is not—but because, for men who are naturally selfish and irrational, it constitutes the only realistic means for creating an effective and safe political authority.[14]

---

[14] Two passages from the *Second Discourse* demonstrate very strikingly both Rousseau's acknowledgment of inequality and distributive justice on the level of theory and his indignant rejection of them on the level of realistic practice. Moral or political inequality, he states, "is contrary to natural right whenever it is not combined in the same proportion with physical inequality: a distinction which sufficiently determines what one ought to think in this regard of the sort of inequality that reigns among *all civilized people*" (p. 180, emphasis added). Therefore the question "whether those who command are necessarily worth more than those who obey, and whether strength of body or mind, wisdom or virtue, are always found in the same individuals in proportion to power or wealth" is "a question perhaps good for slaves to discuss in the hearing of their masters, but not suitable for reasonable and free men who seek the truth" (pp. 101-2). Natural inequality does exist and it would be owed respect but for the fact that it never corresponds to the civil inequalities that men attempt to justify in its name.

In other words, to understand the general will it is necessary to recall once again Rousseau's close kinship, not indeed to Kant, but to Hobbes. In a famous passage of *De Cive*, Hobbes explains the realistic root of his own egalitarianism:

> Whether men be equal by nature, the equality is to be acknowledged; or whether unequal, because they are like to contest for dominion, it is necessary for the obtaining of peace, *that they be esteemed as equal.*[15]

Echoing this statement, Rousseau writes in the *Social Contract*:

> I shall end this chapter and this [first] book with a comment that ought to serve as the *basis of the whole social system.* It is that rather than destroying natural equality, the fundamental compact on the contrary substitutes a moral and legitimate equality for whatever physical inequality nature may have placed between men, and that although they may be unequal in force or in genius, they all become equal through convention and by right. (*SC* I-9: 58; emphasis added)[16]

In sum, to think that Rousseau embraces the general will out of egalitarian moralism or obedience to some preexisting metaphysical or ethical imperative is to misunderstand—to invert—the whole spirit of his political thought. The general will doctrine is based precisely on the realistic dismissal of all transcendent imperatives, the utter liberation of politics from divine or natural standards. Like the state as a whole, the general will is a free human construct, an artificial creation. And just as the Rousseauian state ruthlessly conquers men's natural inclinations, transforming selfish individuals into patriotic citizens, so the general will ruthlessly imposes

---

[15] *De Cive* III-13: 143, Hobbes's italics; see *Leviathan* XV: 120.

[16] When Rousseau uses the term "physical inequality," this includes "the difference of ages, health, bodily strengths, and qualities of *mind* or *soul*" (*SD*, 101, emphasis added). And by "moral equality" he means positive or conventional equality, not equality of intrinsic moral worth (ibid.).

Throughout the *Social Contract* Rousseau repeats the point made in this passage, that the equality at the root of the general will is an artificial creation of the contract. "The social compact *established* an equality between the citizens. . . ." "Since the citizens are all equal *by the social contract*, what everyone ought to do can be prescribed by everyone" (II-4: 62, III-16: 104, emphasis added; see I-6: 53).

Rousseau is not contradicting this view when he states elsewhere that the law "reestablishes, as a right, the natural equality among men" (*PE*, 214; see *GM* I-7: 178). The "natural equality among men" that law "reestablishes" is the freedom from mastery and servitude that prevails in the state of nature, which is different from (and coexists with) the natural *in*equality that men have with respect to their abilities (*SD*, 101-2, 138-39).

upon men—who are by nature both unequal and individually unique—a conventional equality and an artificial equivalence.[17]

Idealistic Realism

Yet this still does not capture the whole spirit of Rousseau's doctrine, for how can this harsh realism explain the "ideal" attributes of the general will or Rousseau's peculiar tone of enthusiasm in describing them. Throughout the *Social Contract*, he can scarcely conceal his admiration for the sheer elegance and power of his new theory.

Once one has done full justice to the spirit of hobbesian realism at the heart of Rousseau's thought, then (but only then) can one go on to see that this realism is of a complex kind: not simply resigned and pessimistic, but also strangely eager, hopeful, and even idealistic. Hobbes, for example, begins as the tough-minded skeptic, demanding that we relinquish our age-old illusions and face the bitter truth about the selfishness of men and the indifference of nature; but if we will only be thus realistic, he enthusiastically continues, well then, taking matters firmly into our own human hands and building at last on what is real and effectual, we can construct a state more stable and secure than the world has ever known, an eternal commonwealth.[18]

Similarly, in Rousseau, a powerful idealism emerges out of (and perhaps ultimately motivates) his initial realism. He begins by attacking the traditional hopes of both the philosophers and priests with their reliance on nature and God, insisting that civilized humanity, orphaned by history, is now abandoned to itself. But while realistically acknowledging these harsh facts, he also ultimately embraces them as a liberation and an opportunity. Liberated from the cumbersome obligation to follow natural or divine justice, we are free at last to construct our own, completely artificial political mechanism—which we can make serve mankind much better. Rousseau's withering skepticism directed at natural and divine politics, then, ultimately prepares a new idealism concerning what man can do on his own, a new humanistic or "technological" idealism.

---

[17]As to the claim that Rousseau must be motivated by doctrinaire moralism because what he demands is so "impractical" (in the sense of difficult to produce), this rather proves that he is skeptical and willing to hold out for what will really work, no matter how hard it may be to create (see *Emile* Preface: 34). The great irony is that Rousseau's extraordinary pessimism about what will work in practice leads him to formulate such demanding requirements for safe or legitimate government that these requirements inevitably appear to his readers—who are much less skeptical than he about the demands of practice—to be an expression of doctrinaire moralism and a reckless indifference to practice. It is his very skepticism, then, that has made him appear utopian. For this reason, too, the doctrine of the general will has always been thought to sacrifice the requirements of "politics" to those of some higher moral law, when just the opposite is the case.

[18] *Leviathan* XXIX: 237.

Specifically, the general will is not only an artificial contrivance that the harshness of nature forces us to invent, but a marvelously elegant and ingenious one, possessed of certain "ideal" attributes. Through the realistic renunciation of all effort to do justice to men's natural inequalities and differences, through the ruthless imposition of an artificial equality and equivalence, it becomes possible for the first time to collapse men together into a single homogeneous unit with a single will—a will that may then be allowed to flow freely where it chooses, a law unto itself, without the need to tie it to or judge it by any external standard of justice; for where there is only a single unit making rules for itself, there can be no injustice and everyone obeys only himself. Thus, even the famous "ideality" of the general will, which is almost always taken to prove its transcendent nature, derives rather from the rejection of all transcendence, which frees us to engineer something perfectly to human needs.

Does the General Will Really Exist?

With this understanding of the spirit of Rousseau's doctrine, we turn to the more concrete question: does the "general will" actually exist, and if so where? Given the great disagreement and confusion that surrounds this issue, it will be useful to try to work our way through the evidence on all sides.

Rousseau maintains that the general will does exist—and not just occasionally or under unique circumstances but somehow permanently or "indestructibly" (SC IV-1: 108-9). Furthermore, it exists as a *will*: it is not, as its permanence might lead one to suppose, a "truth," a Platonic Idea, a moral imperative or standard, like natural law, which shows men what they *ought* to will. Rather, it is itself a will.[19]

The question thus becomes: where does this indestructible will exist? *Whose will* is the general will?

The general will "come[s] from all," Rousseau answers in his very definition. It is also said to be the will of the "whole community" and of the "public person"—which mean, again, that it is the will of every person in the community, for Rousseau makes it clear that the "public person" is an artificial being with no reality beyond that of its individual members

---

[19] SC III-15: 102, II-1: 59. This distinguishes Rousseau from those thinkers, like John Rawls to take a contemporary example, who regard social contract theory as involving only a thought experiment in which the state of nature and the social contract, understood as purely hypothetical constructs, are employed to deduce a fair or rational standard of justice. On this view the "general will" would be such an abstract rational standard and not a will at all.

But Rousseau's doctrine is not a "theory of justice" of this kind, with its abstraction from the harsh facts of politics and history, but rather, as it were, a "theory of politics." The whole purpose of Rousseau's general will doctrine is precisely to replace all such abstract standards of justice— which are not naturally promulgated or enforced—with a "sovereign," a real, publicly recognizable will that can reasonably be relied upon to make up, promulgate, and enforce its own standard of justice.

(*SC* II-4: 62, I-6: 53-54; *Guerre*, 608; *Frags.*, 510-12). Furthermore, if the general will were not the unanimous will of all, then Rousseau could not claim that the citizens obey only themselves. Evidence of every sort, then, supports the view which Rousseau also states explicitly and repeatedly: "the constant will of *all the members* of the state is the general will" (*SC* IV-2: 110, emphasis added). Properly interpreted, I believe this is indeed Rousseau's view.

In spite of all such evidence, however, this view is almost always rejected out of hand, due to the obvious fact that the vote of the sovereign assembly is rarely if ever unanimous. Rousseau even states explicitly that (at least in the popular assembly) "in order for a will to be general, it is not always necessary for it to be unanimous." On the contrary, "except for [the] primitive contract, the vote of the *majority* always obligates all the others" (*SC* II-2: 59n, IV-2: 110, emphasis added; see I-5: 52, II-4: 63). The general will, he thus appears to suggest, is the will of the assembly majority.

This position would seem to be reasonable and even necessary on the following grounds. Outside the assembly there is nothing that can reliably force individuals to generalize their naturally selfish wills; therefore, the general will has its essential existence not within individuals as such, but rather within the assembly, where the mechanism of voting either constrains men to generalize their wills or causes their selfish wills to cancel each other out, leaving the general will as the resultant. A famous passage in the *Social Contract* seems to support this view:

> There is often a great difference between the will of all and the general will. The latter considers only the common interest; the former considers private interest, and is only a sum of private wills. But take away from these same wills the pluses and minuses that cancel each other out, and there remains, as the sum of the differences, the general will. (*SC* II-3: 61)[20]

Thus the general will is the vote or will of the assembly majority.

But this common interpretation is certainly incorrect. Rousseau states repeatedly, including in the sequel to the very passage just quoted, that the mechanism of voting—the mutual canceling out of the "pluses and minuses"—is a very imperfect expedient, easily manipulated by selfish, partisan interests, and that, except where certain very specific moral and institutional conditions prevail, the majority vote will often express a factional rather than a general will (*SC* II-3: 61, II-6: 67, IV-1, 2: 108-11; *PE*, 213, 216). Thus Rousseau is certainly not taking the absurd and dangerous view that the general will is the same thing as the majority will.

The usual response to this objection, however, is simply to retreat to the position that every majority is not a general will, but every general will

---

[20] I have slightly altered the translation. For an exegesis of this notoriously obscure passage, see Gildin (1983) pp. 54-57.

exists in the form of a majority will. Where the requisite moral and institutional conditions prevail, there the general will exists, and it exists, for the reasons stated above, as the assembly majority's will; but where these conditions do not prevail and the majority's will is partisan and unjust, there the general will simply does not exist.

But it is precisely this view that Rousseau means to reject in calling the general will "indestructible."

> When the State, close to its ruin, continues to subsist only in an illusory and ineffectual form; when the social bond is broken in all hearts; when the basest interest brazenly adopts the sacred name of the public good, then the general will becomes mute. . . and iniquitous decrees whose only goal is the private interest are falsely passed under the name of laws.
>
> Does it follow from this that the general will is annihilated or corrupted? No, it is always constant, unalterable and pure. But it is subordinate to others that prevail over it. (*SC* IV-1: 108-9)

Even when morals and institutions have reached their final stage of decay and the assembly wills nothing but "iniquitous decrees," even then the general will continues to exist just as it had before, serenely unmoved and unaffected. Clearly, the general will must exist somewhere other than in the assembly and the majority will.

One is misled on this issue because Rousseau speaks so much about the majority and the mechanism of voting, as in the above passage regarding the "pluses and minuses." But in all of these passages Rousseau is not describing what the general will is in itself but only how it can find practical political expression. The whole activity of voting in the popular assembly is nothing but a means (if also the only and essential means) for expressing, consulting, trying to make contact with the general will—with something "indestructible," that exists and is itself quite apart from the uncertain outcome of all such votes and assemblies (*SC* II-3: 61, II-6: 67, IV-1, 2: 108-11; *PE*, 213, 216).[21]

But then where does this indestructible will exist? It might seem that there is nowhere left to turn but to some metaphysical entity. Instead, let us reconsider Rousseau's explicit answer: "the constant will of all the members of the state is the general will." This view seemed untenable because we tacitly assumed that men can have within them only one will and thus that something cannot be a constant and unanimous will of the community without also being the unanimous vote of the assembly. But this assumption is incorrect. As Rousseau uses the term, a man may have several different and even conflicting wills within him—for a will is produced by an interest and a man often has several different and conflicting interests. In particular,

---

[21] Indeed, Rousseau maintains that even small and informal groups that have *no* assemblies and votes at all still possess a general will (see *PE*, 212).

Rousseau expressly states that "each individual can, as a man, have a private will contrary to or differing from the general will he has as a citizen" (*SC* I-7: 55). These different wills coexist within each citizen, and which one is followed and expressed in the act of voting (or in any other act) will depend on a variety of moral and institutional circumstances. On those occasions when the general will is *not* followed, Rousseau is perfectly prepared to say, as he does in the passage above, that "the general will becomes mute", but this only means that "it is subordinate to others that prevail over it." "Even in selling his vote for money," Rousseau asserts, the citizen "doesn't extinguish the general will within himself, he evades it" (*SC* IV-1: 109). Thus, what is inextinguishable is this "general will *within himself*," that is, within each and every citizen.

In sum, Rousseau's position is as follows: the general will is a real and permanent will existing within every one of the citizens, and this is so regardless of the state's moral and institutional circumstances; however, this will is not necessarily the citizens' only or dominant will and, depending on circumstances, it may or may not be consistently expressed by a majority of the citizens in the popular assembly.

On this understanding, Rousseau's famous doctrine of the sovereignty of the general will turns out to comprise two very different theses: one posits the existence of a unanimous general will, the other explains the means required to give it public expression. We may treat each in turn. *Why* do all members of the community, regardless of the state of mores and institutions, always have within them a general will? And how can this unanimous will—which is only an inner will, one among many, and rarely the strongest—be made into the official public sovereign of the state?

Why Does Every Citizen Possess a Permanent General Will?

The only interpreters of Rousseau who tend to take seriously his thesis regarding the existence of an indestructible general will within every citizen are those who view him through the particular lens of German Idealism, both Kantian and Hegelian. Rousseau's claim is taken to be the expression of a metaphysical dualism: man's soul is not by nature one or unified but contains, alongside the empirical will, a distinct and permanent "Ideal" or "Rational" will—the general will—which is the expression of man's freedom or spirituality.[22]

But this is not at all the explanation that Rousseau himself gives for his claim. In the chapter of the *Social Contract* expressly devoted to the proposition "That the General Will is Indestructible," he argues that each citizen, even at the very moment when he votes for an unjust law, still

---

[22] See Bosanquet (1965), chap. 5; G. D. H. Cole (1950) pp. 8, 46-47; Vaughn (1915) pp. 27-28; Cassirer (1954) pp. 56-57, 63, 76, 96, 126-27.

possesses within himself the general will "unalterable and pure" for the following reason:

> Each person, detaching his interest from the common interest, sees perfectly well that he cannot completely separate himself from it; but his share of the public misfortune seems like nothing to him compared to the exclusive good that he claims he is getting. With the exception of this private good, he wants the general good in his own interest just as vigorously as anyone else. Even in selling his vote for money, he doesn't extinguish the general will within himself, he evades it. (*SC* IV-1: 109)

Rousseau maintains here (consistent with his general spirit of realism) that the general will men have within them is an outgrowth of self-interest, that all citizens have a permanent general will for the simple reason that they all have a permanent selfish interest in the common good.

It is certainly true that everyone has a stake in the continued functioning of the state as opposed to a return to the late state of nature. But even when the existence of the state is not at risk, the common interest, precisely because it is the common interest, always and necessarily constitutes at least *one part* of each man's selfish interest. To be sure, it may not be the largest part, and thus a selfish man may calculate that it is to his net advantage, in certain instances, to sacrifice the common good—including his own share of it—to pursue some exclusive good of his own. Nevertheless, the point is that, whether or not he chooses to sacrifice it, each citizen has a necessary and permanent stake in the common good.

But one can easily grant this premise—almost all thinkers have—without conceding Rousseau's conclusion: that this interest in the common good must produce in each man a "general will." This conclusion rests on two further propositions: first, the common good can be secured only through the rule of the general will and, second, all men somehow know this to be the case. Only on these two assumptions will men's permanent interest in the public good translate into a permanent general will.

The first proposition—that the common good requires the sovereignty of the general will—is of course nothing other than the doctrine of the *Social Contract* as a whole. As for the surprising second claim, that all men already know and feel the truth of this doctrine, that too is in fact something Rousseau has explicitly maintained all along. In the climactic passage of the first book, where Rousseau finally proclaims the unique terms for the social contract, he declares that these terms "although they may never have been formally pronounced, they are everywhere the same, everywhere tacitly accepted and recognized" (*SC* I-6: 53). Rousseau maintains that his official juridical doctrine is not some obscure dream about how things ought to be but rather an empirical description of principles that in some sense everyone already knows and acts upon.

Most interpretations of the *Social Contract* tend to pass over this puzzling assertion in silence, but in doing so they forsake all possibility of understanding Rousseau's later claim that the general will exists permanently within each citizen. In other words, in order to resolve the great mystery concerning the manner of existence of the general will it is necessary to see that Rousseau's juridical doctrine has an additional "descriptive" meaning, that has been almost totally neglected.

The Descriptive Meaning of the Principles of Political Right

Up to this point we have understood the *Social Contract* primarily on the prescriptive level, as an attempt, not to describe what is, but to prescribe what ought to be. But Rousseau's pursuit of this purpose, as I have tried to emphasize, is shaped at every point by a moral commitment to being realistic, to prescribe political conditions that, should they come into being, would really work as promised. For it would indeed be immoral to encourage men to put their faith in unreal or ineffectual forces (like natural law) that cannot protect them. That is why Rousseau is very eager, as he declares at the beginning of the *Social Contract*, to build on "men as they are," to base his doctrine on the most elementary facts of human nature that are known to, and active within, all men (*SC* I-[Preface]: 46). Thus, Rousseau's prescriptive purpose itself requires that his doctrine have a second, descriptive level, that the prescribed ideal grow out of and express real, immanent forces already at work within the world.

There is also, we have seen, a polemical level to Rousseau's doctrine, an effort to have a real practical effect in the world, and this too requires that the doctrine be descriptive and draw upon ways of thinking and behaving to which men are already inclined. All levels of the doctrine, then, point to the descriptive, which in turn is at the root of Rousseau's crucial claim that the general will is something permanently actual in the world.

Rousseau succeeds in making his juridical doctrine descriptive through his choice of first principle, self-preservation, which is not only the most basic right men have but also their most powerful instinct, permanently guiding their behavior.[23] The remainder of Rousseau's doctrine, moreover, simply prescribes the necessary and self-evident means to the end of preservation, which prescriptions men intuitively know and follow. All men instinctively understand, even if they could not give a rational account of it, that it is not safe ever to put themselves at the mercy of another man, and that it is rational truly to cooperate and voluntarily to obey only where one governs oneself and where all members without exception are constrained to obey the same general laws. Indeed, men are almost led to these conclu-

---

[23] *SC* I-2: 47. One sees the dual, prescriptive/descriptive character of the principle of self-preservation with particular clarity in a passage from *Emile*: "Our first *duties* are to ourselves; our primary *sentiments* are centered on ourselves; all our natural *movements* relate in the first instance to our preservation and our well-being" (II: 97, emphasis added).

sions by the very nature of self-love which, in Rousseau's view, makes them self-absorbed, intractable, and genuinely responsive only to what sincerely comes from within. Consequently, Rousseau believes that his prescriptive juridical doctrine is based upon—indeed, it simply describes and makes fully explicit—certain self-evident rules of behavior that everyone already knows, inclines to, and, in some sense, obeys.[24]

But in what sense does everyone obey them? Certainly Rousseau, having proclaimed that man is "everywhere in chains," is not now asserting that the true social contract called for in his doctrine is everywhere respected and in force.

What he does maintain is, in the first place, that his principles of legitimacy are obeyed negatively. That is, wherever and to whatever extent these principles are *not* present in the structure of the state, men will instinctively and unfailingly *withhold* all genuine obedience and cooperation.[25] States that fail to embody these principles may indeed appear to be stable and orderly, but in reality they are only continuations of the state of war by different means, in which the people are not free but the rulers do not rule. This is merely to restate Rousseau's fundamental insight into the contradiction of society: all effort to force the obedience and cooperation of others necessarily leads to a disordered condition of active and passive aggression that enslaves the masters no less than the slaves. Obedience worthy of the name cannot ever be elicited from men except on the basis of the self-evident principles of political right. By nature absorbed in themselves as well as

---

[24] See *PE*, 213-14 and *SD*, 79, where Rousseau presents a summary of his principles as self-evident good sense. He also argues in the *Second Discourse* that barbarous man defends his political freedom because these principles are part of his common sense. Describing how the latter must have reasoned, he states: "in relations between one man and another, as the worst that can happen to one is to see himself at the discretion of the other, would it not have been *contrary to good sense* to begin by surrendering into the hands of a chief the only things they needed his help to preserve?" (pp. 163-64, emphasis added). And in *The Government of Poland*, he states regarding his principles: "God forbid that I should think there is a need to prove here that which a little good sense and some feeling suffice to make perceptible to anyone" (VI: 973).

To be sure, Rousseau knows that these self-evident principles are not found in the writings of the moralists and philosophers, nor are they often seen in the historical behavior of the people. But that is because the former are liars and the latter cowards. Indeed, this striking and seemingly perverse feature of Rousseau's works, that he is constantly accusing other writers of insincerity and bad faith and the people of cowardice and effeminacy, can be fully understood only with reference to the point at hand: he believes the principles of the *Social Contract* are essentially self-evident and known to all. See, for example, SC I-2: 48, II-2: 60-61, III-9: 96n; *PE*, 213-14; *SD*, 101-2, 104, 164-65.

[25] Speaking of these principles in *The Government of Poland*, Rousseau states: "One does not violate this sacred law with impunity, and the state of weakness to which so great a nation finds itself reduced is the work of this feudal barbarism which cuts off from the body of the state its most numerous part [i.e., the serfs]" (VI: 973).

distrustful of others, men will only obey themselves. Self-government is the only real government, consent and freedom the only genuine social bond. In sum, men not only *ought not* but, in fact, *do not* and *will not* truly unite and cooperate wherever the principles of the *Social Contract* are not fulfilled.[26]

There is also a positive sense in which, according to Rousseau, his doctrine is always obeyed. The existence or nonexistence of genuine cooperation is not, after all, a matter of indifference to men in society. Having lost their primitive self-sufficiency, they have a strong selfish need for such cooperation and are driven by this need to form all kinds of artificial groups and associations, of which the state is only the largest and most comprehensive. And in forming these groups, Rousseau claims, men intuitively and spontaneously tend to make use of something like his principles of political right. Although sometimes misled by false doctrines and superstitions, everyone senses on some level that it is safe to cooperate and reasonable to expect others to cooperate only if the common burdens and benefits are distributed on the basis of general rules that are acceptable and applicable to all. If one looks particularly at the smaller and more informal groups found in society, one sees that they are always based on an appeal to this sort of fairness and generality. The principles of political right, then, describe a real, positive tendency everywhere at work in the world.

Of course, Rousseau's principles do not appear to rule the world, but that is only because they do so in a self-hindering form. The selfish needs that impel men to form cooperative groups impel them also to exploit the groups they form. But even effective cheating and exploitation is possible only through the help of loyal allies: one needs a faithful militia to control the state by force, or trustworthy partisans to vote as a block in the assembly, or fellow thieves to put together a loyal gang. And these lesser, exploitative groups, like any groups, must themselves be united on the basis of Rousseau's principles if they are to possess the cohesiveness that alone makes them capable of violating these same principles in the larger group. "Thus the most corrupt men," Rousseau states, "always render some sort of homage to the public faith...[and] even brigands who are the enemies of virtue in the large society worship its semblance in their hideouts" (*PE*, 213). Rousseau does not deny—he rather emphatically asserts—that his principles of right are constantly being

---

[26] Rousseau does not altogether deny that men have a tendency to give their obedience to leaders or elites who assert an inherent right to rule based on moral and religious claims (especially in early times when men were more easily fooled, see *SC* IV-8: 124). But this tendency is not strong in the decisive respect. It is strong enough to give ambitious outsiders the power to destabilize an established state (that is why Rousseau is so eager to refute the exploitative doctrines of natural rule and natural law) and strong enough to add a crucial extra margin of obedience to a legitimate regime (that is why he sees the necessity for a civil religion) but it is not strong enough to ground a state, to produce a stable and lasting obedience, purely on its own.

violated, but all significant violations of these principles presuppose the following of them on a different level.[27] In sum, Rousseau believes that his principles of political right constitute an empirical description of the universal and self-evident rules of human cooperation that are everywhere obeyed and in effect in the world, albeit in a multileveled and self-hindering form.[28]

Returning to the issue of the general will's existence, it appears that if Rousseau's peculiar position has not been adequately understood, that is because it cannot be grasped without a significant reinterpretation of the whole meaning of the *Social Contract*. Rousseau's prescriptive realism as well as his polemical intentions lead him to formulate a doctrine of political right that is also necessarily descriptive. Since all social men have an indestructible interest (among other, contradictory interests) in the common good, and since all intuitively understand the necessary terms of social cooperation—the sovereignty of the general

[27] Rousseau sketches out this group theory of society in the *Discourse on Political Economy* (pp. 212-13, emphasis added). "All political societies are composed of other, smaller societies of different types, each of which has its interests and maxims." And these smaller groups are based, openly or tacitly, on Rousseau's principles: "The will of these particular societies always has two relations: for the members of the association, it is a *general will*; for the large society, it is a *private will*." The disorder of the larger society is due to men's greater loyalty to the smaller: "It is true that since particular societies are always subordinate to those that contain them, one ought to obey the latter in preference to the former. . . . But unfortunately personal interest is always found in inverse ratio to duty, and it increases in proportion as the association becomes narrower." See also *Jugement sur la polysynodie, OC* III: 644-45; *Poland* X: 1000; NH II-14: 233-34; *Dialogues* III: 965n; *SC* III-2: 82.

[28] A number of passages appear to contradict this view. In treating of political right, Rousseau states, "it is not a matter of what is, but of what is suitable and just." And again: "the issue here is less one of history and facts than of right and justice" (*GM* I-5: 174; *Guerre*, 603; see *GM* I-5: 169; *SC* I-2: 47, III-15: 103; *Emile* V: 458; *Guerre*, 616). From such statements, many have concluded that a passionate longing for "right" led Rousseau to an unparalleled indifference to "fact," and that his thought is historically distinctive precisely in causing so great a gap to open up between the "ought" and the "is."

But in these passages rejecting the appeal to "fact," Rousseau is criticizing a specific philosophical practice common in his time, represented above all by "Grotius, the master of all our learned men in this matter" of political right (*Emile* V: 458). Grotius's "most persistent mode of reasoning is always to establish *right by fact*" (*SC* I-2: 47, emphasis added). Rousseau means that Grotius derives his doctrine of right from the authority of the *consensus gentium*, the customary beliefs and established practices of mankind as manifested by the facts of history. It is only this particular use of "facts" that Rousseau is rejecting, as part of his rationalistic dismissal of the authority of custom and opinion (see *SC* I-2: 47n; *Guerre*, 603, 616). His own doctrine of "right" is indeed based on "fact," not in the old sense of accepting all the irrational and abusive institutions hallowed by history, but in the scientific sense of looking to men's empirical needs and universal tendencies.

will—it follows that all social men have within them (among other, contradictory wills) an indestructible general will. That is where the general will exists and why.[29]

How to Make the General Will Sovereign

We turn finally to the concrete political issue of how this inner will can be given a publicly recognizable voice and made to serve as the official sovereign of the state. To raise this question is to see the importance of the one just answered. If the general will exists permanently within each citizen, then, in calling for the sovereignty of the general will, Rousseau is not trying to impose on the world some transcendent ideal from above, nor is he appealing to some feeble conscience within; rather he is identifying and following the immanent principle of the social world, the mechanism already at work everywhere where men engage in moral thinking and group behavior, albeit at work in an unstable and self-hindering form. The concrete significance of this fact will become apparent momentarily.

Rousseau's general answer to our question is, of course, that the power of sovereignty must be vested in a legislative assembly of all the people, and the laws passed by the assembly majority must be taken to be the general will. That is why he declares: "The vote of the majority always

---

[29] The great difference between the views of Rousseau and Kant can be seen clearly at this point. The two thinkers make the striking and strikingly similar assertion that the general will, an ideal entity, forms a permanent element within the soul of every man, regardless of social institutions, patriotism, and so forth. But for Kant this will is the expression of a permanent, metaphysically distinct element in man's nature which, always free and disinterested, acts out of pure respect for the intrinsic worth of all rational beings. For Rousseau it only expresses social man's indestructible selfish interest in the cooperation of other men.

Rousseau's view, one might say, constitutes a psychological and eudemonistic explanation for the phenomenon that Kant believes can only be explained deontologically. If all social men, no matter how selfish, carry around with them an elementary "sense of fairness," that is not because they see that this is inherently "Rational" and necessary for its own sake, but because they intuitively understand the self-evident principles of political right which show that social cooperation, without which they could not survive a day, is possible only on these terms. Civilized man always feels (among other things) an inner imperative to respect the rights of other men, but what he is actually "respecting" in others is not their intrinsic worth stemming from the capacity to transcend selfishness, but rather precisely their selfishness or intractability, which renders them unwilling to cooperate except on the basis of an equal and safe exchange.

obligates all the others. This is a consequence of the contract itself" (*SC* IV-2: 110; see I-5: 52).[30]

And yet Rousseau is keenly aware that the majority can fail to express the general will. After defending his reliance on the majority, he admits: "This presupposes, it is true, that all the characteristics of the general will are still in the majority." And he adds: "When they cease to be, there is no longer any freedom regardless of the side one takes" (*SC* IV-2: 111). Rousseau's precise position on majority rule is this: what is guaranteed is not that the majority vote will express the general will but simply that it—and only it—is at least structurally inclined to do so (through the canceling out of the "pluses and minuses"). Consequently, making the assembly majority sovereign is a necessary condition but by no means a sufficient one for making the general will sovereign.

To make it sufficient, one must add certain supplementary measures which can reinforce the majority's basic structural tendency to express the general will. It is the legislator's task to arrange these additional features, which are not mentioned in the simple formula of Rousseau's juridical doctrine but which are presupposed by it. The reinforcements are essentially of two kinds: moral and institutional.

The moral reinforcements we have already considered in some detail. Notwithstanding certain appearances to the contrary, Rousseau is not proposing a purely "institutional solution" but is perhaps the greatest modern champion of the political importance of moral virtue. If the citizens are not filled with love for their compatriots, their selfishness will inevitably lead them to form factions and parties that will bias the assembly's vote and draw the majority outcome away from the general will. If the general will is to reign in the legislative assembly, then patriotism and virtue must reign in men's hearts.

It need only be added here that, in keeping with the general spirit of

[30] By this statement Rousseau must not be understood to mean that the will of the majority obligates in its own right. Strictly speaking, Rousseau is not a majoritarian; for the vote of the majority obligates only because it is assumed to express something beyond itself, the general will, which all citizens will *unanimously* (IV-2: 110-11). Rousseau's citizen obeys "only himself," not the majority.

If a citizen votes with the minority, that is either because he has followed some partisan will rather than the general will within him, or because his general will was based on a mistaken conception of the common interest. In either case, in being constrained to obey the majority, he is obeying the true general will, which is his own true will (ibid.).

It is not, Rousseau knows, his only will or his strongest or natural will, but it is his only self-consistent will, for in society all private, selfish wills are self-contradictory and enslaving. He is free only through the general will; but he must force himself to be free. The citizen's freedom consists in a kind of enslavement to himself. But all Rousseau ever promised, on the first page of the *Social Contract*, was to show how the chains of society might be made legitimate. Freedom in the most uncompromising sense is possible only outside the bounds of society.

Rousseau's doctrine, he regards this moral requirement as a uniquely realistic one. This would not be the case if the virtue required were the sort that leads men to know their place in a hierarchical order—to obey their betters and grant superior goods to superior men—for virtue of this deferential or "vertical" kind has very little root in human nature. But fortunately the general will requires only that men expand themselves horizontally and feel an essential equivalence with their fellow citizens; and such virtue, in Rousseau's view, is rooted in a real tendency of the human heart, the inclination to *identify* with others. In other words, this turns out to be a second respect in which the principles of political right are rooted in an immanent tendency: not only is there a rational basis for these principles (as the necessary terms of human cooperation) which all men actually know, but also there is an affective basis which all men actually feel: the impulse to identification. Of course, this impulse must be given an elaborate cultivation before it develops into the patriotic virtue required, but the seed is there in human nature.[31]

A second battery of reinforcements—certain measures on the institutional level—are also necessary to ensure that the majority vote consistently expresses the general will. As we have seen, this "indestructible" will is always present within the community. "The natural disposition of the assembly," Rousseau believes, is to express the general will, and if it sometimes fails to do so, that only results from this natural disposition somehow interfering with itself (*PE*, 213). Thus Rousseau's institutional devices have the task of simply rectifying and aligning this immanent tendency.

> If, when an adequately informed people deliberates, the citizens were to have no communication among themselves, the general will would always result from the large number of small differences, and the deliberation would always be good. But when factions, partial associations at the expense of the whole, are formed, the will of each of these associations becomes general with reference to its members and particular with reference to the state. One can say, then, that there are no longer as many voters as there are men, but merely as many as there are associations. The differences become less numerous and produce a result that is less general. Finally, when one of these associations is so big

[31] In Rousseau's view, this is an inclination that even in the state of nature tended to temper the force of men's selfishness, that in civilized private life can serve (if properly cultivated) as the foundation for pity and conscience, and that in the state can produce patriotism (*SD*, 95-96, 132-33). In *Emile*, he states: "When the strength of an expansive soul makes me identify myself with my fellow, and I feel that I am, so to speak, in him, it is in order not to suffer that I do not want him to suffer. I am interested in him for love of myself. . . . Love of men derived from love of self is the principle of human justice" (IV: 235n). For Rousseau, identification is the true affective principle of all human justice.

> that it prevails over all the others, the result is no longer a sum
> of small differences, but a single difference. Then there is no
> longer a general will, and the opinion that prevails is merely a
> private opinion. (*SC* II-3: 61; see *PE*, 212-13; *Polysynodie*, 628)

Men betray the general will only because they follow it on a different
level. The political problem is not that men refuse to form cooperative
associations but that they form too many—misplaced obedience. Thus,
the political task is not arbitrarily to introduce the general will into
human affairs but rather to remove the interfering ones already there, to
rectify this preexisting tendency.

"In order for the general will to be well expressed," Rousseau concludes, "it is therefore important that there be no partial society in the
State" (*SC* II-3: 61).[32] The individual must stand alone before the state,
with no intervening groups or lesser general wills. The legislator must
therefore strive, for example, to discourage the growth of uneven distri-
butions of population, large disparities in income, and great specializa-
tion of labor, for these conditions, among others, encourage the formation of subpolitical associations and interest groups. However, where it
is impossible to eliminate all such associations, Rousseau then recom-
mends: "their number must be multiplied and their inequality prevented,
as was done by Solon, Numa, and Servius" (*SC* II-3: 61-62).[33] Thus the
proper management of subpolitical groups—whether by eliminating
them or multiplying and balancing them—is an essential institutional
precondition for the sovereignty of the general will.

Also essential are certain arrangements regarding the functioning of
the sovereign legislative assembly (who will have the right of convening, who may initiate legislation, how will votes be counted, and so
forth). Although Rousseau gives these practical details only a very
general and desultory treatment (because he believes they need to be
settled differently in each country according to local needs), and although for this reason they are often neglected by his readers, they are
in fact vitally important for ensuring the hegemony of the general will.
Specifically, it is through these crucial details that Rousseau endeavors
to eliminate the most obvious problem with majority rule: the danger of
the tyranny of the majority.

First, a sovereign assembly must be convened. Who should have
the right to do so? The power of convening unscheduled assemblies, he argues, should rest solely in the hands of the executive or
Government, as distinguished from the sovereign (*SC* III-13: 100). It is
by virtue of this arrangement, he points out, that the Roman senate "held
in check a proud and restless people, and appropriately tempered the

---

[32] See also *Jugement sur la polysynodie, OC* III: 644-45; *Poland* X: 1000.

[33] We will see momentarily what "was done by. . . Numa and Servius."

ardor of seditious tribunes" (*SC* IV-4: 117).[34] This right was particularly important later when the people had become corrupt, for then "sometimes an assembly was convoked suddenly, before the candidates had time to arrange their intrigues" (*SC* IV-4: 119). Lest this arrangement give too much power to the Government, however, there must also be regularly scheduled assemblies that the executive is not empowered to prevent.

Once the assembly is in session, who shall have the right to initiate legislation and the right to speak before the assembly? In the *Social Contract*, Rousseau is noncommittal on these questions except to indicate that they are very complex: "this important subject would require a separate treatise, and I cannot say everything in this one" (*SC* IV-1: 109). Elsewhere, he states his preferences: "I would have desired that in order to stop the selfish and ill-conceived projects and the dangerous innovations that finally ruined the Athenians, everyone did not have the power to propose new laws according to his fancy; that this right belonged exclusively to the magistrates [the executive]" (*SD*, 82; for the same point see *Montagne* VIII: 843, 846-47, IX: 872). But as for the right to debate the proposals made by the magistrates, Rousseau holds that it should belong to all (*Montagne* VII: 830).

After a law has been proposed and debated a vote must be taken: should the votes be cast aloud or through secret ballot? In Rome, at first they were cast aloud.

> This practice was good as long as honesty prevailed among the citizens and each was ashamed to vote publicly for an unjust opinion or an unworthy subject. But when the people became corrupt and votes were bought, it was agreed that voting should be done in secret in order to restrain buyers by distrust and provide scoundrels with means not to be traitors. (*SC* IV-4: 119)

In this, as in all other matters, the arrangements must be tailored to the particular character and needs of the people.

Once the votes have been cast, what percentage should be required for the law to pass? Since Rousseau postpones all discussion of this vital question until book IV, chapter 2, his readers invariably assume that when he speaks of rule by the majority, as he does throughout the book, he means a simple majority. This turns out not to be the case. "Between unanimity and a tie there are several qualified majorities, at any of which the proportion can be established, according to the condition and needs of the body politic." As always, the legislator

---

[34] Rousseau implies that the senate attained this salutary power only by manipulating the auguries, which were required to be favorable before an assembly could be legitimately convened.

must look to local circumstances, but "two general maxims" should guide his decision.

> One, that the more important and serious the deliberations, the closer the winning opinion should be to unanimity. The other, that the more speed the business at hand requires, the smaller the prescribed difference in the division of opinions should be. In deliberations that must be finished on the spot, a majority of a single vote should suffice. The first of these maxims appears more suited to laws; the second, to business matters. (*SC* IV-2: 111)

In his *Considerations on the Government of Poland*, Rousseau is more explicit: unanimity should be required to pass or change constitutional laws, but "when it concerns legislation, one can require at least three-quarters of the votes, two-thirds in matters of state, a simple majority for elections and other current and momentary matters" (*Poland* IX: 996-97). In its sovereign, lawmaking capacity, then, the assembly will always require much more than a simple majority.

As surprising as this may seem, a far more shocking question remains to be settled: how much is each citizen's vote to count? It is an explicit requirement of the social contract that every citizen have a vote, and the reader naturally assumes that this means an equal vote. Only in the fourth chapter of book IV does one learn that this assumption is incorrect. This chapter, discussing "the manner in which the votes are cast and collected in the assembly of the people," takes the form of a brief "history of the Roman regulations in this regard" through which Rousseau hopes to "explain more graphically all the maxims I could establish" (*SC* IV-3: 112). In their assemblies, Rousseau explains, the Roman people never voted directly and as a whole but rather as members of smaller groups into which Numa and Servius had divided them, the vote of the whole being determined by the vote among these groups, each taken as a unit. At different times and for various purposes three different criteria were used for defining the groups: tribal identity, geographical location, and wealth. By apportioning the groups in a very unequal fashion (under the pretext of military requirements), it was possible to make the votes of certain elements of the population—for example, the wealthy or the virtuous rural tribes—vastly more influential than those of the others. Rousseau makes clear that it is perfectly legitimate and, under certain circumstances, very useful to take measures of this kind. In particular, he seems to acknowledge that in certain cases it is necessary virtually to disenfranchise the urban poor, the "wretched proletarian[s]," who would have "sold the state to those who stooped to buying the votes of the rabble" (*SC* IV-4: 114, 115).[35]

One last limitation on majority rule needs to be mentioned. In imagining Rousseau's state one should not be thinking of the dynamic, reformist, and future-oriented modern nation-state. Rousseau has in mind an old and conservative state living in more or less unchanging obedience to a code of ancient laws inherited from a distant past when these laws were instituted by a heroic legislator and ratified by the people. [36] Therefore, the role of the present-day assembly majority is not nearly so active or authoritative as one may be supposing. It will be limited to making minor additions to the law when necessary and to protecting the laws from the encroachments of the executive power. If Rousseau's citizen were asked the true locus of the general will, his first answer would be "The Law"; only secondarily would he point to the present-day assembly majority as the ultimate moral ground of the law.

In sum, an ancient code of popularly ratified laws, now watched over and occasionally supplemented by an assembly majority bolstered and qualified

[35] Most commentators, reluctant to attribute such a harsh and plutocratic position to Rousseau, have either ignored this long chapter on Rome's inegalitarian voting institutions or dismissed it as mere historical filler (see the references cited in Masters's note 120 in *SC*: 151). But the chapter is clearly intended to flesh out Rousseau's earlier assertion that, for the general will to be expressed in the assembly, the "partial societies" in the state must be properly arranged "as was done by...Numa and Servius" (II-3: 61-62). Moreover, Rousseau expressly asserts that it embodies "all the maxims I could establish" on the subject of voting regulations (IV-3: 112). In *Poland* (VII: 988), he claims: "this matter of voting [is] one of those which I discussed with the most care in the *Social Contract*." And in the summary of that treatise presented in the *Letters from the Mountain*, he states: "Finally in the last book I examine by means of a comparison with the best government that has existed, to wit that of Rome, the regulations most favorable to the good constitution of the state" (VI: 809).

One should also remember in this connection that, in all his writings addressing and celebrating his homeland, Rousseau never once spoke out against the fact that the right to vote was enjoyed by only two of the four classes of Genevans (and none of the women), less than a quarter of the total population. And while this silence must in part be due to mere prudence, Rousseau also alludes in *Letters from the Mountain* to the same extenuating factors that he mentions in his discussion of Rome (IX: 890).

As for the substance of his position, it is harsh but is it inconsistent? Rousseau's passionate hatred of inequality and oppression derives from his view that the extreme dependence in which the urban poor live utterly corrupts them. It follows that one must do all that one can to prevent the emergence of such a class of destitute men; but, sadly, it also follows that, once such a class does exist, one must for the public good do all that one can to limit its political influence (*SC* I-2: 48, II-11: 75, 75n; *FD*, 64; *Epitre à M. Bordes, OC* II: 1131; *Poland* VI: 974). Once again one is struck by Rousseau's steely consistency in not shrinking from a conclusion that must have been terrible for him.

[36] This point is stated nicely by Cobban (1934, p. 100): "Of the complexities of modern industrialism and the continual demand for fresh legislation to meet ever changing circumstances Rousseau could have no conception. He is all along thinking of the small, simply organized, conservative state, where the inhabitants live as their fathers have lived, and where, once the constitution has been established, the passing of new laws would be a very rare event."

by the elaborate moral and institutional reinforcements described above—that is Rousseau's answer to how one makes the general will sovereign.

Exaggerating the Sufficiency of Majority Rule

We have seen in some detail the extensive, elaborate, and rather tough-minded measures needed, in Rousseau's view, to ensure that the assembly majority shall express the general will. Indeed, only by focusing on these much neglected measures can one ever really make sense of the *Social Contract*, which otherwise seems to display an undefended and indefensible faith in the infallibility of the majority as such. It is now apparent that when Rousseau seems to proclaim the universal necessity of majority rule, and even when he expressly declares that "the vote of the majority always obligates all the others," what he means is this: in those rare cases where a wise legislator has infused the citizens with a spirit of patriotic virtue and put into place all the necessary institutional reinforcements regulating the conduct of the assembly, all tailored to the specific needs of the time and place, then and only then will the vote of the assembly majority reliably express the general will and so deserve to be made sovereign and obligatory.

Yet if, by the insertion of these unstated clauses, we succeed in making sense of Rousseau's politics, we create new difficulties regarding his presentation of them—regarding his "doctrine." For Rousseau never quite says what I say he means. What he says is that the majority *"always* obligates all the others. This is a consequence of the *contract itself"*—always, and not just when buttressed by all of these rare, elaborate, and difficult reinforcements. Moreover, the reinforcements, though indispensable, are scarcely discussed until the very end of the book, and then only in a vague and disordered fashion, and even omitted altogether in the summaries of the *Social Contract* presented in *Emile* and *Letters from the Mountain*. Thus Rousseau's doctrine gives every appearance of calling for majority rule as a universal and unqualified demand.

Indeed, the whole premise of the kind of doctrine Rousseau employs—natural constitutional law—is that certain elementary constitutional conditions can be identified that form, by themselves, the necessary and sufficient conditions of legitimate government, and that it is therefore possible to draw up a list of precise "institutional demands" that are everywhere morally necessary, constituting universally valid grounds for obedience and revolution. Rousseau's "principles of political right" present just such a list of demands, at the heart of which is an unqualified insistence on the sovereignty of the majority.

It would seem, in other words, that if most readers of the *Social Contract* come away with the conclusion that Rousseau tends (albeit inconsistently) to identify the general will with the will of the assembly majority, that is no accident. By certain explicit statements, by downplaying the importance of the moral and institutional reinforcements, and by employing the particular form of doctrine he does, Rousseau gives the misleading impression that majority rule is not only the necessary but also the sufficient condition for the sovereignty of the general will. Whatever his reasons, it seems impossible to deny that Rousseau consciously and systematically exaggerates the sufficiency of majority rule.

Rousseau himself explains his reasons right after making his most explicit statement of the exaggerated view. "The vote of the majority *always* obligates all the others." At first he justifies this statement with a strong defense of the claim that the majority expresses the general will. But then he acknowledges: "This presupposes, it is true, that all the characteristics of the General Will are still in the majority. When they cease to be, there is no longer any freedom regardless of the side one takes" (*SC* IV-2: 111). Rousseau's view seems to be this: the assembly majority, and it alone, is at least structurally inclined to express the general will, and where all the requisite supports have been put into place, the laws passed by the majority will indeed reliably embody the general will. However, where these supports are lacking, the laws will stray from the general will, *but* public questioning of the majority and of the laws will not lead to the general will either. Therefore, nothing is lost by exaggerating or absolutizing the claims of the majority—and something very important is gained.

Without this exaggeration, the door would always remain open for the ambitious or disgruntled to question whether the vague "requisite supports" still remained and whether the majority still spoke for the general will. The definition of justice, thus pried away from its procedural determination, would once again be up for grabs—inevitably to be seized by the two elites that it is precisely the great purpose of Rousseau's doctrine to disarm: the secular and religious ideologues and the executive power.

In order to disarm these elites—to "put law above man"—Rousseau must find some source of law that is relatively just and defend it absolutely. Thus he purposely blurs the distinction between the majority and the infallible general will, purposely exaggerates the justice of the majority as such, in order to discourage questioning of the laws that it enacts, for in any given society such laws will constitute the most just standard possible.

Furthermore, as will be seen in the discussion of the executive power, Rousseau believes that the universal tendency of history is always to strengthen the executive at the expense of the people. It is also to counteract this tendency, then, that Rousseau seeks to defend the legislative rights of the majority in as precise and absolute a manner as possible.

Summary

We may conclude by summarizing the arguments—we have seen five in all—that stand behind Rousseau's most characteristic and important political tenet: in all legitimate states the general will must be sovereign.

First, Rousseau has taken the epoch-making step of fully liberating man from the claims of all objective standards above human will. Based on the dual premise of man's natural asociality and arationality, he rejects all doctrines of natural rule and natural law, which, insufficiently known and enforced, function in the world only as tools of exploitation. In order for the state and morality to escape such ineffectuality and abuse, a *human will* must be sovereign, whose precise and enforced commands shall themselves define the rules of morality.

Second, where is the human will to which such power could safely be given? Although the will of every individual seeks only his own good, men are capable of forming a collective individual with a general will that seeks only the good of the whole. Owing, again, to their liberation from natural standards, men are free to ignore the objective differences and inequalities among them and to unite on the basis of an artificial equivalence. This equivalence enables all to be ruled by a single will that, coming from all, applies equally to each. This general will, through which the whole rules itself as a whole, can safely be given the sovereign power because it and it alone is constitutionally incapable of seeking to harm any part.

Third, all men intuitively know the preceding argument—that the general will is the only will it is safe to obey—and therefore it is also the only will that men ever *do* obey. They will never really follow private wills (which only enslave themselves through their efforts at mastery). Rousseau's prescriptions are descriptive: the general will is not some ineffectual transcendent ideal but an immanent (if self-hindering) social force and indeed the only significant social force. Thus the general will *ought* to be made sovereign because it is the only thing that *can* be made sovereign, the only power that will ever be truly obeyed.

Fourth, in addition to this *rational* basis for men's exclusive willingness to obey the general will—their knowledge that it alone is safe—there is also a dual *affective* basis. Human self-love is such as to make men naturally self-absorbed. Only the inner and immanent, only what sincerely grows and emerges from within, can gain a real hold on men. Hence, only the general will, which is in some sense men's own will, can successfully command them. Moreover, due to their natural self-absorption men have little inclination to look up and to subordinate themselves to what is above them, but, due to the peculiar expansiveness of their self-love, they do have an impulse to look across at their equals and to extend their being over them. This prerational, natural inclination to "identify" with others gives the general will a real, affective force.

Thus, again, the general will ought to be sovereign because it is the only thing that can be, that can acquire a real hold over men's hearts.

Fifth and finally, if we look beyond the issue of preservation to Rousseau's deeper concern, the state of men's souls, this too points directly to the sovereignty of the general will. According to Rousseau's new principle, the unhealthiness of man's soul derives not from any natural dividedness or incompleteness but solely from the contradiction of society. The human problem is social and not metaphysical, and thus the cure requires not uplifting men to some heavenly standard of perfection but simply putting men into better relation with one another. Specifically, since the relation of *personal dependence* is the source of all evil, the rule of impersonal law—of law as such, regardless of content, of pure general will—is the key to man's political salvation. For the sake of the health of men's souls, then, no less than for the safety of their bodies, the "great problem of statecraft [is] to find a form of government that puts law above man"— that makes the general will sovereign.

This is the fivefold root of the sovereignty of the general will.

10

The General Will as the Foundation of a New Science of Politics

To be legitimate, a state must be based on a "social contract" that bestows "sovereignty" on the "general will." Before turning to the final step of Rousseau's juridical argument, the establishment of an "executive" to enforce the laws legislated by the sovereign, we must pause to consider the larger, "descriptive" significance of the theory of the general will. For this theory does not merely present Rousseau's curious new candidate for sovereign in the state, but forms the centerpiece of a comprehensive new science of morality and politics—of what they are, whence they arise, and how they work. Beginning from the theoretical individualism characteristic of early modern political philosophy, Rousseau's new science attempts to generate, on that basis, a more convincing account of the political world in all its complexity.

It can perhaps be brought into sharpest focus by contrasting it with classical "constitutional" theory, with the doctrine of "forms of government" or "regimes" understood as organic political wholes, that was elaborated in its original form by Plato and Aristotle. Classical political science in this form had been the dominant strain of political theorizing in the West (alongside the doctrine of natural law) and although it had been subjected over the centuries to significant challenges or modifications, it was never completely repudiated and replaced until the doctrine of the general will.

The Nonexistence of Leading and Following

Virtually all political theorists prior to Rousseau (although, more unambiguously, all prior to Machiavelli) had taken the commonsense view that the heart of politics lies in the phenomenon of ruling and being ruled. Through this hierarchic power relation—through the respect and obedience paid by followers to leaders—the state constitutes itself and every aspect of life within it. And since everyone cannot rule, "leading and following" has always meant that some particular segment of society asserts its superiority and authority over the rest. Therefore, every state is a state by virtue of being a monarchy, aristocracy, or democracy, that is, by possessing some one "form of government" through which a particular part of society—one, few, or many—exercises authority over the rest. And political theory, the science of the state, has been essentially a science of "forms of government" or "constitutions" or "regimes," list-

ing the different possible ruling classes, describing the different virtues or ends in the name of which they lead, and ranking them in a hierarchy
of better and worse.

All of this, which might seem too obvious to state, Rousseau rejects.
What, after all, does his fundamental insight into the contradiction of
society mean but that where there is ruling and being ruled, one human
will commanding another, there can be neither justice nor genuine obedience, but only disorder and mutual enslavement. Mastery is slavery. In
Rousseau's system, the whole phenomenon of leading and following, formerly considered the very essence of politics and the core of the state, has
only an illusory existence. Politics, in this classical sense, simply does not
take place. Precisely where a "regime" exists, there is *no* state.

Such a thing as a "state" can exist, according to Rousseau, but it will not be
a monarchy, an aristocracy, or a democracy; not a "form of government" at all,
in which some *part* of the community rules over the rest. It will consist in the
rule of something completely new—the "general will"—by which he means
precisely: the unanimous rule of *all* over each, of the *whole* over itself. "What
really is an act of sovereignty?" Rousseau asks, posing the central question.
"It is not a convention between a superior and an inferior, but a convention
between the body and each of its members" (*SC* II-4: 63).[1] This conception
completely inverts the traditional view: the state is constituted and held
together not by creating but precisely by eliminating the vertical phenomenon
of leading and following. The state is a leveled and homogenized whole that,
just because it is such, can rule itself as a whole, all over each.[2]

Rousseau's new conception of what ruling is brings with it a new
understanding of the source of authority and obedience. Where rule is exer-

---

[1] "The social pact is of a particular and unique nature, in that the people contracts only with
itself—that is to say, the people as sovereign body contracts with the individuals as subjects. This
condition constitutes the whole artifice of the political machine and sets it in motion" (*Emile* V:
461; see *GM* I-3: 165). This condition is what produces the "marvel" that the citizens "obey and
no one commands, that they serve and have no master" (*PE*, 214). Similarly, it enables Rousseau's
state to resolve the famous conflict between freedom and authority, a permanent antinomy in the
traditional state, where the ruling part is distinct from the ruled. Having collapsed this distinction,
Rousseau declares: "the essence of the body politic lies in the harmony of obedience and freedom;
and the words *subject* and *sovereign* are identical correlatives, whose meaning is combined in the
single word citizen" (*SC* III-13: 100, emphasis in the original).

[2] Rousseau's radical departure from all earlier political science gets obscured by the fact that,
in practice, his state resembles a democracy and that, for this reason, he himself sometimes calls
his state by that name (see *SD*, 79), as I have as well. But strictly speaking this is not correct. A
"democracy" is still a "form of government," being the rule of a part—the many or majority—over
the whole, whereas the sovereignty of the general will means the unanimous rule of all over each.

Of course, Rousseau speaks of monarchy, aristocracy, and democracy when discussing the
possible arrangements of *executive* power, but this is a secondary matter and does not concern the
state's essence and foundation, the sovereign general will. In the decisive respect there is only one
kind of state, there is only "the state," and not the variety of forms of government assumed by
earlier thought. "The foundations of the state are the same in all governments" (*Montagne* VI:
811; see *SC* II-6: 67).

cised by a part over the whole, the ruling part must justify its authority by some claim to excellence. "Leadership" *is* an assertion of superiority. Thus, if the regime exists and coheres through the leadership of a part, its authority and cohesion derive from something like "admiration," from the general belief among the followers in the superior goodness of their leaders. But Rousseau denies that this is how the state and politics really work. The state is not a "regime"—leaders ruling followers *in the name of the good*—but rather the *self*-rule of all over each, and the latter involves no appeal to the good. For Rousseau, all genuine obeying is obeying only oneself. So, again, he stands the older view on its head: the state's commandments obligate and move you not because they are good but because they are your own.

This is Rousseau's new theory of politics, proudly proclaimed and practiced in the *Social Contract*. It is a comprehensive, horizontal, "non-regime" political science, which is, in effect, only the flip side of his fundamental insight into the contradiction of social power. Rule, if it is to be real and noncontradictory, cannot be something that one party does to an "other," but something that all somehow do to themselves. Hence, the heart of this new science is the replacement of the concept of "regime," "form of government," or "constitution" with that of the "general will." This means replacing the idea of "some ruling others" with "all ruling each," and the call of the good with that of the self.

Having seen Rousseau's "general will science" in outline, we may explore it in greater depth—its new conception of what the state is, how it functions, and in what ways it forms a genuine "whole," greater than the sum of its parts. In the terminology that will emerge momentarily, we need to examine what it means that Rousseau conceives the state no longer as an "organism" but as a "civil person."

The Nonexistence of Order

In the above discussion, the uniqueness of Rousseau's state was brought to light by focusing on the relation between ruler and ruled. But the state is not constituted by this relation alone, which may in fact be seen as only a special case, if the most important case, of the still more fundamental phenomenon of "order." In the political theory of Plato and Aristotle, and in one form or another in the thought of almost all political thinkers prior to the Renaissance, the state was understood as an ordered whole: a collection of functionally differentiated parts, each suited for the performance of some particular job (ruling being one), all fitted together for the common good. It is order in this sense—the principle "one man, one job," the division of labor, "distributive justice," the complementarity of men's different abilities and interests—that makes the state a state by making it a genuine whole with properties beyond those possessed by its parts in isolation. To be sure, one must beware of over-stating this point, since there was also much skepticism regarding the possibility of achieving genuine order, and since the rival consideration of freedom or consent was almost always granted some importance. Still, however diluted, order remained the dominant principle, grounding whatever cohesion, common goodness, and reality the state possessed.[3]

On the basis of this more general formulation, we see again Rousseau's break with the traditional view: he entirely rejects the conception of the state as a functionally differentiated order, just as he rejected the particular aspect of this conception involved in the notion of a separate ruling part. The state can hardly be based on the complementarity of men's interests when, as Rousseau insists, "what private interests have in common is so slight that it will never outweigh what sets them in opposition." Men are so little made for society that "in the social state the good of one necessarily constitutes the harm of another" (*Emile* IV: 312n; II: 105n).[4] Rousseau does not deny that, historically speaking, the division of labor is what gave rise to the so-called state, as he explains in the *Second Discourse*, but the "state" that it created, by making each person dependent on every other, is in reality only a deceitful appearance of order, behind which men ceaselessly exploit and oppress one another.

Once again, the key to Rousseau's new political science is his principle of the contradiction of society, which reverses the fundamental principle of traditional political science: what formerly was thought to constitute the ground of the state's unity and being—an order of mutual dependence, the division of labor, "one man, one job"—not only does not unify and ground the state but, on the contrary, is actually the great hidden cause of all social disorder and instability.[5]

---

[3] See Plato *Republic* 369a-372a, 433a-434d. Aristotle, *Politics* 1261a20-30, 1276b1-15; *Nicomachean Ethics* 1133a17: "For a community is not formed by two physicians, but by a physician and a farmer, and, in general by people who are different and unequal."

[4] "If I am answered that society is so constituted that each man gains by serving the others, I shall reply that this would be very well, if he did not gain still more by harming them" (*SD*, 195; see *Narcissus*, 105). Hobbes makes the same point: "But though the benefits of this life may be much furthered by mutual help...yet those may be better attained to by dominion than by the society of others" (*De Cive* I-2: 113).

[5] *SD*, 151-52, 154-60. In a passage in *Emile* probably modeled on Plato's *Republic* 369ff., Rousseau describes the traditional view he rejects: "Let us suppose ten men, each of whom has ten sorts of needs. Each must, for what he needs, apply himself to ten sorts of work; but, given the differences of genius and talent, one man will be less successful at one sort of work, another man at another.... Let us form a society of these ten men and let each apply himself, for himself and for the nine others, to the kind of occupation which suits him best. Each will profit from the talents of the others as if he alone had them all. Each will perfect his own by continuous practice, and it will turn out that all ten, perfectly well provided for, will even have a surplus for others. That is the *apparent* principle of *all our institutions*. It is not part of my subject to examine its consequences here. I have done it in another writing" (III: 193, emphasis added). By "another writing" he means the *Second Discourse* with its radical critique of the division of labor, a reference made explicit in an earlier version of the *Emile* passage (see *OC* IV: 467, var. 4). In his advice to the Corsicans, Rousseau urges them to minimize the division of labor (*Corsica*, 914, 924-25; see also *d'Alembert*, 61).

The Negative and Secondary Common Good

If there is no harmony among men's private interests, no common good, then how is a true state—a union that is not merely a system of mutual exploitation—at all possible for human beings? What could a genuine state possibly be if it is not a community based on order and mutual complementarity? That is just what Rousseau's new horizontal political science needs and purports to explain.

Rousseau's theory of the state begins by following the radical innovations of Hobbes. Lacking a common good, (social) men are in a state of constant war. But this war, which threatens the preservation of everyone, gives everyone an identical and urgent interest in peace. Consequently, there *is* a common good after all—only it is a "negative" and also "secondary" one, arising precisely from the *lack* of a common good in the "positive" and "primary" sense. The existence of a common good in this crucial new sense makes the formation of genuine states possible despite the fact—or, rather, on the basis of the fact—that men do not naturally fit together into an order of mutual benefit.

The common good that grounds the state is, in the first place, *negative*. So long as men live in pursuit of their natural positive desires they will know only conflict and misery; but if they orient their lives negatively, toward the avoidance of evil, then they can unite around the common goal of avoiding civil war, the greatest of evils. The state is a negative union, a uniting against and not a uniting for. Men form communities not to produce some new, positive social good but to protect the private goods they already have—their lives, liberty, and property. They unite not because all have something to contribute but because all have something to lose.[6]

Men come to this negative union, moreover, not directly (as would be the case if they united against some external enemy) but *secondarily*, on the "rebound"—as a reaction against the disorder resulting from their own primary impulses. The common enemy against which they unite is their own spontaneous, natural selves. Political union does not arise from the direct, forward movement of men's natural

---

[6] Rousseau does not deny, since he is famous for affirming, that once the state is in being it occasions the rise of all sorts of positive benefits—remarkable new developments of mind and heart, as well as new prosperity deriving from the division of labor. But again, these benefits, which by themselves often divide men as much as unite them, necessarily *presuppose* the existence of a framework of law and rule, and thus cannot themselves constitute the foundation of that framework (although they may help to strengthen it where it already exists).

What really unites men in society remains negative: that they all have something to lose. Only by appreciating this fact can one understand why Rousseau endorses, to the surprise of many, the narrow Lockean view that "the right of property is the most sacred of all the rights of citizens" (*PE*, 224). Since property is what is most easily lost, since it is men's greatest vulnerability, it constitutes the single strongest bond for a negative union. That is why "property is the true basis of civil society and the true guarantee of the citizen's engagements" (*PE*, 225; see 229-30; *Emile* II: 99, V: 461; *Frags.*, 483; *SD*, 154). For the same reason, Rousseau is certain that the rich founded society. The poor "had nothing to lose except their freedom," whereas the rich "being so to speak vulnerable in every part of their goods, it was much easier to harm them" (*SD*, 162; see 154) Men unite for the avoidance of harm. To put it differently, the goal of the state consists not in distributive order but civil freedom.

longings and interests, perhaps given form through some image of perfect order, but from a shrinking back from the terrifying absence of order, made palpable through an image of the state of nature. In other words, the traditional state, based on a primary common good, says to men: "you should unite because you naturally fit together." Rousseau and Hobbes tell men: "you must unite because you do not fit together."

To summarize, Rousseau denies the existence of what was formerly thought to constitute the bond of the state—a direct and positive common good based on differential order—but sees that the very absence of such order produces a secondary and negative common good, which forms the true social bond. His succinct formula for the common good is this: "the agreement of all interests is formed in opposition to the interest of each" (*SC* II-3: 61n). The state is a *negative* union because it is "formed in opposition"; and it is a secondary or reactive union because the thing in opposition to which men unite is themselves, their "primary" selves which are naturally at war. Men join together in reaction against their natural opposition.

The State as a "Civil Person"

How is the negative and secondary common good to be secured? All men are in secondary agreement on the need to escape the warlike condition resulting from their primary disagreement. Thus all agree on the need artificially to make themselves agree, which they can do only by appointing a "sovereign" whose single, arbitrary will all contract to obey and to "own" (in Hobbes's term) in preference to their own, natural and conflicting wills. In this way, all wills are artificially collapsed into one.

From this contract arises the state, conceived now as a *single will*. And for this new conception a new term is needed: the state is a "civil person" because, as Hobbes explains, "when there is *one will* of all men it is to be esteemed for *one person*." He therefore defines the commonwealth as "one person, whose will, by the compact of many men, is to be received for the will of them all."[7] The crucial innovation here is that the sovereign will creates the unity of the state not by wisely discovering and enforcing a

---

[7]*De Cive* V-9: 170, emphasis added. See *Leviathan* XVII: 132. Something is a "person" when it has a single legal will, a single source of legally relevant words and actions. This concept of persons and especially of artificial, corporate persons is borrowed, as Hobbes himself explains, from Roman law (*Leviathan* XVI: 125; *De Homine* XV: 83-85). The claim, however, that the state (as distinguished from lesser associations existing within and by virtue of the state) is such an artificial person and that its unity and being consist in its artificial personality is Hobbes's own epoch-making innovation. The concept and terminology of "moral persons" (using "moral" in the sense of "conventional" or "positive") is further developed by Pufendorf, who defines the state as "a composite moral person whose will, formed by the assemblage of the wills of many united by their conventions, is considered the will of all generally" (*Les devoirs de l'homme* II-6.10). For Rousseau too, the state is a "moral person" or "public person" whose unity, self, and life consist in its having a single, unitary will, the general will (*SC* I-7: 55, II-4: 62, II-1: 80, III-5: 86, III-6: 87, III-11: 99). See also the excellent discussion of these terms in Derathé (1950) pp. 397-410.

preexisting social unity, the natural harmony of men's interests, but rather by being itself the unity of the state. As Locke explains, "the essence and union of the society consist in having one will." It is in this will (expressed by the legislature) "that the members of a commonwealth are united and combined together into one coherent living body. This is the soul that gives form, life, and unity to the commonwealth."[8] In this inverted state, men are united not in society but in the ruler, not in the harmony of their interests but in the unitary sovereign will.

Hobbes underlines the difference between the older conception of the state and his own when he chastises Aristotle for calling ants and bees, with their organic societies, political animals: "because their government is only. . . many wills concurring in one object, not (as is necessary in civil government) one will."[9] In the state men unite not in the *object* of their will, but in the *organ*. Indeed, it is because the objects of their natural wills are in conflict that they agree artificially to unite in the organ; that is, to make the sovereign's will their own regardless of *what* he wills. Hence, the unity and being of the political whole is, as it were, not objective but subjective: not the unity of an organized body, an ordered fitting together of functions and interests, but rather the unity of a single source of willing. And thus the state is no longer to be termed an *organism* but a *person*.[10]

In the thought of Hobbes, Locke, and others prior to Rousseau, however, the unity of will that constitutes the life of the state is understood to be a convention or legal fiction. Sovereignty is still to be lodged in some *part*

---

[8] *Second Treatise*, para. 212.

[9] *De Cive* V-6: 168. See *Elements of Law* XII-7, 8: 238-39; *Leviathan* XVII: 131-32.

[10] We broach here a famous controversy. In a well-known passage near the beginning of the *Political Economy*, Rousseau describes the body politic through a detailed comparison to the human organism: "the sovereign power represents the head; the laws and customs are the brain . . . commerce, industry, and agriculture are the mouth and stomach . . . public finances are the blood . . . the citizens are the body and members . . . " (pp. 211-12). Similarly, in the *Social Contract* other such parallels are drawn, and there is much talk of the "life," "vigor," "health," and "death" of the state (I-6: 53, II-4: 62, III-1: 78, III-6: 87, III-11: 98-99, IV-2: 109). Many scholars have therefore concluded that Rousseau held an organic view of the state (see Vaughn [1918] pp. xxviii, xxix [cited by Derathé, 1950, p. 410]).

But a passage almost identical to the one above is found in the introduction to Hobbes's *Leviathan*, certainly a nonorganicist work. In fact, on *any* view of the state, one can divide it into different parts or "organs" that supply its various needs for decision making, economic production, and so forth. The distinctive claim of the organic view is that the heterogeneity of the human species produces groups naturally suited to serve as these different state organs or at least that men's differentiated service is what constitutes their citizenship and grounds the state. But the above passage not only fails to make this claim but implicity rejects it by referring to *all* of the citizens homogeneously as the "body" of the state and to *all* of them again (in their capacity as members of the sovereign) as the "head."

The state in Rousseau's conception is the very opposite of a functionally differentiated order since it arises through a reaction against the lack of order and is constructed through men's renunciation of their natural differences and inequalities. If Rousseau, like Hobbes, is manifestly eager to speak of the state in vitalistic terms and to describe it as an "artificial man," that is because he wants to emphasize the new idea that the state is, not indeed an organism, but a person.

of the whole, one, few, or many; and the will of this sovereign part is not really the actual will of all the citizens but is only by their rational consent "*considered* the will of all generally" (Pufendorf); it is "*to be received* for the will of them all" (Hobbes).

Through the theory of the general will, however, Rousseau argues that the "fiction" is real, that the sovereign's unitary will is indeed the actual will of every citizen. In this way, Rousseau radically transforms Hobbes's conception of the state, a transformation traceable to two differences in their psychological theories.

The theory of the general will, we have seen, derives from a more skeptical psychology, which denies that men ever should or ever will risk submitting themselves to a will outside their own. Rousseau believes that when social men, seeing the conflict that naturally exists among them, realize their need to force themselves to agree, they will also realize that they have no other means but to do so directly, without recourse to an external sovereign. Each feels the need to force himself to will generally and to obey the general rules that all will make for each. Thus, in the psychological world postulated by Rousseau, men's need to escape their natural opposition necessarily produces within the soul of each a general will as the only possible ground of agreement—a real, nonfictional (though artificial) unanimous will that animates the collective person of the state.

Rousseau's alteration of the Hobbesian state is carried still further through a second revision of Hobbes's psychology. The basis of the state for both thinkers is self-preservation, which Hobbes simply equates with the fear of death. But Rousseau, as we have seen, interprets it more positively as a desire to exist and to sense one's existence. And joined to this desire is a capacity for "identification" with others. Therefore, the merging of all wills into a single collective person, the union through legal identification, that remains merely a conventional arrangement for Hobbes, becomes, in Rousseau, something real and rooted in the identification of our selves and existence. Thus, Rousseau's state, precisely because it is based on "self-preservation," is united not only through fear but also through the love of our collective existence, and although lacking a positive common good in the full, organic sense, it nevertheless involves a positive bond of identification.

Rousseau's state emerges, then, from a specific transformation of Hobbes's. Both thinkers, rejecting the notion of an organic or natural political order, see the state as a civil person: a negative and secondary union held together by the artificial creation of a single, unified source of will. But for Hobbes, the state is a "person" only in a purely legal sense, whereas Rousseau adds both a psychological and a vitalistic dimension. His "civil person" is in some sense a *real* person, possessing both a true collective will and also a collective life, self, or existence.

A "real civil person"—that is Rousseau's new image or definition of the state. As we will see, he believes that no human society can ever fully embody this ideal, but it remains his organizing concept of what a state is and how it works. Perhaps the best way of fleshing out its meaning and consequences is in the following terms. By radicalizing Hobbes's political conception in the ways just described, Rousseau found the means to restore to the "civil person" certain vital and lost characteristics of the traditional state. In particular, if one looks either at the justice of the state's conduct toward its citizens or, conversely, at the citizens' devotion toward the state, one finds that Rousseau's "real civil person" reestablishes, from the bottom up as it were, both the aspiration toward moral perfection and the communal "wholeness" that were characteristic of the functionally differentiated organic state.

Rousseau's State and Moral Infallibility

Consider the issue of the state's conduct toward its citizens. In Hobbes's commonwealth, infamous for its amorality, the authority of the sovereign's will derives not from its claim to be good but to be the citizens' own will; consequently, there is already a narrowly legal sense in which Hobbes's sovereign claims infallibility, although this claim's purpose is to liberate the state from any real moral accountability. Whatever the sovereign commands, Hobbes explains, "it can be no injury to any of his subjects," because "every subject is by this institution author of all the actions, and judgments of the sovereign" and "to do injury to oneself, is impossible."[11] But, in this state the monarch's will is the citizen's will only as a legal fiction, and therefore Hobbes concedes the obvious point that "they that have sovereign power may commit *iniquity*," only this iniquity cannot be called "injustice, or injury in the proper [i.e., legal] signification."[12] But in Rousseau's state, where the general will is sovereign, the civil person is real, its will is truly the will of everyone, and therefore what it wills is genuinely infallible.

Rousseau thus reestablishes the moral aspirations of the traditional state, although in an inverted way. Men are not elevated to justice by the call of reason and the good, mediated by the leadership of wise statesmen. That is not how politics works. Justice, when it comes into being, springs up from below, as the spontaneous flow and expression of the collective will, whose moral correctness is guaranteed not by its correspondence to any transcendent standard but by its well-intentioned source, not by the infallibility of the good above us but of self-love within. Again, the morality of the state does not consist in distributive justice or differential order based on the

---

[11]*Leviathan* XVIII: 136. Rousseau will make the same argument: one cannot ask "whether the law can be unjust, since no one is unjust toward himself" (*SC* II-6: 66); "if law cannot be unjust, it is not because justice is its basis, which might not always be true, but because it is contrary to nature for one to want to harm himself, which is true without exception" (*GM* II-4: 191).

[12]*Leviathan* XVIII: 136, emphasis added.

natural complementarity of men's differences. A genuine state is formed through the conscious renunciation of all hopes for such order and the adoption of an artificial equivalence which allows all to will for each. All are collapsed together under the shelter of a single selfishness, which can then flow freely, a law unto itself. Where there is only a single "person" ruling itself, there can be no injustice.

Rousseau's State as a Horizontal "Whole"

The concrete meaning of Rousseau's conception of the "real civil person" comes to light still more clearly if one raises the converse and much more complex issue of the citizen's relation to the state. On the famous "individualistic" view of this issue, found in Hobbes and most social contract theorists, the individual is by nature "prior" to the state. The state, that is, is purely instrumental, external, and atomized: it is a mere instrument or means for the individual; it is created for the satisfaction of his preexisting, private interests or rights; and it consists in a simple aggregation of atomized individuals. Rousseau, on the other hand, manages to return to something like the view of Plato and Aristotle, seeing the relation of citizen and state as more integral, and the state as more of a genuine whole. Specifically, Rousseau, or at least his citizen-patriot, believes the following: first, that the state is not external or posterior to him but is the source of his most important internal characteristics and in some sense of his very being; second, that the state is not atomistic but a genuine "whole," greater in some sense than the collection of its parts; and third, that the state is therefore not a mere instrument or means to his own selfish desires but an end to which he should virtuously dedicate himself. Rousseau sums this all up in one word, alien to the individualist view: the legitimate state is not merely a *pays* (country) but a *patrie* (fatherland).[13]

Rousseau claims that his new political science is meant to demonstrate: "what the fatherland is, precisely what it consists in, and how each person can know whether or not he has a fatherland" (*Emile* V: 466). So what indeed *is* the "fatherland"? Given Rousseau's acceptance of Hobbesian notions of individualism and social contract, given his resolute rejection of the concept of "order," on what are the three "holistic" features, just described, grounded? How are they reinterpreted and reestablished in his science of "real civil persons"?

Let us begin with the first. In Rousseau's theory, the state in some sense creates the citizens, rather than the reverse. For Hobbes, the political sovereign, ruling either by general laws or arbitrary decrees as he sees fit, puts an end to the state of nature and thereby fundamentally transforms men's external, physical relations without, however, particularly altering their characters.

---

[13] *Emile* I: 40, V: 466, 473. In the *Nouvelle Héloïse*, Claire writes from Geneva: "The more I contemplate this little state, the more I find that it is beautiful to have a *patrie*, and God help all those who believe they have one, but only have a *pays*" (*NH* VI-5: 657).

Rousseau's state begins in the same way: selfishly motivated men conclude a social contract in order to transform their external, physical world.
But the unique terms of Rousseau's contract tend also to give birth to a new
world entirely, a moral world within which men come to redefine their
existence and their ends. Because sovereignty is bestowed on the general
will, which must rule through fixed, general *laws*, men in this new state
receive not only immediate physical protection but also grounds for a firm
expectation of their *future* protection, a faith in the abiding security of the
individual. This expectation and faith is embodied above all in the
individual's possession of publicly recognized and guaranteed "rights"
created by the laws or general will. The combination of the longing for
security, the expectation of it, and the legal right to it (guaranteed by the
force of the state and, ultimately, by the civil religion) produces in the
individual's mind a moral idea of his inviolability. And since social men
are governed by foresight and fear, they soon come to cherish this moral
status and security more than any of their particular bodily goods. The
individual is thus transformed from a natural into a moral being. He defines
his existence and identity in a new way: he is not a human being, a mere
speck in the universe, but a "citizen," with standing in the new moral world.
He is a bearer of civil *rights*—which are recognized and defended by the
state, which are a sign of his moral worth, and which ground a faith in his
sacred inviolability (*SC* I-8: 55-56; *PE*, 220-21).

But why, in the citizen's view, is he owed these rights? Again, at first,
only due to an external, selfish, instrumental contract: he receives his rights
in exchange for granting the same rights to others. But in order to carry out
his side of the bargain, which he sees as a necessary evil, he must conquer
his selfish, natural impulses; and in doing so he experiences the moral pride,
the new sense of self-worth that comes from actualizing his distinctive
human capacity for self-conquest. He becomes alive to the beauty of
virtue—of man's inner force or freedom of will—which completes his
transformation into a moral being.[14] And such a being knows himself as
inherently worthy of rights.

In Rousseau's conception, then, the state does not stand in a merely
external relation to its citizens, but reconstitutes their characters and world
view. The social contract may indeed begin as a selfish exchange of
external, physical behaviors, and that is primarily how Rousseau describes
it in the *Social Contract*, but the state that results from it gives rise to
"citizens" who reinterpret themselves and also the social contract itself in
new, moral terms. The citizen defines himself as a bearer of certain inviolable rights—that, and not his natural or biological life, is what makes him
himself—and he believes that these rights were not simply created or

---

[14] SC I-8: 55-56. "It will always be a grand and beautiful thing to be in command of oneself,
even in order to obey fantastic opinions" (*Emile* V: 391).

posited by a selfish exchange, but are owed to him inherently, on the basis of his moral status or virtue, which he understands to consist precisely in his commitment—by freely conquering his natural, animal instincts—to respect these same inherent rights in all citizens generally. "Human beings" may be prior to the state, but the state creates the "citizens."[15]

The transformative effect of the state upon its citizens, conceived in this specific way, enables us to understand the second "holistic" feature Rousseau attributes to his state: it is not a mere aggregation of disconnected atoms, but a genuine whole, greater than the sum of its parts. This is, of course, the most characteristic claim made by the organic theory of the state, which Rousseau repudiates. In that context, it means that, through the phenomenon of "order," the fitting together of functionally differentiated parts, a political "whole" is produced that is a new being, a unique, irreducible, and higher entity. Consequently, there is also a "good of the whole," a "common good," a "public interest," that cannot be reduced to the sum of private good experienced by the individual parts, but is a good realized only by or within the whole. In the face of these traditional claims, Rousseau eagerly embraces the individualistic and atomistic view that no such higher "whole" exists, nor any separate "good of the whole," and that the new common good created by political union consists precisely in a new private good bestowed on each of the individuals comprising the union. Nothing more (*Frags.*, 510-11; *PE*, 220).

But Rousseau's view goes beyond the atomistic position to a new sort of "holism." Understanding the new good bestowed on the individual in the manner described above—the inviolable rights and sanctity of the citizen—

[15] For this reason, many have thought Rousseau grossly inconsistent for clinging to social contract theory, and indeed he would be if one could simply equate his world view with that of his citizen. But ultimately he views the latter's "transformation" in psychological rather than moral or metaphysical terms. The citizen or moral being does not really supplant but rather emerges out of the natural, selfish human being. Rousseau seems to believe that men's natural fear for their bodies is the true psychological root of their moralistic belief that they have transcended them. Men can be made into "moral beings" at all only because, on some level of consciousness, they remain natural beings and are aware of the *selfish* necessity of mutual exchange. That is why Rousseau does not abandon social contract theory, as later thinkers— truer believers in the morally transformative character of the state—would do.

Presumably, it is also why he openly presents the "selfish" interpretation of the social contract and does not fear that this individualistic doctrine will undermine men's moral transformation. (See Strauss [1953, pp. 287-88], who had suggested that the doctrines of the *Social Contract* would have to be forgotten in order to be implemented.) Of course, here and there, Rousseau also gives direct support to the citizens' "moralized" understanding of themselves and of the social contract. He argues, for example, that the contract must leave sovereignty in the hands of the people, not only because this alone guarantees the preservation of each, but also because "freedom being the most noble of man's faculties, it is...degrading one's nature, putting oneself on the level of beasts enslaved by instinct, even offending the author of one's being, to renounce without reservation the most precious of all his gifts" (*SD*, 167; see *SC* I-4: 50, I-8: 56; *Emile* V: 460). But the main argument of the *Social Contract* is, among other things, an account of the logical and psychological genesis of such moral beliefs.

he sees that political union creates a good for the individual that cannot exist, that is strictly unintelligible, for the individual as an "atom." Rousseau's citizen cannot possess his individual good individually; he cannot be himself, by himself. He is constituted precisely by being and knowing himself as one individual alongside many other individuals with identical rights, defined by the general laws that all together have chosen to enforce upon each. Only through this union with others can he be his individual self, a citizen with sacred, inviolable rights of his own.

In other words, whereas there is no such thing as a separate "good of the public," there does exist what might be called a "collective private good," meaning a good of the individual that can exist only collectively, all individuals possessing it being the condition for each possessing it. And, in Rousseau's understanding, it is just such goods—"irreducible" in their own way—that are produced by the political union. One man can possess his own rights only because all have agreed to bestow them on each. Thus, for Rousseau, the political whole *is* after all greater than the sum of its separated parts, yet not because there exists some distinct, irreducible, higher "good of the whole," but because there are private, individual goods that can exist only collectively. The civil person—the fatherland—is not a vertical, organic whole, and yet it is not an atomistic aggregation either. It is something new: a horizontal whole, creating collective individual goods.

Finally, this conception of the fatherland's irreducible wholeness helps to explain Rousseau's third claim: that the state is not a mere means for the selfish interests of the individual (as Hobbes maintains) but an end to which he should virtuously dedicate and even sacrifice himself. Again, at first we find Rousseau fiercely attacking this very claim—in its traditional form. He declares in the *Political Economy* that if someone should put forward the common dictum that:

> the government is allowed to sacrifice an innocent man for the safety of the multitude, I hold this maxim to be one of the most execrable that tyranny ever invented, the most false that might be proposed, the most dangerous that might be accepted, and the most directly opposed to the fundamental laws of society. (*PE*, 220; see *OC* IV: 1126; *Frags.*, 511)

What Rousseau is rejecting so vociferously is the old view, based on organic or other grounds, that the superior dignity of the state means or entails the utter subordination of the individual. The new position that Rousseau puts forward is that the state—being a kind of whole—does indeed have an inherent dignity and constitutes an "end" for the individual (contrary to Hobbes), but—being a horizontal whole—the state's dignity consists precisely in creating and protecting the inviolable worth of each individual citizen (contrary to the traditional view). "Rather than that one ought to perish for all, all have engaged their goods and their lives for the defense of each" (*PE*, 220).

To the political whole, thus conceived, the citizens will indeed devote themselves as to an end, "engag[ing] their goods and their lives"—but again, with a new, "horizontal" devotion or patriotism. The citizen knows he is himself only through his citizenship, and that is the ground of his devotion to the state. But in what does this citizenship consist? Not in knowing his place or doing his job in the larger order, not in a relation of *part to whole*, but in a relation of *particular to general*: he is himself, an inviolable citizen, by being an instance of the generalization that all have willed to apply to each. Therefore, the *object* of his loyalty and devotion will not be the "larger order" but the "generality"—the law and the citizens horizontally united by it, all to each. That is what he loves in loving the "fatherland."

Similarly, his patriotism, though requiring detachment from his self, involves no *vertical* detachment, through which, feeling the smallness and insignificance of his mere individuality, he devotes himself to the greater whole above him. It is rather a horizontal detachment, through which, feeling his importance and sanctity as an individual, he sees the necessity only of detaching himself from his particularity as *this* individual and of devoting himself to the sanctity of the individual as such. In short, the citizen's patriotism takes the form not of an effort to lose himself in the overarching whole but to find and affirm himself in every member.

Rousseau's State as a Unity of Existence

We have seen that Rousseau's political science, by replacing Hobbes's fictional unity of will with a real, unanimous general will, conceives the state as a "real civil person" in which the "holistic" attributes of the classical regime, as well as its aspiration to moral infallibility, are reestablished in a new, horizontal form. Yet there is also a second, "vitalistic" element to Rousseau's transformation of Hobbes's political theory, which attributes to the civil person a unity of "existence." A collection of individuals form a "real union," Rousseau explains, by virtue of *two* unities: "a universal motivation which makes each part act for an end that is general and relative to the whole"—the unity of will just described—but also "a feeling of common existence which gives it individuality and constitutes it as one" (*GM* I-2: 159).[16] This "feeling of common existence," or what he elsewhere calls the "common life" or "common self,"[17] adds a further dimension to the wholeness of the state and especially to the patriotism of its members; for the rational forms of patriotism described above, based on interest and virtue, will be too weak, in Rousseau's view, unless supplemented through the force of this prerational, sentimental unity. A complete analysis of Rousseau's theory of the state, then, must examine the "unity of existence" that forms the second defining characteristic of the "real civil person."

Whatever human lives and selves most truly *are*—clearly that is what

---

[16] The same is true even for the unity of groups within the state: "in order for the body of the government [i.e., the executive] to exist, to have a real life that distinguishes it from the body of the state. . . it must have a separate self, a sensibility shared by its members, [and] a force or will of its own" (*SC* III-1: 81).

[17] *SC* I-6: 53; *PE*, 212; *GM* I-3: 164; *OC* III: 1900.

must be joined together if men are to be united on the deepest level. Now, according to Rousseau's psychology, man's "life," "self," and "self-preservation" are to be understood no longer in terms of any organic form or teleological nature, nor in terms of Hobbesian fear of death, but rather in terms of the fundamental experience of the sentiment of existence. Therefore, to unite men in the state on the deepest level means precisely: "to take his absolute existence from him in order to give him a relative one and transport the *I* into the common unity" so that he "no longer feels except within the whole." When truly united in this way, citizens "perceive their own existence . . . [only] as part of the state's" (*Emile* I: 40; *PE*, 222).[18]

That it is possible (within limits) to unite men in this way—on the level of existence—stems from the fortunate coincidence of two vital facts. First, there is a certain flexibility to where a man locates his existence, as a result of which he is capable of seeing himself in others and merging his existence with theirs. Second, for all the reasons considered above, Rousseau rejects the traditional understanding of the state as based on functional differentiation, arguing that political union is possible only on the basis of homogeneity and mutual "identification" on the legal and moral level. It turns out, then, that the rational structure of Rousseau's state is uniquely suited to allow and promote the psychological process of "existential" identification.

Consequently, Rousseau places great emphasis on the various means for promoting this process, most of which may be summed up in the formula "seeing and being seen." Existence is somehow given and received primarily through the eyes. Thus, on the one hand, the constant "habit of seeing" others—especially if the dress, customs, literature, and resulting "manner of being" of the nation is unique and distinctive—will lead men to find and know themselves in others, to identify with them on the most intimate level, and to mingle their own existence with theirs (*PE*, 219; see *SD*, 79, 149; *Poland* IV: 966). On the other hand, if from birth "all the citizens feel themselves incessantly under the eyes of the public," they will regard the public eye as the very source of their existence (*Poland* XII: 1019; see II: 958; *SD*, 179). Such "seeing and being seen" is brought to a peak in public festivals— which Rousseau elevates to central political importance—where "each sees and loves himself in the others so that all will be better united" (*d'Alembert*, 126).[19] The end result of this unifying process is the citizen whose existence is merged into the common self: "he sees nothing but the fatherland; he lives only for it. As soon as he is alone, he is nothing; when he no longer has a fatherland he is no more, and if he is not dead he is worse" (*Poland*

---

[18] These passages may seem to contradict the previous claim that the citizen's relation to the state is not one of part to whole. The citizen is indeed not a functionally differentiated part fitted into a larger, ordered whole created by the division of labor. He may be considered a "part" in that he identifies with and lives for the homogeneous unity that is the fatherland.

[19] See the interesting discussion of festivals in Starobinski (1971) pp. 116-21.

IV: 966).[20] United on this level, the citizens form a whole, drawing their being from a single source.

Thus, the second dimension of Rousseau's science of "real civil persons," which conceives the state as a unified self or existence in addition to a unity of will, adds to his explanation of the state's wholeness. And again, this reestablished wholeness, like the state's moral infallibility, is understood to spring up from below, from the fountain of a common self, rather than to inhere in some objective organic order. In Rousseau's inverted political science, citizens are joined at the level of existence rather than of function. The "real civil person" is one, not as a common enterprise but as a festival: a community united by nothing more than *being* together—living and feeling a common existence.

Rousseau and Nationalism

A famous and fateful term might be used to characterize the new kind of social unity discovered by Rousseau's political science: "nationalism."[21] Historically, Rousseau has often been credited as the founder of this ideology or movement, and it is not hard to understand why. Not only did he forcefully reassert the practical importance of local attachments and patriotic political unity—in heretical opposition to the cosmopolitanism and atomism of liberal, Enlightenment thought—but he also showed how such unity was theoretically possible precisely on the basis of (transformed) liberal philosophical principles, how the needed patriotism could be produced within the psyche of the naturally asocial individual, indifferent as he is to the call of the ancestral or of the organic whole—the supposed grounds of patriotism in the traditional understanding.

The patriotic unity of existence described in the second part of Rousseau's theory of the state is a devotion, not to the ancestral land or to the regime, but to something that might indeed be called the "nation," that is, to a whole people united by nothing other than the strong tendency of its members to *identify* with one another based upon their similarity of character and culture, as produced by the effects of a common climate,

---

[20] Rousseau certainly believes in the psychological reality and power of these feelings, and he might agree with the citizen that, given how he feels, his life would be worthless and nothing outside the fatherland. But Rousseau is not prepared to concede a metaphysical reality to the "common existence" that is the object and ground of the citizen's feelings. In the final analysis, then, these salutary feelings are based on an illusion.

[21] Rousseau's conception of unity also contains the seed of the longing for the spontaneous "being together," the nonorganic and goalless community, found in much contemporary "communitarian" thought. As Wolin (1960, p. 375) remarks: "The quest for community undertaken by so many writers, who have reflected so many different political persuasions, suggests that Rousseau's conception of community has turned into a specter haunting the age of organization."

history, language, and literature.[22] And for this reason, Rousseau was in fact among the first to emphasize the existence of such culturally distinct nationalities (encouraged also by his unique "historical sense" and insight into human malleability) (*SD*, 148; *Emile* V: 452-53). He was also the first to insist that well-ordered states must cultivate, appeal to, and build upon their unique national character. When forming a state, "the first rule that we have to follow is national character. Every people has or ought to have a national character and if it lacked one, we would have to begin by giving it one" (*Corsica*, 913, see var. a). Again: "It is national institutions that form the genius, the character, the tastes, and the mores of a people, that cause it to be itself and not another, that inspire in it that ardent love of country based upon habits of mind impossible to uproot" (*Poland* III: 960; see 961, 962, XII: 1013).

It is quite true, then, that Rousseau's new understanding of political union has much in common with, and helped give rise to, the theory of nationalism that developed later. Moreover, his science of politics, with its ingenious insights into the complex relation between individualism and political wholes, is most useful for understanding the unanticipated power that nationalism has exercised in the liberal state over the last two centuries.

All the same, one cannot say that Rousseau's own political theory was truly nationalist. Although he emphasizes the importance of nationality, he is not willing to say, as truly nationalist thinkers are, that the nation, the cultural unit, is a stronger and more fundamental phenomenon than the state, or that men can be patriotically devoted to the nation regardless of its political condition. An emphatically political thinker, Rousseau maintains that the quasi-nationalistic "unity of existence" he has discovered cannot exist except in conjunction with the "unity of will," the political liberty, that grounds the legitimate state. "A national education belongs only to free men; for it is only they who have a common existence and are truly linked together by the law" (*Poland* IV: 966). This assertion is required by Rousseau's principles, for where men live in a condition of personal dependence, let them be ever so similar, they will feel only mutual enmity. It is only the free man, made such either by solitude or by the rule of law, who, standing back from the need to use others, is moved

---

[22] For Rousseau, as well as most later nationalist thinkers, the "nation" is identified with the "people," *das Volk*. This new entity is essentially egalitarian in its conception, for two reasons. Since its unity is based on similarity or identity rather than complementarity or organic order, the "nation" is conceived of as fundamentally homogeneous, and thus all traditional aristocratic and hierarchical views tend to be excluded from the outset. Moreover, since the features of national character upon which the unity is based were formed by the effects of ancient events and age-old customs, effects which tend to be effaced in the urban or aristocratic elites who are steeped in modern or alien ways, it is the "people," that is, the backward, simple, rural populations, that most truly represent the nation. "It is the people of the country who constitute the nation," Rousseau asserted, to the scandal of his contemporaries (*Emile* V: 469).

to identify with and love them.[23]

In other words, Rousseau embraces the view, alien to modern nationalism, that patriotic devotion is strictly inseparable from political democracy. And for this reason he is in fact strongly opposed to the modern nation-state—to states large enough to be based on nationality—and in favor of a return, were it possible, to the ancient city-state, which was small enough to be governed democratically. To the extent possible, Rousseau does wish to build on national character and to foster love of the fatherland based on a "unity of existence," but he never doubts that the "fatherland" is a political entity, not a national or cultural one, and that this unity is inseparable from the social contract and the sovereignty of the general will.[24]

The Limits of Political Union

In examining Rousseau's political science we have been preoccupied with its most striking and challenging element, the "holistic" conception of the state that it manages to generate from individualistic, social contract premises. It is important to emphasize, therefore, what has so far only been implied, that Rousseau, like Plato, ultimately doubts the adequacy or genuineness of the particular wholeness he describes. The individual cannot be perfectly integrated into the state, for it is not rational for him to do all the things that it is necessary for the state to demand. This gulf can be bridged and the state united only with the aid of religious belief or myth. "As soon as men live in society, they must have a religion that keeps them there. A people has never subsisted nor ever will subsist without religion" (*GM* III-2: 195).

The limits of political union are most visible in the state's demand that the individual be willing to fight and die for it. Rousseau devotes a chapter of the *Social Contract* to this requirement and, in contrast to Hobbes and Locke, defends it as essential for the survival of the state and as a legitimate element of the social contract. "It is asked how private individuals who have no right to dispose of their own lives can transfer to the sovereign a right they do not have. . . . [But] every man has a right to risk his own life in order to preserve it." Moreover, "whoever wants to preserve his life at the expense of others should also give it up for them when

---

[23] For Rousseau, the love for others can arise only from a certain distance and independence, for then the full energy of one's free and undivided soul can overflow into identification with them. As he states regarding himself (a reclusive humanitarian): "When one lives alone one loves men more." And: "One is truly sociable only to the extent that one loves to live alone" (*LM*, 1114; *Art de jouir, OC* I: 1175). Similarly, citizens will identify with and love one another in the degree to which, protected by the law from all mutual dependence, they are free simply to behold each other alongside themselves. See the moving description of the early Swiss in *Corsica*, 914-15.

[24] Rousseau expressly asserts that the social contract is "the act by which a people becomes a people" (*SC* I-5: 52; see also *Poland* IV: 966; Letter to Colonel Pictet, March 1, 1764, quoted in *OC* III: 1535).

necessary. . . . And when the prince has said to him, 'it is expedient for the state that you should die,' he ought to die. Because it is only under this condition that he has lived in safety up to that point" (*SC* II-5: 64). This argument proves that it is *legitimate* for the individual to contractually consent to his sacrifice and just for the state to demand it. But in this chapter, Rousseau does not even attempt to explain why it would be rational for the individual, who concludes the contract for the sake of his preservation, to continue obeying it (legitimate though it may be) when he is called upon to sacrifice his life. Elsewhere, Rousseau demonstrates that, for the individual's safety and freedom, it is better to join society than to remain in the (late) state of nature, and better to obey the laws than to engage in crime and exploitation (*SC* I-7:55, I-8:55-56). But again, this in no way proves that every sacrifice demanded by the state is good or rational for the individual.

To be sure, we have just seen that the state integrates its members by transforming them into patriots and moral beings who obey the contract for more than self-interested reasons, who cherish the state as the source of their moral being, and who love the fatherland as their common self. Yet in the final analysis, Rousseau considers the rationality and power of such motives questionable, leading him to conclude: "In every State that can require its members to sacrifice their lives, anyone who does not believe in the afterlife is necessarily a coward or a madman" (*GM* III-2: 195).[25] Rousseau's state is clearly much closer to a genuine whole than that of Hobbes or Locke, but ultimately it can be unified only by beliefs that go beyond reason and goods that go beyond politics.

Summary

Rousseau's *Social Contract*, the culmination of early modern theoretical individualism, presents the most rigorous and sweeping reinterpretation of the political world from the standpoint of the belief in man's asociality and arationality. Although one may not accept this premise, everyone recognizes at least an individualistic *component* to human nature, and Rousseau's science of politics is invaluable for the power and ingenuity with which it works through the corresponding dimension of political life. In this it forms the perfect counterpoint to Plato's *Republic*, which envisions the political world from the standpoint of an exaggerated faith in human reason and sociality. Rousseau's theory, to state it formulaically, completely inverts the Platonic view, replacing the transcendent with the immanent, vertical order with horizontal generality, truth with consent, the

---

[25]Anyone who does not accept the civil religion is simply "incapable of sincerely loving the laws, justice, and of giving his life, if need be, for his duty." "If the divinity does not exist, it is only the wicked man who reasons, and the good man is nothing but a fool" (*SC* IV-8: 131; *Emile* IV: 292, the Savoyard Vicar speaks).

good with the willed, objective form with subjective source, and the higher with the inner.

Where naturally asocial individuals have accidentally evolved into a social condition, there can be no natural order or rule, but only chaos and conflict. Wherever genuine states and morality now exist, they are based therefore not on the call of men's natural harmony but on their common fear of their natural opposition. Men naturally agree only on the need to force themselves to agree, which they can do, not through the rule of some over others, but all over each. Legally and psychologically, the many are collapsed into one person, the naturally different and unequal human beings becoming so many identical citizens moving together in unison, with a single will and a common self. They are made one "subjectively," not by being given any particular objective order, purpose, or regime, but being joined at the "source": in their faculty of willing and their sentiment of existence. And similarly, the life of the state, the activity of politics, is not the movement toward what seems good and just, mediated by the leadership of those who seem best, but the autonomous activity and "being itself" of the single "public person" which, whatever commands it gives itself, is always, perfectly absolute, infallible, and united.

11

The Executive Power or "Government"

We come to the final element in the construction of the legitimate state. When men conclude a "social contract" bestowing "sovereignty" on the "general will," they must also create an executive power or "Government" to execute the laws made by the sovereign.

It may seem, as it has to most students of the *Social Contract*, that, having gotten past the general will, we are now moving into a less important, less innovative, and less theoretically demanding area of Rousseau's thought. This is clearly not Rousseau's own view, however, for in expounding this part of his doctrine—to which he dedicates the third and longest book of the *Social Contract*—he makes his most frequent and insistent claims to novelty and he explicitly urges the reader to pay close attention. Executive power is really the most difficult and important subject, he explains in the *Geneva Manuscript*, because:

> just as in the constitution of man the action of the soul on the body is the abyss of philosophy, so too the action of the general will on the public force [i.e. on the executive] is the abyss of political theory in the constitution of the State. It is here that all legislators have gone astray. (*GM* I-4: 168)[1]

Rousseau's theory of executive power will finally clarify the issue that has led all others astray.

It would seem, however, that Rousseau's doctrine has succeeded only in leading his interpreters astray, who have been variously perplexed by his bizarre mathematicism, his unclear stance concerning the separation of powers, and his curious doctrine of political history. Worst of all, there seem to be two wholly distinct and contradictory sides to Rousseau's treatment of the executive. On the one hand, this power is *the* great danger in the state, the exclusive and inevitable destroyer of legitimate regimes, which must be vigilantly watched and controlled. On the other hand (to be treated in the following chapter), Rousseau endeavors to expand the role of the executive, even urging it to manipulate and control the people. It is possible to resolve these perplexities, however, if Rousseau's theory of the

---

[1] I have altered the translation. On the general theme of the emphasis placed by Rousseau on his doctrine of Government, see Masters's note 68 in *SC*: 143.

executive is examined in the context of the doctrines and innovations that have already come to light.

The Meaning of the Legislative-Executive Distinction

Rousseau's account begins from the fundamental contention that "ruling" is not one thing but two. It is composed of legislation and execution, two essentially different functions which must be theoretically distinguished to be properly understood (a point not to be confused with the constitutional issue of whether they should be institutionally separated). But this assertion, with which we are excessively familiar, is by no means self-evident. We need to examine the origin and theoretical basis of the whole legislative-executive distinction.

In Aristotle, one finds a very different division of functions—"deliberative" and "magisterial" (and also "judicial")—which follows directly from his own conception of the state. Political rule, understood as leading and guiding the community, is most essentially characterized by the exercise of wise deliberation regarding issues of common importance, and therefore by the "deliberative" function. And since there is no good reason to assume that all issues requiring intelligent decision-making will be addressable through the making of general laws, the deliberative function is not arbitrarily limited to a legislative power but naturally includes a great deal of what today we parcel off into the executive and judicial powers. Any vital decision that has to be made—whether concerning a general law, a specific policy, an issue of foreign relations, the appointment and evaluation of magistrates, or the most serious crimes—naturally falls within the purview of the deliberative function. It makes no sense, however, to burden those who must deliberate with the carrying out of settled policies requiring little thought, so these responsibilities naturally constitute a separate "magisterial" function. (This function is much less extensive than the modern executive, which is swollen by the addition of all those elements of the deliberative function that cannot be handled by an exclusively legislative power).[2]

This traditional understanding of governmental functions was decisively repudiated when Hobbes, seeking peace and security for naturally asocial individuals, and doubting the power of reason, separated political rule from all claims to wisdom or rational deliberation, redefining it as arbitrary sovereign *will* backed by force. Locke and Montesquieu then added that this sovereign will ought to function only through settled standing laws— ought to be an exclusively legislative power—because the generality, publicity, and predictability of law were necessary to guarantee individual security.

---

[2] See *Politics* 1297b16-1301a18.

Rousseau brings these developments to their ultimate expression. Through his radical doubt of human sociality and rationality, his complete elevation of will above reason as the basis of the state, his theory that men should and can obey only the general will, and his fundamental thesis that the rule of law, by eliminating personal dependence, will restore men to psychic unity, Rousseau elevates the importance of law—of law as such, regardless of content—to the highest imaginable level. Far more than any thinker before or since, he identifies the highest purpose, the sovereign function, and the supreme power of the state not with the deliberative function but with the lawmaking function, the legislative power.

Political rule consists not in mere will, however, but will backed by force. And if the sovereign will must only express itself in the form of law, which can command all citizens in general, but never any man in particular, then the sovereign cannot itself enforce the law that it wills, for enforcement involves judging and commanding individuals. It follows with logical necessity that ruling involves a second, theoretically distinct function, an "executive" power that deals with individuals and applies the state's force to the sovereign's will. It is possible to combine these two functions in the same hands, but they are in their own nature distinct. "The executive power," Rousseau states, "cannot belong to the general public in its legislator's or sovereign capacity, because this power consists solely of particular acts which are not within the jurisdiction of the law, nor consequently of the sovereign, all of whose acts can only be laws" (*SC* III-1: 78).

Rousseau's whole teaching regarding the general will, then, leads to the strictest identification of sovereignty with the legislative power, which leads in turn to the most radical separation of this function from the executive power, of will from force, along the logically precise lines of the distinction between the general and the particular. Although the distinction of these two powers has become familiar to us through Locke and Montesquieu, Rousseau is quite correct in claiming to have formulated it in a new manner, more rigorous and more absolute than any that came before.

The Establishment of the Executive

If it is theoretically necessary that an "executive power" exist in the state, how does it come into being and what is its legal status?

There are only a small number of ways of answering this question. Rousseau is especially eager to find one that will allow him to assert, as he does in the title to one of his chapters: "That the Institution of the Government Is Not a Contract." What he seeks to deny in rejecting the contractual view is, in the first place, the Hobbesian doctrine, according to which the establishment of the Government or executive forms a part of—forms the essence of—the original social contract. For on this view the Government *is* the state, from which it follows that one must never contemplate removing or altering the Government—in order to keep it in check—for this would be tantamount to returning men to the state of nature. Furthermore, since the state is the sovereign source of all law and justice, it would follow that the Government, which is the state, is not subject to the law and justice.

There was also another contractual view, older but still prevalent, according to which the Government is established not by the original "pact of association" that creates the state, but by a second contract, a so-called pact of submission concluded between the people and the Government (*SD*, 169; *SC* III-17: 105). Since this contract is bilateral, establishing mutual obligations, the people are not free to question or renounce it so long as its terms are met.

To avoid these contractual doctrines, which were both theoretically unconvincing and practically harmful, Rousseau devised a new and rather ingenious account of the establishment of executive power. In the official formula for the social contract there is absolutely no mention of executive power—a silence that proclaims Rousseau's rejection of the Hobbesian view. But soon after, he explains that the contract "*tacitly* includes the following engagement, which alone can give force to the others: that whoever refuses to obey the general will shall be constrained to do so by the entire body" (*SC* I-7: 55, emphasis added). Yet still unstated is: who has the right to direct this power? Elsewhere, Rousseau cryptically states that executive power is not a "part" of sovereignty but an "emanation" from it (*SC* II-2: 60). What this seems to mean is the following. The social contract establishes the necessity and legitimacy of an executive power, but does not itself create it. It does create the sovereign, which, being an exclusively legislative power, cannot be the executive. But the sovereign, unable to *exercise* the executive power, does have the capacity to *delegate* it, and must do so if it is to maintain its own existence.

The sovereign creates the executive in a two-step process. First, it passes a law determining the general form of the Government (say, an aristocracy). The next task is to select the specific individuals who are to be members of the Government, but this the sovereign cannot do because it involves particular individuals. Therefore, its next step is to establish a provisional democratic Government, the one form of executive which, including everyone, can be established through a general law. Then the people, switching their legal capacity from sovereigns to members of the provisional Government, exercise the executive function of selecting the members for the permanent Government. Such is the necessary procedure through which the sovereign establishes the executive (*SC* III-17: 105).

Rousseau uses this unique argument to define the rights of the executive power both as precisely and as narrowly as possible. He wants to make clearer than ever before that the existence of the state and the law is not dependent on that of the Government but rather the reverse. The sovereign alone is what is created in the social contract—the sovereign *is* the state—and the Government is merely a creation of the sovereign, owing its whole existence to a revocable law that it has pleased the sovereign to enact.

Therefore the executive can be checked, altered, or removed without in any way destroying the state and without violating any separate contract made with the Government. Furthermore, whereas the state—the sovereign—is indeed the absolute source of all law and justice and therefore superior to them, this is not true of the Government, which is itself a creation of the law and thus wholly subordinate to it (*SD*, 163-70; *SC* I-5: 52, III-1: 79, III-14: 101, III-16-18: 104-7; *PE*, 215).[3]

These principles (at least considered in isolation) go well beyond the right of rebellion defended by Locke, beyond the right to impeach, beyond the right periodically to elect new officials, and even beyond the right to amend the constitution. Rousseau grants the people the right to change their whole form of government, to throw out their constitution, at will. This utter legal subordination of the executive to the legislative power is the most politically radical element of Rousseau's whole doctrine.[4]

The Separation of Powers

Now that there are two powers in the state, the question arises as to their interaction. The extreme legal subordination of the one to the other that we have just witnessed has led most scholars to conclude that Rousseau was opposed to any sort of separation and balance of powers. Indeed, isn't this idea wholly alien to Rousseau's political imagination? As a political dreamer, his conception of the state is a harmonious and static one, not dynamic and conflictual. As an absolutist, he must see divided sovereignty as a contradiction in terms. And clearly he makes no provision for balance, permitting instead a dangerous concentration of unchecked power.

We have arrived at another of the great "disputed questions" of Rousseauian scholarship. This particular disagreement has been intensified by the partisan significance of the separation of powers, that cherished principle of liberal constitutionalism, which, ever since Locke and Montesquieu, has been revered as the necessary condition of free government. Always hovering over the discussion, then, is the earnest demand to know whether Rousseau is a friend or foe of liberty. But even such scholarly and

---

[3] In a well-known passage of the *Second Treatise* (para. 211) Locke remarks: "He that with any clearness will speak of the dissolution of government ought in the first place to distinguish between the dissolution of the society and the dissolution of the government." Rousseau's doctrine is a more radical development of this line of argument. As Paul Bastid remarks (1964, p. 316), "The great originality of the *Social Contract* is the definitive separation of the state (in the current sense of the word) and the government." In other words, Rousseau brings the concept of Government closer to the current parliamentary sense or to the American notion of an "administration."

[4] This seems to be Rousseau's own view (see *SD*, 170; *SC* III-18: 106) as well as that of most of his contemporary opponents. See Derathé (1950-52) on the eighteenth-century refutations of the *Social Contract*.

partisan disputes aside, the issue is very much worth pursuing, for it invites us finally to abandon the abstract, legalistic plane we have been occupying and to confront the concrete practical questions of how Rousseau's state is really going to function. What is more, it will prove to be the key to resolving all the seeming contradictions that surround Rousseau's discussion of the executive.

One aspect of the issue, at least, is beyond dispute and the whole rest of the discussion must take place within the bounds set by it: Rousseau does not establish a clear distinction or separation between the judicial and executive powers. But how damning is this fact if the same point can be made about Locke, whose credentials in this matter are generally not open to question?[5] The main theoretical issue hinges on the relation between the legislative and executive powers. Is the latter to be simply subordinate to the former, or is there to be a real separation and balancing?

One great virtue of Rousseau's thought is that the difficulties we constantly experience in interpreting it usually end up disclosing the inadequacies of our categories of interpretation. In this case, it seems that much of our perplexity arises from insufficient clarity about the separation of powers. In particular, it is necessary to distinguish two very different elements contained in this principle, two wholly distinct ways in which it prevents the rise of tyranny. The first element derives from the benefits of dividing or separating power as such, the second from the benefits of turning these separated powers against each other in a system of mutual "checks and balances."

The latter element, the creation of a balance of powers, is by far the more familiar and easily understood. To prevent governmental arrogance and abuse, one divides it into several parts—almost any parts will do—and arranges them so that "power is a check to power" (in Montesquieu's famous phrase). One uses the government against itself, relying on the ambition of each part to keep the other parts within the bounds of their proper authority.[6] There is nothing

---

[5] But see Laslett (1965, pp. 132-33) who does question them. It is perhaps less excusable for Rousseau than for Locke to have ignored the judiciary since he was familiar with Montesquieu's compelling discussion of this issue. On the other hand, "in a well-governed state," according to Rousseau, "there are few punishments . . . because there are few criminals" (*SC* II-5: 65). The whole role of punishment, hence of the judiciary, is much smaller in Rousseau's virtuous city than in the individualistic liberal state.

[6] Montesquieu *Spirit of the Laws*, XI-4: 150. See Locke *Second Treatise*, para. 107. The balance need not take the form of a fully developed system of checks and balances; that is, it may not check every power equally and the checks need not be built into the daily or routine functioning of the several powers. As W. B. Gwyn (1965) has shown, the earliest arguments for the separation of powers (those of the seventeenth-century English republicans writing in the Interregnum period) called for the separation of legislative and executive simply so that the former could be a check upon the latter (and not the reverse) and so that subjects might have a separate and thus relatively impartial judge to appeal to on the rare occasions when they were driven to seek redress against the executive (pp. 26-27, 47-51, 85-86).

particularly modern or liberal, however, in this idea of checks and balances, which may already be found as an important part of the ancient conception of the balanced constitution or "mixed regime."[7]

The first element, which forms the truly definitive aspect of the modern doctrine of separation of powers, hinges on the fact that it is possible to partition power by *functions* and to do so in such a way that these functions are not susceptible of abuse as long as they are separated. Consider, for instance, the familiar example of two boys dividing a piece of cake. To prevent a tyrannical outcome we could establish "checks and balances," either by giving each boy an equal say in all decisions, or by giving one all authority over cakes, the other the same authority over pies. This balance of power forces each boy to compromise and cooperate with the other, though at the risk of stalemate and conflict. A more elegant solution is to create a "separation of powers." If one boy is given the specific power to cut, the other to choose first, then neither possesses a power capable of being abused in isolation.

The modern doctrine of the separation of powers seeks a similar solution on the political level. By dividing political power along functional lines— as those functions had been newly defined: legislative and executive—it gives to each of the different parts of government a specific power that cannot be abused in isolation from the complementary power. This is precisely Locke's main argument for separating the powers. It is "too great a temptation to human frailty, apt to grasp at power," he states, "for the same persons who have the power of making laws to have also in their hands the power to execute them, whereby they may exempt themselves from obedience to the laws they make, and suit the law, both in its making and execution, to their own private advantage." If the legislative and executive powers are combined, then the members of this united power will be able to make exploitative laws in full confidence that they will not be applied to themselves. Montesquieu's argument is the same: the united power will "make tyrannical laws to execute them tyrannically." Therefore, the legislative body must be separated from the executive because then (to return to Locke) the legislators "are themselves subject to the laws they have made, which is a new and near tie upon them to take care that they make them for

---

[7]Although the concept of the mixed regime tends to be associated with Polybius, who placed such great emphasis on it, it was first formulated by Plato in the *Laws* (from which Polybius' account is explicitly derived) and it was endorsed as the best practical regime by virtually all classical political philosophers. See Plato *Laws* 691b-694a; Polybius *Histories* Bk. VI; Aristotle *Politics* 1293b20-1296b10; Cicero *Republic* Bk I, 45, 69; Thomas Aquinas *Summa Theologica*, I-II, qu. 95, a. 4, qu. 105, a. 1. The classical conception, however, puts less emphasis on "checks and balances" than on mixing the several titles to rule, blending the various virtues, and moderating political power to *forestall* ambition.

the public good."[8] And where the laws are well made and watched over by a separate legislative power, the executive will find it much harder to make unjust use of its power.

Obviously this sort of expedient, which works much better for the legislative than for the executive power, is not sufficient by itself and must rely heavily on the second expedient, the effect of checks and balances. Nevertheless, what is most distinctive and perhaps most important in the modern principle of the separation of powers is the first element—not the external balance that exists between two rival centers of power but the internal safety that these specific "powers" acquire simply by virtue of being kept separate.[9]

With this distinction in mind, let us return to Rousseau. Does he adhere to the separation of powers as regards the first and more characteristic element of that principle? The answer is obviously, resoundingly "yes." In the first place, Rousseau is the one, as he repeatedly declares, who develops the legislative-executive distinction with the greatest precision and force, who grounds it most directly and systematically in first principles, and who makes it the central pivot of his politics. He describes the novelty of his political doctrine as follows: "The democratic constitution [i.e., the legitimate state] has until now been poorly examined. . . . None of those [who have spoken of it] have sufficiently distinguished the sovereign from the government, the legislative power from the executive. There is no state where these two powers are so separate" (*Montagne* VIII: 837-38).

And why must these powers be so carefully distinguished and separated? Because, he argues, in that way one can render them internally safe. That is very nearly the guiding idea of Rousseau's whole political thought. Taking Locke's argument to an extreme, he hopes to rectify, indeed to render virtually infallible, the sovereign power by limiting it to the *legislative* power—to the general will—for then "everyone necessarily subjects himself to the conditions he imposes on others" (*SC* II-4: 63). To remain infallible, this power must be carefully distin-

---

[8] *Second Treatise* para. 143. The *Spirit of the Laws*, XI-6: 152, near the beginning (my translation). Montesquieu's arguments for separating the judicial from the legislative and executive powers are of the same kind, that is, they rely on the benefits of separation as such. Indeed, here there *are* no other benefits since the judicial power, in Montesquieu's understanding, plays no part in the system of checks and balances (see p. 160).

[9] Since Montesquieu seems to regard the separation of the judiciary as the most important (*Spirit of the Laws* XI-6: 152), and since this plays no part in the balance of power (ibid., 160), it seems clear that he considered the first element of the separation of powers the more essential. Indeed, it is necessary to *mix* the powers somewhat in order to produce an adequate balance (for example, the executive must be given a legislative veto), so balance cannot be the primary rationale for separating according to powers.

For a more extensive and somewhat different account of the separation of powers, to which I am indebted, see Pangle (1973, pp. 118-38). See also Gwyn (1965).

guished and separated from the executive power. "It is not good for him who makes the laws to execute them," Rousseau explains, for then the legislators begin to think of their own private interest and "nothing is more dangerous than the influence of private interests on public affairs . . . the corruption of the legislator . . . is the inevitable consequence" (*SC* III-4: 84-85).[10]

If the principle of the separation of powers (in its first aspect) seems somehow more prominent and clearly defined in the works of Locke and Montesquieu than in the *Social Contract*, that is because in the former it remains more of an ad hoc and prudential proposal that must be added on, given a name, and defended. Rousseau has built it into the very foundations of his theory, where it has become less visible but more important. With only some exaggeration one might describe Rousseau's political thought as nothing but the principle of the separation of powers elevated into a theory of the state.[11]

We turn, then, to the second element of this principle—checks and balances. This, after all, is what most people have in mind, rightly or wrongly, when they speak of the separation of powers; and this is the issue on which the scholarly debate has for the most part been focused.

The dominant opinion is that Rousseau neither desires nor provides for a balance of powers. As one scholar states, "the doctrine of *Social Contract*, is there any need to recall, is based on principles that are diametrically opposed to those of the system of balance."[12] And there are some compelling reasons for taking this view.

If Rousseau is in important respects an heir of the absolutist tradition of Bodin and especially of Hobbes, as I have argued, then one might well

[10] "One who has authority over men should not have authority over laws, [and] one who has authority over laws should also not have authority over men" (*SC* II-7: 68; see also III-15: 103, III-16: 104).

[11] Two further reasons can be given for the relative invisibility of the principle of separation of powers in Rousseau. First, in Locke and Montesquieu, this principle is presented as a separate source of civil liberty that functions regardless of who rules, and therefore it steals a certain independent importance from the formerly all-important issue of form of government. Rousseau retreats from this position and does not discuss the arrangement of "powers" apart from the assumption that the legislative power will be exercised by the people. The principles of separation and of popular sovereignty are thus seamlessly combined in Rousseau.

Second, because Rousseau assumes that the people have the legislative power, the whole issue of separation comes down to the question of whether the executive should take the form of a pure democracy. But this is not a question of great practical interest since pure executive democracy is very rare and, strictly speaking, impossible, according to Rousseau (*SC* III-4: 84-85). Thus, given popular sovereignty, the separation of powers becomes more or less a forgone conclusion, neither requiring nor receiving much discussion.

[12] Candaux (1964) p. CXCIV. See also Plamenatz (1963) pp. 403-4; Polin (1971) p. 184. The best presentation of this viewpoint is to be found in Derathé (1950) pp. 280-307, to which my account is heavily indebted.

expect him to share their well-known hostility to the mixed regime and to all other systems of balanced, checked, or limited power. In order for a genuine and unified state to exist, the absolutists maintain, it must contain somewhere an ultimate authority, a single, undivided, supreme power or "sovereign" which, by definition, cannot be limited by any power outside itself. "It is of the essence of the sovereign power," Rousseau maintains, "to not be able to be limited: it can do everything or it is nothing" (Montagne VII: 826).[13] "Limited sovereignty" is a contradiction in terms. And it follows from this, as Rousseau proclaims in the very title to book II, chapter 2, that "sovereignty is indivisible."

Rousseau does, of course, allow, indeed virtually require, a separation of the legislative and executive powers. But as we have seen, he goes to great and ingenious lengths to demonstrate that, since the executive power is not a "part" but only an "emanation" of the sovereign power, its separation in no way constitutes a division of sovereignty, which remains absolute and undivided in the legislative power, the general will.[14]

It follows (according to the argument we are trying to understand) that although Rousseau does separate the powers in a sense, he does not create real checks and balances. The latter requires that the separated powers each have part of the sovereign authority or at least that they be mutually independent so that, neither power being able to alter or abolish the rights of the other, they can remain permanently in a mutually checking equilibrium. But by keeping sovereignty absolute and undivided in the legislative power, Rousseau deprives the executive of all real independence. Utterly subordinated to the sovereign, it can hardly serve as a check upon it. In short, through his particular arrangement for their "separation," Rousseau establishes not indeed a balance but a "subordination of powers."

Such an orderly arrangement of legal subordination, the argument often continues, is perfectly in keeping with Rousseau's political imagination which, idyllic and idealizing, tends to picture the state as a harmonious unity built on a precise, static, juridical order rather than as a dynamic equilibrium among shifting and mutually offsetting

---

[13] See also *SC* II-4: 62-63; *Montagne* VIII: 837, and especially VII: 823-24: "Every political state must have a supreme power, a center to which everything is related, a principle from which everything derives, a sovereign which can do everything." And consider Hobbes (*De Cive* VI-18: 187): "For if his power were limited, that limitation must necessarily proceed from some greater power. . . . Now that confining power is either without limit, or is again restrained by some other greater than itself; and so we shall at length arrive to a power which hath no other limit but that which is the *terminus ultimus* of the forces of all the citizens together." See *SC* III-16: 104 for essentially the same argument.

[14] Rousseau attempts to embed this claim in our very language through one of the many terminological innovations he introduces in the *Social Contract*: "the sovereign," he claims, is the name for the legislative power. See *SC* II-3: 60; *Montagne* VII: 826.

forces. Rousseau's ideal institutions, as one scholar puts it, "presuppose harmony in order to function."[15] In sum, it would seem that Rousseau has no head for the messy realism of liberal constitutionalism, for a pluralistic world of institutionalized conflict and dynamic balance. His thought flows from a different tradition and a different impulse: he is an absolutist with a longing for unity and with a faith in the power of fixed, harmonious, legal forms.

There is an element of truth to this portrayal of Rousseau's opposition to the separation of powers, but the whole truth, I believe, is more complex, more interesting, and quite different. To grasp it we must, as always, try to include all of Rousseau's apparent contradictions on the subject. To begin with the last point made, it is true that Rousseau's most ardent wish and political ideal, which plays an important role in much of his rhetoric, is perfect social harmony and peace (consider, for example, the dedication to the *Second Discourse*).[16] But his actual politics flow from an attitude of vigilant realism which rejects all belief in static forms, which is dynamic in the extreme, and which strongly emphasizes the inevitability of conflict and social turbulence, even, or rather, especially in the best-ordered states. He endorses, for example, the famous dictum of Machiavelli that sustained civil conflict is a frequent and beneficial companion of liberty, adding that "a little agitation gives vitality to souls" (*SC* III-9: 96n).[17] He speaks incessantly of "turbulent liberty," which he contrasts to "the tranquility of despotism." It is not he but others, Rousseau claims, who "would like to join the peace of despotism to the sweetness of liberty. I fear they wish for contradictory things. Repose and liberty seem to me incompatible; one must choose" (*Poland* I: 954-55).[18] That is why he so scorns the cowardice of modern peoples and never tires of warning republican citizens of the heroic and unrelenting courage necessary for the preservation of freedom. In short, the dynamic and conflictual nature of republican politics is one of Rousseau's most frequent and characteristic themes.

If this is so, then Rousseau ought to be very much concerned with the issue of equilibrium and balance in the state. And in fact he is, as becomes perfectly obvious if one simply reminds oneself of the two states that he took as his great models, Sparta and Rome—the two states

[15] Fralin (1978) p. 50.

[16] For a good account of Rousseau's rhetorical ideal or "dream of democracy," see Miller (1984), chap. 2.

[17] See Machiavelli *History of Florence* preface, *Discourses* 1.4.

[18] See *SC* I-4: 49, III-4: 85; *Frags.*, 512-13; *SD*, 80-81, 164-65.

that have stood throughout history as *the* classic examples of the balanced constitution.[19]

But Rousseau also openly and repeatedly declares his interest in balance. In his writing on Poland, he describes in great detail how the Poles must "establish the equilibrium and balance of powers that compose the legislation and administration." In the *Nouvelle Héloïse*, Claire speaks admiringly of "the mutual action and reaction of all the parts of the [Genevan] state that hold it in equilibrium." In the *Letters from the Mountain*, Rousseau asserts: "What government could be better than one in which all the parts balance each other in a perfect equilibrium, where the individuals cannot transgress the laws because they are subjected to judges, and where these judges cannot transgress them either, because they are watched over by people?" (*Poland* VIII: 993; *NH* VI-5: 658; *Montagne* VIII: 844).[20]

But the primary difficulty still remains: how can Rousseau be seeking a balance in the state when he concentrates absolute authority in the legislative power, completely subordinating the executive? The first step is to realize that this contradiction is not unique to Rousseau. Locke and Montesquieu, who clearly desire a balance of powers, also uphold the doctrine of absolute legislative supremacy, since they too see the rule of law as the purpose of the state and the sole possible ground of legitimate authority. "In a constituted commonwealth," Locke asserts, "there can be but one supreme power which is the legislative, to which all the rest are and must be subordinate."[21] Yet they also see that, paradoxically, this principle's actualization requires in certain respects its dilution: the rule of law itself requires that there be a balance of powers, but such a balance,

---

[19] Hobbes, by contrast, attacks republican Rome as fundamentally flawed because "neither senate, nor people pretended to the whole power" (*Leviathan* XXIX: 238). It is true that Rousseau severely criticizes England, the classic modern example of the balanced constitution, but he does so only for alienating the sovereign power to a representative body, whereas he praises it for being "a model of the proper balance of the respective powers" (*Montagne* IX: 874).

Rousseau's great contemporary model is, of course, Geneva, which most people would describe as a mixed aristocracy. It can hardly be cited in support of the view that Rousseau desired the executive to be utterly subordinated to the unchecked power of the sovereign people.

[20] See also *Montagne* VII: 816, 823, VIII: 838, 841, 867, IX: 874; and *SC* III-7: 91, III-10: 96, IV-5: 120.

[21] Locke *Second Treatise* para. 149. Montesquieu is, of course, much less explicit on such issues of abstract right, but it is clear that he regards the executive power as existing in order to put into effect the laws passed by the legislative and indeed as existing only by virtue of such laws. Of these two powers, the one is only "the general will of the state, and the other the execution of this general will" (*Spirit of the Laws* XI-6: 153, my translation). Regarding the dependence of the executive on the legislative power for its existence and rights see XI-6: 152, 157, 159 and see the passage quoted in note 23 below.

in turn, requires that the executive, which in strict right is dependent on the legislative power, be independent enough from that power to balance and moderate it.[22]

Locke and Montesquieu manage to make the requirements of balance compatible with the principle of legislative supremacy by giving part of the legislative *power* to the executive *body*—by giving a legislative veto to the king. "The executive power," Locke explains, "placed anywhere but in a person that has also a share in the legislative, is visibly subordinate and accountable to it and may be at pleasure changed and displaced." In this way, while the legislative power remains supreme, the executive body, possessing a part of that power, can protect its rights from being legislated away, can rise above a position of subordination, and can function as an effective check on the legislature.[23]

Now, Rousseau does the very same thing. He makes the principle of legislative supremacy compatible with the need for a balance of powers by giving two all-important rights to the executive body: that of convening the sovereign assembly and that of legislative initiative. By virtue of the first right, Rousseau notes approvingly, the executive body in Rome "*held in check* a proud and restless people, and appropriately tempered the ardor of seditious tribunes" (*SC* IV-4: 117, emphasis added). As for the right of legislative initiative, or at least the right to veto any proposal prior to its being submitted to the sovereign assembly, Rousseau baldly states: "this right is indeed so essential a part of the democratic constitution that it would generally be impossible for it to maintain itself if the legislative power could always be put in movement by each of those who compose it" (*Montagne* IX: 872). In addition to these formal rights, moreover, the executive possesses a hundred informal means for influencing or manipulating the sovereign, as will be seen in the next chapter. The net result is described in the *Letters from the Mountain*, where Rousseau openly assures the executive power of Geneva (perhaps with some exaggeration, given the context) that his doctrine of legislative sovereignty will not significantly diminish their own power (which was very great) because these two rights, which they possess, "suffice by themselves to hold the General Council [the sovereign] in the most complete dependence." Thus "by not limiting the rights of the sovereign power one does not make it less dependent in fact" (*Montagne* VIII: 838). Clearly, then, Rousseau's espousal of legislative supremacy, just like that

---

[22] See Locke *Second Treatise* chap. 14.

[23] Locke *Second Treatise*, para. 152. See *Spirit of the Laws* XI-6: 157 (my translation): "If the executive power does not have the right to stop the undertakings of the legislative body [through a veto], the latter will be despotic; for, as it will be able to give itself all the power it can think of, it will annihilate all the other powers."

of his two predecessors, by no means precludes his serious pursuit of a balance of powers.[24]

What prevents this fact from being perfectly obvious is that Locke and especially Montesquieu give greater prominence to the need for a balance of powers than to the underlying principle of legislative supremacy, whereas Rousseau reverses this emphasis. He proclaims the sovereign and absolute rights of the legislative power with such novelty, force, and brilliance that one is blinded to the more prosaic signs of his desire for balance. But this difference in rhetorical or doctrinal emphasis, we will see, reflects a different view not of the desirability of equilibrium but of the means needed to attain it—a different analysis and weighting of the various forces to be balanced.

It is clear at this point that the doctrine of the separation of powers, in its two distinct aspects, lies at the very core of Rousseau's politics. But only after more fully examining his theory of the executive, seeing the exact relation of the Government to other forces in the state, can we determine the sort of balance he is aiming at and understand the role that his own doctrines are meant to play within it.

Rousseau's New Science of Forms of Government

Rousseau's account of the executive function emphasizes that, although there is only one legitimate form of sovereignty, there are any number of legitimate forms for the executive power, and therefore the choice of which of these to institute in a given state will depend on circumstances. This whole subject, although vitally important, is no longer a question of principle or strict right, but of expediency. Thus, here we are beyond the competence of the "principles of political right" and Rousseau is compelled to develop a second doctrine, parallel to and supplementing the first, a

---

[24] This fact and the important kinship among these three thinkers has often been obscured due to the excessive attention paid to the Genevan jurist Jean-Jacques Burlamaqui in discussions of this issue. Burlamaqui, the most important interpreter and theorist of the Genevan constitution at the time, was known above all for his elaborate theory of the balance of powers, in which he laid particular stress on the need for dividing *sovereignty* among the different powers (as opposed to legislative supremacy). Burlamaqui is clearly one of Rousseau's primary if unnamed targets in his writings, and while this fact justifies paying him some attention, it has led many to conclude incorrectly that since Rousseau strongly opposed this most recent and seemingly archetypal theory of balanced power he was therefore opposed to all such theories. But in fact Burlamaqui's theory, with its division of sovereignty, was fairly atypical, having perhaps more in common with the classical doctrine of the mixed regime than the modern doctrine of separation of powers. Furthermore, it is clear that, in the concrete context of Genevan politics, Burlamaqui's theory was really an argument for the hegemony of the patrician-dominated "small council," whereas Rousseau's doctrine, with its theoretical assertion of legislative supremacy, was actually pushing for something closer to a genuine balance of powers. See Derathé (1950) pp. 287-91; Fralin (1978) pp. 43, 54, 208 n. 10.

"science of the legislator" or "maxims of politics," with the specific purpose
of characterizing the different forms of Government, of guiding the selection
of the best form for any given state, and of describing the forces within the
body politic that, over time, tend to transform the executive and the state. This
doctrine, elaborated in book III, takes the form of a new, quasi-mathematical
science of the forms of Government.

Students of the *Social Contract* invariably find this "science," upon
which Rousseau himself lays so much stress, to be one of the strangest,
most improbable aspects of the book. Why all of a sudden do we come
upon, tucked away in this eighteenth-century philosophical treatise,
something that might fairly be termed history's first serious attempt at
a quantitative political science? Why would Rousseau—Rousseau of all
people—be eager to describe human interactions with algebraic equations? And why does he think it possible?

Rousseau's eagerness to make this doctrine exact and mathematical
should not strike us as surprising, for it is altogether of a piece with the
spirit of his principles of political right. These two halves of his political
thought both manifest the same determined effort to attain, each in the
way proper to their subject matter, an indubitable and unchallengeable
precision—one through extreme legalism, the other through extreme
mathematicism.[25] It is by precision that one dispels both skepticism and
partisanship—and that one conquers, intellectually.

As to what makes such precision—both legal and mathematical—
possible in the study of human affairs, the answer lies in the transformation brought about by Rousseau's new science of politics, described in the preceding chapter. For most earlier political theorists,
there is a fundamental variety of forms of government, which are
seen not as different behavior systems but, so to speak, as different
cultures—qualitatively distinct communities, constituted by the hegemony of different types of men who claim and exercise their leadership
in the name of fundamentally different ways of life. Thus, any adequate
political science, descriptive or prescriptive, must engage in the necessarily imprecise effort to evaluate the human ends and communal purposes that constitute and result from the various forms of government.

Rousseau, as we have seen, rejects this whole conception of politics and
character formation. All these vague, competing conceptions regarding excellence and the common good, which political philosophers have been busily
comparing, are just so many lies through which naturally selfish individuals
attempt to oppress other such individuals. Wherever genuine states (and
healthy souls) exist, they are not based on a positive common good, but on two
things: a unified will that men have artificially consented to obey, and some

[25] See Strauss's (1953, pp. 194-96) discussion of this point in the context of Hobbes's
thought.

particular arrangement for enforcing this will. The single form that this sovereign will must take can be stated in a precise juridical deduction, and that is what Rousseau does in his "principles of political right." The sovereign will being everywhere the same, legitimate states differ only in their arrangements for enforcement, that is, in their forms of Government. And since all such forms—democracy, aristocracy, monarchy—have the exact same goal or purpose, they are qualitatively identical; they differ only in quantity of force and certain other features of enforcement behavior, which tend to vary with size. Therefore, when Rousseau raises the central question in the title to one of his chapters—what is "the Principle that Constitutes the Various Forms of Government"—he does not answer as Plato would have: the human end or concept of virtue in the name of which the different ruling classes lead; but rather: "the number of members composing them" (*SC* III-3: 83; see *Montagne* VI: 808).[26] Rousseau has completely drained the formerly crucial issue—form of government—of all question of principle or way of life, leaving only these generally quantifiable differences of executive force, differences suitable for treatment by a new, quasi-mathematical science of Governments.[27]

In sum, as a result of Rousseau's revolutionary new approach to politics, there are no principled or qualitative distinctions to be made among genuine states: they are all identical in their ends and differ only quantitatively. Having reduced the state to a composite of sovereign will and force, Rousseau

---

[26] Rousseau finds it convenient to continue using the traditional names for the different forms of Government: democracy, aristocracy, and monarchy. But to make it clear that he rejects the traditional assumption underlying them—that they represent qualitatively distinct wholes—he states that: "there is a point at which each form of government is indistinguishable from the next, and it is apparent that under these three names, government really admits of as many diverse forms as there are citizens in the state" (*SC* III-3: 84).

[27] Rousseau's reduction of the variety of forms of Government to purely quantitative differences is intended as a rejection even of the more limited qualitative distinctions made by Montesquieu. Elaborating a familiar distinction, the latter identifies three different forms of government: republics, monarchies, and despotisms, which are fundamentally distinct by virtue of the different "principles" (as Montesquieu calls them) through which they function—virtue, honor, and fear (*Spirit of the Laws*, II and III). Rousseau objects that, because Montesquieu "failed to make the necessary distinctions [i.e. between the sovereign and Government], this noble genius often lacked precision, sometimes clarity; and he did not see that since the sovereign authority is everywhere the same [i.e. the general will], the *same principle* [virtue] ought to apply to every well-constituted State, albeit to a greater or lesser *degree* according to the form of government" (*SC* III-4: 85, emphasis added).

Rousseau collapses these most elementary distinctions and even tries to enshrine these changes in a new political terminology. Every genuine or legitimate state is to be called a "republic," regardless of its form of Government. Thus, provided that the general will is sovereign, even "monarchy itself is a republic" (*SC* II-6: 67, 67n). And regardless of the form of Government, the members of the executive power "are called magistrates or *kings*, that is to say, *governors*; and the body as a whole bears the name *prince*" (*SC* III-1: 78-79, emphasis in the original). Monarchic and republican terms are purposely mixed together to show that, in a proper view of things, there is no longer a principled difference between them.

reduces political philosophy to the "precise" composite (still prevalent today) of legalistic natural constitutional law and semiquantita-
tive, behavioral political science.[28]

Let us briefly consider the most important theses of Rousseau's new
science of Governments (without getting mired down in its more obscure
details).[29] The central claim of Rousseau's science is that the various parts
of the state should be understood in terms of a "continuous proportion,"
that is, in terms of a ratio of the form A is to B as B is to C. This is "no
arbitrary idea," Rousseau insists, "but rather a necessary consequence of
the nature of the body politic" (*SC* III-1: 80). A state, for Rousseau, is not
the rule of some over others but all over each. But such rule is impossible
without the mediation of a middle term, the Government or executive,
which takes the general laws made by the people in their sovereign capacity
and applies them to the people as individual subjects. Thus, on the functional level, a state necessarily operates like a continuous proportion: the
sovereign does to the Government (gives commands) what the Government
does to the people. And for these functional relations to operate correctly
the quantity of force in each of the three parts must be exactly proportionate
or in equilibrium; that is, the Government must have enough force to control
the people, and the sovereign to control the Government. "None of the three
terms could be altered without simultaneously destroying the proportion"
(*SC* III-1: 79).[30]

The amount of force required to control the people will vary as a function
of several factors, but Rousseau emphasizes population. The larger the
population, the smaller each citizen's influence on the drafting of the laws
and thus the weaker his spontaneous agreement with or loyalty to these
laws—necessitating greater force in the Government. "Thus, in order for
the government to be good, it ought to be relatively stronger in proportion
as the people is more numerous" (*SC* III-1: 80).

The factors that make the Government stronger again relate primarily to
size. As it grows larger, the executive, like a state, grows less internally
cohesive, and, needing to expend more of its force on its own members,
it has less for the exercise of its executive functions. "Therefore, the

[28] It should be emphasized that Rousseau's new science is still only *quasi*-mathematical.
"If I momentarily borrow the vocabulary of geometry in order to express myself in fewer words,
I am nevertheless not unaware that geometric precision does not exist in moral quantities"
(*SC* III-1: 80). It will become particularly clear in the next chapter that Rousseau's full
conception of the legislator's science involves forms of wisdom that are not at all quantifi-
able.

[29] For a more detailed discussion that elaborates Rousseau's mathematical conceptions,
see Masters (1968) pp. 340-48.

[30] Rousseau's doctrine of the "continuous proportion" is precisely a theory of the equilibrium and balance of powers in the state. He is so far from neglecting this aspect of politics that
he may claim to be the first in history to have attempted an exact, scientific account of it.

more numerous the magistrates, the weaker the government" (*SC* III-2: 82).

From these maxims regarding relations of force Rousseau draws the following conclusions. In each different state the continuous proportion requires a different but determinate value for the Government's force, so that "there is no unique and absolute constitution of government" suitable for all states, but at the same time "there is no more than one good government possible in a [given] State" (*SC* III-1: 79-80). And the most basic rule for identifying that one good Government is this: in order for an equilibrium of forces to be maintained "the ratio of magistrates to government should be the inverse of the ratio of subjects to sovereign, which means that the more the State grows, the more the government should shrink, so that the number of leaders diminishes in proportion to the increase of people." Rousseau concludes, in other words, that "in general democratic government is suited to small States, aristocratic to medium-sized ones, and monarchical to large ones" (*SC* III-2: 83, III-3: 84).[31] Such is the general guidance provided by Rousseau's new science of Governments.

The Executive as the Source of Danger in Politics

The purpose of Rousseau's science of Governments is not merely to help find the best form of executive for a given state—to fix the proportion for one moment in time—but also to identify the forces that tend to destroy this equilibrium. The concern with stability over time as distinguished from intrinsic goodness forms a necessary part of any complete political philosophy. For Rousseau, however, it assumes special importance since the state is contrary to nature, hence inherently unstable. The body politic, he laments, "begins to die at the moment of its birth." It is vitally important, then, to understand the forces of decay in the state and how they may be counterbalanced so as to render the state not only good but lasting (*SC* III-11: 98).[32]

Rousseau addresses this issue as an integral part of his discussion of the executive power, for he will argue that it is the Government which, though a necessary part of the state, relentlessly works to destroy it. This is, of course, a highly debatable and partisan thesis, for in one way or another most earlier

[31] The passage continues: "This rule is derived directly from the principle; but countless circumstances can furnish exceptions." Later, on additional grounds, Rousseau will argue that elective aristocracy is the best form of Government simply.

[32] The distinction between the good and the lasting is particularly clear in the *Letters from the Mountain*. At one point, Rousseau states that if he had been present in Geneva two centuries earlier he would have given the following advice: "The constitution that you are forming is good for the present, and bad for the future; it is good for establishing public liberty, bad for conserving it, and that which now creates your security will in a short time be the source of your chains" (VII: 816).

philosophers had argued that the major source of instability, especially in
republics, lay in the legislature or the people.[33] But Rousseau clearly hopes
that the new precision of his science of Governments can force an end to
this eternal debate by rigorously demonstrating that the true source of evil
in politics is the Government's natural tendency to tyranny.[34]

Rousseau claims in fact to have discovered three behavioral laws that,
taken together, make it inevitable that every state eventually decline into
executive tyranny. The first law asserts that within the Government there
inevitably develops a will or desire to dominate the sovereign.

Within every individual member of the Government, Rousseau argues,
one must distinguish three essentially different wills.

> First, the individual's own will, which tends only toward his private
> advantage. Second, the common will of the magistrates, which
> relates uniquely to the advantage of the prince; which may be called
> the corporate will, and is general in relation to the government and
> private in relation to the State.... Third, the will of the people or
> the sovereign will. (*SC* III-2: 82)

A perfect state, or at least one containing no inherent tendency to destroy
itself, could exist if the strength of these several wills were in direct
proportion to their generality. Tragically, just the opposite is the case.

> According to the natural order, on the contrary, these different wills
> become more active as they are more concentrated. Thus the general
> will is always the weakest, the corporate will has second place, and
> the private will is the first of all. So that each member of the
> government is first himself, and then magistrate, and then citizen—
> a gradation that is exactly opposite to the one required by the social
> order. (*SC* III-2: 82)

This is the fundamental source of evil within the body politic, the fatal and
inescapable flaw within the structure of every state, necessitating its decline.

> Just as the private will acts incessantly against the general will,
> so the government makes a continual effort against sover-
> eignty.... sooner or later the prince must finally oppress the sov-
> ereign and break the social treaty. That is the inherent vice which,

[33] See Montesquieu *Spirit of the Laws* XI-6, 13, 14, 15, 16; *The Federalist* nos. 10, 48, 49.
Tocqueville *Democracy in America* I-1 (8): 122: "This dependence of the executive power is
one of the inherent vices of republican constitutions. The Americans could not eliminate that
tendency which leads legislative assemblies to take over the government."

[34] Rousseau takes the same approach to another classic and endless dispute, that between
the partisans of monarchy and republicanism. He attempts permanently to settle the issue by
reducing it to something quantitative and thus unchallengeable: population growth. "Calcula-
tors, it is up to you now. Count, measure, compare" (*SC* III-9: 96). Rousseau's great hope
throughout is to use precision as a cure for men's partisanship and dishonesty.

from the emergence of the body politic, tends without respite to destroy it. (*SC* III-10: 96; see *Montagne* IX: 888-89, 891-92, 891n)

That is why the state "begins to die at the moment of its birth, and carries within itself the causes of its destruction" (*SC* III-11: 98).

Yet, just because the executive must seek to dominate the sovereign, that does not mean that it must succeed. The sovereign, after all, has the means to resist; it has the power as well as the right to inspect the Government's actions and to keep it in line. Hence the importance of Rousseau's second law: over time, the sovereign s power must necessarily weaken in relation to the executive.

In the early period of a state's life, Rousseau argues, new laws are needed often, and therefore the sovereign assembles frequently and plays a continuous, active, and vigorous role in the conduct of public affairs. But later, when the task of lawmaking has been more or less completed, there is less obvious need for the sovereign to assemble and it slowly grows accustomed to a greater passivity (*Montagne* VII: 815-16, VIII: 843). This tendency is greatly reinforced by the gradual slackening of the people's republican morals, which, always contrary to inclination, naturally tend to decay. As patriotism declines and men become caught up in their private interests, they come to regard the political rights and duties, for which their forbears fought and died, as a burden and are only too willing to entrust the management of public affairs to others. After a time, of course, they begin to realize the disadvantages of being ruled by others, but by then they have become too cowardly, too divided, and too much in love with ease to undertake the difficult and dangerous actions that would then be necessary to restore their power. They think of reconvening the sovereign assembly, but Governments, full of the will to dominate,

> never spare efforts, nor objections, nor obstacles, nor promises to discourage the citizens from holding them. When the latter are greedy, cowardly, pusillanimous, fonder of repose than of freedom, they don't hold out long against the redoubled efforts of the government. (*SC* III-14: 101; see *SC* III-15: 101-4; *SD*, 172-73; *Montagne* IX: 881)

In this way, as public morals gradually decay, the sovereign power necessarily slackens. Therefore, "as the sovereignty tends always to slacken, the government tends always to strengthen," so that in the end the latter inevitably realizes its ambition to master the former (*Montagne* VI: 808).

Rousseau also discerns a third historical law which, reinforcing the effects of the first two, makes their operation—and their tyrannical outcome—all the more certain. Over time, Rousseau asserts, the Government necessarily tends to shrink in size, going from democracy to aristocracy and from aristocracy to monarchy. What makes this progression toward monarchy (and ultimately tyranny) necessary is that over time "all governments tend continually to weaken" and because they weaken they must grow

smaller in order to increase and restore their force (*PE*, 227). "The government never changes its form," Rousseau explains, "except when its worn
out mechanism leaves it too weakened to be able to preserve itself. . . . The
mechanism must therefore be wound up and tightened in proportion as
it gives way; otherwise the State it supports would fall into ruins" (*SC*
III-10: 97; see *Montagne* VI: 808; *Polysynodie*, 621).

The claim that the Government must continually shrink to counteract its
natural tendency to weaken might seem to contradict the argument just
made that the executive tends to strengthen over time. The difficulty is
resolved by distinguishing between the two relations that the Government—the mean proportional in Rousseau's "continuous proportion"—
maintains in the state. Over time the Government strengthens in relation to
the sovereign (the people as a legislative body); but it also weakens in
relation to the subjects (the people as individuals who must be constrained
to obey). And the cause of the Government's strengthening in the first
respect is the same as of its weakening in the second: the gradual decay of
virtue. The decline of patriotism and the growth of selfishness progressively
weaken the executive by decreasing its internal coherence at the same time
as they increase the proclivity of the subjects to disobey. To counteract this
growing weakness, the Government must shrink, because, as Rousseau's
science has shown, executive force is inversely proportional to size. Thus,
over time, Governments necessarily grow smaller.

This third tendency reinforces and, as it were, summarizes the other two.
First, as the Government grows smaller, it must desire all the more to
dominate the sovereign general will, for "the more numerous the body of
magistrates, the closer the [government's] corporate will is to the general
will, whereas under a unique magistrate, this same corporate will . . . is
merely a private will" (*SC* III-2: 83).[35] Second, the smaller the Government,
the more it can act with unity, speed, and secrecy, and thus the stronger it
is in its contest with the sovereign. Thus, these three demonstrable tendencies, taken together, produce what Rousseau considers to be an iron-clad
law of history: from the moment of their birth, all states necessarily
progress toward executive tyranny.

The Cycle of Regimes

Having used his science of Governments to analyze the interplay of forces
within the state and to discover the source and law of its decline, Rousseau
will propose various measures for strengthening the state and holding back
the forces of decay.

Before examining these measures, however, it is necessary to appreciate
the uniqueness of Rousseau's analysis of forces and proposed law of
history. It is not merely new but directly contradictory to the most widely

---

[35] "Kings want to be absolute" (*SC* III-6: 88).

accepted view. In classical times and continuing more or less up until Rousseau, political thinkers were in considerable agreement regarding the trends of secular political history and the ways in which forms of government change over time. Whether one looks in Plato or Polybius or Machiavelli one finds more or less the same view of political decline: the famous doctrine of "the cycle of regimes." This doctrine holds—in agreement with Rousseau—that all regimes, or at least all unmixed ones, are internally unstable and tend to decay into other regimes. But the order of this decay is precisely opposite to the one Rousseau describes, going from smaller to larger, from monarchy to aristocracy to democracy. And whereas oppressive or tyrannical regimes may exist at any stage, toward the end of the process the primary danger is the slide toward extreme democracy (which finally leads to tyranny). According to this older view, Rousseau has it perfectly backwards: history is a process of progressive democratization.[36]

These are the sorts of dispute that bring intellectual historians to despair. How can there be such complete and utter disagreement regarding what seems to be a relatively simple question of fact? The answer lies, however, in the new way of interpreting facts entailed by Rousseau's political thought. Much of our discussion of his philosophy has proceeded on a very abstract plane, but the remarkable difference existing between his law of history and the traditional view provides a concrete illustration of the true revolution in thinking about political phenomena that his new theory entails.

Consider first the case of a single regime about which the basic facts are clear. Everyone agrees that fifth-century Athens was an extreme democracy, indeed a classic case of such democracy verging at times on mob rule. But Rousseau claims: "Athens was not in fact a democracy." What was it then? "A highly tyrannical aristocracy, governed by learned men and orators" (*PE*, 213). Looking at the same object, why does he see something so different?

A democracy, in the classical view, is the rule of the common people asserted in the name of freedom, just as an aristocracy is the domination by a privileged class justified in the name of good birth or virtue, and in general every form of government consists in the leadership of some particular sociopolitical class defended through some claim to superiority. In this sense, Athens was very much a democracy, with the *demos* having all the power and the aristocrats suffering from its lack.

But Rousseau dismisses as fundamentally irrelevant the whole magnificent melodrama of politics: the rivalry of classes, the conflicting public claims for leadership, the open clash of principles regarding distributive justice and the common good. Wherever and to whatever extent a genuine

---

[36] More precisely, history moves toward democracy until the end of the cycle is reached. See Plato *Republic* Bks. VIII and IX, *Laws* Bk. III; Polybius *Histories* Bk. VI; Machiavelli *Discourses* I.2. See also Isocrates *Aeropagetica* 3-5; Cicero *Republic* Bk. I, 65-68.

state exists, commanding true obedience, its real basis, whatever the public claims may be, is in the agreement of the people to obey the laws as embodiments of the general will. The real issue of principle—the definition of legitimacy and of human virtue—is settled in the same way in every genuine state and all that differs from one to another is the form of executive power. Consequently, if one desires scientifically to understand a given state or to compare several different states—to know how they really function and how they affect men's lives—one must resolutely ignore the seeming variations in principles and names, cut through the pompous and irrelevant surface of partisan ideologies, and fix one's gaze on the one significant thing: the distribution of real executive power, the location and size of the Governmental clique, the executive "power elite." It is Government in this technical sense, drained of all traditional reference to principle or class basis, Government as purely an arrangement of executive force, that Rousseau focuses on both in his quantitative science of Governments and in his new historical law of political change. For this alone is real, causal, and humanly significant; the rest is mere superstructure.

Thus, in the case of Athens, Rousseau reverses the traditional description because, ignoring the public principles, ends, and class basis of the state, which were indeed "democratic" in the old sense, he directs his attention solely to those who, through whatever means and pretexts, exercise the real executive power. In Athens it was exercised by a shifting cabal of demagogic "learned men and orators." And since this power elite was small in number, it was an aristocracy, regardless of everything else.

Similarly, the famous republic of Venice, which was commonly regarded as an aristocracy, Rousseau now redefines as a mixed Government much like Geneva, with a strong democratic element, because its grand council, although reserved for the "aristocracy" (in the qualitative, sociopolitical sense), is as large in *number* as the assembly of the people at Geneva (*SC* IV-3: 112).[37]

The Roman Republic is the most important example of Rousseau's redefinition or reinterpretation of regimes. In the context of stating his law of history, Rousseau remarks that Rome "will not fail to be cited as an objection for supposedly following a completely opposite development, changing from monarchy to aristocracy and from aristocracy to democracy" (*SC* III-10: 97n). Everyone knows that the aristocratic patrician class eventually lost power to the plebs and their representatives the tribunes. How can this be a movement toward aristocracy? Rousseau responds:

> As the patriciate abolished itself in a sense, the aristocracy no longer consisted in the body of patricians . . . but in the body of the senate, composed of patricians and plebians, and even in the body of the tribunes when they began to usurp active power. For words do not change things, and when the people has leaders who govern for it,

[37] Rousseau does also argue that the aristocracy's privileges do not amount to much.

whatever name these leaders may assume, they are always an aristocracy. (Ibid.)

It is clear, in sum, that Rousseau's comprehensive new political science—
by dismissing all principled titles to leadership as both humanly and
politically irrelevant, and by reducing the state to a sovereign will that is
everywhere the same and an executive force (defined purely quantitatively) that is the sole subject of variation among genuine states—leads
to a radically new way of interpreting and categorizing states, a way that
tends to reverse the most elementary judgments of earlier political thought.

With this in mind, we can begin to understand Rousseau's new law of
history and its diametrical opposition to the traditional theory of constitutional change. The classical doctrine of the cycle of regimes is, of course,
a theory about "regimes"—the rule of certain classes in the name of certain
virtues. Over time, it claims, regimes tend to evolve from monarchy to
democracy due to a historical tendency that Rousseau also perceives. The
strenuous, austere, and reverent morals of earlier times tend always to
weaken, becoming more relaxed, indulgent, and inclusive. Consequently,
over time, the class of men who can make a credible public claim to "virtue"
and thus also to worthiness to rule gradually increases. This is a fairly
commonsensical view. Old-fashioned severity and elitism inevitably give
way to more liberal values: awe and reverence diminish, hierarchies are
leveled, authority weakens, deference declines, and the human types and
pursuits that formerly were despised now claim equal public respect.
History is a process of moral and political relaxation, a constant movement
toward the liberation and then the dominance of the more common human
ends—freedom and comfort—and thus toward the rule of the lower, larger,
and naturally more powerful classes that live for these ends.[38] Therefore,
all regimes naturally tend to expand and not shrink, to evolve toward
democracy and not monarchy.

Rousseau's view of history begins from the same premise: morals tend
to loosen over time. Perhaps he also would grant that this leads to a gradual
change in the sorts of justifications or titles that ambitious men employ in
their bid for political power, a change in the direction of less elitist and
more democratic titles to rule. But since he believes that all such titles are
deceptive (mere pretexts for exploitation) and ineffectual, he regards the
progressive democratization of these titles as fundamentally irrelevant,
as a mere change in the ideological superstructure that leaves the real
events more or less unchanged.

On the level of real events, genuine states consist of a sovereign
general will plus some form of executive power. The first of these
elements, the sovereignty of the general will, tends to be strongest,

---

[38] See Plato *Republic* Bks. VIII and IX.

according to Rousseau, in the earlier stages of history. "Few weeks went by," he points out, "in which the Roman people was not assembled, and even several times. . . . By going back to the earliest periods of nations, it would be found that most of the ancient governments, even the monarchical ones like the Macedonians and the Franks, had similar councils" (*SC* III-12: 100). These democratic institutions were strongest in earlier times because the need for them—the need for the people to distrust their leaders at least to the extent of keeping the legislative power in their own hands—is a virtually self-evident truth, obvious to all healthy human beings; and human beings were healthier in the earlier times when their morals were more pure and austere. Of course, these old-fashioned morals may encourage deference and hierarchy in certain respects—as the classics emphasize—but they also give men the simplicity, strength, and courage to recognize the obvious limits to all deference: the clear necessity for popular sovereignty. It is only over time, as these morals decay, that the people allow their sovereignty to slip away. The decline in mores may indeed bring a decrease in *moral* deference or inequality, but it also brings an increase in *political* inequality, because corrupted men—selfish, slavish, and cowardly—allow themselves to be half-bullied and half-tricked out of the sovereign rights that their deferential forbears had the simple clear-sightedness and courage to defend.[39]

As to the executive power, the same moral changes compel it to shrink toward monarchy. As men become less deferential, patriotic, and obedient, the Government is compelled to increase its force, which it can do only by decreasing its size. It may be that the ideological justifications and even the social classes in the name of which men seek power become progressively more democratic—as the traditional view asserts—still, that power itself tends to concentrate in fewer and fewer hands. The pretexts grow broader at the same time as the underlying power structure, the executive elite, becomes narrower. Thus, Rousseau reverses the classical view of political history because the same loosening of morals and decline in deference that produce an evolution toward democracy on the surface level of principles and ends, creates a movement toward monarchy on the real level of the size of the executive elite.

To summarize the point in somewhat more general and contemporary terms, Rousseau's new science of politics originates "elite theory," which condemns the naivete of categorizing governments primarily with reference to the public principles or even the larger class interests in the name of which they rule. The true determinant of society's fate and

---

[39] See *SD*, 163-65. It is not reasonable to believe, Rousseau claims, that "the first means of providing for the common security imagined by proud and unconquered men [of early times] was to rush into slavery" because "barbarous man does not bend his head for the yoke that civilized man wears without a murmur" (p. 163; 164).

the government's behavior is the interest and power of the governmental clique itself. Furthermore, when governments are defined in this new way, one sees that their natural tendency is to shrink toward monarchy. In other words, Rousseau is the first to have discovered what is now called the "iron law of oligarchy": over time, although the pretexts may change or move toward democracy, real power tends to concentrate in ever smaller groups.[40]

Holding Back Decline

We have spent considerable time examining Rousseau's doctrine of political history, not only because of its general theoretical interest but also because of its immense practical implications. Once one has identified the forces of corruption in the state, then one can devise means to balance them; once one has determined the direction of historical decline, then one knows which way to lean.[41]

The more optimistic or "progressive" one's view of history, of course, the less will be one's preoccupation with forces of decline. But for the deeply pessimistic Rousseau, for whom the state is an unnatural creation that begins to die at the moment of its birth, this subject is absolutely crucial, pervading the whole of his political thought and occupying fully a

---

[40] See Michels (1915) who, like Pareto and Durkheim, was greatly influenced by Rousseau. The contrast between the traditional view of politics and history and Rousseau's approach can be seen in two rival intellectual positions within America today. Social critics with a more traditional orientation maintain that the direction of American history has clearly been toward ever greater equality and democracy, as Tocqueville observed two centuries ago. Over the long term there has been a continual extension of the suffrage; the subjection of ever more elements of the political process to direct popular control; the progressive reduction of "discrimination" in every sense; and the relentless decline of every sort of deference, distinction, and hierarchy, be it between parent and child, male and female, heterosexual and homosexual, priest and layman, teacher and student, criminal and noncriminal, promiscuous and chaste, alien and citizen, and so forth. If America has a characteristic danger, then, it consists in too much equality and democracy.

A rival camp asserts that American history has been tending in exactly the opposite direction. If one does not allow oneself to be distracted by these cultural changes, this democratization on the level of ideas and of apparent participation, if one ignores everything but the pure question of force, then one sees that power has always been concentrated in a small elite which has tended continually to shrink over time. Our great historical danger, therefore, is not excessive equality and democracy but rather the opposite: the arrogance of power, the corporate clique, the power elite, the military-industrial complex, the imperial presidency—the constant slide toward governmental tyranny. This form of argument, this inverted reading of history, is Rousseau's invention.

[41] After his own discussion of the cycle of regimes, Cicero remarks: "The foundation of that political wisdom which is the aim of our whole discourse is an understanding of the regular curving path through which governments travel [i.e., of the laws of historical change], in order that, when you know what direction any commonwealth tends to take, you may be able to hold it back or take measures to meet the change" (*Republic* II-25).

third of the *Social Contract*. No other major work of political philosophy gives this issue as much space and importance.[42]

Rousseau also gives it a revolutionary new content. Just as his law of history completely reverses the prevailing understanding of political decay, so also his proposals for resisting decline push in an opposite direction. Wherever the classical doctrine of the cycle of regimes held sway, political thinking and writing was always colored by the belief that the great, relentless political danger looming on the horizon, which will ultimately lead to tyranny or destruction, is the progressive decay of hierarchy and authority, the inexorable slide toward extreme democracy and mob rule. And thus one detects especially in many classical writers (as Rousseau himself complainingly points out) an eagerness to lean the other way, to exaggerate the merits of monarchy and aristocracy, describing them under ideal conditions while depicting democracy through lurid accounts of its worst excesses.[43] In somewhat crude contemporary terms, classical thinkers may be said to have viewed political decay as coming from the "left," which gave them a motive (in addition to their intrinsic preferences) to lean "right."

Rousseau brings about a hundred and eighty degree shift in the "leaning" of political thought. The danger pressing down upon us, he shouts, is coming from the other direction, from the growth of inequality, the relentless concentration of executive power in fewer and fewer hands.

Thus, men of good will who seek to hold back the forces of decline will praise and perhaps even exaggerate the virtues of democracy, while warning against the ever growing danger of tyranny. Indeed, we have seen in chapter 9 that Rousseau exactly reverses the practice for which he blamed previous writers: his account of the general will and majority rule tends to describe them under ideal conditions, to quietly presuppose all sorts of supporting conditions, whereas his discussion of monarchy dwells on its worst abuses.[44]

---

[42] Perhaps Machiavelli's works might be cited as an exception. As for the *Social Contract*, the last nine chapters of book III are explicitly devoted to the issue of preserving the state from decline, and all of book 4 addresses the same subject, though in a more general and less explicit manner. See *Dialogues* III: 934-35, where Rousseau states in so many words that holding back the forces of decay was the purpose of *all* his writings. This theme will be treated at greater length in chap. 13.

[43] See *SC* III-6: 90, III-10: 98n; Plato *Republic* Bks. VIII, IX, especially 555b-58d; Cicero *Republic* I-43, 44, 45 (and the remarks on this passage by the editors, Sabine and Smith, p. 58).

[44] See *SC* I-4: 49, III-6: 87-91. In chap. 9 we attributed Rousseau's exaggerated praise of the majority primarily to his need to combat the ambitious ideologues who seek to erect their own opinions as the standard of justice. Here we see that he is also combatting the executive power. These are the two enemies of law in Rousseau's view: those who claim wisdom and those who wield force.

For an opposite interpretation—that Rousseau does not exaggerate but cautiously understates his preference for democracy—see Miller (1984) pp. 65-75 and Gildin (1983) chap. 5.

More generally, if students of the *Social Contract* have always noticed with great frustration that Rousseau boldly sets forth clear egalitarian and democratic principles at the beginning of the book only gradually to qualify and compromise them in the details that follow, that may be attributed to this polemical need to take an exaggerated public stand against the swelling tide of inequality. "It is precisely because the force of things always tends to destroy equality," Rousseau writes, "that the force of legislation should always tend to maintain it"—and what is true of legislation is true of Rousseau's doctrines as well (*SC* II-11: 75). Rousseau is in fact an extremely inegalitarian thinker in many important respects, as will become clear toward the end of our discussion of the executive and the legislator, but he tends to understate this side of things, to let it sit quietly in his maxims of politics, while gloriously enshrining his democratic views as principles of political right. This is his rhetorical contribution to the balance of powers.

When interpreting any political thinker, it is important to know his views not only on what makes the state good but also on what makes it stable and lasting, to know his account of the direction of decline and of the means through which it might be resisted. This is true above all of Rousseau. Without understanding his "leanings" as well as his ideal, one will never grasp the meaning of his political thought and doctrine or appreciate the extent of his originality. Rousseau revolutionized not only the prevailing conception of the highest political goal, as is often recognized, but also that of the immanent political danger and of the proper "leaning" for political thought, which is less often seen. As the inventor of the iron law of oligarchy, Rousseau is the first to argue that political decline comes from the "right" and that to hold it back one must push to the "left" both institutionally and rhetorically.

The Balance of Powers

The measures Rousseau devises for holding back the forces of decline are, of course, not limited to the level of rhetoric or public principles, but also include certain constitutional arrangements. Specifically, he proposes three institutional means for maintaining a balance of powers between the sovereign and the executive.

The first expedient is to weaken the executive power by dividing it. Employing the terms of his science of the continuous proportion, Rousseau states:

> When the executive power does not depend enough on the legislative power, that is when there is a greater ratio between prince and sovereign than between people and prince, this defect in the proportion must be remedied by dividing the government. For then all of its parts do not have any less authority over the subjects, and their division makes all of them together weaker when opposed to the sovereign.

Rousseau calls this form of executive "mixed government" and cites England and Poland as examples (*SC* III-7: 91).

But this expedient is not a particularly good one in Rousseau's eyes. "The invention of this division by chambers or departments is modern," Rousseau points out, employing a favorite term of derogation (*Poland* VII: 977). It is not really possible, he believes, to divide executive power in a perfectly balanced and lasting manner, and, over time, with the shifting of personalities and events, one of the parts will eventually gain effective dominion. What is worse, where this has not or not yet occurred, there will be a constant competition and tug-of-war among the several parts of the administration which will make it weak and inefficient. And Rousseau, for all his fear of Governmental tyranny, strongly insists on the necessity for a forceful and vigorous executive. Therefore this modern extension of the principle of separation of powers to *within* the executive power itself is a very imperfect, if sometimes necessary, expedient. The Roman Senate—unicameral, with members elected for life—remains Rousseau's ideal (*SC* III-7: 91; *Poland* VII: 975-77).

The second means Rousseau proposes to "balance the two powers and maintain their respective rights" is not to weaken the executive but to create a third, intermediary power, the "tribunate," which would shift its weight as necessary to hold the other two in equilibrium (*SC* III-7: 91). Without either legislative or executive power, it would have the power to nullify the actions of the sovereign or Government when it judged them to violate the constitutional laws. The tribunes of the people in Rome, the ephors of Sparta, and the Council of Ten in Venice are the examples given (*SC* IV-5: 120).[45] This expedient, to which Rousseau devotes a whole chapter, is said to be "the firmest support of a good constitution" (*SC* IV-5: 120; see also *Montagne* IX: 879-80, 880n). Its drawback, however, is that once the constitution has begun to degenerate, the tribunate itself tends strongly to tyranny, which it did, according to Rousseau, in both Sparta and Rome.

Rousseau's third and final proposal—which he claims he is the first ever to have put forward, which he calls the "true secret" for keeping the Government in line, and to which he devotes no fewer than five chapters—is to strengthen the sovereign by establishing periodic popular assemblies which the executive is not empowered to prevent or postpone.[46] In a sense, of course, this institution is hardly new—either to history or to the reader at this late point in the *Social Contract*. We already know that popular assemblies are necessary in the legitimate state for the purpose of making laws and giving expression to the general will.

[45] Masters (1968) p. 407n suggests the American Supreme Court as a vague contemporary parallel. See also Gildin (1983) pp. 174-76 for a useful discussion.

[46] The assemblies are discussed in *SC* III-12-15, 18. For Rousseau's claims of originality and of having found the "true secret" see *Poland* VII: 978.

What stands behind Rousseau's claim to originality is that he structures this existing institution for an important new function: that of watching over the Government in its execution of the laws. To be sure, assemblies in the past have also exercised this second function, but Rousseau now grounds it directly in first principles. Furthermore, he gives this function a new prominence, as exemplified by the striking fact that the five chapters in which Rousseau delivers his famous encomium of the popular assembly occur not, as one might expect, in the first book, in the discussion of popular sovereignty, but rather here in the third, in the context of controlling the executive. Indeed, if everyone takes it for granted that the popular assembly is the centerpiece of the *Social Contract*, that it is *the* characteristic institution of the Rousseauian city, that is because of the important role that Rousseau gives it here as guardian of the laws and of the executive. Finally, Rousseau also introduces certain concrete innovations in the functioning of the assemblies: they should be periodic, and in their presence the authority of the Government (which, as Rousseau has proved, derives from a revocable law and not a contract) should be wholly suspended (*SC* III-13: 100, III-18: 106, III-14: 101).

Let us consider, then, how such assemblies—the "true secret" for keeping the executive in check—will accomplish their new mission. On the most obvious level, the periodic assemblies will be just like periodic elections. At an appointed time that cannot be postponed, the executive will be held to account, grievances will be heard and debated, and the tenure of the magistrates will be put to a vote. Yet, if this were all, Rousseau would have no reason for insisting, as he does, on assemblies as distinguished from elections. What assemblies add, beyond institutionalized "accountability," are certain moral effects—and it is on the latter, we should not be surprised to learn, that Rousseau is primarily counting. When men gather together, they make "the people" and "the sovereign" into things that can be seen and heard; they transform "the whole" into a perceptible reality. In the assemblies, therefore, the citizens are reminded of the pettiness of their daily individual pursuits and are moved to rededicate themselves to their political duties and public lives.

By socializing and invigorating the citizenry, popular assemblies help to hold back the two processes at the root of the drift toward executive tyranny. First, the tendency toward the growth of private selfishness and disobedience is slowed, which diminishes the pressures that constrain Governments to increase their force and thus decrease their size. Second, the periodic assemblies eliminate or check the sovereign's tendency to grow weak and passive through inaction. Given an ongoing or at least periodic role in the conduct of affairs, the sovereign people stays in shape: it develops a firm sense of its rights and public identity, and keeps alive the courage and constant vigilance needed to hold the executive in check. Thus the periodic assemblies, by making the people at once more obedient as subjects and more active as sovereigns, block the two roads to Governmental usurpation.

One further moral effect of this institution derives from the fact that the popular assembly is not only the gathering of the people but also the suspension of the Government. On every other day of the year the people, as individual subjects, experience their inferiority and subordination to the magistrates. It is therefore very important that periodically there be an occasion when, united together as sovereigns, they experience their ultimate superiority to the magistrates. In the assembly, the abstract relations of right on which the state rests are made to take on flesh and everyone is reminded again of what they naturally tend to forget: that the sovereign *is* the state; that the Government, for all its superiority to individuals, exists only as an emanation and servant of the people as a whole. Like a moment of self-recollection in the life of the individual, the gathering together of the people is a precious time of self-renewal in which the city puts itself back into right shape by re-enacting its origins and re-establishing contact with the true source of its existence, which always tends to get covered over in the course of daily life.

By virtue of these moral effects, in combination with institutionalized accountability, the periodic popular assemblies—*the* central Rousseauian institution—will strengthen the sovereign, stabilize the balance of powers, and thus counteract *the* central political danger, the decline toward executive tyranny.

Conclusion

We have considered only the first part of Rousseau's strangely two-sided treatment of the executive power, and yet perhaps we have already seen enough complexity and originality to justify Rousseau's warnings and boasts. At any rate, the one issue it is important to summarize concerns the theory of the balance of powers. Near the beginning we observed the great originality of Rousseau's theory concerning the legal establishment of the Government, a theory that, by totally subordinating the executive power to the legislative, seemed to have both the intention and effect of precluding any possibility of balance between the two. But in addition to the fact that Rousseau quietly supplies the Government with sufficient rights to protect itself, his science of Governments, leading to his law of political history, demonstrates that he was very much concerned with the balance of forces but that he understood the primary danger in a new way, as coming from the progressive weakening of the sovereign, the shrinking of the executive, and the eventual triumph of the latter over the former. This fact, combined with other evidence we have seen, makes it fairly clear that Rousseau's unique emphasis on legislative supremacy is not intended to preclude the balance of powers, as has been generally assumed, but rather to maintain it.

Still further evidence will emerge in the next chapter; for the theory of balance stands at the very heart of Rousseau's politics, and only in terms of this theory will it prove possible to resolve the great contradiction in Rousseau's doctrine of executive power that we are about to confront.

12

The Executive, the Legislator, and the "Authoritarian Rousseau"

A massive contradiction presides over Rousseau's discussion of the Government. One well-defined "side" of his account, which we have just examined, clearly subordinates the executive to the legislative power. It also attacks the executive as the great danger within the state, the source of all decline, and it urges the sovereign people vigilantly to maintain its rights and legal superiority. The second side, embodied in Rousseau's "maxims of politics," contradicts not only this view of the Government but indeed everything we have seen regarding the necessity for consent, popular sovereignty, freedom, and equality—the whole of the "principles of political right." It holds that the executive, like the legislator, must be active, elitist, and almost "authoritarian" in its behavior. Not limiting itself to its official, passive role of enforcing the laws handed down by the assembly, it should venture to guide, manipulate, and control the people.

To appreciate the magnitude of the dilemma posed by this strangely elitist side to Rousseau, one must see that it is not a minor inconsistency confined to his political works. As Judith Shklar has shown with particular force, the authoritarian longing for the intervention of a wise, absolute, and transforming leader is a major Rousseauian theme found consistently throughout all his writings. "He firmly believed in his Plutarchian heroes, and such figures as the legislator, Emile's tutor and M. de Wolmar in *La Nouvelle Héloïse* show how well he could imagine men capable of reordering the lives of others."[1] Lester Crocker goes so far as to label Rousseau "a perfect model of what we now refer to as 'the authoritarian personality.'"[2] To put it somewhat differently, alongside the modern, voluntaristic strain in Rousseau's thought, emphasizing freedom, consent, and popular sovereignty, there is also a pervasive "Platonic" strain, recognizing the need for the absolute rule of wisdom.

---

[1] Shklar (1972) p. 335.

[2] Crocker (1968) p. 36; see pp. 9, 163-64.

Since this troubling "other side" to Rousseau has been largely neglected, it will be useful to begin with a simple accounting of the textual "facts."[3] This theme is expressed most clearly and radically in Rousseau's discussion of the great legislator. Of course, the lawgiver does not really constitute an integral part of the state, appearing only at its beginning to found and order it. Still, since the active, elitist side of the executive power—with which we are more narrowly concerned as a permanent element of the state—results from its taking over and continuing some of the functions of the lawgiver, it is best to begin with the latter.

The Legislator

What compelled Rousseau to resort to the strange expedient of a "great legislator"? The answer follows from his view that the sovereign assembly will reliably embody the general will only under certain strict conditions, above all the prevalence of a high degree of virtue or public-spiritedness. But virtue, a highly unnatural condition, can exist only where men have been raised under a system of transforming laws and institutions. Obviously, then, such a system of laws cannot be created by the people, who will lack the virtue that arises only as its effect (*SC* II-7: 69).

Furthermore, at *any* period in their history, the people would lack the wisdom necessary to devise such a comprehensive system of legislation.

> How is it to be expected that a blind multitude, which often does not know what it wants because it rarely knows what is good for it, can formulate and carry out by itself such a difficult undertaking as a system of legislation, which is the most sublime effort of human wisdom and foresight? (*GM* I-7: 178)[4]

The point is less that the people are stupid than that lawmaking is extraordinarily difficult—the creation of artificial order from natural chaos—requiring a degree of genius and insight never found in large numbers of

---

[3] Lester Crocker's work, *The Social Contract: An Interpretive Essay* (1968), is, so far as I know, the only book-length treatment of this "authoritarian" side of Rousseau. There are, to be sure, many books that point to the unlimited authority of Rousseau's *sovereign* (as distinguished from the Government), but this is still part of the first, egalitarian side of Rousseau (as I would use the term), for the sovereign's power is only the power of the whole community over itself. It is *democratic* absolutism or, if you prefer, totalitarian democracy. But what Crocker and Shklar have pointed out is that there is also in Rousseau a tendency to *undemocratic* absolutism, to genuine authoritarianism, to the longing for salvation through the unsupervised and unfathomable activity of some great man or elite.

Again, many scholars have argued that, in practice, the actual but surely unintended result of Rousseau's doctrine would be the rise of an authoritarian elite. The thesis of Crocker's book is that there is evidence suggesting that such an elite is precisely what Rousseau desires. This evidence constitutes the perplexing "other side" of Rousseau that we seek to understand.

[4] "One who dares to undertake the founding of a people," Rousseau maintains, "should feel that he is capable of changing human nature, so to speak" (*SC* II-7: 68; see 67).

people. The task, after all, is not to establish mere law and order but to transform human nature, and this is done not by direct command—otherwise it would be easy—but only by molding institutions that in turn mold the men who grow up within them. As Rousseau explains, one must arrange not only the "constitution" in the narrow, political sense, but also the religious rites and beliefs, the manner of education, the economic practices, public festivals, athletic games, and so forth. One's concern is less with immediate behavior than with the establishment of salutary mores, customs, and opinions. Moreover, all of this must be arranged with an eye to local circumstances: the particular character and temperament of the people, their inherited prejudices and traditions, the climate, the fecundity of women, the nature of the soil, the state's location, size, population, neighbors, and so forth. Read *The Spirit of the Laws*, Rousseau suggests, if one wants to get some feel for what is involved (*Poland* II, *SC* II-7-12: 67-77). Lawmaking does indeed demand "the most sublime effort of human wisdom and foresight." It is clearly not for the people.

Rousseau is therefore compelled to introduce the great legislator, who is capable of resolving these two problems of virtue and wisdom. Like the people prior to their subjection to good laws, he too is naturally selfish and lacking in simple virtue; but the sheer power and grandeur of his selfish ambitions—the desire for the immortal glory of being the founder of a great nation—will lead him to strain every fiber for the common good. Second, he is a man of transcendent ability, combining the contemplative genius of a philosopher, the practical wisdom of a statesman, and the inspirational qualities of a prophet. Chance must bring together an extraordinary man such as this and a people ripe for receiving good laws (which is almost as rare) if a good state is ever to come into being (*SC* II-7: 67-70; *GM* II-2: 179-183).

This doctrine, so alien to modern sensibilities, tempts us to go looking in Rousseau's biography for its sources. Yet, like so many things in his writings that seem strange to us, it is merely a commonplace of ancient political theory. If modern liberal thought has dispensed with such a doctrine, that is because it no longer needs or desires a comprehensive system of legislation that can mold men to some strenuous ideal of virtue. It seeks only to command or forbid behavior, not to transform character. For this no genius is required. Although beginning with Burke there is a return to the emphatic concern with character, customs, and socially imbedded morals, the function of the legislator is now taken over by history, by the spontaneous growth of usage and tradition, which is thought far wiser than any individual rational planner. But Rousseau, who sees a need to reorder human nature, who has no faith in history or progress, but who still maintains a rationalist belief in the philosophical powers of the rare individual—Rousseau returns to the classical conception of the great legislator.

This doctrine is not inherently strange or unreasonable, then; and the real question is only whether it is consistent with the rest of Rousseau's thought. Does it not flagrantly contradict the great principle of popular sovereignty which he has so staunchly defended? Rousseau himself raises this question and answers emphatically that it does not—for the simple reason that the legislator will not claim any sovereign authority.

> He who drafts the laws . . . does not or should not have any legislative right. And the people itself cannot, even if it wanted to, divest itself of this incommunicable right, because according to the fundamental compact, only the general will obligates private individuals, and one can never be assured that a private will is in conformity with the general will until it has been submitted to the free vote of the people. I have already said this, but it is not useless to repeat it. (*SC* II-7: 69)[5]

Here, in the very heart of the chapter on the legislator, Rousseau reaffirms his adherence to the principle of popular sovereignty: in order for the system of legislation drafted by the lawgiver to bind the citizens it must, like any other law, be submitted to and adopted by "the free vote of the people."

As Rousseau acknowledges in the immediate sequel, however, there is a small problem with this position. The same lack of intelligence and original virtue that makes the people incapable of drafting laws by themselves also makes them incapable of recognizing the wisdom of the laws drafted by the legislator. Thus, if the latter must rely solely on rational argument, he will find it quite impossible to convince the people to consent to his salutary but necessarily strange, austere, and demanding system of laws. The need for a legislator is, after all, incompatible with the principle of popular sovereignty.

But there is still one way out, Rousseau contends. The legislator will "persuade without convincing" the people, by claiming to speak for the gods; he will place his code "in the mouth of the immortals in order to win over by divine authority those who cannot be moved by human prudence" (*SC* II-7: 69-70, I have altered the translation). The solution, in short, is to use fraud, to win the people's consent through religious deceit.

Rousseau had actually prepared us for this surprising suggestion in the preceding chapter when describing the people's need for a legislator: "The general will is always right, but the judgement that guides it is not always enlightened. It must be made to see objects as they are, or sometimes *as they should appear to be*" (*SC* II-6: 67, emphasis added). Similarly, when addressing the issue of the citizens' mores, customs, and opinions, Rousseau asserts that these are matters "to which the great legislator attends *in*

---

[5] See *GM* II-2: 180-82: in this earlier discussion of the legislator, Rousseau spends a full page and a half reasserting the principle of popular sovereignty.

secret while *appearing* to limit himself to . . . particular regulations" (*SC* II-12: 77, emphasis added). Again, Rousseau points out approvingly that when the lawgiver Servius divided up the Roman voting population so as greatly to weaken the influence of the large lower class, he cleverly disguised his intentions. "In order that the people would have less understanding of the consequences of this last division, Servius pretended to give it a military appearance" (*SC* IV-4: 115). More generally, perhaps we should not be surprised that a great legislator engaged in the project of "changing human nature" will find it necessary occasionally to deceive men.

But what *is* genuinely surprising is that Rousseau presents this course of action as perfectly compatible with—indeed, as the great means for pre-serving—the principle of popular sovereignty. It is through the legislator's deceit, Rousseau states admiringly, that the people are induced to "obey *with freedom* and bear with docility the yoke of public felicity" (*SC* II-7: 69, emphasis added). For some reason Rousseau is willing to claim that so long as the people actually consent to the laws, even though they have been tricked into doing so, they remain free and sovereign.

The chapter on the legislator has made clear how Rousseau expects the two seemingly opposite sides of his thought to be combined. The legal right of sovereignty will belong to the people alone, and their consent will be the sole source of legitimate authority; but the legislator, without ever chal-lenging the principle of popular sovereignty or asserting a title to rule in his own right, will exercise an *indirect* power by manipulating the people as they exercise their direct power.

If it is not yet apparent *why* Rousseau desires the state to function in this strange manner, it would be difficult to deny *that* he desires it—at least at the state's founding. But what about afterwards? With this question we return to the examination of the executive.

The Active Executive

Perhaps the legislator's task could be completed once and for all at the state's founding in the case of a very small, primitive, and isolated people. Thereafter, the Government would have nothing more to do than enforce the laws. The sovereign people would oversee the executive and add new laws if some minor issue of policy should arise, and the egalitarian mech-anism of the state would coast along easily without any further need for the sort of human superiority that first invented it and set it in motion. Where innocence and moderation rule, Rousseau is fond of pointing out, every-thing becomes simple: "Good public mores replace the genius of leaders. And the longer virtue reigns, the less necessary are talents" (*PE*, 218; see *SC* IV-1: 108).

But in less primitive or idyllic circumstances, the state will not run forever on the order and wisdom at its beginning, and the need for superior talents will remain as an ongoing feature of the state. Order is not natural and must constantly be renewed—that is the master fact of Rousseauian politics. Hence, there must be continuously present in the state, if not another legislator, at least genuine statesmen, a man or group of superior wisdom who can understand and restore the spirit of the original founding.[6] This continuous need for order-creating wisdom is what gives rise to the "other side" of Rousseau's account of the Government, to what we may call the "active executive."

There is considerable evidence showing that Rousseau intends the executive to have, on an informal and unofficial level, a more active, elitist, manipulative role in the state. Consider, first, the powers that the Governmental body will have. As we have seen, Rousseau gives it not only the executive power but also a part of the legislative power (without calling it that): the power of convening the assembly and of legislative initiative. From this fact alone it is obvious that the Government will not simply execute the sovereign's laws as its mere agent but will have an enormous power to influence or manipulate the outcome of the sovereign assembly.[7]

Rousseau also points to this more active role in describing the specific qualities or virtues that an executive body must have to carry out its functions in the state. On the official level, the "subordinate" Government, having no role other than enforcing the laws, need have no virtues other than force and obedience to the sovereign's will. But when Rousseau turns, in the particular chapters on democracy, aristocracy, and monarchy, to a detailed evaluation of the three forms of Government, he actually speaks about much more than number and force. He puts the greatest emphasis, in fact, on the quality of wisdom, which suggests that this power is meant to play a more active, legislator-like role in the state. The suggestion is greatly strengthened when, in these few chapters on the Government, just as in those on the legislator, Rousseau suddenly reintroduces the fact of human inequality and proclaims its crucial political importance, which he had all but denied earlier, in his discussion of sovereignty. Whereas in the beginning of the *Social Contract* he

---

[6] See Masters (1968) p. 357: "Since the need for innovation in the laws is ever present, the problem of the founding is thus merely the problem of all government in its most radical form."

[7] In his admiring account of Rome in the *Social Contract*, Rousseau indicates that the senate exercised its salutary power over the convening of assemblies by means of religious deceit—by manipulating the auguries, which were required to be favorable before an assembly could be legitimately convened (IV-4: 117). He also mentions other tricks that, especially in Rome's decline, were employed to control the people: "Sometimes miracles were invented; but this means which could fool the people, could not fool those who governed it. Sometimes an assembly was convoked suddenly, before the candidates had time to arrange their intrigues. Sometimes an entire session was consumed by talk, when it was seen that the people was won over and ready to make a bad choice" (IV-4: 119-20).

makes his famous proclamation that all men are born free and equal, here, in the context of the executive, he actually goes so far as to speak of "those men who are born to govern"! (*SC* III-6: 89).

Moreover, earlier he had emphasized that different forms of Government are best for different sized states, but here he adds that elective aristocracy is the best simply. It is best because "there is more wisdom in a senate" and because "it is the best and most natural order for the wisest to govern the multitude, as long as it is certain that they govern for its benefit and not for their own" (*SC* III-6: 90, III-5: 86). Thus, the specific qualities Rousseau attributes to the well-ordered executive—wisdom and natural superiority—no less than the powers he gives it suggest a more active, guiding role for it in the state.

To get to the bottom of this question, however, we should examine Rousseau's explicit, thematic discussion of the Government's proper role in the state. Strangely, no such discussion occurs in the *Social Contract*, perhaps because Rousseau already undertook it in the earlier *Discourse on Political Economy*, a work wholly devoted to this subject.[8] All that is said in the *Social Contract* of the proper function of the executive is this: "What is the government then? An intermediate body . . . charged with the execution of the laws and the maintenance of civil as well as political freedom" (*SC* III-1: 78). The *Political Economy* makes exactly the same point, but then explains in detail what these simple sounding tasks really involve.

Precisely what does it mean to "enforce the laws"? Due to the natural intractability of man, Rousseau believes, one can never gain hold of men through so crude and external a means as the use or threat of punishment. "Anyone who manages to defy remorse will not long delay in defying corporal punishment . . . .whatever precautions are taken, those who are only waiting for impunity to do evil, will hardly lack means of eluding the law or escaping a penalty" (*PE*, 217). "If you want the laws to be obeyed," Rousseau concludes, you must "make them beloved" (*PE*, 216-17). There is no other way. When Rousseau charges the Government with the seemingly simple role of enforcing the laws, then, he does not have anything very simple in mind.

> Although the government is not the master of the law [only the sovereign people is], it is no small thing to be its guarantor and to dispose of a thousand ways of *making it beloved*. The talent of reigning consists of nothing else. . . . An imbecile who is obeyed can, like anyone else, punish crimes. The true statesman knows how to prevent them. He extends his respectable dominion *over wills* even more than over actions. . . . It is certain . . . that the greatest

---

[8] This work declares its subject matter as follows: "I urge my readers also to distinguish carefully *public economy*, about which I am to speak, and which I shall call *government*, from the supreme authority, which I call *sovereignty*" (p. 211, emphasis in the original).

talent of leaders is to *disguise their power* to make it less odious, and
to manage the State so peacefully that it *seems* to have no need for
managers. (*PE*, 215, emphasis added)

As this remarkable passage makes clear, the executive power will be far
more than a passive agent of the people's will and far more than a
mere police force and judicial system, punishing crimes. It will—and, on
Rousseau's principles, it must—engage in what might be called active,
positive enforcement. Like the legislator, it will endeavor to gain a "dominion over wills" to mold them to a love of the laws.

This passage recalls the chapter on the legislator also in that right in the
very act of urging the executive to mold and manipulate the people,
Rousseau reiterates the principle of popular sovereignty, as if to reassure
his puzzled readers that, however things may appear, he does not mean to
renounce it. "The government is not the master of the law": the executive
power must scrupulously respect the people's legal sovereignty. But the
talented executive disposes of a thousand means of disguising his power so
as to control the people indirectly and unofficially. The executive will
manipulate the people while obeying them.

Lest there be any lingering uncertainty on these points Rousseau restates
them in even stronger terms. If "enforce the laws" means "make them
beloved," then the true mission of the executive power, as Rousseau now
declares, is to "make virtue reign" (*PE*, 217). But that was precisely the
legislator's central task, which, since virtue is an antinatural condition
tending to decay, can never be completed.

> The government will have difficulty making itself obeyed if it limits
> itself to obedience. If it is good to know how to use men as they are,
> it is better still to make them what one needs them to be. The most
> absolute authority is that which penetrates to the inner man and is
> exerted no less on his will than on his actions. It is certain that the
> people are in the long run what the government makes them.
> Warriors, citizens, men when it so pleases; mob and rabble when it
> wishes. And every prince who scorns his subjects dishonors himself
> by showing that he did not know how to make them worthy. (*PE*, 216)[9]

In this passage, the mission of the Government and of the legislator are all
but indistinguishable. And here, as in the passage above, Rousseau is only
stating what follows necessarily from his principles. To enforce the laws
among naturally intractable men, and to maintain the strength of an artifi-

---

[9] In order to encourage the executive to mold the people, Rousseau seems here to exaggerate considerably their capacity for doing so. In the *Social Contract*, he explains that even
the great legislator himself cannot make the people into "Warriors, citizens, men when it so
pleases" but only under certain very demanding and rare historical conditions (*SC* II-8, 9, 10:
70-75). The *Political Economy* exaggerates the capabilities of the executive just as the *Social
Contract* exaggerates those of the sovereign majority.

cial and ever decaying virtue, the executive must carry on the wise, manipulative role of the great legislator.

Thus, there is indeed a massive contradiction presiding over Rousseau's political thought. In his official "principles of political right," he indignantly rejects all supposed natural titles to rule based on superior merit or wisdom and founds the state on the egalitarian principle of consent or popular sovereignty. But in his "maxims of politics," Rousseau takes a strongly elitist view, emphasizing the state's absolute need for men of superior wisdom, and calling upon such men to guide and control the people. Rousseau is obviously conscious of this division and seems to believe that the two opposite sides are both correct and must be brought together if a well-ordered state is to be formed. And they can be brought together, he implies, so long as the superior men—the legislator and the executive—never disobey or usurp the legal right of sovereignty, which belongs inalienably to the people, but undertake to mold the people through informal, indirect, or secret means.

Further evidence that Rousseau desires the state to function in this manner will emerge shortly. But let us turn to the question of *why* he desires it.

Consent and Wisdom

It may help to put the question in perspective. That Rousseau's political thought should revolve around the problem of reconciling the egalitarian principle of consent and the elitist principle of wisdom is hardly surprising. Virtually all premodern thinkers regarded the reconciliation of these rival principles as *the* fundamental political problem. For example, Plato, in the *Republic*, begins his political analysis by absolutizing the principle of reason and calling for the unlimited rule of the wise man. But he shows by means of this very discussion that such a scheme is utopian and that he too must acknowledge an "other side" to things. The people cannot be expected to obey without some measure of consent or self-rule, because, being unwise, they cannot see the value of the wise man's commands or tell him apart from all the false claimants to wisdom, and because, rationally or irrationally, they desire freedom for its own sake. Therefore, the consideration of pure merit or wisdom must be mixed with the different and contradictory consideration of consent, freedom, egalitarian popular sovereignty. This fundamental dualism, ultimately reflecting the dualism of mind and body or reason and inclination, defines the political problem for Plato. How is one to reconcile the authority of reason and of one's own will, the claim of the good and of the self, the value of rational order and of subjective freedom, the need for wise rule and for self-rule?[10]

If this issue's centrality is no longer so obvious to us that is because the modern liberal state, which has forsworn the direct effort to lead men to moral wisdom, has let go of one pole of the contradiction and thus reduced the political problem to the tension within freedom itself: the freedom of each needs to be reconciled, not with the demands of wisdom, but only with the equal freedom of others. Today, this formula—freedom versus "authority"—is almost universally accepted as the central issue of politics and the guiding question of social thought. But Rousseau, whose state requires wise institutions capable of transforming human nature, returns to something like the larger classical view. Thus, the seemingly idiosyncratic fact we are trying to explain, that his thought contains a systematic tension between two different and opposing "sides," expresses a contradiction not in Rousseau but, as it were, in the nature of things. In struggling to reconcile the eternal rivals of wisdom and consent, he is doing nothing other than addressing the political problem in its most classic and comprehensive form.

That being said, however, there is also something radically new in Rousseau, both in the way he *speaks* about this classic problem and in the way he *solves* it. He does not speak about the problem in a single, open, thematic discussion, but, strangely, makes his case for each element separately and without explaining its relation to its opposite. That is why his writings appear contradictory and not merely complex. In other words, his thought takes the form not of a single presentation of a two-sided issue, but rather of two different, unreconciled presentations, two contradictory "sides."

And the solution he proposes is unique in just the same way. The classical solution is to reconcile the two rivals openly through a "mixed regime," in which both principles receive a share of public authority and of official recognition and respect. In Rousseau's solution, by contrast, the public title of wisdom is completely rejected and all official respect and legitimacy is given exclusively to the principle of consent; but at the same time, wisdom, which is indispensable to the state, is quietly urged to exercise a vast indirect power, through the covert manipulation of the single official authority, the popular will. Granted that Rousseau is confronting the classic problem of wisdom and consent, the question is: why do both his discussion and his solution take this curious, two-sided form?

Wisdom and Indirect Rule

The answer involves four distinct but interrelated reasons, all of which simply build upon the arguments Rousseau used in rejecting natural rule and natural law, and in establishing the sovereignty of the general will.

First, wise statesmen, as enlightened and patriotic as they may be, are

---

[10] See Plato *Republic* 487b-496a; *Laws* 690a-e, 693d-694c. Aristotle *Politics* 1270b20, 1296b15, 1309b15. Strauss (1953) pp. 140-42.

nevertheless human beings, and their wills naturally tend to stray in the direction of their own benefit. Therefore, as much as the state may need their guidance, it cannot acknowledge their title to rule or give them official sovereignty, for such direct power would lead to exploitation. But if these superior men are concentrated in the Government, as they will be in a well-ordered elective aristocracy, then through their example, their persuasion, their leadership, and, when necessary, their covert manipulation, they can exercise a strong influence over the sovereign people without their ever attaining a degree of power that would be corrupting and dangerous. And to make sure that even this indirect, manipulative influence—at which Governments become extremely adept—does not give the executive too much power, Rousseau compensates by weighting the formal, official powers heavily in the sovereign's favor (as we saw in the previous chapter). Thus, Rousseau's desire to prevent exploitation and to maintain a balance of powers is the first cause of the curious arrangement we are examining—a realistic balance maintained between the near-total public rights of the sovereign legislative assembly and the unofficial, manipulative powers of the wise executive.

Second, wisdom can have no natural title to rule because rationality or truth has no natural support, being both insufficiently known and enforced. Indeed, wherever a right to rule of wisdom or natural law has in fact been acknowledged the inevitable result has been to institutionalize sophistry and subversion by ambitious ideologues. If this age-old evil is to be avoided and political authority to be placed at last on a firm basis, impervious to ideological assault, then all such unsupported transcendent standards must finally be swept away in favor of something clearly promulgated and enforced—the commands of a sovereign will. For the sake of *juridical stability*, then, public authority must be based on will and not rationality, on consent and not wisdom.

But here is the great irony that pushes Rousseau's thought in contradictory directions: the very same fact that makes it impossible for wisdom to rule openly—the weakness of men's reason—makes it all the more imperative for wisdom to guide men. Thus, it must find some other, less destabilizing means of doing so—indirect rule. The wise elite, knowing that its rule is problematic for the same reason that it is indispensable, will not attempt to rule openly and in its own, always uncertain name; but rather, like a "power behind the throne," it will seek to rule indirectly by influencing the will of the official sovereign.

Third, wisdom cannot rule in its own name because it is incapable of providing not only a stable juridical basis for the state, as we have just seen, but also a firm *psychological* foundation, a genuine and effective social bond. Since men are naturally selfish and intractable—untrustworthy and untrusting—the only will that in practice they will ever truly obey is the general will. A genuine state cannot be the open rule of some over others but only of all over each. Therefore, any effort by the wise few to rule over the rest would necessarily be ineffectual and self-defeating. Masters are slaves. But again, the guidance of wisdom is made all the more necessary by the condition—men's natural unfitness for political order—that makes it so problematic. Therefore, the wise elite should acknowledge, indeed actively promote, the official sovereignty of the popular will—which it knows to be the only source of genuine social cohesion—and it must content itself with manipulating this will from behind the scenes.[11]

The last of Rousseau's reasons for requiring wisdom to rule indirectly is in a sense his most fundamental, following as it does directly from the principle of natural goodness. If the wise should attempt to exercise formal public authority, if they should expel the principle of consent, as Plato would have them do, to rule and command others in the name of wisdom, then they would create a condition of personal dependence, the source of all injustice and disunity of soul. Thus, the wise man must never attempt to help the people, who are greatly in need of his guidance, by directly commanding them, by openly confronting their wills with his own will, his wise and well-intentioned but nevertheless *personal* will. To have a salutary effect, he must work behind their backs, secretly molding the will without ever openly confronting it. He must leave them the experience of freedom, the feeling of only obeying themselves, so as not to corrupt them through his very efforts to help. In short, because of the central importance of personal dependence, the first act of genuine wisdom is always to hide one's power.

To summarize in somewhat more general terms, Rousseau's most fundamental principles reveal to him men's original solitude and goodness and their tragic corruption, their blind, helpless victimization, by the accidental forces of history. It is hardly surprising, then, that Rousseau has an "authoritarian side" (perhaps even stronger than Plato's) depicting human beings as helpless and lost when abandoned to themselves and as desperately in need of salvation through the intervention of some wise and transforming authority.

But the same modern, individualistic principles that reveal men's need for this transforming rational authority also reveal the unnaturalness both of rationality and of authority, so that the traditional solution of the rule of wisdom contains for Rousseau a new and exquisite dilemma. How can a wise man use his authority to save men if precisely what their salvation

---

[11] In his discussion of the legislator in the *Geneva Manuscript* (II-2: 182), Rousseau explains: "Since the general will is the continuing bond of the body politic, the legislator is never allowed . . . to prescribe anything to private individuals that has not first received the sanction of general consent, for fear of destroying from the outset the very essence of the thing one wants to form, and of breaking the social tie in trying to strengthen the society." The legislator must get the people's consent, although he can trick them into it, because the appearance of freedom and self-rule is the social bond.

requires is rejection of wisdom's dangerous title to rule, which might corrupt the wise and which, at any rate, is always stolen and abused by the unwise; if it requires a genuine and heartfelt social cohesion that is only possible through *self*-rule; and if it requires, above all, freedom from every form of personal authority and dependence? In short, how can a wise authority cure men if the essence of the cure is freedom and self-rule? This is the ironic new twist that Rousseau's principles give to the classic problem of wisdom *versus* consent.

The bizarre and ingenious political arrangement outlined in Rousseau's works is his solution—probably the only possible solution—to the political problem defined in these terms. In his formal "principles of political right" (with its characteristic "exaggerations"), he wholly expels the consideration of wisdom and builds the state on the exclusive basis of consent or popular sovereignty, in order to give the state the most unchallengeable juridical structure, to give it the strongest psychological foundation, and to free men from every experience or overt relation of personal dependence; but on the "other side," particularly in his "maxims of politics," he arranges for the secret return of wisdom—its indirect rule through the unofficial, manipulative role of the legislator and of the "active executive."[12]

Indirect Rule in Rousseau's Other Writings

The foregoing analysis carries a certain look of implausibility, even if it does seem to be supported by a number of striking passages, to be entailed by Rousseau's principles, and to be required in order to explain what is otherwise a massive contradiction at the heart of his thought. Can it be, one wants to ask, that Rousseau's political thought, which seems to be so passionately direct, is in reality so complex and artful, that this apostle of sincerity is really recommending a kind of duplicity, and that the great champion of freedom is calling for some measure of secret manipulation of the people? The briefest glance at some of Rousseau's other works suffices to remove such misgivings.

Throughout Rousseau's various writings one meets the same fundamental dilemma we have identified in his political works: men are desperately in need of the guidance of a wise and benevolent authority, but, being naturally "individuals," they are also unresponsive to, rebel-

---

[12]Although the general phenomenon of indirect rule—secret manipulation, the power behind the throne, the grey eminence, puppet government, and so forth—is probably as old as politics itself, it only becomes recognized as an essential element of the state and thus elevated to a primary theme of political philosophy starting with Machiavelli, with his well-advertised intention to describe politics the way it is. For the all-important role of this concept in Machiavelli, Hobbes, and all theorists of "representative government," see the brilliant series of studies by Harvey C. Mansfield, Jr. (1968, 1971, 1979).

lious against, and corrupted by any attempt at direct guidance or control. And everywhere in Rousseau one finds the same general response to this problem: secret or indirect rule. To be sure, as Lester Crocker puts it, "Rousseau's motto was 'To risk one's life for the truth'; but one of those truths was the usefulness, the necessity, of duplicity and 'illusion.'"[13]

In the *Nouvelle Héloïse*, for example, the godlike Wolmar rules over a model estate, Clarens, and his rule is effective and salutary because it is hidden, leaving everyone with the feeling of freedom. In ruling servants, for instance, there is usually need for "constraint and hindrance"; but "the whole art of the master," as Wolmar is said to practice it, "is to hide this hindrance under the veil of pleasure or interest so that they believe they will everything one requires them to do" (*NH* IV-10: 453).[14] The primary focus of the novel, of course, is Wolmar's rule over and effort to cure the lovesick St. Preux. "How does Wolmar proceed?" writes Judith Shklar. "He never preaches, never reproaches, never punishes. What he does is to arrange situations which force St. Preux to face reality.... These situations are created with infinite care, the environment being structured in advance. Often it is done against the wishes of Julie and St. Preux. . . . Sometimes it involves deception." In short, in everything Wolmar undertakes, he acts indirectly: his "guiding hand is felt but never seen. It is invisible, yet omnipresent."[15]

This same description could be applied with equal justice to the tutor in *Emile*, the third of Rousseau's great authority figures. What, after all, is the great innovation and central technique of Rousseau's whole educational project? It is precisely the idea of indirect rule. The wise tutor will abdicate all "authority," hide his will, and control his pupil through secret manipulation. Never commanding or forbidding anything, never

[13] Crocker (1968), p. 14. Crocker gives an excellent brief survey of Rousseau's major works, showing in each one the use of "his favorite technique of *la main cachée*, or the hidden hand, which strangely, his commentators seem scarcely to have noticed." An exception to this last observation is made, correctly, for Burgelin, who (in Crocker's words) "speaks of the universality, in Rousseau's character and thought, of dissimulation, trickery, lying, duplicity, ruse, illusion" (p. 38 n. 26). See Burgelin (1952) pp. 298-303, 557-58. See also Starobinski (1971) pp. 122-26; Blum (1986) pp. 66-68; and especially Shklar (1972) pp. 343, 352-53, 354, 360-61.

[14] Commenting on this passage, Starobinski (1971, pp. 125-26) writes: "This enemy of opinion, masks and veils nevertheless accepts that the master should hide the constraint he exercises.... The servant is treated here as Emile will be by his tutor: the man of reason imposes his will through artifice, and disguises the violence he does, thus leaving the pupil or servant the feeling of acting freely." The passage is also strikingly similar to one we have seen in the *Political Economy*: "It is certain . . . that the greatest talent of leaders is to disguise their power to make it less odious, and to manage the State so peacefully that it seems to have no need for managers" (p. 215).

[15] Shklar (1972) pp. 352; 354.

confronting the child's will or telling him what to do, the tutor will keep the child free of all personal dependence, free to be himself and follow wholeheartedly his own inner will. But behind the scenes, the tutor will shape and arrange the whole environment so as to control his pupil's every action and mold the content of this inner will. As Rousseau advises the tutor:

> Let [the pupil] always believe he is the master, and let it always be you who are. There is no subjection so perfect as that which keeps the appearance of freedom. Thus the will itself is made captive. . . . Do you not dispose, with respect to him, of everything which surrounds him? Are you not the master of affecting him as you please? Are not his labors, his games, his pleasures, his pains, all in your hands without his knowing it? Doubtless he ought to do only what he wants; but he ought to want only what you want him to do. (*Emile* II: 120)[16]

The tutor's method is exactly the same as Wolmar's and the legislator's. All rule indirectly, through a covert manipulation that maintains the appearance of freedom.

From this brief discussion it should be clear that in suggesting that "indirect rule" plays an important part in Rousseau's political scheme we are not forcing on him some alien theory constructed to fill a gap in the argument. Rather we are revealing in his political thought an idea that is found throughout his writings, that constitutes one of the most striking and characteristic features of his thinking, and that follows with clear necessity from his most basic principles.

One could, however, raise the following objection. These parallels with Rousseau's other writings do indeed strengthen the suggestion that the great legislator, like the tutor and Wolmar, will trick the people and rule them indirectly, yet this was never particularly in doubt. But the truly controversial claim—that the officially subordinate executive power is also meant to exercise some degree of indirect rule—is actually rendered less plausible by the parallel with *Emile*. For does not the tutor's total control of Emile as a child have the precise purpose of making him genuinely, and not just apparently, free as an adult? So similarly, shouldn't one suspect that the legislator's control of the people in its "youth" is meant to prepare it for genuine freedom and sovereignty later, without any ongoing indirect rule by the executive?

One could simply reply to this objection that after the initial, youthful stage, the parallelism between Emile and the people breaks down,

[16]Again, note the similarity to the *Political Economy* (p. 216): "The most absolute authority is that which penetrates to the inner man and is exerted no less on his will than on his actions."

that, whatever may be the case in *Emile*, the *Discourse on Political Economy* leaves very little doubt that Rousseau wants the Government to continue the legislator's role of manipulating the people, if in a more limited way. But in fact the parallelism does not break down, because the adult Emile will not live alone and free, but rather in partnership with Sophie, his wife, who, just like the executive, is meant to continue the tutor's manipulative role, if in a more limited way. As the tutor tells Emile on the day following his wedding, "a man needs advice and guidance throughout his life. Up to now I have done my best to fulfill this duty toward you. Here my long task ends, and another's begins. Today I abdicate the authority you confided to me, and *Sophie is your governor* from now on" (*Emile* V: 479, emphasis added). The correspondence between Emile and the people extends beyond the immature stage of tutor and legislator, to blossom into a striking parallel between Rousseau's theory of the family and his doctrine of the state.

Rousseau's discussion of the family turns out to contain exactly the same "contradiction" as his political theory. In certain places he declares that the husband (like the sovereign people) should have the supreme power in every respect and that the wife (like the Government) should be wholly subordinate. If the family is to be stable and well ordered, he argues, then, like the state, it must have a single sovereign and that sovereign must be the man because he is physically stronger, because he, unlike the woman, needs assurances that his children are his own, and because man's pride and eroticism are such that he can truly love only where he feels he is in control (again, like the people) (*PE*, 210; *Emile* V: 357-60, 370, 382).[17] Hence, Rousseau flatly asserts, "it is part of the order of nature that the woman obey the man" (*Emile* V: 407). At this point, Rousseau seems to be as extreme a partisan of male supremacy as of legislative supremacy.

But there is a contradictory "other side" to Rousseau's discussion, a doctrine of the "active executive," as it were, which maintains that women should rule men, that "Sophie is your governor from now on." Certainly women need some power in the family, he acknowledges, so as not to be wholly enslaved to men. Moreover, since women have a kind of practical intelligence that men lack, since they have a strong interest in the virtue of their husbands, and since "women are the natural judges of men's merit," their rule has a naturally salutary effect (*Emile* V: 390; see V: 360-61, 371, 377, 387, 433, 479). Rousseau now asserts that women are "that half of the human race which governs the other," and

---

[17]On this whole issue see the excellent study by Schwartz (1984).

that "this ascendancy of women. . . is a gift given them by nature for the happiness of the human race" (*FD*, 52n). The great defender of male sovereignty somehow also calls for the rule of women over men.

The two contradictory sides can be reconciled through the same means used in the state, the combination of direct and indirect rule. And here Rousseau makes this completely explicit. Having just asserted that the man should rule, he adds:

> I expect that many readers, remembering that I ascribe to woman a natural talent for governing man, will accuse me of a contradiction here. They will, however, be mistaken. There is quite a difference between arrogating to oneself the *right to command* and *governing him who commands*. . . . She ought to reign in the home *as a minister* [i.e., the executive power] does in a state—by getting herself commanded to do what she wants to do. (*Emile* V: 408, emphasis added)

This passage says it all. Rousseau states as clearly as one could wish how the seeming contradictions are to be resolved, how the family and also the state will really function. The man (or the people) will possess the legal sovereign power, the "right to command," and on this official level the woman (or the executive) is subordinate and must simply obey. But formal sovereign power is not everything, and in vehemently insisting that this power must belong exclusively to the man (the people), Rousseau by no means intends to exclude the woman (Government) from every form of dominion. Unofficially and indirectly, the latter will "reign" by dint of "governing him who commands." While publicly affirming the man's right to command and her duty to obey, she will use her various feminine wiles to manipulate him into commanding what she desires.[18]

Rousseau does not imagine or desire, it should be added, that the woman will completely control the man. "It is by means of this superiority in talent" for manipulation, he contends, that the woman "keeps herself *his equal* and that she governs him while obeying him." Thus, "in the harmony which reigns between them . . . each follows the prompting of the other; each obeys, and both are masters" (*Emile* V: 371, emphasis added; V: 377). The well-ordered family, like the well-ordered state, will be constituted by a relation of rough equality, an artful balance of powers struck between the public, official sovereignty of the

---

[18] *Emile* V: 387. See Schwartz (1984) pp. 43-45. Women, according to Rousseau, are natural masters of indirect rule. "Guile is a natural talent with the fair sex," a talent which (we should no longer be surprised to discover) Rousseau thinks "should be cultivated like the others" (*Emile* V: 370).

man (the people) and the informal, manipulative power of the woman (the executive).[19]

Summary: Rousseau's Politics

The question that naturally agitates the practical-minded reader after working his way through the *Social Contract* is this: beneath all these legalistic distinctions and abstract doctrines, who is really going to rule in this state? Most readers conclude that Rousseau is a radical democrat seeking to put control in the hands of the people. Others have objected that, on examination, the people's power does not really seem to amount to much and that, strangely, Rousseau appears to allow a Governmental elite to have the real power. Much dispute has thus been generated by this simple question, and for a good reason. The answer is that *no one* will "really rule." Rousseau's state is precisely meant to be a system, a *balance of powers*, in which no part "rules" in the full, traditional sense. In the language of *Emile*, "each obeys, and both are masters." The phenomenon of "balance" is at the center of Rousseau's practical politics.

The importance of this concept has been obscured and almost universally denied, paradoxically, because of the very radicalness with which Rousseau embraces it. He appears simply to reject the liberal constitutional tradition with its realistic mistrust of absolute power and static forms, and its concern for a

---

[19] This equality between the people and the Governmental elite is, of course, a very inegalitarian arrangement. Still, what is surprising about this whole interpretation is not that it suddenly reintroduces inequality into what had seemed an egalitarian theory, for we have seen all along that, notwithstanding an increased humanitarianism, Rousseau is a fundamentally inegalitarian thinker, recognizing vast differences among men in intellect and character, who embraces strict equality only due to certain practical necessities—which, as we now see, he has found an ingenious method of getting around.

What is surprising is rather that it contradicts Rousseau's emphatic claim that the people have self-rule and free will—political and moral freedom. Rousseau clearly thinks that the people must believe in their own freedom if they are to be patriotic and virtuous, but in light of the manipulative role that he urges upon the legislator and executive, one is driven to conclude that he considers this belief to be more or less a salutary illusion. This is one more reason why it seems impossible to make sense of Rousseau on a Kantian interpretation.

Indeed, the passage in the *Second Discourse* (pp. 113-15) where Rousseau makes his famous assertion that freedom is man's specific difference must be reexamined in this light. For here again we find the "two sides." It seems that man has free will, Rousseau asserts, but since this is very unclear, he will only insist that man is free in a second sense, extreme malleability. But the second sense contradicts the first, showing men to be mere creatures of their environment. Man has fallen from his original goodness and become evil, the *Discourse* goes on to argue, *not* through the conscious abuse of free will (which was the biblical view) but due to accidental changes in the environment which mutilated man's malleable nature without his knowing it. Indeed, the whole point of the doctrine of natural goodness is that men are innocent victims of the contradiction of society. They are good precisely because they are not free. And therefore men can be saved only from the outside—by a legislator who, believing in human malleability, remakes men into virtuous citizens who believe in free will.

dynamic balance of forces; but, once again, he rejects liberalism only by pushing its own insights to an extreme. The liberal tradition is still not realistic enough in thinking the state's competing political forces can be kept in equilibrium by balancing their formal, legal rights. Rousseau rejects the lingering "formalism" that still hopes to impose a balance *from above* through constitutional laws, whether inscribed in philosophical treatises or on parchment. This is to ignore all the informal, manipulative means through which, in real life politics, men get outside and beyond their legally defined powers. Rousseau, remaining closer to the level of immanent forces, recognizes these informal powers, sees in particular that they always tip the balance toward the executive, and thus compensates by giving the great preponderance of visible, legal rights to the sovereign people—although creating thereby the appearance of being opposed to the system of balance. Rousseau's system is less visible because more realistic. It balances not only the two *functions* of government—legislation and execution—but also the two *kinds* of rule: direct and indirect, public authority and private manipulation.

But this transformation of the theory of balance opens the way, in turn, to a still more radical change. It shows how the balance of powers may be turned into a means not only for preventing the concentration and abuse of power—its standard purpose—but also for solving in a new way the fundamental problem of *consent versus wisdom*. The classic solution, the "mixed regime," which publicly recognizes and reconciles the two rival principles, openly dividing political authority between them, is not workable in Rousseau's individualistic political science. The public claims of wisdom must be wholly repudiated, and those of consent absolutized, if one is to produce unchallengeable legitimacy, real social solidarity, and freedom from personal dependence among individuals who are by nature arational, solitary, and selfish. And yet just because the state is so unnatural, it absolutely requires the rule of wisdom, without which the will of the popular assembly itself is likely to be both unenlightened and corrupt. Rousseau's solution is to bestow on wise statesmen the official rights, not indeed of wisdom but of "execution," which gives them great opportunities for indirect rule. In this way he combines and balances the two necessary principles, and yet without a public reconciliation, without officially recognizing the claims of wisdom or compromising the indispensable absolute sovereignty of the general will. In sum, it is in order to combine wisdom and consent covertly, as well as to create an equilibrium of forces realistically, that Rousseau establishes his unique, "invisible" balance of powers between formal legislative authority and indirect executive manipulation.

Finally, this understanding of Rousseau's state also explains the contradictory, two-sided character of his writings. Rousseau's state solves the problem of consent and wisdom not through an open reconciliation, as in the mixed regime, but through a covert combination of contradictory principles. Therefore, in his writings about the state Rousseau cannot present a single discussion describing the proper way of adjudicating and mixing the two principles (as found, say, in Aristotle's *Politics*) but must simply leave it at two essentially contradictory and unreconciled discussions.

More generally, the same political premises that compel Rousseau to set up his state as a balance between two separate and oppositely partisan powers also compel him to write about the state in the form of two separate and oppositely partisan "sides." Rousseau's writings, after all, are a form of political action through which he seeks a kind of rule. Therefore he must apply his new science of politics to his own activity. His writings must be so constructed as to function properly within the world as they themselves describe it. Specifically, Rousseau cannot hope, through any doctrine, to "lead," to impose rational forms from above, to preach his ideal constitution to the world and expect it to follow. A philosopher may rise above partisanship in his thinking, but every published doctrine, if it isn't ignored, will be seized upon as a weapon by some partisan interest (as Rousseau explained to the preachers of natural law). Thus, if a philosopher has an ideal he wishes to promote, his writings must not attempt to command it from on high, nor even to describe it, but rather to *produce* it—by identifying, appealing to, and manipulating the partisan forces immanent in the world. It must give to each side just the right ideological ammunition and encouragement so that the desired order results as an outcome, without the partisan actors ever necessarily understanding or intending it. That is just what Rousseau is doing: his state is a balance between two sides, and his writings are designed, not to describe that balance (which they rather obscure), but to produce it by addressing a different message to each side.

The first side, constituted by the "principles of political right," takes to an extreme virtually every partisan claim that the people or its defenders ever made for it. Consider Rousseau's innovations: regarding the necessity for popular sovereignty (all else is slavery), regarding its form (the people must rule directly; representation is slavery), regarding its extent (the people's will is absolute, the source of all morality, and unlimited by natural law, constitutional law, or private rights), regarding its benefits (the popular will is infallible; it leaves one as free as before; one only obeys oneself), and regarding its superiority to the executive (a mere agent of the sovereign and deposable at its will; it is the source of all political decline). Through a combination of juridical precision and rhetorical passion, as well as a certain systematic exaggeration, Rousseau calls upon the people as never before to know and defend their sovereign rights.

The second side corresponds more or less to Rousseau's "maxims of politics," which are indicated in the chapters on the legislator, aristocracy, and Roman institutions in the *Social Contract*, but presented fully only in the separate *Discourse on Political Economy*. Here Rousseau gives his partisan advice to the intelligent statesman and executive, emphasizing the necessity of wisdom, the shortsightedness of the people, and the need to manipulate and mold the latter to virtue. Indeed, he systematically exaggerates the executive's power to mold the people and repeatedly blames it (especially the modern executive) for being too passive and unenterprising on this score (*PE*, 216-17). He does repeat his warnings to the Government not to violate the people's public, sovereign rights, but he does so by appealing to its own interests: "Ambitious leaders! . . . Respect freedom, and your power will be increased daily. Never exceed your rights, and soon they will be limitless" (*PE*, 221).

It is Rousseau's hope that the sovereign people, newly aroused and strengthened by his "principles of political right," and the executive power, uniquely enlightened and instructed by his "maxims of politics," will together form a stable and realistic system of balanced power as well as an effective if covert union of consent and wisdom.

13

Rousseau's "Mission" and the Practical Intention of His Writings

In examining the philosophical meaning of Rousseau's doctrines, we have often made use of the claim, without pausing to substantiate it, that they were composed for a practical as well as theoretical purpose. It is pretty obvious, after all, that Rousseau, like other philosophers of the Enlightenment, was eager to be useful to his fellow man. His writings fairly brim with reformist schemes and projects, ranging from the opposition to swaddling and a lifelong campaign to revive maternal breast-feeding, to an effort to calm the fierce conflict then raging between the Church and the *philosophes* (one of the primary purposes, he asserts, of the *Nouvelle Héloïse*; *Confs*. IX: 435-36).[1] Above all, it is clear from Rousseau's *political* writings—which are more openly radical in content, more rigidly doctrinaire in form, and more inflammatory in style than those of any major philosopher before him—that he wrote his books not only to state the truth but to change the world.

We have examined Rousseau's solutions in a general, theoretical sense; it remains to ask what concrete reforms he thought possible in his time and how his various writings were designed to promote them. Although it would be important to raise these questions for any thinker with a practical intention, it is particularly so in the case of Rousseau, who saw himself as having not merely a project but, as it were, a personal "mission." Moreover, his writings turned out in fact to have an immense, perhaps unparalleled, historical effect. It is important, then, to ask whether the effect he produced is the same as the one he intended.

The Philosopher and the World of Practice

No doubt works of moral and political theory—of "practical philosophy"— have always had some practical influence on their readers, but it is generally conceded that, starting in the period of the Renaissance, philosophers began to show a programmatic interest in having a large-scale practical effect, and

---

[1] The novel served this purpose by depicting the mutual love and respect of Julie, a believer, and her husband Wolmar, an atheist.

philosophical treatises began more and more to have the character (if not always the appearance) of political pamphlets or "tracts for the times." It is plausible to suppose that this change resulted largely from a diminished faith in theoretical reason, which, inclining philosophers to doubt the possibility or worth of the detached, contemplative life, turned them back to the world of action and to a greater concern for humanity or glory, or both.[2]

Rousseau greatly extends both the attack on theoretical reason and the resulting desire to benefit humanity, but also brings out the ultimate tension between the two: the doubt of reason renders questionable whether one can know what will benefit mankind. Since reason is unnatural, the more the philosophers develop their minds, the more artificial they make themselves, and the further they move from knowledge of humanity's true nature and good (*SD*, 92). Furthermore, since reason is not independent but a slave of our interests and passions, and since "in the social state the good of one necessarily constitutes the harm of another," it follows that within society men cannot ever escape partisanship and its illusions, cannot ever stop lying and being lied to (*Emile* II: 105n). Rousseau concludes that, ironically, these humanitarian modern philosophers—just because their intellects are so highly developed, and just because they are so eager for practical influence in society—are precisely the last ones able to know or, if they knew, willing to proclaim the elusive truth regarding the good for humanity.

But Rousseau believed himself to be a crucial exception to all this: "I am not made like any other man that exists" (*Confs.* I: 5; *Dialogues* III: 936). A solitary by inclination, a misfit by character, a vagabond and outcast by circumstance, Rousseau felt he was detached from society as perhaps no civilized man had ever been. From this unique perspective, he was able to restore contact for the first time with the lost traces of our true nature, which had been disfigured by centuries of civilization. Moreover, from this withdrawn and lonely position, he was also moved to expand his sentiment of existence into a love of all humanity—a love that was genuine, as distinguished from the hypocritical form proclaimed everywhere in society, because he was above the partisanship and enmity that are inseparable from life within society. Thus, having

---

[2] The article "Philosopher" in the *Encyclopedia* describes this new attitude: "The common run of philosophers who reflect too much, or rather reflect badly, behave in the same manner toward everyone: they flee men, and men avoid them. But our philosopher, who knows how to divide his time between solitude and social intercourse, is full of humanity." "From this it is easy to conclude how far removed the impassive sage of the Stoics is from our philosopher: the philosopher is a man while their sage was only a phantom. They were ashamed of their humanity, he takes pride in his." "Our philosopher does not think that he lives in exile in this world; he does not believe himself to be in enemy territory. . . . He is an *honnête homme* who wishes to please others and to render himself useful" ([1965] pp. 287, 288-89, 286).

found the lost truth of human nature and, by the same means, a true love for humanity, Rousseau was moved to promulgate his truths in a way that would be beneficial to mankind.

Rousseau viewed himself, then, in a manner quite unlike that of all previous philosophers, who tended to believe that their discoveries were in principle accessible to all men, and that their own individuality was more or less irrelevant philosophically. Rousseau believed he was in possession of both truths and motives that were attainable only because of certain accidents of his character and circumstances, historical accidents that might never have occurred and might never occur again. He felt that his character, perspective, and life were, so to speak, a unique and precious human resource that he was called upon to share with mankind. A secular prophet, he was chosen by fate for a special revelation and thus for a special "mission," for if he did not bring this truth to mankind no one else would do so in his place. Hence Rousseau became a man with an official motto: *vitam impendere vero* (dedicate life to truth) and took on "the sad job of telling the truth to men," being "called to this sublime vocation" (*Emile* V: 474; Letter to Perdriau, September 28, 1754).[3] In this way, the modern philosophic orientation, with its characteristic combination of theoretical skepticism and the desire for practical influence, when thought through more radically, became in Rousseau the assumption of a personal "mission."

But ultimately Rousseau's "thinking through" could not stop at this point. His doubt of the naturalness of reason and society finally led him to an opposite, though no less radical conclusion: the best life for man is that of the solitary dreamer, a life in which the expansiveness of the soul is indulged through communion with nature or through idle dreams of perfect fellowship but not through activist humanitarianism.

> The contemplative life disgusts one with action. There is no charm more seductive than that of the fictions of a loving and tender heart which, within the universe that it creates to its liking, expands and extends itself freely, delivered from the harsh fetters that oppress it within this one. . . . All the wearying cares of the active life become insupportable to him and seem superfluous; for why give oneself so many troubles in the distant hope of a success so poor, so uncertain, when one can from this very moment, in a delicious reverie, enjoy at one's ease all the happiness of which ones feels within oneself the power and the need. (*Dialogues* II: 822)

Rousseau's internal critique of modern thought ultimately brings him back,

---

[3] See *d'Alembert*, 131-32n; *Bordes*, 112-15. Rousseau believed himself to be "the only author of my century and of many others who wrote in good faith" (*Beaumont*, 965).

albeit on a subrational level, to the posture of the classical philosopher
with his extreme detachment from society and from the life of action.

In view of this, however, the question necessarily arises why Rousseau in fact spent most of his life not in solitary reverie but in pursuit of
his "mission," why, although his conception of the best life was even more
solitary than, say, Plato's, did he live his own life in a far more activist
manner.[4] This question is made all the more pressing by the extreme danger
necessarily attending his activism; for, in Rousseau's system, the truth can
be seen and proclaimed only from a standpoint of absolute vulnerability.
From his lonely and exposed position outside all human society, supported
by no parties and attacking all of them, Rousseau in a sense invited the
enmity and persecution of all mankind. Thus "what is most difficult in this
enterprise is the courage" (*Beaumont* fragment, 1019; see 1021-22). Given
this theoretical fact, as well as the actual persecution Rousseau experienced, what motivated him to persevere in his mission? Can Rousseau's
own life, and especially the practical uses to which he put his philosophical
system, be explained in terms of that system?

Despite the number and length of Rousseau's autobiographical writings,
his reasons for acting as he did remain rather unclear. He seems to have
been moved by a complex combination of motives which, in addition to the
love of humanity stemming from natural expansiveness mentioned above,
included the love of popular glory and an "intoxication" with virtue.

"The wise man does not chase after riches," Rousseau remarks, "but he
is not insensitive to glory" (*FD*, 58). This passion arises partly from the
natural desire to expand one's existence or to make it immortal, but partly
also from *amour-propre*, which Rousseau had not completely transcended.
It is the noblest and freest expression of *amour-propre* since it liberates one
from the accidental prejudices of one's time in attaching one to what is
enduring because rooted in truth.[5] As Rousseau experienced it, this motive

[4] In perfecting his rational nature, the Platonic philosopher withdraws from political engagement but not from all human society. His philosophic method, dialectics, even makes converse
with other men necessary in some degree. His Rousseauian counterpart, however, fulfills human
nature precisely by returning to complete solitude, which is required also by his philosophic
method of detached introspection. Plato, moreover, was greatly preoccupied with the
various preconditions of and approximations to the philosophic way of life and thus was
led back to some concern for political matters in the very name of philosophy. But Rousseau
could have no parallel motive since his conception of the peak of human perfection, the solitary
dreamer, has essentially no political conditions or expressions. Thus, Rousseau's practical
involvement, while far more extensive than Plato's, is also much harder to understand, since it
involves concern for a political world that is irrelevant or even hostile to the way of life that is
both highest and his own.

[5] *FD*, 33; *Mals.*, 1131, 1145; *Dialogues* II: 822; see Kelly (1987) pp. 191-93. Rousseau was
obviously obsessed with how later generations would judge him and wrote his *Confessions* and
Dialogues for the express purpose (among others) of ensuring his future reputation (*Reveries* I:
4, 7, II: 20; *Dialogues* Preface, 661-64, III: 956; *OC* I: 1186). He also points to glory as a primary
motive of philosophers in general (FD, 58, 63-64; *SD*, 175, 212).

was also closely connected to the love of humanity, for the more one takes human beings seriously, the more one can credit the importance of being remembered or celebrated by them. And it was through his love of humanity, through the unprecedented sincerity and benevolence of his intentions, that Rousseau expected to win such glory.

But the sincere effort to benefit mankind is both difficult and dangerous, and to sustain it Rousseau had to lift himself above the mere, spontaneous "goodness" of his love of humanity to something resembling self-sacrificing "virtue," the third element of his motivation (*Confs.* VIII: 356-57, IX: 416-17). The complex interconnection among Rousseau's three motives, and especially between the passion for virtue and for glory, is described most clearly in a revealing fragment for the *Letter to Beaumont.*

> Certainly I do not believe, nor wish another to believe, that I myself am without passion in speaking to men and without other love than that of the truth. I am eager, on the contrary, that one read at the base of my heart all the pride that animates me. I am eager that one see there all the energy of the most noble passion that can swell the heart of a man of good will. I aspire to glory without doubt; it is, after the good witness of oneself, the most worthy recompense of virtue. But this glory to which I aspire . . . is the only one to which opinion has not given being. . . . All prejudices can change . . . but one has never seen [a people] among whom the zeal for justice was not in esteem and among whom true courage was despised. . . . My own self-interest is to say what is useful to others without any concern for my own utility, and this honor which I will possess alone among the authors of my century will always distinguish me above them all. . . . They will, if you like, be better philosophers or better wits . . . but I, I will be more disinterested in my maxims, more sincere in my sentiments . . . more bold in saying the truth when it is useful to others. . . . [Today] they may win pensions, employments, positions in academies and I will have only injuries and affronts . . . but no matter, my disgraces will honor my courage, [someday] one will see that I did not merit them and that I knew how to endure them. (Pp. 1021-22; see 1019; *Beaumont,* 965-66)

This complex passage indicates that, on the one hand, Rousseau was moved by an enthusiasm for virtue for its own sake. He even implies that without this passion he could not have loved glory in quite the way he did—as something to be merited and not merely attained—nor could he have been psychologically capable of the disinterested intentions from which he expected his renown to come.

Yet, on the other hand, it seems clear that the love of virtue by itself is not a sufficient motive. Being painful and self-sacrificing, virtue is in need of "recompense" and, in the absence of divine rewards, of which no mention is made, glory seems to supply the needed compensation. At times the passage even seems to indicate that Rousseau cherishes virtue as a means to glory. Virtue is the surest means of raising himself above all of his contemporaries, for it is the rarest as well as the best loved of human distinctions. "There is a vulgar for heroes as well as for kings, there is none for virtuous men. And the latter are the only ones who, after lifting themselves above the crowd of the people, cannot fall back into the crowd of their similars" (*OC* III, 1898). We also see on the basis of this combined interest in virtue and glory how Rousseau is able not merely to endure but to welcome his persecution, for it will enhance his popular glory by proving his sincerity, displaying his courage, and covering these virtues with the further luster of martyrdom.

If these three interrelated passions are what moved Rousseau to undertake his practical mission, can one say that they are justifiable or rational motives from the standpoint of his theoretical system? The active love of humanity stemming from natural expansiveness is certainly a rational or healthy passion on Rousseau's principles, but only so long as it does not undermine, as his mission ultimately did, the preservation or repose of the existence one is expanding. The desire for glory is a more questionable motive, based as it is on the unnatural and irrational passion of *amour-propre*. It may be the freest and least distorting form of *amour-propre* but, as Rousseau knows well, it still fosters illusions about the eternity of fame and about the possibility of controlling one's future reputation. It also biases one in the direction of doctrines flattering to human hopes and vanity, and it makes one draw the sentiment of one's existence from the opinions of others rather than from oneself.[6]

Finally, the enthusiasm for virtue, as we have seen, is a most ambiguous phenomenon for Rousseau. It is clearly something indispensable for society as well as for the psychic unity of the citizen, but it requires a painful self-conquest that is justifiable and psychologically possible only on the basis of certain beliefs which Rousseau's system ultimately renders doubtful. The virtuous man must believe that he is free of external control and responsible for his own character and actions, that he also rises above the internal force of instinct and passion to follow pure duty, and that duty is something more important than his happiness or life. Yet Rousseau clearly implies that men are not self-determining and free but creatures of their environment; that virtue is itself a passion;[7] and that duty is binding on us only if it is fundamentally good and conducive to happiness.

Accordingly, Rousseau asserts in the *Dialogues* and *Reveries*, in some contrast to what we have just seen, that he himself has never been genuinely capable of virtue because he was always incapable of real self-conquest. And this "incapacity," he argues, is not only a product of his indolent

---

[6]*SD*, 179; *Hero*, 1265; *Emile* II: 82-83. Consider also what Rousseau refers to as "my old maxim": "The uncertainty of the future has always made me regard projects of long execution as lures for fools" (Confs. IX: 413, IV: 146).

[7]See *Emile* V: 397, 445; *NH* IV-12: 493; *Frags.*, 501.

temperament but is also rational and would be shared by the inhabitants of an "ideal world" that he describes (*Dialogues* I: 668-71, II: 822-25; *Reveries* VI: 77). To be sure, the ideal people, like himself, will love to *dream* about virtue. "Who is there with an imagination more lively who will paint for himself better the divine simulacre [of virtue]? Who is there with a heart more tender who will intoxicate himself more with love for it?" (*Dialogues* II: 824, see I: 670-71). However, they will not act upon these romantic dreams of virtue and heroism because ultimately they do not believe this "divine simulacre" to be real. Indeed, Rousseau is so far from subscribing to the reality or moral necessity of virtue that he repeatedly proclaims himself "the best of men" even while denying that he is virtuous (*Confs.* X: 517; see *Dialogues* III: 952; *Mals.*, 1133). Virtue, like love, is a beautiful illusion which nourishes the romantic imagination of the solitary but does not guide his actions.

Thus, none of the motives that led Rousseau to undertake his mission are fully justifiable on his theoretical principles. One can perhaps see some acknowledgment of this fact in the regrets he expresses for having embarked on his mission. After the "illumination of Vincennes," he recounts, Diderot "exhorted me to develop my ideas and compete for the prize. I did so and from that moment I was lost. All the rest of my life and of my misfortunes were the inevitable effect of that misguided moment" (*Confs.* VIII: 351). The constant theme of Rousseau's autobiographical writings is that the period of his greatest happiness was that prior to his literary career when he lived in idleness and obscurity, a happiness recovered only in his old age in renouncing the world and returning to solitary self-absorption (*Confs.* VI: 225, VII: 277-79; *Dialogues* II: 828; *Reveries* V, VII, VIII, X; *FD*, 32). If, during the middle period of his life, Rousseau pursued his mission goaded by somewhat irrational passions, that is presumably because he was unable to liberate his character from everything that his new theoretical insights told him was a corruption or illusion.

Thus, he sought glory, despite his principles, because he remained in the grips of *amour-propre* and because he had not yet managed to recover man's natural resignation to the necessity of death. Similarly, he was irrationally moved by an enthusiasm for virtue—although, if alerted by his later denials, one can see that his claims regarding this motive were always strongly qualified. In describing the moment he first dedicated himself to his mission, he states: "Up until then I had been good, from that point I became virtuous, or at least *intoxicated* with virtue" (*Confs.* IX: 416, emphasis added).[8] He explains that this "intoxication," which lasted almost six years and which was a violent and unnatural state for his soul, came over him partly as a result

---

[8] See the editor's note to this passage (*OC* I: 1474-75). Also, in recounting the first act of virtue in his life, Rousseau again qualifies his claim: "pride had perhaps as large a part in my resolution as virtue; but if this pride is not virtue itself it has effects so similar that it is pardonable to confuse them" (*Confs.* VI: 260).

of the resounding and unanticipated success of his *First Discourse* which kindled his ambitions. "In the illusion of my foolish pride I believed myself born to dispel all these prejudices" (ibid.; see VIII: 356). The other source of his intoxication was the terrible indignation he felt at the spectacle of human injustice which confronted him every day in Paris. When he finally withdrew from Paris to live in retreat, he ceased to hate men and, returning to himself, he soon lost this "ardent enthusiasm that had transported me for so long" (ibid., 417).[9]

This discrepancy between Rousseau's theoretical principles and his pursuit of his mission actually poses more of a difficulty for the former than the latter. His actions would seem to give unwitting testimony to the inadequacy of his ideas, to the unsatisfying thinness or irreality of the solitary dreamer's pleasures. And the discrepancy throws into doubt Rousseau's central claim to have discovered the truth through the most sincere knowledge of his own uniquely natural self. In his defense one might say that he is keenly aware of his own volatility and predisposition to illusion and, as any reader of the *Confessions* knows, he by no means vouches for the rationality of his actions. What he does claim is that he knows how to ride out the violent but brief storms of his exquisitely sensitive temperament and, in moments of calm recollection, to extract from his experiences what is natural and true. Yet at issue here is not some isolated action but Rousseau's great "mission," his choice of how to spend his life. Faced with his acknowledgment that he was moved by less than rational motives in this most momentous decision, one cannot but wonder whether these motives did not also taint his theoretical insights.

One is particularly suspicious of what Rousseau acknowledges to be the main source of his "intoxication": his uncontrollable indignation at the spectacle of oppression. "The sight of injustice and wickedness still makes my blood boil with anger" (*Reveries* VI: 81; see *Mals.*, 1145; *Confs.* I: 20, IV: 164, IX: 416; *OC* I: 1177). To be sure, Rousseau does not indulge such indignation within his theoretical system, which is not that of an angry moralist or even a proto-Kantian, as I have been at pains to show. He calmly acknowledges that injustice is condemnable if and only if it is also bad for the oppressors. This condition is met, he shows, because the masters of others are greater slaves than they. This ultimately means that the wicked are naturally good but unknowingly corrupted by the contradiction of society. Conse-

[9] There is a parallel to Rousseau's "intoxication" with virtue in his attitude toward romantic love. His clearly stated theoretical view is that "in love everything is only illusion. I admit it" (*Emile* V: 391). Yet despite this admission he allowed himself to fall in love—and with the mistress of a good friend, which cost him the friendship of many others. "She came, I saw her, I was intoxicated with love without an object, this intoxication enchanted my eyes, the object fixed upon her, I saw my Julie in Mme d'Houdetot, and soon I saw only Mme d'Houdetot, but adorned with all the perfections with which I had just embellished the idol of my heart" (*Confs.* IX: 440). It is possible to fall in love while knowing on some level that the perfections one sees are illusory. The same would seem to be true of Rousseau's love of virtue.

quently, the rational and healthy response to the spectacle of injustice, the response Rousseau expressly attributes to Emile and the "ideal people" of the *Dialogues*, is not uncontrollable anger and resentment but mainly pity and sorrow. Impressively, Rousseau's theoretical system forcefully repudiates the passionate indignation that he himself happened to feel.[10] And yet this system, proceeding in its calm and rational way, does culminate in the view that oppression is the source of all human misery. One is forced to wonder, therefore, whether Rousseau's seething resentment, which he excludes from his theoretical system as irrational, may not still have played a crucial role in shaping that system from the outside, especially given its admitted role in motivating his mission. Having first examined Rousseau's system from the inside, we have at least earned the right to raise this psychologizing question. It could be answered, if at all, only after evaluating the system on its own terms, as will be attempted in the next chapter.

Returning then to the practical level, it is at least clear that Rousseau adopted a personal "mission" and why he did so. Yet, as soon as we ask what that mission was, we find ourselves back in the middle of controversy. Given the long history of fervent quoting and counter-quoting on this subject, it will be useful to begin by working our way through the most commonly held positions.

Rousseau the Revolutionary

Barring strong evidence to the contrary, it is natural to assume that the immense historical effect that Rousseau's writings actually had—the spread of doctrinaire republicanism and revolutionary fervor through much of Europe—bears some resemblance to the effect he desired to have.[11] And from a first reading of his works, it usually seems obvious that he did indeed seek to promote revolution.

In the first place, his *Social Contract* is not a "utopia" like Plato's *Republic*, idly speculating about an impossibly perfect society, but a rigid, uncompromising statement of the "principles of political right," which

---

[10]*Emile* II: 96, IV: 236-37, 243-44; *Dialogues* I: 669-70. Moral indignation, Rousseau explains, is the characteristic reaction to society's vices of one who himself partakes of them. The savage, by contrast, "looks at us *without emotion* and says, 'You are mad.' He is right. No one does the bad for the sake of the bad." In other words, moral indignation is a selfish and contradictory passion: "It is *our* passions which arouse us against those of others. It is *our* interest which makes us hate the wicked. If they did *us* no harm, we would have more pity for them than hate. The harm the wicked do us makes us forget the harm they do themselves. We would pardon them their vices more easily if we knew how much they are punished by their own heart. . . . The passions we share seduce us; those that conflict with our interests revolt us; and, by an inconsistency which comes to us from these passions, we blame in others what we would like to imitate" (*Emile* IV: 243-44, emphasis added).

[11] Of course, there is also much dispute as to the extent of Rousseau's influence in the period of the French Revolution. See especially McDonald (1965), McNeil (1952-53), Blum (1986), and Miller (1984, chap. 6).

proclaim the strict minimum requirements for legitimacy. And by the demanding standards it establishes, virtually every existing state is illegit- imate, as Rousseau does not hesitate to proclaim on the very first page of the *Social Contract*: men are now "everywhere. . . . in chains." Further- more, in such circumstances men have a right of revolution. "The despot is master only as long as he is the strongest, and as soon as he can be driven out, he cannot protest against violence" (*SD*, 177; see *SC* I-6: 53, III-10: 98, III-18: 106-7). How can one deny, then, that Rousseau intends to promote revolution?

In fact, Rousseau's writings do not simply justify revolt but foster those messianic revolutionary longings that found expression for the first time in the French Revolution. His principle of natural goodness reduces all evil to oppression, so that repressive government can no longer be justified as necessary to control naturally unruly men or as a punishment sent by God for man's sinfulness. On the contrary, repression is now to be blamed for the things that used to excuse it: it has itself made men unruly and caused man's Fall. The political system is the source of all evil and therefore, through revolution, men can aspire not only to change rulers but to trans- form the human condition itself. Such political messianism, at the heart of most modern revolutions, grows directly out of the thought of Rousseau.

It appears, then, that Rousseau represents not just an obvious but a classic case of the revolutionary. As Jacob Talmon writes:

> Rousseau represents the most articulate form of the esprit revolutionnaire in each of its facets. In the *Discourse on Inequality* he expressed the burning sense of a society that has gone astray. In the *Social Contract* he postulates an exclusively legitimate social system as a challenge to human greatness.[12]

This famous interpretation, however, has a fatal flaw. Rousseau explic- itly and repeatedly condemned revolution, describing himself as "the man in the world who has the greatest respect for the laws, for national consti- tutions, and who has the greatest aversion for revolutions and plotters of all kinds" (*Dialogues* III: 935). Regarding France, for example, he states:

> Consider the danger of once rousing the enormous masses that compose the French monarchy! Who will be able to restrain the disturbances once begun or foresee all the effects they could pro- duce? Even if all the advantages of the new plan were incontestable, what man of sense would dare to abolish the old customs, change old principles, and give a form to the state other than the one to which it has been successively led over a period of thirteen hundred years? Whether the present government is still that of former times, or whether, over the centuries, it has imperceptibly changed nature,

---

[12] Talmon (1952) p. 49.

it is equally imprudent to touch it. If it is the same, one must respect
it; if it has degenerated, it is by the force of time and circumstance, and human wisdom can do nothing. (*Jugement sur la
Polysynodie, OC* III: 638)[13]

These statements by themselves are perhaps not conclusive, since they
might merely be the cautious lies of a revolutionary (although the second
one appears in a work written for posthumous publication). But they render
it likely, and further evidence will confirm, that Rousseau genuinely opposed revolution.

Indeed, despite the fame of the "revolutionary Rousseau," this conclusion is not at all new. After 1789, many books and pamphlets were written
in France enlisting the authority of Rousseau in support of the revolution,
the most famous being S. M. Mercier's *De J.-J. Rousseau considéré comme
l'un des premiers auteurs de la révolution* (1791). But at this time an equal
number of works had already appeared pointing out Rousseau's opposition
to revolution, and even Edmund Burke, who blamed Rousseau for causing
the revolution and for much else besides, apparently did not believe that he
had actually desired it. Of recent Rousseau scholars almost all acknowledge
his opposition to revolution.[14]

Rousseau the Progressive

But then what *was* Rousseau's great "mission"? And if he was actually
opposed to revolution, as he insists, then why did he write in the
undeniably subversive and revolutionary manner just described? This
question is clearly the most vexing and puzzling aspect of the whole
issue and stands as a Gordian knot before those who would try to make
sense of Rousseau's practical intention.

The most commonly suggested solution is that Rousseau is simply an
ardent "progressive" who, although opposed to violent, revolutionary
change, is nevertheless in favor of radical evolutionary reform. If his
writings appear subversive and revolutionary, that is only because he
sometimes overshoots his true intention, which is to encourage the
incremental progress of Europe toward justice, republican liberty, and
the restoration of man's natural goodness.[15]

---

[13] See *Polysynodie*, 590, 600; *Montagne* VIII: 836, 851-52, 851 var. e; *Confs.*, IX: 424; letter
to Ivernois, January 29, 1768; *Observations*, 51; *GM*, 174.

[14] See McNeil (1952-53). Edmund Burke, *Reflections on the Revolution in France*, p.
167. For the view that Rousseau did desire revolution, see especially Hippolyte Taine,
L'Ancien Régime, pp. 351-58; Hilaire Belloc, *The French Revolution*, pp. 7, 14-21; Maine,
Ancient Law, pp. 84-85.

[15] Those who see a progressive Rousseau include Grimsley (1973) pp. 163-64, Cassirer
(1963) pp. 26-27, Gay (1963) pp. 27-29, Hoffding (1930), Chapman (1956) p. 106, Hendel
(1934) vol. I, pp. 188-89, and Mornet (1933) pp. 92-96.

Rousseau the Conservative

But the "progressive Rousseau," a construction actually far more current than the "revolutionary," is no less a myth. Abundant evidence, drawn from every period of Rousseau's career, suggests that his opposition to revolution, indeed his political thought in general, was fundamentally conservative. "Let us never lose sight of the important maxim," he asserts, "never to change anything, either to subtract or add, unless necessity requires it" (*Poland* VII: 985; see I: 954, V: 971, XIV: 1031; *d'Alembert*, 74).

One misinterprets Rousseau on this point because one is unaccustomed to a thinker who combines such a strong sense of the evil of certain institutions with so clear a sense of their necessity. He vehemently denounces the abuses of economic inequality, for example, but he nevertheless opposes any tampering with property rights, which are "the most sacred of all the rights of citizens, and more important in certain respects than freedom itself" (*GM*, 229-30; see 224-25). Similarly, he sees that established social hierarchies are often brutally unjust and yet he opposes social mobility because "nothing is more pernicious for mores and for the republic than continual changes of status and fortune among the citizens" (*PE*, 225). In general, Rousseau's keen perception of social evils—which, for some as yet unexplained reason, he chooses to speak about so openly—makes him doubtful rather than hopeful of the possibilities for change.

Furthermore, like Edmund Burke, Rousseau especially disdains the progressivist inclination to promote change in the name of abstract, universal principles, for "with respect to political establishments, time and place are all important" (*Observations*, 51; see letter to Mirabeau July 26, 1767). Thus he chastises earlier thinkers who "have always argued a great deal over the best form of government, without considering that each of them is the best in certain cases and the worst in others." And he maintains, along with Montesquieu, that: "Freedom, not being the fruit of every climate, is not accessible to all peoples" (*SC* III-3: 84, III-8: 92; see *Montagne* VI: 811).

Above all, Rousseau insists that one must respect ancient customs and inherited institutions. He would "not have wished to live in a newly instituted republic, however good its laws might be," but rather in a "tranquil republic, whose antiquity was in a way lost in the darkness of time" (*SD*, 80-81). Old laws and practices, having withstood a test of time, have also had the chance to become rooted in the people's habits and beliefs. Thus "the slightest change in customs, even if it is in some respects advantageous, invariably proves prejudicial to morals. For customs are the morality of the people; and as soon as it ceases to respect them, it is left with no rule than its passions" (*Narcissus*, 107; see *SC* II-12: 77, III-11: 99). Change as such is to be avoided. Rousseau, it would appear, was no progressive, but a staunch conservative opposed to reform as well as to revolution.[16]

The Pessimist

If this conclusion were true in an unqualified sense, it would be impossible to explain why Rousseau—now a "Burkean conservative"—would write such unquestionably radical, doctrinaire, and subversive books. In fact, "conservatism" is still not quite an adequate description of Rousseau's posture toward history and political practice.

Conservatism of the sort just described remains, in many respects, optimistic and even progressive. Its preference for old over new often turns out to imply the superiority of the present over the past, for things are older today than yesterday. The conservative is like a progressive in believing that the state improves with age; only, it progresses not by changing but precisely by not changing. In other words, conservative thinkers like Burke and the members of the historical school tend to have a faith in the march of history and a deep respect for the institutions and traditions it has bestowed on us.

Rousseau, on the other hand, while condemning novelty and change like a conservative, has no such faith in history and tradition. In any given period, he believes, the old institutions men have inherited are probably the best of which they are capable—so they should not be changed—but they are still likely to be contemptibly bad. And whereas states have some tendency to improve with age, they have a still stronger, countervailing one to decay. In short, Rousseau's thought is steeped in historical pessimism. He seriously regarded the prehistoric age when men lived in small tribes as "the veritable prime of the world," and all subsequent history as so many steps toward "the decrepitude of the species" (*SD*, 151). Civilization reached its peak in the ancient republics of Greece and Rome and has been deteriorating ever since. Thus Rousseau is not a "conservative"—with the cautious optimism or complacency, the deep respect for the status quo, that this label implies—but rather an extreme historical pessimist, a radical philosopher of decadence.

Unlike the other views considered above, the sustained interpretation of Rousseau as a historical pessimist is a fairly recent development.[17] Yet plainly the true practical purpose of Rousseau's writings could not be determined without understanding this aspect of his thought, for one cannot begin to guess what Rousseau was trying to do for his contemporaries

---

[16] This view of Rousseau, although surprising to many, is in fact quite old. The engaging idea, for example, that Rousseau and Burke had a great deal in common was already the subject of an anonymous pamphlet published in London in 1791, *A Comparison of the Opinions of Mr. Burke and Monsr. Rousseau*. See also Osborn (1940) and Cobban (1934) pp. 228-35.

[17] See especially de Jouvenel (1947 and 1961-62), and Shklar (1969).

unless one knows how he conceived their particular historical situation. Do they live at the dawn of a new age of freedom, or at a time of universal and permanent despotism? We turn briefly to Rousseau's theory of history, then, to reconstruct his conception of the world to which he was speaking.

Rousseau's Theory of History and of the Ancien Regime

Scholars have been slow to take full cognizance of Rousseau's theory of history probably because its radical pessimism is so opposed to the prevailing views of his time and ours. But this theory, far from being a mere idiosyncrasy, follows directly from his fundamental principle. Men were originally good and originally asocial; over time, in becoming social, they became bad. It is possible for social men to become good again, but only through the adventitious intervention of a wise legislator, who suppresses their innate selfishness and fills them with austere and public-spirited "republican morals." Thereafter, men's fate is the fate of these morals—unnatural, strenuous, and thus fragile. "History" is essentially the process of their corruption through the inevitable reemergence of men's natural selfishness.

History, it is true, tends to bring economic development and the progress of the arts and sciences. Therefore, those thinkers who believe that men's unity and goodness can be founded upon the harmony of their economic interests or the enlightenment of their minds will conclude that history brings social progress. But Rousseau, who rejects these two beliefs and judges everything from the standpoint of virtue, sees rather that economic development weakens virtue by heightening economic inequality and class conflict, by producing wealth and luxury that seduce men away from the public good to the indulgence of private pleasures, and by softening men so that they lose the moral vigor and stamina necessary for energetic public-spiritedness. This process of corruption is only accelerated by the progress of the arts and sciences, for these activities are private pursuits that are nevertheless able to challenge the nobility of public devotion. Through them, selfishness, which heretofore had been ashamed of itself, acquires a clear conscience; and patriotism, which had become too difficult, comes to be debunked as too low. In this way, thinking to improve themselves, men eagerly abandon the austere virtue that alone could keep them free and healthy. Thus, by stimulating material and cultural development, the historical process tends to bring moral corruption.[18]

With this general account of the historical process in mind, let us turn to Rousseau's conception of Western history in particular. The republics of Sparta and Rome constituted the twin peaks of all recorded civilization. The decline of Rome, stemming from the usual causes, was particularly has-

---

[18]Although strange to our ears, this view of history is of course quite common among classical thinkers (see, for example, Plato *Republic* book VIII, *Laws* book III). Rousseau's version is somewhat more extreme, however, owing to the fact that the state and republican virtue are less natural in his eyes and therefore more subject to decay.

tened and deepened by the rise of Christianity which, through its extreme otherworldliness, universality, and gentleness, sapped the power of republican virtue. By leading to the rise of an independent priestly class, it also dangerously weakened the power of political authority (*Montagne* I: 705; *SC* IV-8: 128-29).

As a result of Christianity, then, in combination with the more general causes of decadence, it came to pass that, in the centuries after the fall of Rome:

> Europe had sunk back into the barbarism of the first ages. The people of that part of the world which is today so enlightened lived, a few centuries ago, in a condition worse than ignorance. A nondescript scientific jargon, even more despicable than ignorance, had usurped the name of knowledge, and opposed an almost invincible obstacle to its return. A revolution was needed to bring men back to common sense. (FD, 35; see *Observations*, 42-43)

The "revolution" was, of course, the Renaissance followed by the Enlightenment. Rousseau acknowledges here that this unique effort to revive, then to popularize, the arts and sciences had become a necessity for Europe in order to overcome the historically unique evils of Scholastic Christianity.

But this revolution, although necessary, still brought with it all the morally corrupting effects of the arts and sciences—and in an intensified form that was also historically unique. In the Enlightenment, the praise of hedonism, high culture, luxury, individualism and self-interest—of everything that destroys republican virtue—had become a fervently held dogma of the philosophers in their battle with the church. "Until the present time," Rousseau points out, "luxury, although often prevalent, had at least always been viewed as the fatal source of infinitely many evils"; the praise of it as politically salutary was a novelty of modern philosophy (*Last Reply*, 88; see *Frags.*, 517-18). Similarly, through its open skepticism, materialism, atheism, and cosmopolitanism, the new Enlightenment philosophy undermined the moral beliefs necessary for patriotic citizenship: belief in virtue, free will, and divine support for the laws. All these modern philosophers "smile disdainfully at the old-fashioned words of fatherland and religion, and devote their talents and philosophy to destroying and debasing all that is sacred among men" (*FD*, 50; see 60; *Emile* IV: 312n; *Observations* 41n; *Dialogues* III: 968-69). It is the sad fate of the West, in sum, that the natural process of moral corruption has been vastly strengthened and deepened first by the rise of Christianity and then, in reaction to it, by the misguided efforts of modern philosophy.

Rousseau describes the tragic result of all this:

> Men nourished since infancy in an intolerant impiety approaching fanaticism, and in a libertinism without fear or shame; youth without discipline, women without morals, peoples without faith; kings without law or a Superior they fear, delivered from every

kind of restraint; all the duties of conscience annihilated, patriotism and loyalty to the Prince extinguished in all hearts, finally, no social bond other than force. (*Dialogues* III: 971)[19]

Rousseau believed that, with the exception of a few tiny islands of republican freedom (such as Geneva), all of Europe was in a state of utter debasement.

The crucial question, however, is how he conceived of the future. Many thinkers regarded Europe of the *ancien regime* as decadent, but saw in this fact a promise of revolutionary change and improvement. Rousseau himself certainly agreed that the current order could not last. "We are approaching a state of crisis and the age of revolutions," he wrote. "I hold it to be impossible that the great monarchies of Europe still have long to last" (*Emile* III: 194n, 194).[20]

Could Europe's decadence perhaps be reversed by the coming "age of revolutions"? In a passage of the *Social Contract* often cited by proponents of the "revolutionary Rousseau," he asserts:

There sometimes occur during the lifetime of States violent periods when revolutions have the same effect on peoples as do crises on individuals; when horror of the past is equivalent to amnesia, and when the State, set afire by civil wars, is reborn so to speak from its ashes and resumes the vigor of youth by escaping from death's clutches. (*SC* II-8: 70-71)

Rousseau did not believe, however, that such revolutionary rebirth was possible for Europe. In the sequel to this passage, he explains that a people "can liberate itself as long as it is merely barbarous, but can no longer do so when the civil machinery is worn out. Then, disturbances can destroy it, but revolutions cannot reestablish it." *Civilized* decadence is by its very nature irreversible.

Corruption might be reversible if it were merely a problem of institutions rather than of character; or if what men's characters lacked were only some quality of compassion or sensitivity that could be relearned. But in Rousseau's view, "decadence" is at bottom a weakening and enervation of the soul itself, a loss of that psychic strength that enables men to rise above their innate selfishness and reconstitute their souls around the strenuous ideal of virtue and the public good. When this strength of soul has been lost, men have no means for restoring it, any more than a coward has the means for making himself courageous.

Barbarous peoples, by contrast, sometimes decline into despotism due to their immoderation and untamed energy which renders them incapable of free government. But the same wildness that causes their enslavement

---

[19] See II: 890; *Frags.*, 538, 518; *Extrait du projet de paix perpetuelle*, *OC* III: 568; *Confs*. XI: 546; *Poland* XI: 1003.

[20] For Rousseau's list of the causes of the coming revolution in France see *Confs. XI: 565.*

preserves them from its most corrupting effects, thus permitting them to be saved through revolution. In the case of civilized peoples, however, the vices and enslavement themselves stem from weakness, so there is no counterpoise. "I do not accuse the men of this century of having all the vices; they have only the vices of cowardly souls; they are only rogues and knaves. As for vices requiring courage and fortitude, I believe that they are incapable of them" (*Last Reply*, 72; see *SC* I-2: 48; *LM*, 1090; *Emile* IV: 335; *FD*, 54-56). Weakness of this kind cannot be reversed.

Furthermore, while men's souls grow feeble and cold their minds become sophisticated as they employ them to discredit or refute the virtues they can no longer practice.

> All barbarous Peoples, even those that are without virtue, nevertheless always honor it; whereas learned and Philosophic Peoples by dint of progress eventually succeed in turning virtue into an object of derision and to despise it. Once a nation has reached that point, its corruption may be said to have reached its zenith, and it is past remedy. (*Last Reply*, 69; see *Observations*, 47; *Narcissus*, 108 n. 1)

What has been learned cannot be unlearned (especially since the invention of printing), so the progress of the arts and sciences also renders irreversible the progressive decline of morals. "Human nature does not go backwards and one can never return to the times of innocence and equality when one has once left it; that is one of the principles on which [I have] insisted the most" (*Dialogues* III: 935).[21] Thus Europe of the *ancien regime* is not only decadent, in Rousseau's view, but irreversibly so.

What then did he expect the future to look like? And what did he mean by the strangely ominous warning he placed near the beginning of the *Second Discourse*?

> Discontented with your present state for reasons that foretell even greater discontents for your unhappy posterity, perhaps you would want to be able to go backward in time. This sentiment must be the eulogy of your first ancestors, the criticism of your contemporaries, and the dread of those who will have the unhappiness to live after you. (*SD*, 104)

As we have seen, Rousseau expected a period of revolutions, although not salutary ones. The fate of the West would probably be like that of ancient Greece in its decline: "Greece, always learned, always voluptuous, and always enslaved, no longer experienced anything in her revolutions but a change of masters" (*FD*, 40). But what of England, one wants to ask, the home of liberty and constitutional government? In Rousseau's view this overly large, overly commercial, representative state was never more than half-free, and it is "easy to foresee," he wrote, "that, twenty years from now,

---

[21] See *Observations*, 51; *Narcissus*, 107-8; *SD*, 80; *GM* II-3: 188.

England with all its glory will . . . have lost the rest of its liberty" (*Extrait du projet de paix perpétuelle, OC* III: 573n). He seems to have dismissed the prospects of England's American colonies with equal assurance, at least to judge from the fact that his writings contain not a single reference to them. Thus everywhere in the West, with a few isolated exceptions, the future promised nothing but further corruption and tyranny.

Yet perhaps a still worse fate was in store for our "unhappy posterity." In the *First Discourse*, Rousseau repeatedly emphasized that the fate of large, decadent nations was to fall prey to small and vigorous ones. And in the *Social Contract* he prophesied: "The Russian empire would like to subjugate Europe and will itself be subjugated. The Tartars, its subjects or its neighbors, will become its masters and ours. This revolution appears inevitable to me" (*SC* II-8: 71). Whether or not Rousseau was completely serious in this final prediction, it is clear that he was extraordinarily pessimistic about the present and future of the West. The stage of human history when political freedom was possible, the era of republican morals, of strength and greatness of soul, was now as permanently lost to mankind as was the state of nature or the epoch of the primitive tribe. History had run its course and the *ancien regime* of Europe was now the veritable old age of the world, a time of moral and political decline akin to that of the late Roman Empire, only more universal and therefore more permanent.

The Duality of Rousseau's Practical Intention

Great misunderstandings have been generated by the ironic fact that, since 1789, Rousseau's readers have naturally tended to think of him as having lived at the great dawn of the "age of freedom," whereas he himself was certain that he lived rather at its end. To understand his practical intention we must begin from the latter premise. Living in a world that was so hopelessly corrupt, to whom was Rousseau addressing his doctrines and for what possible purpose?

The inexorable march of history does not necessarily proceed everywhere at an equal pace, and a few exceptional states can be preserved from the general decline through their fortunate location or size or some other historical accident. In Rousseau's view, Corsica—because it was small and an island—and, to a much lesser extent, Poland—because of its semi-anarchic constitution—had remained fairly vigorous and unformed, and although their situations were perilous and uncertain, they might still be capable of receiving good laws if a wise legislator could be found (*SC* II-10: 75; *Poland* I). More importantly, the Swiss republics, isolated in their mountains, and especially the republic of Geneva—Rousseau's beloved native city—with its wise laws drawn up by Calvin, had succeeded in remaining relatively healthy and vigorous republics (*SC* II-7: 68 n. 2). Thus, Rousseau's pessimistic theory of history led him, in practice, to see a radical division among existing states, to see the West as essentially comprised of two different and opposite worlds: on one side, the tiny, threatened world of actual and potential republics, and on the other, the vast, decadent, politically hopeless world of monarchic Europe.[22]

The primary addressee of Rousseau's political writings was in fact only this tiny republican world, and principally Geneva. His mission was to strengthen their free political institutions. Secondarily, Rousseau endeavored to address the distinct world of monarchic Europe, where his purpose was simply to promote among individuals certain limited moral reforms.

In other words, Rousseau's writings are characterized by an abrupt dualism on the level of practical intention, just as they are on the theoretical level. And his two practical missions correspond roughly to the theoretical opposition between the political and individualistic solutions. Only by carefully distinguishing Rousseau's two very different audiences and purposes, while keeping his general pessimism in mind, is it possible to decipher the practical meaning of his writings.

Rousseau's Primary Audience and the Puzzle of His Revolutionary Rhetoric

"It is a very remarkable thing," wrote d'Alembert in his *Encyclopedia* article on Geneva, "that a city which numbers hardly twenty-four thousand souls...is nevertheless a sovereign state and one of the most flourishing cities in Europe" (*d'Alembert*, 141-42). It is even more remarkable that Rousseau's major political writings, which have had such an extraordinary effect on the Western world for two centuries, were actually written primarily for this tiny Swiss city.

If one wonders how a philosopher, who speaks constantly of the love of all humanity and the pursuit of universal truth, could have composed his major writings for so provincial an audience and so narrow a purpose, the answer lies in Rousseau's historical pessimism. He believed that Geneva, bravely holding back the tide of history, was desperately in need of his help and was eminently worthy of it, despite its small size, since it represented one of the last precious embers of freedom in a darkening world. As Rousseau explained (speaking of himself):

> Human nature does not go backwards. . . . Therefore, his object could not be to lead numerous peoples or large States back to their first simplicity, but only to stop, if possible, the progress of those who were preserved by their smallness and location from such a

---

[22] Rousseau was, of course, aware that Europe is not the world: "the whole earth is covered with nations of which we know only the names" (*SD*, 212). Although the major civilizations of the East and Middle East were just as decadent as that of the West, in his view, there was still some hope for the more isolated and backward peoples. Rousseau seems to have considered the possibility that his writings might somehow find their way to such peoples, but his primary concern naturally remained with his immediate and direct audience in Europe (see *Frags.*, 474).

rapid procession toward the perfection of society and toward the deterioration of the species. . . . He worked for his fatherland and for the small States constituted like it. (*Dialogues* III: 935)

That his fatherland was indeed his primary addressee can also be seen by a quick survey of his writings. Just as, toward the end of his life, Rousseau wrote the *Considerations on the Government of Poland* and the *Constitutional Project for Corsica*, so in his major political writings he also devoted his attention to a particular state, although without naming it in the title. The *Letter to d'Alembert* and the *Letters from the Mountain* (which is by far Rousseau's longest political work) were both expressly written to and about Geneva. In the *Social Contract*, a far more abstract and universal work, Rousseau was also primarily speaking of Geneva. After summarizing the book in *Letters from the Mountain*, he remarked: "There is the history of the Government of Geneva. . . . I took, then, your Constitution, which I found beautiful, as a model of political institutions, and . . . revealed the means of conserving you" (*Montagne* VI: 809).[23] Finally, even the *Second Discourse* was intended primarily for Geneva, just as it is formally dedicated to that city. As Rousseau stated in a letter to the *Mercure de France*:

> Those for whom this work is written, those to whom it is dedicated . . . will not ask me what it is useful for. . . . They will see in it, I dare to believe, strong reasons for loving their government, and means for conserving it. . . . As for the inhabitants of other countries, if they do not find in this work anything useful or amusing, it would be better, it seems to me, to ask them why they read it than to explain to them why it was written. (January 1756, reprinted in *OC* III: 1387; see *Philopolis* 235-36; *Mals.*, 1143)

Rousseau could hardly have been more explicit about his intended audience.

It has been necessary to argue this point at some length because of its extreme importance and because, despite all these explicit assertions, Rousseau's contemporaries, and most subsequent scholars, have been very reluctant to believe that, in their practical intention, these major works were addressed to such a specific and tiny population. As Rousseau observed: "The foolishness of vanity—which inclines each man to think that one is always occupied with him even when one gives him no thought—[has] made the large nations apply to themselves what was meant to apply only to the small republics" (*Dialogues* III: 935). And this particular error has been extremely important, he continued, for it has led people to see "a promoter of revolts and disorder in that man who . . . has the greatest aversion for revolutions and plotters of all kinds."

Here, from Rousseau's own lips, is the solution to our great puzzle. The writings of this conservative have appeared—and, historically, have been— so subversive and revolutionary only because of a tragic misunderstanding

---

[23] See *Confs.* IX: 406; *SC* I: 46; Letter to Duchesne, May 23, 1762.

of their intended addressee. These doctrines were never meant to be applied to the world at large, to the monarchies that all but cover the earth, but only to Europe's small, dwindling republican population, for whom they would be nonrevolutionary and beneficial.

There is one problem, however, with this solution. The *Social Contract* is not a book that can "apply" to some states and not to others. It proclaims universally binding principles—principles which rendered all European monarchies illegitimate. And Rousseau neither could nor did confine the publication of his books to Geneva and the other republics, but, on the contrary, shouted his doctrinaire republicanism to the four corners of Europe. Thus, even if he composed his doctrine only for the purpose of "applying" it to the few small republics, the great question remains why this self-professed conservative was not restrained by the delegitimizing and subversive effect his doctrine was likely to have on the monarchies.

The answer lies, once again, in Rousseau's historical pessimism. He believed that the deterioration of monarchic Europe had reached such a point—the people's courage was so enervated and their opinions so cynical—that, politically, it no longer mattered what one said. As he states quite clearly in a fragment for the *Letter to Beaumont* (his reply to the condemnation of *Emile* as subversive by the Archbishop of Paris):

> The people are not as duped as one thinks. If one did not use force with them, ruse would hardly accomplish anything. . . . In this regard, there are no more secrets to keep nor truths to hide. . . . My writings will not teach them anything about the wickedness of the powerful. . . . The true spring of governments is in the cowardice of men, and this cowardice grows from roots that my books will not tear out. (*Beaumont* fragment, 1020)[24]

The ruling classes of his time underestimated the people's intelligence and overestimated their courage in believing that the charade of legitimacy was still effectual and necessary. The great nations of Europe no longer were and nevermore would be based on the people's belief in their legitimacy, but solely on force. That is why Rousseau now felt free to promulgate his radically democratic doctrines without fearing their consequences for monarchic Europe.

Furthermore, Rousseau's political writings, while strongly denying the legitimacy of the large European states, also denied that they could be made legitimate. Precisely by setting the requirements for legitimacy so impossibly high—and by speaking with such radical pessimism about historical practice—Rousseau expected actually to *discourage* would-be reformers or revolutionaries. This lesson is drawn explicitly for Emile, who is made to study the doctrine of the *Social Contract* as part of his quest for a nonoppress-

[24] See *Beaumont*, 966, 937 var. b; *Fragment sur la liberté* in *OC* III: 1895; *Emile* I: 41, IV: 295n; *Dialogues* III: 971.

ive country in which to settle with his family. As a result of this study, the tutor explains, "you will be cured of a chimera. You will console yourself for an inevitable unhappiness, and you will submit yourself to the law of necessity" (*Emile* V: 457-58).[25] Rousseau expected his radical doctrine to foster an attitude of political resignation in monarchic Europe, not of radical hope.

In sum, Rousseau's seemingly revolutionary writings were actually in the service of a conservative intention, for their purpose was not to overthrow the monarchies—which could no longer be harmed or helped by what he wrote—but rather to conserve the few last remaining republics. Ironically, it was not revolutionary hopefulness but extreme historical pessimism·that turned Rousseau into a "revolutionary" writer.

Rousseau's Mission for Republican Europe

If Rousseau was primarily addressing Geneva and the other republics, what was he hoping to do for them? What was their need—and his mission?

On the most immediate level, Rousseau was trying to strengthen their free political institutions which, he believed, were on the verge of declining into tyranny owing to the encroachments of the executive power. Indeed, by the time he wrote the *Letters from the Mountain* (1764), he considered Geneva's battle all but lost: "Nothing is more free than your legitimate state; nothing is more servile than your present state" (*Montagne* VII: 813).

Earlier, Rousseau could see this danger approaching and the possible remedies, but he also saw that the Genevan people could not, since they lacked an adequate understanding of the basis of their own republican constitution. The Genevans, he discovered during his return there in 1754, did not have "ideas of the laws and of liberty that were just and precise enough for my liking," so he decided to write the *Social Contract* because "I believed that this indirect manner of giving them to them was the best suited to manage their *amour-propre* and to secure their pardon for having been able to see in this matter a little further than they" (*Confs*. IX: 405).

Through this abstract treatise, Rousseau hoped to bring the Genevans to understand that, contrary to the reigning interpretation of their constitution (expressed in the Act of Mediation of 1737), the people, as embodied in the "General Council," were truly sovereign; that this council was not simply one governmental body alongside the others (the "Syndics," the "Small Council," and the "Grand Council") with certain limited, delegated powers, but the fundamental source of all powers; that it was not merely one body within the state, but rather the state itself. Not that Rousseau wanted significantly to alter or expand the powers that, in practice, the General Council exercised, but only to reinvigorate this body by giving it a more just and precise conception of its rights and a keener awareness of the

---

[25] Emile will endeavor to benefit his immediate neighbors, but will try to avoid all political involvement. See V: 474-75.

relentless threat to it posed by the ambitions of the small council (the executive power) (*Montagne* VII: 813-17, 823-26, VIII: 836-39, IX: 880-91). In other words, Rousseau saw that Geneva and the other republics were in very great danger owing to the passivity and disunity of the sovereign people. Thus, the practical mission of the *Social Contract* was to arouse the people's vigilance—by demonstrating the inevitable historical tendency toward executive encroachment—and to give that vigilance focus and unity—by presenting a clear and precise definition of the people's rights.

It hardly needs to be stressed that this republican mission, which would have been necessary in any age, was particularly urgent in the monarchical age in which Rousseau lived. Europe's reigning intellectuals, books, universities, pulpits, and academies—all issued nothing but monarchist propaganda, all conspired to bury the elemental truths and beliefs necessary for a healthy republic. Everywhere, the ruling ideas were those of the European ruling classes. Indeed, Rousseau saw himself as virtually the only major thinker of the previous few centuries who had not been corrupted or bought off by the established powers, and thus as the only man who stood in the way of the final obliteration of truth as well as liberty. This perception is what caused Rousseau to set forth his democratic principles in the passionate, uncompromising, and "revolutionary" form that we see in his works.

Rousseau's mission for the republics of Europe was not limited, however, to this strictly political or institutional level and to the *Social Contract*, for there was also a different kind of danger pressing down upon them: the decline of their austere and patriotic morals. This decay was being accelerated by the example of the enlightened and corrupt monarchies surrounding them, all of which "shine with that brilliance which dazzles most eyes, the childish and fatal taste for which is the most mortal enemy of happiness and freedom" (*SD*, 90). In Rousseau's time, France, above all, acted as a cultural magnet drawing the rest of Europe to imitate its splendid vices. As Claire writes to Julie, in the *Nouvelle Héloïse*, during a brief visit to Geneva: "Oh your France, your France! It poisons and corrupts all its neighbors. It has more than one manner of making conquests, and its armies are less to be feared than its mores" (*NH* VI-5: 662, var e). How could Geneva's citizens, and especially its youth, be made to cling to their simple ways, to treasure their homely freedom and equality, after they had been exposed to the dazzling spectacle of imperial greatness, monarchic splendor, and courtly sophistication? Due to the "cultural imperialism" of French civilization—which, of course, was only strengthened by the Enlightenment philosophers—the Genevans, who used to feel proud of their political liberty, now only felt ashamed of their backwardness and simplicity. Their freedom would not long survive this loss of republican pride and austerity.[26]

---

[26] Claire observes: "The luxury of other peoples makes [the Genevans] despise their ancient simplicity; proud liberty seems to them ignoble; they forge shackles of silver for themselves, not as a chain, but as an ornament" (*NH* VI-5: 658; see *d'Alembert*, 132-33).

Thus, a second and no less urgent part of Rousseau's mission for republican Europe was to combat the fateful prestige of everything that was "Paris," the ruinous allure of luxury and talent that was casting moderation and liberty into contempt. That was the great republican purpose of his doctrine of natural goodness. On the one hand, by showing dependence to be the root of all evil and so freedom the foundation of all good, it formulated the strongest and noblest defense of liberty ever made. On the other hand, by defending "backwardness" against "civilization," it attacked monarchic brilliance at its root. As he explains in *Rousseau Juge de Jean-Jacques*, in order to slow the tragic decline of virtue he used his writings:

> to destroy this illusory prestige that gives us a stupid admiration for the instruments of our miseries, and to correct this mistaken valuation which makes us honor pernicious talents and despise useful virtues. Everywhere he [Rousseau] makes us see the human race better, more sensible and happier in its primitive constitution; blind, miserable and wicked in the degree to which it moves away from it. His goal is to correct the error of our judgments in order to retard the progress of our vices, and to show us that there where we seek glory and brilliance we find, in fact, only errors and misery. (*Dialogues* III: 934-35)[27]

Here we see the practical purpose of the writings other than the *Social Contract*. The *First Discourse* begins Rousseau's attack on our misplaced admiration for the arts and sciences, emphasizing the harm this mistake has done to civic virtue. The *Letter to d'Alembert* continues and elaborates this attack, now making explicit and thematic the goal of protecting Geneva from the dangerous allure of French high culture. The *Discourse on Political Economy* urges the executive power to be more active and resourceful in strengthening the people's morals. Finally, in the *Second Discourse*, Rousseau presents the most far-reaching and rhetorically powerful attack ever made on the value of progress and civilization. It is true that, to make this attack in the most radical way possible, Rousseau overshoots the mark, going back beyond the citizen to a praise of the prepolitical and "individualistic" savage. But Rousseau clearly believed that, as presented in his discourse, the savage constituted a compelling and salutary model for the citizen, for his freedom and happiness were shown to derive precisely from his remarkable moderation and simplicity, from his utter indifference to everything that the Parisian lives for. This central lesson is, in fact, made the subject of the frontispiece to the work: a young savage, simple, proud, and free, is shown spurning the splendors of civilized decadence. Rousseau's practical intention in all these works was to inspire the Genevans to save their republic by reenacting this scene.

---

[27] See I: 687; *Confs.* VIII: 388-89; *Mals.*, 1136; *Philopolis*, 232.

According to Rousseau's theoretical analysis, the growth of executive power and the deterioration of virtue are the two interrelated evils that eventually destroy all legitimate states. True to this analysis, we have seen that the major practical purpose of his writings was to combat precisely these two evils in their particular contemporary manifestations.[28]

Rousseau's Moral Mission for Monarchic Europe

There were two worlds of Europe, as Rousseau saw it, and although his primary project clearly centered on the republics, it would be surprising indeed if he had no practical interest in the other, vastly larger world of the monarchies. From a quick glance at Rousseau's works it is obvious that he did intend for them to be read in France and the other monarchies, as in fact they were.[29] The first two *Discourses* were written for French academic prize competitions, the *Discourse on Political Economy* for the *Encyclopedia*. *Emile*, which also contains a detailed summary of the *Social Contract*, is about the education of a Frenchman; and the *Second Discourse*, written in "a language that suits all nations," expressly addresses the reader as "man, whatever country you may come from, whatever your opinions may be" (*SD*, 103). Finally, in the preface to the *Nouvelle Héloïse*, Rousseau declares: "Entertainments are necessary in large cities, and novels for corrupt peoples. I saw the mores of my time and published these letters. If only I lived in a century where I would have had to burn them!" (*NH* Preface: 5). Thus, although the republics were the primary audience of his works (except for the *Nouvelle Héloïse*),[30] clearly Rousseau also desired to address the "corrupt peoples" of monarchic Europe.

On the political level, Rousseau certainly had no hopes of moving the monarchies toward republican legitimacy; but did he therefore have no political advice for them at all? Was there no better and worse for these states? In the *Social Contract* Rousseau had argued that the worst form of government was not monarchy but hereditary aristocracy, and in practice he seems to have favored the further consolidation of monarchical power at the expense of the nobility and the clergy (*SC* III-5: 86, IV-8: 126-28).[31]

[28] Rousseau's involvement in Genevan politics is a long and complex story. For a fuller account see Fralin (1978) and especially Launay (1971).

[29] In the *Letters from the Mountain*, Rousseau boasts that his writings "are printed in all countries, are translated into all languages, and even two translations at the same time have been made of *Emile* in London, an honor given no other book except the *Nouvelle Héloïse*, at least so far as I know" (V: 800).

[30] Rousseau pointedly refused to sign the *Nouvelle Héloïse* with his accustomed title "Citizen of Geneva" and he urged his publisher not to distribute it in that city. See *NH* Second Preface: 27; and Guehenno (1966) vol. 2, p. 40.

[31] See Gildin (1983) pp. 110-12.

278   Chapter Thirteen

In his famous letter to Mirabeau, he states that if legitimate government and its goal of placing "law above man" is not possible, then:

> my view is that one must go to the other extreme and abruptly place man as far above law as possible, one must establish an arbitrary despotism and as arbitrary as possible: I wish the despot could be God. In a word, I see no acceptable middle ground between the most austere democracy and the most perfect hobbism: for the conflict of men and laws, which produces a continual civil war in the state, is the worst of all political conditions. (Letter to Mirabeau, July 26, 1767)

From this characteristic exclusion of middle ground, this stark dualism, it would seem that Rousseau's political advice for the monarchic world was not democratic reform but, on the contrary, something like the *philosophes'* goal of consolidated and enlightened despotism. Rousseau did often praise China, for instance, which was the *philosophes'* favorite example of enlightened despotism.[32] And the *First Discourse* ends with an eloquent plea to kings that "learned men of the first rank find honorable asylum in their courts" (*FD*, 63).

Rousseau seems to have believed that by this means, and especially by the accession of a genuinely enlightened ruler, certain political and economic reforms would be possible that could somewhat improve the lot of the people. The *Social Contract* and the *Discourse on Political Economy* certainly contain general principles and even concrete advice that could guide a thoughtful and well-intentioned monarch in the devising of such reforms, and it may have been among Rousseau's hopes that his writings would one day serve this purpose (see *Frags.*, 473-74).

But one has only to read the chapter on monarchy in the *Social Contract* to see that Rousseau considered the probability of there ever being a genuinely philosophic king as negligible. And as for the sort of enlightened despotism that was actually possible, as in the standard case of China, Rousseau believed that despite the wisdom of many of its laws and policies, China was still "populated by slaves and wicked men" (*FD*, 41; see *NH* IV-3: 413-14). Thus, while probably favoring movement toward enlightened and consolidated monarchy, Rousseau had extremely limited expectations for it, and it is perhaps for this reason that, with the exception of a few hints, Rousseau's writings offer essentially *no* political hope and *no* political advice to decadent Europe.

Whether enlightened or otherwise, despotism was now the master fact of the world in this age of iron, and therefore the practical issue that engaged Rousseau was no longer political but moral: could he find a way

---

[32] "Oriental despotism," he writes, "sustains itself because it is more severe on the nobles than on the people: it thus draws from itself its own remedy" (*Montagne* VIII: 843n; see *PE*, 216, 232, 234).

to shelter men in some degree from the further corrupting and psychologically degrading effects of their inescapable political enslavement? That was Rousseau's "mission" for monarchic Europe.[33] A
modern Tacitus, he wrote to teach men how to live under permanent
tyranny.[34]

This moral mission was to be carried out by promoting a popular-
ized version of the "individualistic solution." When the enervation and
selfishness of men, as well as the decay of political institutions, lead
them to withdraw from communal dedication and energetic citizenship, then the only way to prevent their utter corruption at the hands
of tyranny and personal dependence is to push them still further in the
direction they are tending: let them withdraw from society altogether,
retreat into the bosom of family and friends in rural isolation. Rousseau
described this project in the preface to the *Nouvelle Héloïse*:

> to give men the love of a uniform and simple life; to cure them
> of the whims born of opinion, and give them a taste for true
> pleasures; to make them love solitude and peace; to hold them at
> some distance one from another, and, instead of prompting them
> to crowd into cities, bring them to spread out equally over the
> land to vivify all its parts . . . to show men of leisure that the
> rustic life and agriculture have pleasures which they cannot
> know . . . that a man of merit who would like to retire to the
> country with his family . . . could lead as pleasing a life as among
> the amusements of the cities . . . that the sweetest sentiments of
> the heart can make a more agreeable society there than the
> affected language of social clubs where our mordant and satirical
> laughter is a sad replacement for the gaiety one no longer feels.
> (*NH* Second Preface: 21)[35]

All of Rousseau's different writings (even the *Social Contract*, as we
will see) were designed to contribute in different ways to this moral
reform, to this ethic of withdrawal and inwardness. The powerful attacks
contained in the *First* and *Second Discourses* and the *Letter to d'Alembert*

---

[33] In the *Dialogues*, just after asserting that the primary purpose of his writings was to
help the small republican states, he continued: "if [my] doctrine could be of some usefulness
to the others [the large monarchies], it was in changing the objects of their esteem and thus
perhaps retarding their decadence which they accelerate by their false valuations" (III: 935;
see *Philopolis*, 232).

[34] The influence or echo of late Roman authors (especially the Stoics), which has often been
noticed in Rousseau, stems in large measure from this fact that Rousseau saw his situation and
task as essentially akin to theirs.

[35] The *Nouvelle Héloïse*, the work of Rousseau's most widely read in his lifetime, was central
to this project because, as Julie herself explains in one of her many disquisitions, "Novels are
perhaps the last form of instruction that can be given to a people so corrupt as to be incapable
of receiving any other" (*NH* II-21: 277).

directed against luxury, ostentation, politeness, high culture, and all
the other corrupting creations of Parisian selfish sociability—attacks which served the Genevans by protecting their genuine, patriotic sociability from the growth of selfishness—served the
monarchic world by withdrawing their selfishness from the allures
of vain sociability. The lyrical praise of wilderness and isolation in the
Reveries and other works, and in a different way Rousseau's botanical
writings, helped to foster the new romantic cult of rustic retreat, of
solitude and reverie, of communing with "nature" defined as the nonhu-
man world. At the same time, *Emile*, with its praise of chaste romance,
marrying for love, motherhood, breast-feeding, and child rearing, became one of the founding documents of the inward-turning, child-cen-
tered, sentimental, bourgeois family—of the family conceived not as a
position within society but as a haven outside of it. Through the
remarkable "Profession of Faith of the Savoyard Vicar," Rousseau
hoped to spark a revival of Christianity, for which he believed the time
was now especially ripe. It would be a revival, however, in a newly private
and personal form, with sincerity replacing doctrinal faith as the essential virtue. In conjunction with this he promulgated a new doctrine
of "conscience" as an infallible internal voice and inner witness, in
order to give the individual moral self-sufficiency and encourage him
to live his life with eyes turned inward. By writing the *Confessions*, the
Reveries, and *Rousseau Juge de Jean-Jacques*—by writing more auto-
biographically than any previous philosopher—he conferred new dignity on introspection, individuality, and the fascination with one's self.
Similarly, through his emphasis on the primacy and power of feeling,
Rousseau sought to impress upon men that the intimate, personal, subjective world of sentiment and imagination had as much reality and more
charm than the social world of honor and status. In every possible way,
he endeavored to expand and validate the private inner world—as a
refuge from the public.

Yet, could this really work? "No people," Rousseau himself had
insisted, will "ever be anything except what the nature of its government
[makes] it" (*Confs.* IX: 404). When the government made men feel every
day that they were slaves and worthy of being so, how could they ever
free their minds and self-understanding from this official judgment,
which seems to carry the weight of reality itself? Thus, the attempt to
build up a private refuge could not succeed if one did not also find some
way of weakening the moral influence of the public, political world.
That was Rousseau's great purpose in addressing his political writings
to the monarchies. That is why he was not only unafraid (for the reasons
we have seen) but eager to proclaim his subversive political doctrines
to the whole of Europe. He sought to subvert not the government but the
political world itself. Through the *Social Contract*, Rousseau accused
and denounced virtually all established governments, not in order to

produce a political revolution but a moral one: to drain the existing public world of its impressiveness and authority.

This second, quasi-political part of Rousseau's mission for monarchic Europe was particularly important because it had to overcome the nearly universal attitude of the intellectual elite, which believed that since monarchy was inevitable in the large nations of Europe there was no point in attacking it or questioning its legitimacy. Prudence dictated that one put as good a face on it as possible. Rousseau's radicalism consisted in taking the opposite view on this issue of how one should speak. Precisely because monarchy or despotism was now inevitable, it was necessary to acknowledge, indeed to proclaim, its illegitimacy. He fully agreed that the people should obey their despotic governments as the only ones possible under current circumstances, but they should also know that these governments are unjust and despicable. As Rousseau put it in the *Second Discourse*, they should "scrupulously obey the laws. . . . But they will nonetheless scorn a constitution . . . from which . . . always arise more real calamities than apparent advantages" (*SD*, 202-3). Only if they scorn as well as obey can men be saved from degradation.

That is why Rousseau took so strangely uncompromising a position in the *Social Contract*, refusing to grant any legitimacy to imperfect regimes even while affirming that no real alternative to them was possible under most circumstances. That is why he went even further, questioning the legitimacy of civil society as such, openly revealing the "secret of governments" that past philosophers had only hinted at: that in its very essence the state is a trap set by the rich for the poor, and "those specious names, justice and order, will always serve as instruments of violence and as arms of iniquity" (*Emile* IV: 236; see *SD*, 158-59). Again, the point was not to correct the unjust distribution of power but rather, by ensuring that "injustice and violence do not impudently use the name of right and equity," to drain it of all moral authority (*Guerre*, 610). As Rousseau stated his purpose in a fragment for the *Letter to Beaumont*:

> I penetrated the secret of governments, and I revealed it to the peoples, not so that they might throw off the yoke, which is not possible for them, but that they might become men again in their slavery, and though enslaved to their masters they might not also be so to their vices. If they can no longer be citizens, they can still be wise men. Epictetus the slave was one. (*Beaumont* fragment, 1019)

The greatest evil of enslavement is that it transforms men into slaves. With his radical political doctrine Rousseau sought to combat not the enslavement but the transformation—by delegitimizing the political world as such.

Conclusion

The natural goodness of man, as a theoretical doctrine, led Rousseau to conceive two opposite solutions to the human problem. It also led him to a pessimistic theory of history which revealed a Europe divided into two opposite worlds. And it turned out that the urgent practical needs of these two worlds more or less corresponded to the two theoretical alternatives. The great complexity and seeming contradictoriness of Rousseau's writings, then, derive not only from their theoretical but also their practical dualism: their need to say different things to different audiences at the same time. Thus, the natural goodness of man, as a practical or polemical doctrine, has two opposite meanings.

For the world of small republics, it is a passionate defense of free, republican government as something morally necessary, because dependence is the source of all evil. It is also an attack on the brilliant egotism of the "civilized" monarchies, designed to protect the "backwardness," simplicity, and austerity of republican patriotism.

In the monarchic world, on the other hand, Rousseau's principle encourages not public-spiritedness but withdrawal—to shelter men in some measure from the degrading effects of their political enslavement. The claim that man is naturally good grounds all of Rousseau's efforts to expand the worth and reality of the inner world of sentiment. And the claim that society itself makes man evil constitutes the greatest attack ever made on the dignity of the public realm.[36]

---

[36] Rousseau's estimate of the chances for success of his two missions seems to have varied considerably in the course of his life. See *Last Reply* 88; *Bordes* 112-13; *Extrait du projet de paix perpétuelle OC* III: 563, 590; *Mals.*, 1143; *Frags.*, 474 and var. a; *Confs.* VIII: 388-89, IX: 416, 436; *Dialogues* II: 828-29; Letter to Tscharner, April 29, 1762.

14

Conclusion: A Brief Evaluation

The present work has been an attempt to make good, as it were, on Rousseau's claim that his thought and writings form a unified system—for he also claimed that they could not be fully understood unless grasped in this manner. This does not mean, of course, that the entire value of his thought stands or falls with the validity of his system. Indeed, I have attempted to show that, right or wrong, his system has much to teach us about the genesis of our present ways of thinking. It also demonstrates the importance of thinking comprehensively, "systematically," about the seemingly disconnected "issues of philosophy," and clarifies the inner articulation of the problems even when it fails to solve them. It will be fitting but not comprehensive, then, to conclude with a brief evaluation of Rousseau's system.

A philosophical system, no matter how internally consistent, can still be both arbitrary and false. Rousseau's system, I believe, is indeed false but not arbitrary, that is, not accidental or historically *sui generis*. Although at times it may appear merely the idiosyncratic vision of a rather peculiar man, it is in fact no less systematic "externally" as "internally," standing in a precise and necessary relation to the larger, historical movement of Western political philosophy. Before examining the ways in which the system is false, let us consider the ways in which it was necessary, to gain a final, synoptic view of Rousseau's project and to appreciate what is at stake in its failure.

The Historical Place of Rousseau's System

Every theory that would explain the history and structure of modern philosophy must face as one of its thorniest tests: can it account for Rousseau? With his complexity and paradoxes, he is the great wrecker of theories and categories. Indeed, we have seen that the most comprehensive of his "contradictions" is that he appears, at times, to be a modern Enlightenment figure—with his reductionism, individualism, and voluntarism—and, at others, to be a disciple of the ancient world—with his adulation of Roman virtue, his collectivism, and his "authoritarianism."

In other words, everywhere in his writings, one discovers the competing influence of Hobbes and Plato. Where does this Janus-headed system
really belong, then, and how did it ever arise?

The question of Rousseau's historical place is most often addressed in
terms of the common view, mentioned in the first chapter, that the history of political philosophy is a perennial battle between the pessimistic
or "tough-minded" view of human nature and the optimistic, "tender-
minded" view. While useful in certain respects, this approach ultimately
obscures the most important distinctions by neglecting the fact that
human nature is multiform and complex, and that most philosophic postures toward it are correspondingly complex.

Saint Augustine, for example, and other Christian thinkers, as well as
Plato and most classical philosophers, take a harsh and pessimistic view
of man, emphasizing the sinfulness or baseness of his selfish, bodily
passions. But at the same time they are also "idealistic" in recognizing a
higher spiritual or rational element in man's nature which they consider
to be his true natural end and a source of ultimate happiness. In short,
they are skeptical regarding the "low" but optimistic regarding the "high"
in human nature.

Thomas Hobbes is also famous for taking a harsh and pessimistic view
of man and therefore many have suggested that, in the decisive respect,
his psychology remains essentially Christian. But, on the contrary, his
pessimism is "humanistic," having a diametrically opposite target and
meaning. He emphasizes man's innate selfishness or "baseness" not to
turn men toward their higher end but rather to prove that no such higher
end exists. Such a conclusion would be cause for nihilistic despair, however, were it not accompanied by Hobbes's new idealistic belief that
man's lower nature is not quite as hopeless as had formerly been thought.
Human beings lack not only a higher nature but also the need for one.
The Hobbesian view of human nature, then, is an inverted, humanistic
one of skepticism toward the high redeemed by a new optimism toward
the low.

He achieves this position through a form of argument that I have
called "idealistic realism." There is surely nothing new in a limited skepticism regarding the high, which one can find, for example, in the classical and biblical traditions with their denunciations of sophistry and of
false gods and prophets. Nor was it unheard of among classical thinkers
to doubt the very existence of everything higher and transcendent. What
is distinctive in Hobbes is that he pushes his skepticism to the point of
blaming the "high" as the hidden cause of most of man's evils, which has
the new consequence of exonerating man's lower nature. Hobbes argues
that the false but beautiful claims of philosophy, morality, and religion
have unnaturally extended the power of the ambitious minority, enabling
them to bewitch the innocent majority and lead them into violence, persecution, and revolt. And then these very evils have been cited throughout

history to demonstrate the incurable wickedness of man's lower nature—and of the masses ruled by it—and the critical importance of
leading men up to their higher end, with the aid of the "virtuous"
minority. Hobbes unmasks this historical calumny, placing the blame for
man's degradation where it really belongs—on our illusions regarding the
noble and sacred—thus demonstrating that man's elemental nature is
better than had been thought. The argument of idealistic realism,
then, supplies the inner connection between the two changes that
constitute Hobbes's view: his radical skepticism concerning the high
itself generates the new idealism regarding the low that redeems it.

The specific "redemption" promised by Hobbes is that true peace and
civility can at long last be attained, not by following but by dismissing all
appeals to God; not by building on our higher nature, but by creating a
man-made state based on the lowly, bodily passion of self-preservation
and on vulgar, calculating reason. Similarly, the whole period of the
Enlightenment, which embraced some version of Hobbes's reductionist
psychology and his moral and religious skepticism, is famous for its new
optimism concerning man's economic rationality and secular progress in
a disenchanted world. In other words, idealistic realism, owing to its
doubt of the high and hope for the low, culminates in the untraditional
and counterintuitive hope—definitive of humanism—that precisely by
lowering man one elevates him, that by liberating him from his age-old
delusions about himself and his place in nature, by unmasking all false
and corrupting claims regarding the noble and divine, and by putting man
back in touch with his lower but truer self, one can raise him above his
past degradation and indeed make him better than ever before—although,
admittedly, not nearly so good as was falsely promised by mankind's past
exalters.

Here Rousseau enters the stage. He is impressed by this argument's
power but also by its shortcomings. On the one hand, its extreme skepticism toward the high cannot theoretically explain or practically satisfy
what seems to be man's genuine intimation of and longing for ultimate
happiness. On the other hand, its extreme optimism about the political
stability and progress to be produced by building on man's lower, selfish
nature seems unwarranted. Many conservative or reactionary thinkers of
the time also perceived these difficulties. Rousseau's distinctiveness lies
in his being the first to seek the solution to these problems of early
humanism in more humanism, in a more radical application of idealistic
realism.

Rousseau's crucial "move" is to lower man still further in order to
raise him still higher, to increase Hobbes's pessimism concerning the
high in order to radicalize his optimism regarding the low. He argues that
Hobbes, no less than Plato and Saint Augustine, still sees men as bad
only because he too has exalted them too much. Hobbes's famous skepticism, which mercilessly debunks all transcendent ideals, comes to an

abrupt halt before the state, that "mortal god," and before calculating
reason upon which it is based. Civil society and reason are the true
source of humanity's salvation and dignity, according to Hobbes and
the Enlightenment, for they enable men to rise above the ignominious
savagery of the state of nature and to pursue a truly civilized life of
security, useful industry, and cultivation of the arts. Rousseau simply
demands that we maintain our skepticism in the face of this new, modern,
bourgeois version of the "high," this worship of rationality, society, and
progress. He attacks these new idols of the Enlightenment (so useful
to absolute monarchs and wealthy urban elites) with exactly the same
argument that Hobbes employed against the old, Christian and classical
idols (used by priests and aristocrats): these supposed agents of man's
salvation are in fact the very forces that have secretly corrupted him and
engendered all his evils—the evils which have then mistakenly been
blamed on man's elemental nature. It is society and calculating reason—
no less than the old morality and religion—that unnaturally pervert man,
who, free of all such "greatness," would be good for himself and others. Hobbes was too cynical because not yet cynical enough.

More ruthlessly and consistently than Hobbes, Rousseau humbles
man, revealing how unnatural, how vain, how deceitful, and above all,
how corrupting are all those things on which civilized human beings
have always most prided themselves. He shows men that "in their
pretended perfection [lies] the true source of their miseries" (*Confs.*
VIII: 388).[1] And by more fully uncovering the secret corrupting power
of these "higher" things, thus more completely shifting onto them the
blame for all evil and imperfection, he also more completely exculpates that part of man that has been falsely condemned and despised
throughout history: the bodily, the animal, the instinctive, the sentimental, the passionate. This he reveals for the first time as the most
real and valuable part of us, the seat of a primal, natural goodness.

To the extent that this natural goodness can be preserved or recovered by civilized men, the exalted goals of unity and happiness—
which Hobbes discarded as simply impossible, and which Plato and
Saint Augustine sought through the repression and transcendence of
man's lower, sensuous nature—are in fact possible based on that lower
nature itself, on the preservation of man's animal goodness. Rousseau
thus completes the humanistic inversion, showing that the animal in
man is in fact the angel in him. Evil exists not because of man's Fall
from God or the Good but because of his accidental "Rise" from animality. The task of life, therefore, is no longer to transcend the lower

---

[1] "I am sensible of how important it is," Rousseau asserts, "that pride not deceive us
regarding what ought to make for our genuine greatness, and how much it is to be feared that
by dint of trying to raise ourselves above our nature we may relapse beneath it" (*Bordes*,
113-14; see *Dialogues* III: 934-35).

self for the sake of the higher, but on the contrary, to prevent all false ideas of the higher from corrupting or alienating us from our original natural goodness. Politically, Rousseau promises to bring true unity and happiness to men not by uplifting them to some divine or natural standard, but simply by imposing on them the rule of law—general will—so as to prevent them from ruining each other through mutual dependence. He translates all of the supposed benefits of the divine and transcendent—the "vertical" dimension—onto the level of the immanent, the "horizontal," the merely human.

The final twist, however, is that due to the power of corrupting social or historical forces, especially in the modern world, the preservation of this naturally good self turns out to require as much wisdom and to be as rare and difficult as the perfection of the soul had formerly been thought to be. When all the dust has finally settled from his bold and inventive restructuring of the human problem, Rousseau's thought comes to light as a study in the pessimistic consequences of humanism.

Rousseau's philosophical system, then, is in no sense arbitrary, an idiosyncratic product of his "unique vision," but stands in a systematic relation to the larger, historical movement of Western political philosophy. Indeed, the very same philosophical structure that forms the key to the internal coherence of his system—idealistic realism—turns out to be the key to its external coherence as well. Faced with the striking insights and shortcomings of the Enlightenment thinkers, Rousseau does not oppose but *defects* from their camp, attacking them dialectically with a radicalized version of their own principles. He takes the precise and, one might almost say, inevitable step of applying to their thought the very same philosophical move, the same inverting argument of idealistic realism, that they themselves had used in their break with prior moral philosophy. Rousseau shifts the blame for all man's evil onto the "higher things" that were supposedly its cure, thereby exculpating man's lower, bodily nature and establishing this lower nature as the true basis of man's happiness and perfection. This radicalization of the humanistic inversion is what produces the ingenious but disorienting dual movement—the Platonic Hobbesianism—that defines Rousseau's thought both internally and externally. By lowering man even further than Hobbes did, he discovers a new, bodily route back to the transcendent heights of Christian and classical thought.

The relation of Rousseau's thought to the future course of Western philosophy can also be understood in these terms. Through his general philosophical "move" as well as his personal stance of socio-moral protest, Rousseau revealed or set in motion the theoretical instability and self-devouring tendency inherent in the modern, humanistic revolution. Since his time, the temptation to defect from the modern camp in favor of some still more advanced form of modernity, to find some more radical way to blame the high and exculpate the low, has been a constant feature of moral and political thought, on both the left and the right.

Thinkers of the socialist and the anarchist left have repeatedly used this argument to turn the tables on all who would assert the need for hierarchy or political rule. The clearest example is Marx, at the core of whose philosophy we find this same thought structure: a fierce and unparalleled cynicism directed at every elite class and elite phenomenon, combined with—and preparing the way for—a utopian optimism directed at the liberated proletariat and at man's material existence. On the right as well—that is, the modern, atheistic right, epitomized by Nietzsche—we also find this transvaluing argument: a radical skepticism directed at both Christianity and rationalism, which shifts onto them all the blame for nihilism and modern debasement, and which, by thus exculpating the beast in man, generates an extravagant new idealism. Nietzsche promises that the creativity and strength of will growing out of men's liberated bestial or dionysian energies will enable them to create a new world of meaning, to posit new goals and values, purely on their own, without the support of God or nature.

While Rousseau did not originate it, he was the first fully to unleash this technique and temptation for discovering ever new resources in the merely human—and for standing outside and against one's culture in the name of this discovery.

Rousseau's Predictions

In assessing the validity of a philosophical system as abstract and complex as Rousseau's, it is best to start with those claims that are open to simple, empirical verification. Three such claims come to mind.

In the *Social Contract*, self-preservation is the fundamental end of the state and the goal from which the terms of legitimacy are deduced. This commonly accepted premise, Rousseau adds, points to an obvious empirical test for measuring whether a government is legitimate, and for settling the endless dispute between the partisans of republics and monarchies. "All other things being equal, the government under which . . . the citizens populate and multiply the most is infallibly the best. One under which a people grows smaller and dwindles away is the worst" (*SC* III-9: 96).[2] Rousseau is quite confident that his principles of political right will pass this empirical test, that legitimate republics as defined in the *Social Contract* will be found to increase and monarchies to decline in

---

[2] This is a constant theme and preoccupation of Rousseau's. See *Poland* XI: 1008-9; *Emile* V: 468; *Corsica*, 904-5; *Montagne* VIII: 843n; *Frags.*, 475, 527-28. But see Gildin (1983) pp. 122-25, who argues against its importance.

population. Indeed, he heartily subscribes to the view, made current by Montesquieu and Mirabeau some years earlier (and mocked by Voltaire and Hume), that the ancient world of republics was far more populous than the modern world of monarchies, which continues dangerously to decline in population. In monarchic Europe, Rousseau goes so far as to assert, "the population diminishes everywhere by one tenth every thirty years" (*Montagne* VIII: 843n).[3]

Republics of the sort that Rousseau favors are indeed conducive to population growth (although only if they are not constantly engaged in sanguinary wars and civil conflicts as the ancient republics were). Even Hume grants this much, citing a contemporary example that must have been at the forefront of Rousseau's mind:

> Switzerland alone and Holland resemble the ancient republics; and though the former is far from possessing any advantage, either of soil, climate, or commerce, yet the numbers of people with which it abounds . . . prove sufficiently the advantages of their political institutions.[4]

But Rousseau is certainly wrong in holding that Europe in the mid eighteenth century was less populous than in ancient times. And France, in particular, although a decadent and corrupt monarchy on the verge of revolution, was nevertheless undergoing something of a population boom at the very time Rousseau was writing.[5] Thus, this central and oft-repeated tenet of Rousseau's ardently republican system, that kings slowly devour their subjects, that monarchies are patently illegitimate because inimical to human self-preservation as proved by a decline in population, is demonstrably false.

A second testable hypothesis of Rousseau's system concerns his understanding of the social bond. He insists that people will only obey where they obey only themselves—the general will. True patriotism and public devotion can exist only within a small, democratically

---

[3] See *Emile* I: 44-45; *SD*, 197, 199-201, letter to Mirabeau, July 26, 1767. Montesquieu, *Persian Letters*: "After a calculation as exact as can be made in these sorts of matters, I have found that there are on earth hardly a tenth part of the men who were there in ancient times" (Letter 112; although Montesquieu does not speak in his own name in this fictional work, the view expressed would seem to be his); see letters 113-22; *Spirit of the Laws* XXIII; Victor R. Mirabeau *L'Ami des hommes, ou Traité de la population*; Voltaire "Population" in *Dictionnaire philosophique*; David Hume "On the Populousness of Ancient Nations" in *Essays Literary, Moral and Political*.

[4] "On the Populousness of Ancient Nations," p. 236. Machiavelli also claims that republics are particularly conducive to population growth, see *Discourses* II.2.

[5] In 1789 the population of France was approximately 26 million, up from about 21 million in 1700. The population of the entire European portion of the Roman Empire in 14 A.D. is estimated to have been around 23 million. See Cépède (1964) p. 38 and United Nations (1973) pp. 15, 23.

ruled state. But the modern phenomenon of nationalism, which thrives in
large and nondemocratic states, would seem to refute this thesis. It
is true, as we have seen, that the nationalist movement, which
caught most thinkers by surprise, was prepared or encouraged by
certain aspects of Rousseau's own thought, but it is also the case that
no other thinker ever stated so systematically and unequivocally that
human beings, naturally asocial, can be transformed into genuine
patriots only in the context of a small, face-to-face, egalitarian, non-
commercial, highly intrusive, democratically ruled city-state.
Rousseau's conception of the political preconditions of obedience and
patriotism (as of the requirements of preservation) is clearly too narrow.

The most massive, most revealing, and also the most damning prediction that Rousseau is led to make on the basis of his principles,
however, is his whole pessimistic assessment of the future of Europe.
He considered all of the major civilizations existing in his time, those
of the Orient and Middle East as well as that of Europe's *ancien
regime*, to be in an advanced state of corruption and decline. That was
perhaps not an unfair assessment. But also in his time the ideas were
being formulated and events prepared that would lead to the extraordinary renewal and self-regeneration of the West, and eventually to the
spread of this regeneration around the globe. Of these monumental
developments—to which, of course, his own writings greatly contrib-
uted—Rousseau had not the slightest inkling.

Because of his belief in the psychological irreversibility of enervation and decadence, also his conception of the rare and historically
irretrievable conditions required for political legitimacy, and, above
all, his fundamental principle that society based on self-interest and
mutual dependence is the very source of human evil, Rousseau's philosophical system necessarily culminates in the view that there was no
political hope for the West and that "modernization," the emerging
order of liberal, welfare-capitalist, representative, mass democracy,
could not possibly work. Rousseau does not merely think that this
order, while stable and efficient, would be bad for human character,
or, like Marx, that it would be productive for a while but ultimately
destroy itself; he believes that from the start it would produce nothing but
gross injustice, moral decay, social instability, political despotism, economic collapse, population decline, and military defeat. Thus, the whole
course of events of the last two centuries, starting with the French Revolution eleven years after his death, testify against his political descriptions and predictions. At least in these respects, Rousseau, even more
than Marx, stands refuted by history.

The Natural Goodness of Man

The essential defect of the constructive part of Rousseau's system, as the evidence just considered makes clear, is that it takes a far too narrow and skeptical view of what is possible in politics. It simply cannot account for the possibility of a relatively decent monarchy, of modern nationalism, or of liberal democratic capitalism. This striking defect, moreover, follows directly from and so corroborates the theoretical defect we discerned earlier in Rousseau's proof for his fundamental principle: his skeptical assumption that man is not naturally social. If Rousseau had been willing to acknowledge, as most premodern as well as contemporary theorists have, that man has within him at least the potential for genuine sentiments of cooperation, deference, emulation, and obedience which are not reducible to motives of selfish exchange or identification, then he would also have formed a less skeptical, more capacious, and so more accurate conception of the range of viable political forms.

But, as we have seen, Rousseau's extreme skepticism regarding man's sociality and the possibilities of politics forms the crucial premise for his extreme optimism regarding human nature. Only on the supposition that society is completely unnatural, only on the view that men are so inherently unfit for mutual cooperation that they find it contradictory and deforming, can the blame for evil be shifted from human nature onto society. Thus, if Rousseau is mistaken in his skepticism regarding society, as an analysis of both the theoretical and constructive parts of his system show, then his central argument for the natural goodness of man cannot be sustained.

What follows? Obviously, the rejection of Rousseau's particular argument for the natural goodness of man does not settle the question of the source of human evil. On the one hand, it may be that some less radical version of Rousseau's argument which does not make the questionable assumption of the unnatural and contradictory character of mutual cooperation might succeed in finding some other "hidden contradiction" in the structure of society that would account for all human evil. On the other hand, even if one accepts that the source of evil is in man himself, the question would still remain as to the nature of that source. Is it original sin; or the composition of the soul out of two metaphysically distinct and antithetical substances; or the presence in man of aggressive instincts alongside his social ones owing to his primitive carnivorousness, territoriality, or concern with the social "pecking order"; or the existence of groundless fears and irrational modes of thought formed in childhood which still linger in the subconscious adult mind; or the deranging effect of the simple fact that man's every instinct and longing push him toward life while his unique gift of reason shows him that he and everything he loves must die?

After having read and studied Rousseau, we are still left to ponder these questions on our own. But the effort to understand his thought does help to clarify how we ought to think about them. If Rousseau's attempted proof of man's natural goodness is so radical, assuming the unnaturalness of society, that is because he sees that only a radical argument could succeed. Given the extremity and ubiquity of human evil, and given the multitude of plausible sources of evil in the human soul and the human condition, it is very clear to him that man stands strongly accused and that a heavy burden of proof lies on those who would blame society.

Today, much of our social and political thinking tends to be guided by a kind of reflexive and easygoing Rousseauianism that has quietly shifted the burden of proof, blaming society first. This approach is sometimes thought to be justified by our hard-headed new insight into the prevalence of social injustice and oppression. But this insight is hardly new, as Rousseau was certainly aware. The question is whether the general injustice of society is the cause or merely the effect of man's evil. Similarly, today many tend to assume that the social or cultural origin of evil has been proved by our scientific anthropology which has revealed the great diversity of human cultures and discovered primitive tribes in which people appear to be good. But, again, cultural diversity has been well known since Herodotus; and the ancient tradition of primitivism long ago pointed out that there are conditions under which men's evil will not tend to emerge. The real question is why. If the goodness of primitives, like the innocence of children, is due simply to the limited development of their minds and hearts, or to gross illusions about the human condition, then it proves little about the compatibility of goodness with our fully developed humanity. In short, we incline to Rousseauian answers, but perhaps without always posing the questions in as sharp and uncompromising a manner as he did.

Finally, most of our thinking about man's nature and situation continues to be shaped by the tendency of thought unleashed by Rousseau, the seductive intellectual posture of idealistic realism. Everyone today is "tough-minded"; no one will admit to anything else. Yet this first reflex of the mind both conceals and prepares a deeper idealism. We are full of doubt regarding both reason and revelation, but expect salvation from our mere humanity. Ruthless in questioning everything that people used to live by, we cling unquestioningly to the faith that we can live without it. And perhaps we are right. But to think clearly about the matter we need to be conscious of the habits that condition our thinking. We are indeed all unconscious Rousseauians, and rather tender-minded ones at that.

References

Acton, John E. 1967. *Essays in the Liberal Interpretation of History: Selected Papers.* Edited by William H. McNeill. Chicago: University of Chicago Press.

Althusser, Louis. 1972. *Montesquieu, Rousseau, Marx: Politics and History.* Translated by Ben Brewster. London: Verso Editions.

Anonymous. 1791. *A Comparison of the Opinions of Mr. Burke and Monsr. Rousseau.* London.

Aristotle. 1962. *Nicomachean Ethics.* Translated by Martin Ostwald. Indianapolis: Bobbs-Merrill Co.

———. 1984. *The Politics.* Translated by Carnes Lord. Chicago: University of Chicago Press.

Atkinson, Geoffroy. 1924. *Les relations de voyages du XVII siècle et l'évolution des idées.* Paris: Librarie Ancienne Edouard Champion.

Atkinson, Geoffroy, and Abraham C. Keller. 1971. *Prelude to the Enlightenment.* London: George Allen & Unwin.

Barker, Ernst. 1964. *Greek Political Theory: Plato and His Predecessors.* 5th ed. London: Methuen.

Barth, Hans. 1965. "Volonté général et volonté particulière." *Annales de la philosophie politique* 5:35-50.

Barth, Karl. 1959. *From Rousseau to Ritschal.* Translated by Brian Cozens. London: SCM Press.

Barzun, Jacques. 1947. *Romanticism and the Modern Ego.* Boston: Little, Brown & Co.

Bastid, Paul. 1964. "Rousseau et la théorie des formes de gouvernement." In *Etudes sur le Contrat Social,* pp. 315-28. Paris: Société Les Belles Lettres.

Belloc, Hilaire. 1911. *The French Revolution.* London: Oxford University Press.

Bergson, Henri. 1935. *Two Sources of Morality and Religion.* Translated by R. A. Audra and C. Brereton. Garden City, N.Y.: Doubleday.

Bevin, Edwyn. 1913. *Stoics and Skeptics.* Oxford: Clarendon Press.

Bloom, Allan. 1979. Introduction to *Emile, or On Education.* New York: Basic Books.

Blum, Carol. 1986. *Rousseau and the Republic of Virtue.* Ithaca, N.Y.: Cornell University Press.

Bosanquet, Bernard. 1965. *The Philosophical Theory of the State.* London: Macmillan. First published in 1899.

Bradley, F. H. 1968. *Appearance and Reality.* Oxford: Clarendon Press.

Brochard, Victor. 1926. "La théorie du plaisir d'apres Epicure." In *Etudes de philosophie ancienne et de philosophie moderne.* Paris: Librairie Philosophique J. Vrin.

Burgelin, Pierre. 1952. *La philosophie de l'existence de Jean-Jacques Rousseau.* Paris: Presses Universitaires de France.

Burke, Edmund. 1910. *Reflections on the Revolution in France.* London: J. M. Dent.

Burlamaqui, Jean-Jacques. 1791. *Principes du droit naturel.* Paris: Guillaume Junior.

Candaux, Jean-Daniel. 1964. Introduction to *Lettres écrites de la montagne.* In *Oeuvres complètes* III. Paris: Gallimard, Bibliothèque de la Pléiade.

Carlyle, Thomas. N.d. *Heroes, Hero Worship, and the Heroic in History.* New York: A. L. Burt.

Cassirer, Ernst. 1954. *The Question of Jean-Jacques Rousseau.* Translated by Peter Gay. New York: Columbia University Press.

———. 1963. *Rousseau, Kant, and Goethe.* Translated by J. Gutmann, P. Kristeller, and J. Randall, Jr. New York: Harper & Row.

Cépède, Michel, François Houtart, and Linus Grond. 1964. *Population and Food.* New York: Sheed & Ward.

Chapman, John W. 1956. *Rousseau: Totalitarian or Liberal?* New York: AMS Press.

Charvet, John. 1974. *The Social Problem in the Philosophy of Rousseau.* Cambridge: Cambridge University Press.

Chinard, Gaston. 1913. *L'Amerique et la rêve exotique.* Paris: Librairie Hachette.

Cicero, Marcus Tullius. 1929. *On the Commonwealth.* Translated by George H. Sabine and Stanley B. Smith. Indianapolis: Bobbs-Merrill.

———. 1971. *De Finibus Bonorum et Malorum.* Translated by H. Rackham. Cambridge, Mass.: Harvard University Press.

Clark, Grahame. 1979. "Primitive Man as Hunter, Fisher, Forager, and Farmer." In *The Origins of Civilization.* Edited by P. R. S. Moorey. Oxford: Clarendon Press.

Cobban, Alfred. 1934. *Rousseau and the Modern State.* London: Allen & Unwin.

Cole, G. D. H. 1950. Introduction to *Social Contract, Discourse in Arts and Sciences, Discourse on Inequality, Political Economy, Considerations on the Government of Poland*, by Jean-Jacques Rousseau. New York: E. P. Dutton.

Comte, Auguste. 1929. *Systeme de politique positive.* 5th ed. Paris.

Cranston, Maurice. 1983. *Jean-Jacques: The Early Life and Work of Jean-Jacques Rousseau, 1712-1754.* London: Allen Lane

Crocker, Lester G. 1968. *Rousseau's Social Contract: An Interpretive Essay.* Cleveland: Case Western Reserve University Press.

———. 1963-65. "*Julie* ou la nouvelle duplicité." *Annales de la Société Jean-Jacques Rousseau* 36:105-52.

———. 1961-62. "The Priority of Justice to Law." *Yale French Studies* 28:34-42.

Davy, Georges. 1953. *Thomas Hobbes et J. J. Rousseau.* Oxford: Clarendon Press.

―――. 1964. "Le corps politique selon le *Contrat Social* de Jean-Jacques Rousseau et ses antecedants chez Hobbes." In *Etudes sur le Contrat Social,* pp. 65-93. Paris: Société Les Belles Lettres.

Derathé, Robert. 1950. *Jean-Jacques Rousseau et la science politique de son temps.* Paris: Presses Universitaire de France.

―――. 1950-52. "Les réfutations du *Contrat Social* au XVIIIe siècle." *Annales de la Société Jean-Jacques Rousseau* 32:7-54.

―――. 1964. Introduction to *Du Contrat Social.* In *Oeuvres complètes* III. Paris: Gallimard, Bibliothèque de la Pléiade.

Descartes, René. 1969. *The Philosophical Works of Descartes.* Translated by Elizabeth S. Haldane and G. R. T. Ross. 2 vols. Cambridge: Cambridge University Press.

Diogenes Laertius. 1972. *Lives of Eminent Philosophers.* Translated by R. D. Hicks. 2 vols. Cambridge, Mass.: Harvard University Press.

The Encyclopedia. Selections. 1965. Translated by Nelly S. Hoyt and Thomas Cassirer. Indianapolis: Bobbs-Merrill.

Fairchild, Hoxie N. 1961. *The Noble Savage: A Study in Romantic Naturalism.* New York: Farrar, Straus & Giroux.

Fralin, Richard. 1978. *Rousseau and Representation: A Study of the Development of His Concept of Political Institutions.* New York: Columbia University Press.

Fried, Morton. 1967. *The Evolution of Political Society.* New York: Random House.

Fritz, Kurt von. 1954. *The Theory of the Mixed Constitution in Antiquity: A Critical Analysis of Polybius' Political Ideas.* New York: Columbia University Press.

Furet, François. 1981. *Interpreting the French Revolution.* Translated by Elborg Forster. Cambridge: Cambridge University Press.

Gay, Peter. 1954. Introduction to *The Question of Jean-Jacques Rousseau,* by Ernst Cassirer. Bloomington: Indiana University Press.

Gierke, Otto von. 1934. *Natural Law and the Theory of Society.* Translated by Ernest Barker. 2 vols. Cambridge: At the University Press.

Gildin, Hilail. 1983. *Rousseau's Social Contract: The Design of the Argument.* Chicago: University of Chicago Press.

Goldschmidt, Victor. 1974. *Anthropologie et politique.* Paris: Librairie Philosophique J. Vrin.

Goodall, Jane. 1986. *The Chimpanzees of Gombe: Patterns of Behavior.* Cambridge, Mass.: Harvard University Press.

Gough, John W. 1957. *The Social Contract.* Oxford: Clarendon Press.

Gould, Josiah B. 1970. *The Philosophy of Chrysippus.* Albany: State University of New York Press.

Grimsley, Ronald. 1972. "Rousseau and the Problem of Happiness." In *Hobbes and Rousseau: A Collection of Critical Essays,* pp. 437-61. Edited by Maurice Cranston and Richard S. Peters. Garden City, N.Y.: Doubleday.

————. 1972. Introduction to *Du Contrat Social*, by Jean-Jacques Rousseau. Oxford: Clarendon Press.

————. 1973. *The Philosophy of Rousseau*. London: Oxford University Press.

Grotius, Hugo. 1925. *The Law of War and Peace*. Translated by Francis Kelsey. Oxford: Clarendon Press.

Guehenno, Jean. 1966. *Jean-Jacques Rousseau*. Translated by John Weightman and Doreen Weightman. 2 vols. London: Routledge & Kegan Paul.

Gurvitch, Georges. 1932. *L'idée du droit social. Notion et système du droit social. Histoire doctrinal depuis le XVIIe siècle jusqu'à la fin du XIXe siècle*. Paris: Libraire du Receuil Sirey.

Gwyn, W. B. 1965. *The Meaning of the Separation of Powers: An Analysis of the Doctrine from Its Origin to the Adoption of the United States Constitution*. Tulane Studies in Political Science 9. New Orleans: Tulane University Press.

Haas, Jonathan. 1982. *The Evolution of the Prehistoric State*. New York: Columbia University Press.

Hall, John C. 1973. *Rousseau: An Interpretation of His Political Philosophy*. London: Macmillan & Co.

Hartle, Ann. 1983. *The Modern Self in Rousseau's Confessions*. Notre Dame, Ind.: University of Notre Dame Press.

Haymann, Franz. 1943-45. "La loi naturelle dans la philosophie du J.-J. Rousseau." *Annales de la Société Jean-Jacques Rousseau* 30:65-109.

Hegel, G. W. F. 1974. *Lectures on the Philosophy of History*. Translated by E. S. Haldane and Frances H. Simson. 3 vols. New York: Humanities Press.

Hendel, Charles W. 1934. *Jean-Jacques Rousseau: Moralist*. 2 vols. Indianapolis: Bobbs-Merrill.

Hobbes, Thomas. 1962. *Leviathan; or the Matter, Forme, and Power of a Commonwealth Ecclesiasticall and Civil*. Edited by Michael Oakeshott. London: Collier-Macmillan.

————. 1962. *De Corpore*. In *Body, Man, and Citizen: Selections from Thomas Hobbes*. Edited with an introduction by Richard S. Peters. London: Collier-Macmillan.

————. 1962. *The Elements of Law*. In *Body, Man, and Citizen: Selections from Thomas Hobbes*. Edited with an introduction by Richard S. Peters. London: Collier-Macmillan.

————. 1972. *De Homine*. In *Man and Citizen*. Edited with an introduction by Bernard Gert. Garden City, N.Y.: Doubleday.

————. 1972. *De Cive*. In *Man and Citizen*. Edited with an introduction by Bernard Gert. Garden City, N.Y.: Doubleday.

Hoffding, Harold. 1930. *Jean-Jacques Rousseau and His Philosophy*. Translated by W. Richards and L. E. Saidla. New Haven: Yale University Press.

Holmes, Stephen. 1984. *Benjamin Constant and the Making of Modern Liberalism*. New Haven: Yale University Press.

Hubert, René. 1928. *Rousseau et l'Encyclopédie*. Paris: Gamber.

Hume, David. N.d. *Essays Literary, Moral, and Political*. London: Ward, Lock, & Bowden.

James, William. 1955. *Pragmatism and Four Essays from the Meaning of Truth*. Cleveland: Meridian Books. First printed in 1907.

Jouvenel, Bertrand de. 1947. "Essai sur la politique de Rousseau." In Jean-Jacques Rousseau, *Du contrat social*, pp. 15-160. Geneva: Editions du Cheval Aile.

——. 1961-62. "Rousseau the Pessimistic Evolutionist." *Yale French Studies* 28:83-96.

Kelly, Christopher. 1987. *Rousseau's Exemplary Life: The Confessions as Political Philosophy*. Ithaca, N.Y.: Cornell University Press.

Keohane, Nannerl. 1978. "'The Masterpiece of Policy in Our Century': Rousseau on the Morality of the Enlightenment." *Political Theory* 6:457-84.

Kraynak, Robert. 1990. *History and Modernity in the Thought of Thomas Hobbes*. Ithaca, N.Y.: Cornell University Press.

Lanson, Gustave. 1912. "L'unité de la pensée de Jean-Jacques Rousseau." *Annales de la Société Jean-Jacques Rousseau* 8:1-32.

Laslett, Peter. 1965. Introduction to *Two Treatises of Government*, by John Locke. New York: New American Library.

Launay, Michel. 1971. *Jean-Jacques Rousseau, écrivain politique*. Grenoble: A.C.E.R.

Lévi-Strauss, Claude. 1962. "Jean-Jacques Rousseau, fondateur des sciences de l'homme." In *Jean-Jacques Rousseau*, pp. 239-48. Neuchâtel: Editions de la Baconnière

——. 1984. *Tristes tropiques*. Translated by John Weightman and Doreen Weightman. New York: Atheneum.

Levine, Andrew. 1976. *The Politics of Autonomy: A Kantian Reading of Rousseau's Social Contract*. Amherst: University of Massachusetts Press.

Locke, John. 1952. *The Second Treatise of Government*. Edited with an introduction by Thomas P. Peardon. Indianapolis: Bobbs-Merrill.

——. 1959. *An Essay concerning Human Understanding*. Edited by Alexander Campbell Fraser. 2 vols. New York: Dover Publications.

Lovejoy, Arthur O., and George Boas. 1935. *Primitivism and Related Ideas in Antiquity*. Baltimore: Johns Hopkins Press.

——. 1961. *Reflections on Human Nature*. Baltimore: Johns Hopkins Press.

Löwith, Karl. 1967. *From Hegel to Nietzsche: The Revolution in Nineteenth Century Thought*. Translated by David E. Green. Garden City, N.Y.: Doubleday.

Lucretius. 1910. *On the Nature of Things*. Translated by Cyril Bailey. Oxford: Clarendon Press.

McDonald, Joan. 1965. *Rousseau and the French Revolution, 1762-1791*. London: Athlone Press.

Machiavelli, Niccolò. 1950. *The Discourses of Niccolò Machiavelli*. Translated by Leslie J. Walker. New Haven: Yale University Press.

———. 1985. *The Prince*. Translated by Harvey C. Mansfield, Jr. Chicago: University of Chicago Press.

MacIntyre, Alasdair. 1981. *After Virtue*. Notre Dame, Ind.: University of Notre Dame Press.

Maclay, George, and Humphrey Knipe. 1972. *The Dominant Man*. New York: Dell Publishing.

McNeil, Gordon H. 1952-53. "The Anti-Revolutionary Rousseau." *American Historical Review* 58:808-23.

Maine, Henry Sumner. 1917. *Ancient Law*. London: Everyman's Library, J. M. Dent.

Manent, Pierre. 1977. *Naissances de la politique moderne*. Paris: Payot.

Mansfield, Harvey C., Jr. 1968. "Modern and Medieval Representation." *Nomos* 11:55-82.

———. 1971. "Hobbes and the Science of Indirect Government." *American Political Science Review* 65:97-110.

———. 1979. *Machiavelli's New Modes and Orders: A Study of the Discourses on Livy*. Ithaca N.Y.: Cornell University Press.

Maritain, Jacques. 1929. *Three Reformers: Luther—Descartes—Rousseau*. New York: Charles Scribner's Sons.

Masson, Pierre-Maurice. 1916. *La religion de J.-J. Rousseau*. 3 vols. Paris: Plon.

Masters, Roger D. 1968. *The Political Philosophy of Rousseau*. Princeton: Princeton University Press.

———. 1978. Introduction to *On the Social Contract with Geneva Manuscript and Political Economy*. Translated by Judith R. Masters. Edited by Roger D. Masters. New York: St. Martin's Press.

Mauzi, Robert. 1960. *L'idée du bonheur dans la littérature et la pensée françaises au XVIIIe siècle*. Paris: Librairie Armand Colin.

Mercier, L.-S. 1791. *De J.-J. Rousseau considéré comme l'un des premiers auteurs de la révolution*. 2 vols. Paris: Buisson.

Michels, Roberto. 1915. *Political Parties*. Glencoe, Ill.: Free Press.

Miller, James. 1984. *Rousseau: Dreamer of Democracy*. New Haven: Yale University Press.

Millet, Louis. 1967. "Le Platonisme de Rousseau." *Revue de l'enseignement philosophique*, June-July, 1967.

Mirabeau, Victor R. 1756. *L'ami des hommes, ou Traité de la population*. Avignon.

Montesquieu. 1966. *The Spirit of the Laws*. Translated by Thomas Nugent. New York: Hafner Publishing.

Morel, Jean. 1909. "Recherches sur les sources du Discours de l'inégalité." *Annales de la Société Jean-Jacques Rousseau* 5:119-98.

Mornet, Daniel. 1933. *Les origines intellectuelles de la Revolution Française*. Paris: Libraire Armand Colin.

Nichols, James H., Jr. 1976. *Epicurean Political Philosophy: The De rerum natura of Lucretius*. Ithaca, N.Y.: Cornell University Press.

Norris, John. 1978. *Treatises upon Several Subjects*. New York: Garland

Publishing. First published in 1698.

Orwin, Clifford. 1980. "Compassion." *American Scholar* 49, no. 3: 309-33.

Osborn, Annie. 1940. *Rousseau and Burke.* New York: Russell & Russell.

Pangle, Thomas. 1973. *Montesquieu's Philosophy of Liberalism: A Commentary on the Spirit of the Laws.* Chicago: University of Chicago Press.

Pascal, Blaise. 1958. *Pascal's Pensées.* Translated by W. F. Trotter. New York: E. P. Dutton.

Pire, Georges. 1956. "Jean-Jacques Rousseau et les relations de voyages." *Revue d'histoire littéraire de la France* 56, no. 3 (July-September): 355-78.

Plamanetz, John. 1963. *Man and Society.* 2 vols. New York: McGraw-Hill.

Plato. 1968. *The Republic of Plato.* Translated by Allan Bloom. New York: Basic Books.

———. 1980. *The Laws of Plato.* Translated by Thomas Pangle. New York: Basic Books.

Plattner, Marc F. 1979. *Rousseau's State of Nature: An Interpretation of the Discourse on Inequality.* DeKalb: Northern Illinois University Press.

Polin, Raymond. 1971. *La politique de la solitude: Essai sur la philosophie politique de Jean-Jacques Rousseau.* Paris: Editions Sirey.

Polybius. 1922-27. *The Histories.* Translated by W. R. Paton. 6 vols. Cambridge, Mass.: Harvard University Press.

Poulet, Georges. 1956. *Studies in Human Time.* Translated by Elliot Coleman. Baltimore: Johns Hopkins Press.

———. 1978. "Le sentiment de l'existence chez Rousseau et ses prédécesseurs." *Studi Francesi*: 36-50.

———. 1980. "Le sentiment de l'existence et le repos. In *Reappraisals of Rousseau: Studies in Honor of R. A. Leigh*, pp. 37-45. Edited by Simon Harvey et al. Manchester, England: Manchester University Press.

Pufendorf, Baron Samuel de. 1734. *Le droit de la nature et des gens.* Translated by Jean Barbeyrac. Amsterdam: Chez la Veuve de P. de Coup.

———. 1735. *Les devoirs de l'homme et du citoien, tels qu'ils lui sont prescrit par la Loi Naturelle.* Translated from Latin by Jean Barbeyrac. Amsterdam: Chez la Veuve de P. de Coup.

Riley, Patrick. 1986. *The General Will before Rousseau: The Transformation of the Divine into the Civic.* Princeton: Princeton University Press.

Ritter, Allan, ed., and Julia Conaway Bondanella, ed. and trans. 1988. *Rousseau's Political Writings.* New York: W. W. Norton.

Rommen, Heinrich A. 1947. *The Natural Law: A Study in Legal and Social History and Philosophy.* St. Louis: Herder.

———. 1969. *The State in Catholic Thought: A Treatise in Political Philosophy.* New York: Greenwood Press.

Russell, Bertrand. 1945. *A History of Western Philosophy.* New York: Simon & Schuster.

Sagan, Eli. 1985. *At the Dawn of Tyranny.* New York: Knopf.

Sahlins, Marshall. 1972. *Stone Age Economics*. Chicago: Aldine Atherton.

Schwartz, Joel. 1984. *The Sexual Politics of Jean-Jacques Rousseau*. Chicago: University of Chicago Press.

Seneca. 1932. *Seneca's Letters to Lucilius*. Translated by E. Phillips Barker. 2 vols. Oxford: Clarendon Press.

Service, Elman R. 1975. *The Origins of the State and Civilization: The Process of Cultural Evolution*. New York: W. W. Norton.

Shklar, Judith N. 1969. *Men and Citizens: A Study of Rousseau's Social Theory*. Cambridge: Cambridge University Press.

———. 1972. "Rousseau's Images of Authority." In *Hobbes and Rousseau: A Collection of Critical Essays*, pp. 333-65. Edited by Maurice Cranston and Richard S. Peters. Garden City, N.Y.: Doubleday & Co.

———. 1973. "General Will." In *Dictionary of the History of Ideas*, 2:275-81. Edited by Philip P. Weiner. New York: Charles Scribner's Sons.

Silverthorne, M. J. 1973. "Rousseau's Plato." In *Studies on Voltaire and the Eighteenth Century*, cxvi:235-49. Edited by Theodore Besterman. Banbury Oxfordshire: Cheney & Sons.

Spink, John. 1978. "Les avatars du 'Sentiment de l'existence' de Locke à Rousseau." *Dix-huitième siècle* 10:269-98.

Starobinski, Jean. 1971. *Jean-Jacques Rousseau: La transparence et l'obstacle*. Paris: Gallimard. First published in 1957.

Strauss, Leo. 1952. *The Political Philosophy of Hobbes: Its Basis and Its Genesis*. Translated by Elsa M. Sinclair. Chicago: University of Chicago Press.

———. 1953. *Natural Right and History*. Chicago: University of Chicago Press.

———. 1959. *What Is Political Philosophy? And Other Studies*. Westport, Conn.: Greenwood Press.

Taine, Hippolyte A. 1876. *Les origines de la France contemporaine: L'ancien régime*. Paris: Libraire Hachette.

Talmon, Jacob L. 1952. *The Rise of Totalitarian Democracy*. Boston: Beacon Press.

Taylor, Charles. 1975. *Hegel*. Cambridge: Cambridge University Press.

Taylor, E. G. 1965. "Rousseau's Debt to Hobbes." In *Currents of Thought in French Literature*. Oxford: Blackwell.

Temmer, Mark. 1958. *Time in Rousseau and Kant*. Paris: Libraire Minard.

Thomas Aquinas, Saint. 1964-76. *Summa Theologica*. 60 vols. London: Blackfriars.

Tocqueville, Alexis de. 1969. *Democracy in America*. Edited by J. P. Mayer. Translated by George Lawrence. Garden City, N.Y.: Doubleday.

United Nations. 1973. *The Determinants and Consequences of Population Trends*. New York: United Nations.

Van Laere, François. 1968. *Une lecture du temps dans la Nouvelle Héloïse*. Neuchâtel: Editions de la Baconnière.

Vaughn, C. E. 1915. Introduction to *The Political Writings of Jean-*

Jacques Rousseau. 2 vols. Cambridge: Cambridge University Press.

———. 1918. Introduction to *Du Contrat Social.* Manchester: University Press.

———. 1925. *Studies in the History of Political Philosophy before and after Rousseau.* Manchester: University Press.

Voltaire. 1883. "Population." In *Dictionnaire philosophique. Oeuvres complètes de Voltaire,* vol. 20. Paris: Garnier.

Wolin, Sheldon S. 1960. *Politics and Vision: Continuity and Innovation in Western Political Thought.* Boston: Little, Brown & Co.

Index

Mercier, L.-S., 263
Michels, Roberto, 225 n. 40
Miller, James, 111 n. 24, 210 n. 16, 226 n.
44, 261 n. 11
Millet, Louis, 24 n. 12
Mirabeau, Victor R., 289
Monarchy, 20, 217, 226, 277-82, 288-89
Montaigne, Michel de, 56, 105 n. 15
Montesquieu, Charles de Secondat, Baron
de, 40 n. 20, 110, 151 n. 1, 201, 205-8,
211-13, 215 n. 27, 218 n. 33, 234, 264,
288-89
Morel, Jean, 56 n. 15
Mornet, Daniel, 263 n. 15

Nationalism. *See* State
Natural constitutional law, 116-18, 142-43,
176, 216
Natural goodness of man, meaning of, 15-
26, 56-57, 82-85, 276, 281-82. *See also*
Goodness
Natural law, 30 n. 1, 97, 116, 118, 121, 124-
25, 128-43, 146-49, 165, 167 n. 26, 177
Natural man, 16, 50-51
Natural rule, 118, 123, 126-28, 156, 167 n.
26, 177, 238, 240-44
Nature, 49, 89-90, 92, 94, 96, 125, 131 nn.
22-25, 132-35, 143 n. 36, 177-79
Nichols, James H., 122 n. 6
Nietzsche, Friedrich, 18, 61 n. 1, 63, 64, 288
Noble savage, 55
Norris, John, 41 n. 22

Oppression, xi, 60-63, 82-85, 97, 108, 115,
260-61
Organism. *See* State
Original sin, 17-20, 26
Orwin, Clifford, 93 n. 4
Osborn, Annie, 265 n. 16

Pangle, Thomas, 207 n. 9
Pascal, Blaise, 24 n. 9, 43 n. 25
Pastoral poetry, 55, 81
Patriotism, ix, 3, 19, 79, 91, 95, 106-8, 110,
170-71, 192-97, 219-20, 266, 289-90
People, the, 3, 22-23, 126, 144-45, 153 n. 8,
156, 166 n. 24, 173, 177, 229, 233-34,
237 n. 7, 273, 275
Perfectibility. *See* Malleability
Person, civil. *See* State
Personal dependence, 62, 70-85, 90-93, 96-
113, 149, 178-79, 196, 243, 246, 250.

See also Contradiction of society
Philosophy, 9-12, 16, 32, 89-90, 93, 116,
136-38, 142, 148 n. 44, 156, 166 n. 24,
251, 253-61
Pire, Georges, 56 n. 14
Pity, xi, 16-17, 19, 30 n. 1, 50, 91, 93, 130
n. 20, 171 n. 31, 261
Plamanetz, John, 24 n. 12, 208 n. 12
Plato, 4, 17, 20-26, 32-34, 36, 60, 67, 69 n.
1, 74 n. 3, 104 n. 14, 107, 115, 142, 160,
180, 182, 183 n. 3, 189, 197, 198, 206 n.
7, 215, 221 and n. 36, 223 n. 38, 226 n.
43, 232, 240-41, 243, 256 and n. 4, 261,
266 n. 18, 284-88
Plattner, Marc F., 17 n. 2, 20 n. 5, 51 n. 3,
129 n. 17
Pluralism, 95, 109, 172, 210
Plutarch, 56
Polin, Raymond, 208 n. 12
Polybius, 206 n. 7, 221
Poulet, Georges, 40 n. 20, 41 n. 22, 66 n. 7
Precision, 10, 116-17, 214, 218 n. 34
Prévost, abbé de, 40 n. 20, 56
Primitivism, 56, 81, 292
Principles of political right, 114-19, 142,
165-69, 176, 214-15, 227, 232, 244, 251,
261. *See also* Rousseau's doctrine
Progress, 135-42, 266-70, 285-86
Property, 139, 184
Pufendorf, Baron Samuel de, 129-42, 143
nn. 36-37, 151 n. 1, 185 n. 7, 187

Rawls, John, 160 n. 19
Realism, 19, 24-26, 108, 110-12, 116, 157-
60, 164, 165, 171, 210, 242, 249-52, 284-
88
Reason, 39 n. 19, 45-46, 124, 129-42, 201-2,
242-44, 254-55, 284-88
Religion, 93, 105-6, 147-48, 167 n. 26, 190,
197-98, 198 n. 25, 235, 237 n. 7. *See
also* Christianity; God
Republicanism, 20, 23, 30 n. 1, 115, 210,
273-77, 288-89
Riley, Patrick, 151 n. 1
Romanticism, 41 n. 23, 92, 157, 259, 280
Rome, 63, 79, 108, 172-75, 210, 222, 228,
237 n. 7, 266-67
Rommen, Heinrich A., 123 n. 8, 130 n. 19,
145 n. 39
Rousseau: contradictions of, *see* Contradictions; doctrine of, *see* Rousseau's doctrine; as admirer of ancients, 25, 100,

CPSIA information can be obtained
at www.ICGtesting.com
Printed in the USA
LVHW05s0155290918
591815LV00017B/218/P